POWER TO THE PEOPLE

POWER TO THE PEOPLE

The Political Thought of M.K. Gandhi, M.N. Roy and Jayaprakash Narayan

Primary Texts
and Critical Readings

Selected and Edited by

R.M. Pal
Meera Verma

Volume I
M.K. Gandhi

GYAN PUBLISHING HOUSE
New Delhi - 110002

Power to the People

ISBN : 81-212-0927-7 (set)
ISBN : 81-212-0949-8 (Vol.I)

Rs. 1800 (set)

Published in 2007 in India by
Gyan Publishing House
5, Ansari Road, Daryaganj,
New Delhi - 110002
Phone : 23282060, 23261060
Fax : (011) 23285914
e-mail : books@gyanbooks.com
website : gyanbooks.com

Laser Typesetting at : Vinayak Printers, Delhi
Printed at : Salasar Imaging System, Delhi

Contents

Preface

The concept of this book started with a seminar to celebrate JP's Centenary in March 2002. The seminar was organized by me on behalf of the Delhi Branch of the Radical Humanist Association, Delhi PUCL of which I was President, and the ICSSR, Northern Branch. The JP Centenary Committee of Delhi and I thought that instead of organizing a meeting to be addressed by a few leaders, the proper way to pay homage to JP would be to examine his political ideas, which I have always admired.

I may narrate an incident when I met JP sometime in the winter of 1952. JP wrote a letter to M.N. Roy saying that he would like to meet him to discuss the idea of partyless democracy. JP wrote this letter from somewhere in Punjab where he was engaged in an election campaign. Roy was in a coma at that time after an attack of cerebral thrombosis. Mrs. Roy had no way to inform JP that Roy was not well. JP dropped in one evening. If I remember right, he was staying with his nephew at the Doon school. JP was pained to see Roy lying in a coma. Mrs. Roy and JP talked about partyless politics and Radical Humanism while having tea. I was present there throughout. Later in the evening I went to the Railway station to see JP off. The CPI had brought out a book on the history of the communist movement in India in the formative years 1920-33. In the volume the editors do refer to M.N. Roy, but according to them Roy had nothing to do with either the Kanpur Conspiracy case or the Meerut Conspiracy case. However, there is no reference to his Marxian theoretical classic *India in Transition*, which used to be treated by Indian Communists at one time as their Bible and as laying out the future of Indian politics. The book established him as the sole spokesperson of the International. Roy was expelled by the International in 1929. This again is history available in documents.

Mrs. Roy prepared sandwiches for JP to be given to him after he settled down in the train compartment. On the way JP commented on how sad he was to see a real revolutionary and political thinker like Roy lying helpless. After JP's arrival in Delhi, Mrs. Roy received a letter from Pandit Nehru enquiring about Roy's health and arrangements for his treatment. This was done at on the request of Dr. Rajendra Prasad that the state do something for Roy's treatment. JP later attended a couple of summer camps organized by Mrs. Roy on behalf of the Radicals. Later I read two significant essays by JP in which he elaborates his political ideas and thoughts.

'Power to the People: An Indian View' was the topic of the seminar already referred to. It aimed at understanding the political philosophy of Gandhi, Roy and JP. I worked very hard to make the seminar a success. It turned out to be a reasonably good seminar and very well attended. Professor Bimal Prasad, Mr. Surendra Mohan, Professor Jayanti Bhai Patel and many others presented papers. After a few days I had an attack of cerebral thrombosis. As soon as I recovered I started thinking about publishing the proceedings of the seminar with the help of a political science academic. Mrs. Meera Verma, Reader in political science at Janki Devi Memorial College, Delhi University, agreed. Apart from the seminar papers included in the book, much of the paper selection and the Introduction are hers.

I must express my gratitude to Professor Sibnarayan Ray and Professor Bimal Prasad for their generosity in allowing us to use several of their publications. Both of them are devoted to the idea of Power to the People as propounded by Roy and JP. I have no doubt they would be happy that Meera and I have brought out this volume, which should be of help to students of Political Science. Readers having interest in democracy and decentralization will also find the book interesting and useful.

On behalf of both the editors, I would like to thank all our contributors: we wish to acknowledge the encouragement given by Madhuri Pal and Rajiva Verma. They were helpful in many different ways and without them the book would not have seen the light of day. For reading the initial draft of the Introduction we are grateful to Dr. Moitree Bhattacharya. We also wish to thank Mrs. Santwana Nigam and Mr. B.D. Sharma for granting copyright permission for the article by R.L. Nigam, who unfortunately is no more. We would like to acknowledge here the support given by different publishers who gave copyright permission for material published by them. Details about such material are given separately. We are grateful to Dr. Gautam Thaker, Mr. N.D. Pancholi and Dr. N. lnnaiah for their help in getting some copyright permissions. We would also like to thank Mr. Pramod Mishra, who assisted us in many different ways.

R.M. Pal

Acknowledgements

The Editors would like to express their gratitude to individuals and publishers for granting permission to us to reproduce their articles in the present book. We wish to thank the following :

1. **Professor Sibnarayan Ray for :**
   (a) Sibnarayan Ray, 'MN. Roy and the Mahatma', in *The Radical Humanist*, Vol. 63, No.7, (October 1999), pp. 4-14.
   (b) Jayaprakash Narayan, 'Gandhi and the Politics of Decentralisation', in Sibnarayan Ray (Edited), *Gandhi, India and the World* (Bombay, Nachiketa Publications Limited, 1970), pp. 226-241, 372-373.
2. **Indian Renaissance Institute for :**
   (a) Santi Devi (Evelyn Roy), 'Mr. Gandhi, An Analysis' in I.R.I. Essays and Monograph (No. 11) *Radical Essays on Gandhi and Gandhism* (Calcutta, Renaissance Publishers Private Limited, 1986), pp. 14-30.
   (b) M.N. Roy, 'Morality in Political Practice - Marx and Gandhi' in *The Marxian Way,* Vol. III, No. 2, 1948-49. Also in R.M. Pal (edited), *Selections from The Marxian Way and the Humanist Way* (Delhi, Ajanta, 1999), pp. 252-260.
3. **Gandhi Peace Foundation and *Gandhi Marg* for :**
   (a) Anthony J. Parel, 'Gandhi's Idea of Nation in *Hind Swaraj*' in *Gandhi Marg* (October-December 1991), pp. 261-281.

(b) Anil Dutta Mishra, 'Sources and Implications of Sarvodaya in Gandhi's', in *Gandhi Marg* (July-September, 2004), pp. 167- 186.

(c) Bidyut Chakrabarty, 'Gandhi's Writings in *Harijan:* A Plan of Action or Mere Philosophical Moorings' in *Gandhi Marg* (July-September, 2003), pp. 132-153.

(d) Vandana Shiva, 'The Spinning Wheel and the Seed: Gandhi's Legacy, Humanity's Hope' in *Gandhi Marg* (April-June 2004), pp. 19-30.

(e) Ronald J. Terchek, *Problematizing Modernity: Gandhi's Decentering Impulse'* in *Gandhi Marg,* (April-June, 2001), pp. 5-20.

4. **Professor T.K. Oommen For :**

'Bringing Gandhi back to Independent India', Gandhi Peace Foundation Annual Lecture (2006), delivered by him and published by the Gandhi Peace Foundation, Delhi, 2006, pp. 1-14.

5. **Navajivan Trust, Ahmedabad (India) for :**

M.K.Gandhi, *Hind Swaraj* (Ahmedabad, Navajivan Publishing House, seventeenth Reprint, 2005).

6. **Sage Publications India Private Limited for :**

Thomas Pantham, 'Beyond Liberal Democracy: Thinking with Mahatma Gandhi' in Thomas Pantham and Kenneth L. Deutsch (Edited), *Political Thought in Modern India* Copyright: Thomas Pantham. All rights reserved. (Delhi, Sage, Publications), pp. 325-346.

7. **Oxford University Press, New Delhi for :**

A.L. Basham, 'Traditional Influences on Gandhi' in R. Kumar (Edited), *Essays on Gandhian Politics: The Rowlatt Satyagraha of 1919* (London, OUP, 1971), pp. 17-42.

8. **Professor Bhikhu Parekh for :**

Bhikhu Parekh, 'Critique of Modern Civilisation', in Bhikhu Parekh *Gandhi's Political Philosophy: A Critical Examination* (Delhi, Ajanta Publications, 1991), pp. 11-35, 226-227, First published 1989 (UK).

Contributors

R.M. Pal taught English at Rajdhani College in the University of Delhi. He has been closely associated with the Radical Humanist movement and was personally close to M.N. Roy and Ellen Roy. He was honorary managing editor and also editor for some years R.M. Pal is co-editor of a book Human Rights and Society of *The Radical Humanist* and editor of the *P.U.C.L. Bulletin.* He has published several articles and books.

Meera Verma studied at the universities of Delhi and Warwick and was Reader in the Department of Political Science, Janki Devi Memorial College, University of Delhi. She has co-edited a journal and a book and published several articles on Indian government and politics.

A.L. Basham was the Dean of the Faculty of Oriental Studies (known as the Faculty of Asian Studies since 1970) from 1968 to 1970, at the Australian National University, Canberra. He had a wide knowledge of Indian languages. Among his publications one of the most acclaimed is the book *The Wonder that was India* (1954). Professor Basham died in Calcutta in 1986.

Bidyut Chakrabarty is Professor and Head, Department of Political Science, University of Delhi. He is the author of several books, the more recent of which include *Communal Identity in India* (2003) and *Social and Political Thought of Mahatma Gandhi* (2006).

Bhikhu Parekh, Professor of Political Theory at the University of Hull and former Vice-Chancellor, M.S.University,

Baroda, (1981-84), has been a prolific writer, whose publications include *Gandhi* (2001); *Rethinking Multiculturalism: Cultural Diversity and Political Theory* (2000); *Gandhi's Political Philosophy* (1989) and *Hannah Arendt and the Search for a New Political Philosophy* (1981). Professor Parekh is a member of the House of Lords and a fellow of the Royal Society of Arts. He is vice-chairman of the Gandhi Foundation.

Anthony J. Parel is Professor Emeritus of Political Science at the University of Calgary, Canada. He specializes in the philosophies of Machiavelli and Mahatma Gandhi. His recent publications include *The Machiavellian Cosmos* (1992); *Gandhi: Hind Swaraj and Other Writings* (1997).

Anil Dutta Mishra is Assistant Director, National Gandhi Museum, New Delhi. Earlier he taught and served in IIPA (Delhi), TERI, WSDC Delhi University and in Rajasthan. Among his publications are *Problem and Prospects of Working Women in Urban India* (1994); *Gandhian Approach to Contemporary Problems* (1996); *Rediscovering Gandhi* (2002).

Thomas Pantham till recently was Professor of Political Science at the University of Baroda. He has been a Visiting Fellow at the University of Essex and has written and co-edited many books on politics and Indian political thought. His publications include *Political Theories and Social Reconstruction* (1995); (co-edited), *Political Thought in Modern India* (1986); *Political Parties and Democratic Consensus* (1976).

Ronald J. Terchek is Professor of Government and Politics at the University of Maryland. His focus is on liberal democratic theory. His recent publications include *Gandhi: Struggling for Autonomy* (1998) and *Republican Paradoxes and Liberal Anxieties* (1996).

T.K. Oommen was professor at the Centre for the Study of Social Systems, Jawaharlal Nehru University, New Delhi. He also served as the President of the Indian Sociological Society, and the International Sociological Association and Secretary-General of the XI World Congress of Sociology. He has been visiting professor and Fellow at several universities in the USA, France, Germany, Australia and Sweden. He is a prolific writer. Among his various publications *are : Alien Concepts and Asian Reality:Responses and Reformulations* (1995); *Citizenship and National Identities: From Colonialism to Globalism* (1997); *Nation, Civil Society and Social Movements* (2004).

Vandana Shiva, a physicist, ecologist and author of many books, is better known as an environmental activist and founder of Bija Vidyapeeth and Navdanya. Her publications include *Earth Democracy; Justice, Sustainability, and Peace* (2005); *Globalization's New Wars: Seed, Water and Life Forms* (2005); and *Patents: Myths and Reality* (2001).

Santi Devi (Evelyn Roy) married M.N. Roy and remained his close intellectual companion. She had a deep interest in music and literature. She has written and co-edited *The Radical for Humanist* during the 1960s' when it was brought out as a weekly from Calcutta.

Professor Sibnarayan Ray has taught at the Universities of Bombay and California and was Chairman of Indian Studies at the University of Melbourne. A colleague of M.N. Roy in his later years, Ray is Research Director of the Indian Renaissance Institute, Calcutta. He has authored over twenty books and has edited *Jijnasa,* a quarterly journal of ideas, since 1980.

Introduction

Meera Verma

In keeping with India's reputation for its spiritual tradition and philosophy, ancient Indian thought was considered to be essentially non-secular. The discovery of Kautilya's *Arthashastra* established its thought as containing a rigorous political analysis as well-contributing such concepts as the *saptang* and the *mandala*, apart from the all pervasive principle of *dharma*, that were relevant not only in the field of religion but also, as *rajdharma*, in the realm of politics. The discovery of the treatise and its translation in 1905 contributed greatly to further strengthening the national confidence that had already begun to be reflected in the process by which a nationalist *(Swarajist)* and anti-colonial position was replacing the 'mendicant' posture of the late nineteenth and early twentieth century moderates.

The development of political thought in the modern period, especially the early twentieth century, must be seen in the context of colonialism and the fast growing discontent it produced. However, it is important to remember that the theoretical concerns expressed were not confined to these. In the nationalist debate the impact of westernisation had to be met with an equal dose of national pride and independence. Thus Vivekananda talks of equality in relation to the West - if we are to learn from 'them', then 'we' must also be able to teach them something. According to Vivekananda, Vedantic philosophy is universal in application, encompassing the entire humanity. The Vedantic concepts of 'spiritual freedom', nationalism, internationalism and humanism are things that India could teach the West. As Arnold Toynbee states, 'of all the surviving civilizations, the Hindu differs most fundamentally from the Western Christian, and it is the civilization which has experienced the most intimate, and in many ways the most disturbing, contact with the West.'[1]

Colonialism provided the historical context in which the debate/dialogic took place. But the Indian responses to the western civilization and concepts were varied and complex. Bhikhu Parekh classifies these responses into three broad categories, which he terms 'modernism', 'critical modernism' and 'critical traditionalism'. While the traditionalists valorised the native tradition of thought and the critical modernist or 'syncretists' argued for 'a creative synthesis of the two civilizations', the modernists maintained that the only way to salvage Hindu society was through 'radical reconstruction along modern or European lines'. While none of the social and political thinkers of modern India can be assigned exclusively to any one of these categories, Parekh maintains that 'most of them fall more easily under one rather than the others.'[2]

Is the encounter between the East and the West a clash or a coalescence of civilizations and ideas? Gandhi's *Hind Swaraj* (which, though he had written it as early as 1909 he stood by till the end of his life) makes it sound like a clash rather than coalescence, though Gandhi was too sensitive and intelligent to present the two civilization as 'us and them'. 'A glimpse into Gandhi's western intellectual sources should go a long way towards correcting the view held by some that the Mahatma was opposed to western civilization as such.'[3] 'By 1909 Gandhi had integrated all the essential ingredients of his political philosophy into a coherent whole, ingredients that were derived from the East and the West.'[4] Gandhi himself in a letter to H.S.L.Polak (14 October 1909), clarified that there was no impassable barrier between the East and the West. His objection was not to the British as such but to modern civilization. Before the advent of modern civilization, argued Gandhi, the people of Europe had much in common with the people of the East. It was not the British people who ruled India but modern civilization through its railways, telephone, etc. The East and the West could meet again if the West could throw modern civilization overboard. European civilization as modern civilization was doomed. In a further letter to Polak (November 22, 1909), Gandhi claimed that his views on modern civilization were upheld not only 'by many Indians not touched by what is known as civilization', but also 'by thousands of Europeans'. According to Anthony J. Parel this suggests that Gandhi's criticism of western civilization 'is not inspired by any Indocentric animus.'[5]

There is no dearth of individual thinkers who have acknowledged their debt to western thought - both religious and secular - including among others Ram Mohan Roy, Vivekananda, M.N. Roy and M.K. Gandhi. However, there is a wide range of variations in the perception of the relative merits of the Indian and Western traditions. While Vivekananda represents one extreme in placing Vedantic Hinduism at the top in the scale of hierarchy of religions and philosophy, M.N. Roy, who is perhaps the most uncompromisingly western in his approach, whether in his Marxist or his Humanist phase, represents the other extreme. His *New Humanism*, which he himself described as a manifesto, takes the reader through the different evolving traditions of western philosophy through the ages. Sudipta Kaviraj regards M.N. Roy as the 'most radical' among the nationalists of his generation. However, according to Kaviraj, in spite of his sincerity, Roy's radicalism suffers from 'heteronomy', that is, the 'tendency to see events through an overriding primacy of European history', so that for him India becomes merely 'a theatre of re-enactment' whether of a socialist transformation or of radical humanism.[6]

Describing the traditional influences on the thought of Mahatma Gandhi, A.L. Basham argues that though Gandhi explicitly acknowledges his debt to western books, authors, ideas and religions, the emphasis in his concepts are very 'un-western'. Therefore his concept of truth is used not only as 'trust' and 'troth' (the English equivalent of the meaning) but as 'satya', semantically akin to the word 'sat', 'existence', 'being', the first property of the Absolute, Essence or Brahman according to Vedantic philosophy. Truth for Gandhi seems to incorporate some of the content of the pregnant Indian word *dharma*. His concept has overtones which are more metaphysical than those of the English word. It is the same with Gandhi's concept of Ahimsa (non-violence), of which he said: '[It] is the first article of my faith. It is also the last article of my creed'. It is of course a common concept in ancient Indian thought, as Basham points out, but Gandhi also read it 'in the teachings of all greatest teachers of the world - Zoroaster, Mahavira, David, Jesus, Muhammad, Nanak and a host of others.[7] Anthony J. Parel also traces the concept of 'swaraj' to the *Gita*.[8]

The concept of history and of its interpretation are important in the writings of the thinkers of the twentieth century in order to construct the idea of an Indian 'nation' – something that could both explain India's falling prey to foreign invasion, its existing subservience to British colonial rule and its struggle to emancipate itself. There is a general agreement amongst historians of different shades that nationalism does not predate the coming of British rule in India.[9] M.N. Roy and the Marxists have treated the economic factor as important in creating forces which had a stake in national reconstruction. In *The Transition of India* (1922) Roy argues that India has entered the orbit of capitalism and the proletariat already has taken the task of waging a class war and will soon take the major responsibility of bringing about a nationalist as well as a socialist revolution in the country. The Indian bourgeoisie is likely to reconcile its interests with an increasingly accommodating imperialist bourgeoisie and jointly exploit the masses. The workers and the peasants, who are already waging a class war, are likely to be left to carry on the dual struggle of emancipating themselves and the nation. The accuracy of this analysis and prediction has of course been questioned.[10] Roy himself revises his 'decolonisation' thesis (in the late 1920s) on the ground that ... renaissance hadn't taken place in India because of the nationalist pre-occupation which prevented the questioning of religious obscurantism and fatalistic beliefs. The masses therefore continued to be inert and resigned and unable to play their historical role. India's religious and spiritual past was therefore nothing to be proud of. In his later writings (1947-1948) however, Roy shifts his attention to the reconstruction of society to make individual freedom possible. He treats all forms of collectivism such as nationalism, communism and socialism as threats to freedom.[11]

In contrast to Roy, Vivekananda and Gandhi place greater weight on cultural and religious factors in creating the sense of Indian nationhood - traced back in history to ancient times, especially to the Hindu past. Gandhi challenges the view that India is merely a 'geographic expression' – that it was never a nation, nor can ever become one. He attributes this impression to British historiography which many Indians had started to believe in. To Gandhi India was a nation even before the advent of Islam in India. Though ancient Indian civilization was overwhelmingly Hindu, it had an accommodating capacity, and in establishing places of pilgrimage in various parts of the sub-continent, the acharyas of the past laid the basis for the evolution of an all-India consciousness.[12] Thus nationalism is not a leaf from western thought or western education.

Early twentieth century thinkers were at pains to explain Hindu-Muslim antagonism in terms of history as well as religious differences. Vivekananda, Gandhi *(Hind Swaraj)*, Nehru *(The Discovery of India)* and others tried to grapple with the question. Nationalist construction was to be achieved through an attempt at assimilation and synthesis of different faiths, cultures, peoples and schools of thought. 'Co-existence', 'pluralism', 'tolerance' and 'unity in diversity' are still represented as virtues of our cultural history and also as aspects of the construction of the Indian Nationalist ideology, especially in the writings of Gandhi and Jawaharlal Nehru. In a letter dated 15 September 1944, Gandhi wrote to Muhammad Ali Jinnah, who was advocating the two-nation theory on the ground of the distinct and separate culture and civilization of the Hindus and the Muslims, that 'India was one nation before the advent of Islam, it must remain one in spite of the change of faith of a very large body of her children.'[13] Change of religion in Gandhi's view, did not lead to a new nationality, because if it did, there would be many more such claims, and that would lead to an insoluble problem. Gandhi finds Jinnah's claim 'alarming' and 'wholly unreal'. He argues further that there is no parallel in history for converts and their descendants claiming to be a nation apart from the parent stock.[14] Gandhi pleads for respect for each other's religion. He presents an 'inclusivist' view of Indian nationhood and never argues for the superiority or predominance of any particular religion including Hinduism. Asked in an interview why he did not convert to Christianity as he was so impressed by it, Gandhi replied that there was nothing in the Christian scriptures which was not there in Hinduism and 'that to be a good Hindu also meant that I would be a good Christian'.[15] However, the view of separate Muslim and Hindu nationalisms as against the concept of a common Indian nationalism continued to persist in Indian thought.

An interpretation based on a communal perception of religious and cultural practices constitutes a part of the historical and literary writings and of the oral tradition of India. It has been maintained that the oral perceptions were crystallised in the writings of earlier British historians (e.g., J.S. Mill). British historiography tried to project British rule as better than Muslim rule in India as the Hindus were made to suffer under the latter. Shashi Joshi and Bhagwan Josh have argued at length about the presence of 'a fault line' prevailing between Hindus and Muslims since medieval times.[16] Ziauddin Barani, a fourteenth century political thinker and historian, gives vent to his communal prejudice in unqualified terms. This prejudice has been recorded in history and in contemporary writings of modern India as well. Secularism even in contemporary India suffers from the burdens of past history and the 'identity traps' that both the Hindus and the Muslims seem to fall into[17]. Identity formation along regional, religious, linguistic and caste lines in the nineteenth and twentieth century is well recorded in history and is seen as a problem in the nationalist construction of politics. The introduction of electoral politics encouraged the process even more. The establishment of the Muslim League in 1906 and the willing concessions given by the British government to the Muslims in the form of separate electorates went a long way in emphasising the separateness of Hindu-Muslim identities. These differences have been further formalised/institutionalised through the communal writings of Jinnah, Sawarkar, Golwalkar and several others. The problem of synthesising identities and interpreting one's history in which Muslim-Hindu animosities do not appear either as persistent or inevitable was and is still being worked out – an attempt in which several historians of medieval and modern India, apart from groups and members of the civil society including the intelligentsia and the media, are actively engaged. Several scholars have argued that a communal interpretation of medieval history has been overemphasised to the detriment of other developments, especially the syncretic attempts made at the level of society and politics. A cultural rather than a political interpretation, a subaltern rather than an elitist/dynastic approach, the little rather than the big picture in the representation of life in historical writings on the medieval period, could help us to understand the assimilative aspects of Indian culture and history. Z. M. Quraishi argues that in the wake of Indian resurgence, historians carried useful research on ancient Indian political thought, but medieval Indian political thought was neglected in view of the conflicting interpretations of medieval history. While several historians regarded medieval thought as absolutely irrelevant to the national aspirations, others found in it the 'the very essence of India's composite culture'.[18] Although it was primarily influenced by religious beliefs, it was often syncretic rather than exclusivist and communal. The Sufi order and the Bhakti mystics made 'the greatest contribution to the enrichment of medieval political thought and, in fact, charted the course of the pluralist ideology which came to be known as secularism in India.'[19] As Quraishi argues, Medieval Indian history has suffered at the hands of historians and the political scientists have not ventured very much into this area.

M.N. Roy suggests that 'a critical investigation of the internal as well as the external causes of the Muslim conquest of India is of practical value today'.[20] He contends that the political disintegration of India was a process parallel to the rise of Islam and cites Havell's explanation of the proselytization of the lower castes of the Hindus that took place because of the severity of Brahmanical law with regard to the 'impure' classes and, in contrast, the equality before law courts offered to all those who embraced Islam.[21] Roy therefore argues that the communal question will never be resolved unless 'a radical change of attitude is brought about by a sober sense of history'. The Hindus, he goes on to argue, 'will never be able to see the Muslims as integral parts of the Indian Nation until they come to appreciate the contribution they made towards the emergence of Indian society out of chaos caused by the breakdown of the antique civilization.'[22] Knowledge of the contribution of Islam to human culture, however is necessary for the Muslims as well for, as Roy argues, not only will it 'shock the Hindus out of their arrogant self-satisfaction' but also 'cure the narrow mindedness of the Muslims of our day by bringing them face to face with the true spirit of the faith they profess'.[23]

Interpretation of history, especially of the medieval period, which witnessed the arrival of Islam and Muslim rule in India, became important in the construction of an Indian identity. Aware of the problem of the Hindu-Muslim relationship, Gandhi during the Satyagraha movement of 1919 wanted vows of Hindu-Muslim unity to be taken every day individually. Vows could also be taken collectively in the name of God that both Hindus and Muslims were children of the same parents who would share and remove the sorrows of each others; that religious feelings would not stand in the way of their respective religious practices; and that they would always refrain from violence against each other in the name of religion.[24] Jawaharlal Nehru argued that religious identity could not be the basis for nationalism and ought not to be that of the polity. He stood for a concept of Indian nationalism as against the concept of Hindu, Muslim or Christian nationalism.

Though modern Indian thought grapples with the problem of Hindu-Muslim relationship, there is an attempt to separate it from a consideration of Islam as religion. Raja Ram Mohun Roy, Vivekananda and Gandhi see in Islam many illuminating ideas and values. M.N. Roy has written on the historical role of Islam. 'Although Islam came to India after it had played out its progressive role, and its leadership had been wrested from the learned and cultured Arabs, the revolutionary principles of the days of its origin and ascendancy were still inscribed on its flag.'[25] Islam's 'revolutionary significance and its ability to lead the masses out of the hopeless situation created by the decay of the antique civilisations not only of Greece and Rome but of Persia and China - and of India' was the reason for its phenomenal success, argues Roy.[26] It brought with it 'the idea of social equity that was unknown in all the lands of ancient civilisation.'[27]

Sharing a common historical background of intense political events (World Wars, the rise of Fascism, the Bolshevik revolution, imperialism and anti-colonial movements in the third world, especially India) both on the national and the international stage, the thinkers of this period are driven into political participation as well. Their thoughts and ideas have therefore evolved, developed and even changed over a period. This is especially so with regard to M.N. Roy's thought, which undergoes a dramatic change from revolutionary Marxism to Radical Humanism in the mid 40s, and also the thought of Jayaprakash Narayan, who moves from a Marxian position in the 1930s to a position of socialism which is a 'half-way house' between Gandhism and socialism from the mid 1940s onwards. One of the first to offer a Marxist analysis of the rise of nationalism in India, Roy argued in his book *India in Transition* (1922) that the new economic forces released by imperialism and World War I generated a quicker pace of capitalistic development that transformed the whole character of Indian politics by bringing new classes into the struggle against imperialism. However, Roy predicted a limited success for the Congress as a vehicle of social transformation because of its essentially bourgeois character. The class represented by the Congress often collaborated with the British government in the exploitation of the masses and was seen as much too keen to join government through electoral politics. Hence the need arose for the working class to play its historical role of fighting imperialist and exploitative forces. Gandhi on the other hand sought the cooperation of groups and people across classes to give the nationalist movement a mass character. Gandhi rejected the idea of a class struggle on ethical and philosophical grounds. He was also critical of the utilitarian ethic of liberalism/individualism. Communitarian living was a serious experiment he conducted both in South Africa and India. He was quick to distinguish the method of civil disobedience he employed in his political campaigns from the western notion of passive resistance. Gandhi exhibited an ability to experiment in that he was always adept at reconciling a historical reality with the requirements of the times. However, he also showed a steadfastness or 'stubbornness' in his convictions; for example, as mentioned earlier, he continued to refuse to change his position on the civilizational question that appeared in his writing as early as 1909 in *Hind Swaraj*.

Roy and Gandhi, therefore, represent different ways of looking at history, politics and philosophy. But Roy, like Gandhi, realises the importance of the need for morality in political practice. Writing in 1948-49 in the after-years of his Marxism, Roy sees Marxian dialectics as an 'unmitigated evil' and its materialism as degenerating into a position where the principle of the end justifying the means leads to depriving human life of its humanness. On the other hand, Roy sees Gandhism as leading to a 'blind alley'.[28] Roy concedes that though Gandhi's doctrine of non-violence did try to introduce morality in political practice, he 'failed' to do so as he offered no solution to 'the crisis of modern culture': 'The remedy is ineffective because it is antiquated. It does not take into account the causes of the disease it wants to cure. It is quackery.'[29] If the proof of the pudding lies in the eating, argues Roy, 'Gandhism should be judged by the atmosphere in India, which is its creation.' Comparing Gandhi to Jesus Christ, Roy argues that unlike Jesus Christ, Gandhi has no takers.[30]

However, though it is possibly true that in the corridors of power today there are no Gandhians, Gandhi's views have greatly influenced movements emerging from the civil society both within India and the world. J.P. Narayan has been credited with advancing the uses of Gandhian techniques such as satyagraha to issues of socio-economic justice through the Bhoodan movement. Some recent movements such as the Chipko Movement, the Narmada Bachao Andolan and SEWA draw direct inspiration from Gandhian thought. Several other pacifist, environmental, anti-apartheid and anti-nuclear movements at the global level, such as END (i.e. the organisation for European Nuclear Disarmament, 1980s), Greenpeace (1980s) and Peace Brigades International (1980s) also acknowledge their debt to Gandhian thought.[31] Thus the Gandhian influence continues to be an important force in society.

According to Thomas Pantham, in the literature of the social and political sciences, five different interpretations of the Gandhian way of socio-political transformation can be identified. These are :

(a) that Gandhian values and strategies are functional to the modernisation of the Indian tradition and to the traditionalization of (western) modernity in India, e.g., in the writings of Rudolf and Rudolf;

(b) that on the contrary, these values and strategies contribute to the political appropriation of the peasantry by/for the passive bourgeois-nationalist revolution, which defers or deflects the socialist revolution in India, e.g., in the writings of Evelyn Roy, Partha Chatterjee and Ranjit Guha;

(c) that Gandhian sarvodaya could be revised and extended into a strategy of Total Revolution;

(d) that some aspects of Gandhian thought can be and have been used to subserve the Hindu nationalist ideology;

(e) that the Gandhian programme of sarvodaya through swaraj and satyagraha is superior to the Liberal and Marxist-Leninist paradigms of development and governance.[32]

One may add that the concept of satyagraha lends itself to multiple uses, whether to support a green or a peace revolution or to support the notion of sustainable development, as in the various social and environmental movements mentioned above. T.K. Oommen in the article included in this book brings out the increasing relevance of Gandhi in contemporary India in the context of a globalising world. There is an increasing growth of literature, including the works of Thomas Pantham, Lloyd Rudolph and Robert Terchek, that attempts to read Gandhi in the context of post-modernism, with a shift of emphasis from the state to civil society.

Surprisingly Gandhi discourages/opposes the use of satyagraha on the question of temple entry, which made him suspect in the eyes of B.R. Ambedkar. Ambedkar emerges as a strong critic of Gandhi. The Gandhi-Ambedkar correspondence therefore acquires special significance not only for the politics of the 1930s but also for contemporary India in its search for equality and justice. Unlike Gandhi, Ambedkar sees the dalit question not just as a social problem but also as a political one. The dalit intellectual life today draws its inspiration from Ambedkar and not Gandhi, even though the latter treated the 'Harijan' question as an important part of his constructive programme. Ambedkar is a reference point in the description of the dalit movement even though there are others who have contributed to the uplift ment of the dalit community. According to Gopal Guru three tendencies in the intellectual life of dalits can be perceived in the twentieth century: one, the 'essentialization' of Ambedkar's thought; two, the ideologization of Ambedkar to enable a criticism of Gandhi and Marx; and three, the inability to defend or accept a creative interpretation of Ambedkar. The twenty-first century, argues Guru, will continue to read more of Ambedkar, even if only to redefine him and also to compare him to Marx, Periyar and Gandhi.[33] On the eve of Independence the Indian Constitution and the people generally recognised the need for treating the 'dalit' question as a historical problem requiring a national initiative and solution. Gandhi's contribution to the creation of this climate of thinking is widely recognised, in spite of the heated debate between Gandhi and Ambedkar and in spite of Roy's qualified criticism of the Congress on its approach to the subject, which he sees as one of 'ethical propagandizing'.[34]

The subaltern approach to the study of history has highlighted the subaltern concerns of the period including the concern regarding the status of women in society. Gandhi is credited with bringing women in a big way in the arena of politics, which had earlier been almost exclusively a male concern. Gandhi's mahatma image along with the nature and the purpose of the civil disobedience movement encouraged women to enter 'public spaces' traditionally forbidden to them. Even prostitutes contributed greatly in terms of money and jewellery to the fund raised for the movement. However, after the movement was over, most women, like the peasants, returned to their 'original' areas of functioning. Gandhi did consider the family to be the main area of a woman's concern, though he also considered the 'feminine' qualities as specially enabling them to qualify as satyagrahis. He considered himself too to be endowed with a few of these feminine qualities. Gandhi considered men and women to be complementary to each other. The artificial divide between men and women in terms of feminine and masculine qualities did not hold any sanctity. In spite of such views, Gandhi has been seen as reflecting a 'patriarchal bias and prejudice' in his views on the role of women in society and within the family and in his treatment of his wife on certain occasions (e.g., his harsh treatment of Kasturba Gandhi in the ashram on the question of toilet cleaning and his later decision to observe celibacy in married life). However, while Feminists may see Gandhi as a 'patriarch' lording over the decisions of his wife and family, there is some evidence from his personal life which presents a picture of a household where men too are assigned daily household chores. Gandhi himself was seen to be a good 'nurse' and a 'serious, sensitive, intensely earnest, high-minded and self-sacrificing' man who nevertheless had a sense of humour.[35] Gandhi can be seen as a critical traditionalist adept at adjusting tradition to the demands of modernity, though on some issues, including especially the issue of birth control, his position is clearly opposed to modernity. Roy describes Gandhi's advice of abstention and sexual denial as the impossibility of 'married celibacy'. In one of the last pieces written by him in jail (1936) as a response to Gandhi's interview to Margaret Sanger, Roy questions the concept of 'the ideal of Indian Womanhood'. Influenced by the critique of women's position during the period of the nineteenth century Bengal renaissance, by Marxian writings and by the women leaders in the earlier phase of the International Communist Movement with whom he had worked, Roy finds Hindu society, the scriptures and Manu's laws as offering only 'protection' to woman, no proprietary rights, and treating her as a 'possession'—first of the father, then of the husband and subsequently of the son. Women's 'elementary human rights' are not recognised by the Hindu society and family discipline is converted into 'bondage' for women, making the concepts of equality between men and women and of 'love' and 'companionship' in marriage merely distant dreams. He further argues that the contribution of the lower class women in the struggle for existence is not recognised, thereby reducing them to 'chattel-slavery'. According to Roy, a position of true equality for women cannot be achieved without a radical reconstruction of society. Indeed, as Roy believes, 'the freedom demanded by the modern woman alone can prevent the dissolution of the family as a necessary social institution and head off the danger of a social chaos'.[36]

The concept of Satyagraha is an important contribution of Gandhi to modern political theory and has acquired widening areas of relevance beyond the exclusively political. In history, changes brought about by violence have proved to be unstable and have failed so far to bring about the professed aim of justice and power to the people. But while one may agree with the value of satyagraha as a weapon of protest against colonial rule, the question is often asked whether satyagraha continues to be relevant in an independent, democratic India. A liberal may argue that there is no place for non-cooperation and civil disobedience in a democratic country. However, Jayaprakash Narayan used the techniques of non-co-operation and civil disobedience during the politics of the 1970s and asserted its continuing relevance *(Prison Diary)*. Even in the West several thinkers continue to support the concept of civil disobedience, which in any case was derived from Thoreau's writings. Amongst contemporary writers John Rawls and Peter Singer regard civil disobedience as a non-coercive plea to authorities and an appeal to their sense of justice. Such a concept is, supposedly, workable in a country where there is a premium and national consensus on the values of freedom and justice. But Gandhi's concept of civil disobedience can be applied to all situations, even against tyranny, for the satyagrahi's objective is to 'convert' and not to 'coerce the wrong-doer'. Both Gandhi and Rawls argue that the civil disobedients should be willing to submit to penalties under law. However, while Rawls and Singer 'would not deny that sometimes coercion and even violence may be justified', Gandhi ruled out resort to coercive tactics altogether. He deeply regretted his 'Himalayan blunder' (in his various campaigns, in Champaran 1917, against the indigo planters and in the Non-Cooperation Movement 1920-22 against the colonial Indian government), in not taking sufficient precautions to prevent the movements from becoming violent.[37] As Vinit Haksar points out, according to Gandhi there are two reasons why one should not be a party to a wrong: sometimes Gandhi uses a 'non-consequentialist' line that it is simply one's duty to dissociate oneself from evil; at other times he gives a 'consequentialist' justification for his position, namely that by doing so one could 'wean the ruler from his wickedness'.[38] While appreciative of Gandhi's attempt to introduce morality into politics, M.N. Roy offers a trenchant Marxist criticism of Gandhi's satyagraha: 'Since the day Non-Cooperation was hedged in by the cult of non-violence, it has lost all its potentialities; its revolutionary possibilities have been sacrificed on the altar of sentimental pacificism, born of the dread that the interests of the respectable upper-class will be equally jeopardised by the systematic development of mass-action.'[39]

In India, M.N. Roy addressed himself to a limited and select audience, both before and after Independence, even though unlike other Indian leaders he had worked on a world canvas not experienced by others. His followers are still trying to reckon with his writings on politics and political theory, disseminate knowledge of his impressively erudite and wide-ranging work (through *The Radical Humanist* and through editions of collected works undertaken by individual authors, especially Sibnarayan Ray) and individually take up causes of social justice, rationalism and humanism that were dear to his heart. Commenting on Roy's writings, especially *India in Transition*, Sudipta Kaviraj treats it as a 'remarkable' book, the first 'exhaustive treatment of Indian politics in a Marxist way', an 'interesting intellectual exercise executed to prove wrong conclusions about the present and the future of politics in the 1920s.' Wrong, according to Kaviraj, because his predictions went wrong – for example, Roy announced a premature obituary on Gandhi's leadership of the movement; he expected the Indian bourgeoisie to go over to the side of imperialism and he believed that the proletariat would bring India's freedom after the bourgeoisie's betrayal.[40] Kaviraj writes that 'since he openly broke with Marxism shortly afterwards his theories have a gradually shortening circle of influence'.[41] Royists such as R.L. Nigam and Philip Spratt express similar views about the restricted or confined political influence of Roy in India, though Roy himself did not care about popularity and mass following. Sibnarayan Ray argues that Roy's attempt to work through the Congress and convert it to a socialist and democratic agenda met with a fate similar to Subhas Chandra Bose's similar attempt very largely because of 'Gandhi and Gandhism'. Roy took time to realise that Gandhi had established himself as a leader in the Congress as nearly absolutely as Stalin over the Russian Communist Party and the Comintern. Further, Roy's opposition to Gandhi and Gandhism was rooted in his 'total rejection of the so called spiritualist tradition of India'. Even the Communists voted against him and the Congress Socialists abstained from voting, which caused his defeat in the Congress presidential election of 1939.[42]

All the three thinkers were concerned with the future of India and the nature of the future Indian polity. Though Gandhi does not provide a political blueprint, he has written on the India of the future. The Gandhian concept of development is related to his attempt to view man as a whole and not just as 'economic man'. He warns against 'technological determinism' and the consequent dehumanisation of man and his alienation from work, environment and fellow human beings. As B.R. Nanda states, 'economists may have laughed at Gandhi's ideas in his lifetime; they do so no longer.'[43] A few Gandhians put forward Gandhi's political ideals before the Constituent Assembly but they were rejected as too idealistic and not appropriate for a fast-changing modern world. His views on anti-alcoholism, cow protection, untouchability and panchayati raj did find a place in the Constitution, but, with the exception of untouchability, they were initially included only in the Directive Principles of State Policy, which are a non-justiciable part of the Constitution. Like the anarchists, Gandhi is theoretically suspicious of the state, which for him is a soul-less machine through which it is impossible to get rid of violence. Indeed, for him, its very existence depends upon violence. When he concedes the existence of the state he wishes it to be decentralized, with democratic rights from the grassroots level, and to be based on non-violence and social welfare. The state established by the Indian Constitution does incorporate the welfare concept, but only in the Directive Principles of State Policy. As for the idea of decentralization, though the Constitution does provide for a federal structure, there is a strong centralizing bias in it.

M.N. Roy too presented his followers of the Radical Democratic Party with a draft of a constitution for free India (1944) for debate and discussion. J.P. Narayan also presented his own different views on the political restructuring of India, especially during the post-independence period. What is common to all three thinkers is that they all stand for democracy, decentralisation, accountability, a kind of partyless democracy and a deep concern for ethics in politics, though their views on economic re-structuring differ considerably. M.N. Roy gives primacy to the principle of a federal structure, local self governing institutions, peoples' committees, declaration of rights and fundamental principles, apart from including methods of direct democracy such as initiative, referendum and recall. He also envisages an economic system in which land and other natural resources are owned by the state.[44] Jayaprakash Narayan calls for far-reaching electoral reforms and distribution of land to the landless and later organises a 'total revolution' to make the existing government more accountable. However, like Gandhi, neither of them was part of the efforts of the Constituent Assembly and its debates nowhere reflect their influence.

The preference for democracy or 'power to the people' in all the three thinkers, is marked by a criticism, verging on rejection, of the western notion of parliamentary democracy. For Roy the fundamental defects of parliamentary democracy are rooted in the 'contradiction between the philosophy and the practice of liberalism'. For while liberalism, 'true to its Humanist tradition', proclaimed freedom of the individual, 'the economic doctrine of *laisser-faire*, with its political corollary, place the individual in a helpless position in the wilderness of cut-throat competition'.[45] Labouring under economic disadvantages, the individual citizens have very little chance of exercising effectively the sovereign right which formally belongs to them. Under a parliamentary system, democracy cannot control the executive and, given its majority in the parliament, the ruling party can constitutionally assume dictatorial power. To Jayaprakash Narayan the 'most serious fault' of parliamentary democracy from the point of view of democracy itself is its 'inherent tendency towards centralism'. Between the nation state on the one end of the political spectrum and the atomised individual on the other, there are blank spaces. The local bodies have little self-governing powers and no influence on the nation state. Critical of the party system and expensive elections, Jayaprakash Narayan advocates the concept of communitarian democracy.[46] Gandhi describes even the 'Mother of Parliaments' as a 'sterile woman' and a 'prostitute'.[47] All the three thinkers present a preference for a communitarian concept of democracy as against the notion of democracy as majority rule.

The idea of this collection of essays is not merely to put together scattered material on the three thinkers - M.K. Gandhi, M.N. Roy and Jayaprakash Narayan. The book attempts to bring out through a selection of their own writings as well as of commentaries on them the essential aspects of their intellectual development and their contribution to contemporary Indian political thought. The writings and thought of these thinkers are of seminal importance for several reasons. Their work provides us with a glimpse of the historical debates at a time of tremendous activity in the making of the nation and the transformation of the world and are related to some of the most important theoretical concerns of politics today – war and peace, identity formation and multiculturalism, nationalism and its limits, secularism, development and justice, and the problem of inequality — whether social, economic or political, whether regional, national or international. Gandhi is being presented increasingly as a post-modern thinker as he espoused the cause of civil society rather than the state and challenged not only the British empire in India but also the rule of the state and of corporate bureaucracies; he re-invented satyagraha and sarvodaya, and without denying the market he realised that individuals would need to limit consumption and materialist pursuits if society was to protect itself from the alienation of unrestrained commodification.[48] In spite of the differences in their world view it is interesting to note that the ideas of both Roy (to a limited extent) and JP (almost entirely) start to resemble the Gandhian communitarian notions of democracy in their later writings. One can see that Gandhi thus emerges as the most influential thinker and leader of the time. This is apparent also from the writings of both Roy and JP, who are compelled to react to Gandhi's ideas and politics, even if at times only to refute them. Their ideas and views also provide us with a glimpse of the historical debate and contestation of ideas among the tall thinkers of the nationalist and the internationalist movements of the first half of the twentieth century and even later in India. Another important dimension of their writings, especially those of Jayaprakash Narayan, is the expression of a growing concerns about the way Indian democracy has developed and discussions of remedial measures to be taken. The last but not the least important reason for the inclusion of these three writers in the volume is that all three of them, for different reasons, preferred to stay away from active power politics and that they were led to this by the logic of their theoretical positions and not merely by personal or temperament factors.

The selected articles, especially those by Gandhi and M.N. Roy and to a lesser extent Jayaprakash Narayan, also provide a study in contrast – broadly representing a secular and a non-secular view of man, society and politics. Gandhi is of course the obvious representative of the non-secular view insofar as he considers religion to be an essential part of human life. The secular tradition emerges with the advent of the Russian Revolution and the growing influence of Marxist philosophy on the Indian freedom movement. Nehru, Roy and J.P. may be taken as representatives of the secular tradition, the purest form of which can be seen in the writings of Roy, whose unrelenting rationalism sets him apart from the other thinkers. Broadly speaking, the secularists (a) do not wish to mingle religion and politics, (b) explain historical processes in terms of material factors, (c) view colonialism primarily in economic terms, (d) see the freedom struggle as dominated by the middle classes, (e) see a socialist revolution as necessary to accomplish the aim of national freedom and independence, and (f) consider rationality rather than religion as the basis of morality. Reflections on religion constitute a part of their writings though only to undermine its importance. To Roy 'no religion is based upon any eternal, immutable and absolute truths...the basis of all religions being the material conditions of life, not only are the forms bound to change from time to time, but religion itself, that is faith in some super-natural agency, becomes useless when the spiritual development of man attains a sufficiently high level'.[49] In India, Roy argues, religious ideology retained its dominance over culture even after its historical usefulness had been exhausted as it was not subjected to the criticism born of scientific knowledge. Thus spiritualism was not exposed to all its absurdities and retained its 'pristine purity' – supposedly a special genius of Indian culture. The domination of religious ideology was merely the result of 'a prolonged period of social stagnation' and was nothing to be proud of.[50] The impending renaissance in India will take place, not under 'great men' or their moralising mysticism but 'under the banner of a revolutionary philosophy'.[51] Therefore one has not to return to the imaginary Golden Age of India's past (the past according to Roy cannot inspire, it only teaches lessons) but remember our journey forward. Roy has immense faith in the endless potentialities inherent in human being – and as man gains confidence in himself, 'spiritualism ceases to be an intellectual necessity'.[52]

This book should interest a wide spectrum of readers, from students, teachers and, researchers to journalists and the common reader interested in ideas and in India. Many of the articles included in this volume have been published before. A few of the articles were originally presented in a seminar on 'Power to the People' organised under the joint auspices of The Radical Humanist Association, P.U.C.L. Delhi, The J.P. Centenary Committee and The ICCSR (North Range) in March 2002. The name of the book 'Power to the People' is derived from the title of the seminar as much as from contemporary political concerns. The thinkers included in the book have amply reflected on different dimensions of the issue – both structural as well as conceptual. Their concepts such as 'lokniti', 'people's committees', 'satyagraha' suggest a flavour which is 'un-western', but they are nevertheless globally applicable.

The selection of articles, both primary and secondary, becomes difficult given the constraints of space – especially when the thinkers have been both prolific and profound and have impacted the events of their times and raised several issues which continue to be of significance even today. In the selection of the primary writings of the three thinkers we have kept in mind their central concerns and the evolution of their ideas, though we realise that it is not possible to do full justice to them merely through such a selection as this. The sheer quantity of the available secondary material, particularly on Gandhi, is mind-boggling and makes selection even more difficult.

Summary of articles in Volume I

The primary material consists of Gandhi's *Hind Swaraj* which he wrote in a 'frenzy' aboard a ship from South Africa to India. This book is considered important because it brings out not merely his critique of the western civilization, his comments on the revolutionary movements in India and the rejection of the use of violence in politics, but also his ideal of a society based on *ahimsa*, *dharma* and *Ramrajya*. Gandhi argues that a society based on non-violence cannot be built on a foundation of a 'factory civilization' but can only be established in self-contained villages. He discusses the concept of swaraj not just as self-government but as self-rule. He subscribes to an 'inclusivist' view of Indian society and an 'assimilative' concept of Indian culture. According to Bidyut Chakrabarty, his later writings in *Harijan* (1933 onwards) are 'less philosophical' and more in the form of commentaries on contemporary issues such as untouchability and gender.

Bhikhu Parekh discusses Gandhi's critique of western civilization as a modern civilization characterised by materialism and consumerism. India is a battleground, the modern *Kurukshetra*, on which modern and ancient civilizations are 'locked in a momentous battle for the future'. Gandhi lists the dehumanising factors of modern civilization and dismantles its supposed achievements in the fields of science and technology, law and education, and social relations and the system of governance, thereby providing a 'fresh perspective' on the critique of western civilization.

A. J. Parel argues that Gandhi conceives of a nation as *praja* (the people of the community) rather than as *rashtra*, which has an underlying notion of power, or as a modern nation-state based on brute force, exclusiveness and national interest. Anil

Dutta Mishra highlights the sources, both Western and Indian, of the Gandhian concept of Sarvodaya and argues that it can be an alternative to other existing political systems, including the communist, socialist and liberal systems. He further argues that the Gandhian concept of Sarvodaya offers an alternative solution to the 'malady' of present day existence.

A.L. Basham argues that even though Gandhi explicitly acknowledges his debt to western thinkers, crucial Gandhian concepts like truth, satyagraha and ahimsa have their roots in the Indian philosophical tradition, especially as mediated through his experiences as a child and youth in nineteenth-century Gujarat. Only two major ideas in his conceptual framework – namely the dignity of manual labour and the emancipation of women seem to have no prototypes in India's past. Basham concludes that Gandhi's genius consists in harmonising ideas from different traditions.

Thomas Pantham draws attention to the fact that so far little attention has been paid to the relevance of Gandhi in a post-liberal, 'post-capitalist' scenario. Given the growing realisation of the limitations of liberalism as an institutional arrangement and as a set of values, it is important to recall Gandhi, who can be seen as providing a way out of the liberal-democratic impasse. In his analysis of the role of the capitalist state and his view that a technocratic model of politics is always at the expense of democracy, Gandhi, according to Pantham, anticipates Habermas.

This analysis is supplemented by Ronald J.Terchek's representation of Gandhi as a thinker who anticipates post-modernism in his criticism of some of the central axioms of modernity, namely the tendency to 'homogenise' and establish one universal standard to judge politics, society and culture. By opposing these tendencies, argues Terchek, Gandhi stands for the preservation of the autonomy of individuals and for a robust diversity in society. However, Terchek qualifies his argument by suggesting that though in his 'decentring impulse' Gandhi may resemble the post-modernists, yet he cannot be bracketed with it entirely, primarily because the post-modernists would see Gandhi's 'cosmos' as 'too much like a *telos* with its own imperatives.. .and its unwitting openness to domination'.

In a world of corporate globalisation ('the suicide economy') one needs to defend life's freedom and diversity. Vandana Shiva's article represents the continued relevance and inspirational value of Gandhi in a context in which man's arrogance and greed prevent him from realising the need to live in harmony with nature.

T.K. Oommen discusses the continued relevance of Gandhi in present-day India, where the vast majority of the population continues to live in the villages. The growing inequalities in a globalising world between nations and amongst peoples call for a serious re-thinking of Gandhi's writings.

Several articles bring out the persistent ideological criticism of Gandhi by the Royists, who were equally concerned with the concept of individual freedom, the analysis of the relationship between the individual and society and the need for power to the people. In 'Mr. Gandhi: An Analysis' (first published in *The Vanguard of Indian Independence*, Vols. 1&3: May 15 and June 15, 1922), Evelyn Roy, writing under the name of Santi Devi, offers a balance sheet of the 'defects' and 'achievements' of Gandhism from the point of view of radical humanism. Presenting Gandhi as a 'saintly man who purifies us at sight', she compares him to Thomas Aquinas and St. Francis of Assisi. His personal example gives force to his moral precepts. But in those more worldly faculties of political leadership, she argues, Gandhi is not so conspicuously successful. As a philosophy Mr. Gandhi's is 'neither original nor unique'. M.N. Roy critically examines both Gandhi and Marx's position on the question of means and ends, but acknowledges Gandhi's contribution to political theory in raising the question of morality in politics.

Sibnarayan Ray's article 'M.N. Roy and the Mahatma' offers, as its sub-title suggests, a radical critique of Gandhi and Gandhism. Placed in their respective historical contexts and areas of functioning, Gandhi and Roy are presented as professing very different world-views. Out of the three persistent critics of

Gandhi – namely Jinnah, Ambedkar and M.N. Roy, the author focuses essentially on Roy's critique of Gandhi. Though Gandhi's martyrdom did make him reconsider his view of Gandhi's personality, ideas and methods, Roy still continued to believe that in spite of the 'vaguely visualised humanist' idea, Gandhi remained groping in the 'twilight of medievalism'. Ray brings out many contradictions seen by M.N. Roy in Gandhi's ideas and argues that at no time does he find any evidence that Roy was even remotely influenced by Gandhi or even aware of any possibility of a confluence of ideas in the future.

JP in his article 'Gandhi and the Politics of Decentralization' argues that Gandhi's political system is only a part of a larger whole which demands a comprehensive change in all aspects of society. He therefore finds Indian democracy, despite its many successes, a failure when seen from the Gandhian standpoint of communitarian democracy. Panchayati Raj has not been able to take off because of a highly centralised administration inherited from the past, and 'Power to the People', the goal of many modern revolutions, remains unrealised.

References

1. Quoted in Norman Palmer, 'Indian and Western Political Thought: Coalescence or Clash?', *American Political Science Review*, 49:3(1955), p. 747.
2. Bhikhu Parekh, *Colonialism, Tradition and Reform: An Analysis of Gandhi's Political Discourse*, revised edition (New Delhi: Sage, 1999; first published 1989), p. 42.
3. Anthony J. Parel (ed.), *Gandhi: Hind Swaraj and Other Writings*, (C.U.P.1997, Asian Education, 1997), Introduction, p. xivii.
4. *Ibid.*, Introduction, p. l.
5. *Ibid.*, p. 11.
6. Sudipta Kaviraj, 'The Heteronomous Radicalism of M.N. Roy', in *Political Thought in Modern India*, edited by Thomas Pantham and Kenneth L. Deutsch (New Delhi: Sage Publications, 1986), pp. 234- 235.

7. Gandhi, quoted by A.L. Basham, 'Traditional Influences on the Thought of Mahatma Gandhi', in R. Kumar (ed.), *Essays on Gandhian Politics: The Rowlatt Satyagraha of 1919* (Oxford: Clarendon Press, 1971), p. 28.
8. A.J. Parel, Gandhi: *Hind Swaraj and Other Writings*, Introduction, pp. xlix, xlvii.
9. Rajat Ray, 'Three Interpretation of Indian Nationalism', in B.R. Nanda (ed.), *Essays in Modern Indian History* (New Delhi: OUP, 1980), p. 5.
10. Sudipta Kaviraj, 'Marxian Theory and Analysis of Indian Politics', in *A Survey of Research in Political Science: Political Thought*, Vol. IV, Indian Council of Social Science Research (New Delhi: Allied Publishers, 1986), p. 149.
11. M.N. Roy, 'Rationalist Humanism: An Alternative' (1947-48), in R.M. Pal (ed.), *Selections from The Marxian Way and The Humanist Way* (New Delhi: Ajanta Publications, 1999), p. 249.
12. A.J. Parel, 'Gandhi's Idea of Nation in *Hind Swaraj*', *Gandhi Marg* (October-December, 1991), p. 263.
13. 'Gandhi', in A. Appadorai (ed.), *Documents on Political Thought in Modern India*, Vol.1 (Bombay: OUP, 1973), p. 527.
14. *Ibid.*, p. 527.
15. National Archives, Gandhi-Polak Papers, Vol.V, Part I, Press Clippings, *The Baptist*, 17th September, 1931.
16. Quoted by Satish Saberwal in 'Anxieties, Identities, Complexity, Reality' in Mushirul Hasan (ed.), *Will Secularism Survive?* (Gurgaon: Imprint One, 2004); See also Amalendu Misra, *Identity and Religion: Foundations of Anti-Islamism in India* (New Delhi: Sage, 2004), and Peter Van der Veer, *Religious Nationalism: Hindus and Muslims in India* (New Delhi: OUP, 1994).
17. Pratap Bhanu Mehta, 'Secularism and the Identity Trap', in M. Hasan (ed.), *Will Secularism Survive?* (Gurgaon: Imprint One, 2004).

18. Z.M. Quaraishi, 'Political Thought in Medieval India', in *A Survey of Research in Political Science: Political Thought*, Vol. IV (New Delhi: Allied Publishers, 1986), p. 94.
19. *Ibid.*, pp. 98-99.
20. M.N. Roy, *The Historical Role of Islam* (Calcutta: Renaissance Publishers, 1939; third impression 1958), p. 87.
21. *Ibid.*, p. 82.
22. *Ibid.*, p. 88.
23. *Ibid.*, p. 91.
24. M.K. Gandhi, 'The Vows of Hindu-Muslim Unity', *Young India* (7 May 1919), in Raghavan Iyer, *The Moral and Political Writings of Mahatma Gandhi*, Vol. 1 (Oxford: Clarendon Press, 1986), p. 527.
25. M.N. Roy, *The Historical Role of Islam*, p. 81.
26. *Ibid.*, p. 6.
27. *Ibid.*, p. 13.
28. M.N. Roy, 'Morality in Political Practice: Marx and Gandhi', in R.M. Pal (ed.), *Selections from 'The Marxian Way' and 'The Humanist Way'* (New Delhi: Ajanta Publications, 1999), p. 257.
29. *Ibid.*, p. 259.
30. *Ibid.*, p. 258.
31. See David Hardiman, *Gandhi: In his Time and Ours*, (New Delhi: Permanent Black, 2003), Chapter 9.
32. Thomas Pantham, *Political Theories and Social Reconstruction: A Critical Survey of the Literature on India* (New Delhi: Sage, 1995), p. 102.
33. Gopal Guru, 'Dalits in Pursuit of Modernity', in Romila Thapar (ed.), *India: Another Millennium* (New Delhi: Viking, 2000), p. 135.
34. M.N. Roy, 'India's Problems and its Solution', in

Sibnarayan Ray (ed.), *Selected Works of M.N. Roy*, Vol. I (Delhi: OUP, 1987), pp. 554-555.

35. National Archives, Gandhi-Polak Papers, Volume V, Press Clippings from abroad and India (*The Hindu*), Mrs. Millie Graham Polak, 'Mr. Gandhi the Man'.
36. M.N. Roy, 'The Ideal of Indian Womanhood' (published by Roy in 1941 as the second volume of *Fragments of a Prisoner's Diary*), included in Sibnarayan Ray (ed.), *Selected Works of M.N. Roy*, Vol. IV: 1932-1936 (Delhi: OUP, 1997), p. 562.
37. Vinit Haksar, *Rights, Communities and Disobedience: Liberalism and Gandhi* (New Delhi: OUP, 2001), p. 140.
38. *Ibid.*, p.139.
39. M.N. Roy, 'Constructive Programme' (Selections from *The Vanguard of Indian Independence*, 1:2 (1 June 1922), Editorial, in Sibnarayan Ray (ed.), *Selected Works of M.N. Roy*, Vol. I : 1917-1922 (Delhi: OUP, 1987), pp. 386-387.
40. Sudipta Kaviraj, 'Marxian Theory and Analysis of Indian Politics' (see note 10 above), p. 148.
41. *Ibid.*, p. 151.
42. Sibnarayan Ray, 'In Freedom's Quest: Life of M.N. Roy' in *The Radical Humanist*, 69:11 (February 2006), pp. 2-5.
43. B.R. Nanda, *Gandhi and his Critics* (Delhi: OUP, 1995; first published in 1985), p. 128.
44. Rajendra Prasad places a summary of M.N. Roy's Draft Constitution among other documents in *India Divided* (Bombay: Hind Kitabs Ltd., 1946; third revised edition, 1947), Part VI: 'Alternatives to Pakistan'.
45. M.N. Roy, 'Inadequacy of Current Ideologies', in *New Humanism: A Manifesto*, (Delhi: Ajanta Publications, 1987), pp. 8-9.
46. Jayaprakash Narayan, 'A Plea for the Reconstruction of the Indian Polity', in Bimal Prasad (ed.), *A*

Revolutionary's Quest: Selected Writings of Jayaprakash Narayan (Delhi: OUP, 1980), pp. 224-225.

47. M.K. Gandhi, *Hind Swaraj*, Chapter V, in A.J. Parel (ed.), *Gandhi: Hind Swaraj and Other Writings* (Cambridge University Press, 1997; 1st South Asian Edition, Delhi: Foundation Books, 1997), p. 30.

48. Lloyd Rudolph, 'Post Modern Gandhi', in *Gandhi Marg*, 27:1 (April-June, 2005), pp. 101-104.

49. M.N. Roy, 'Preconditions of Indian Renaissance', in M.N. Roy (ed.), *The Marxian Way: A Quarterly Journal Devoted to Enquiry and Learning*, Vol. III (1948-1949), p. 369.

50. *Ibid.*, p. 377.

51. *Ibid.*, p. 377.

52. *Ibid.*, p. 365.

M.K. Gandhi

M. K. Gandhi (1869-1948)

Mohandas Karamchand Gandhi was born in Porbandar in Gujarat. The importance of 'ahimsa' and morality in his thought is often traced to his early upbringing, especially the influence of Jainism. In 1883 he was married to Kasturba Gandhi, who remained his life long companion and who also became his partner in his political life. In 1888 he left for England to study law. There he became interested in the study of different religions. In 1893 he went to South Africa to work for an Indian Muslim trading company and experienced racial discrimination at the Pietermaritzburg railway station. This commenced his political career as he played a leading role in protesting against discriminatory laws. In 1904 he read Ruskin's *Unto this Last,* which inspired him to experiment with communitarian living in the Phoenix Settlement the same year and to establish the 'Tolstoy Farm' in 1910. Upon his return to India in 1915, he continued the experiment by establishing the Sabarmati Ashram in Ahmedabad in 1915 and the Sevagram Ashram near Wardha in 1936. He also developed his idea of 'satyagraha', which became an effective weapon to fight for economic and political justice, including the settlement of the grievances of indigo plantation workers in Champaran, Bihar (1917) and of the peasants in Kheda (1918) and the resolution of the textile workers' disputes in Ahmedabad in the same year.

Gandhi is better known the world over for converting the freedom struggle into an anti-colonial mass movement. The Rowlatt Satyagraha (1919), the Non-Cooperation Movement

(1920-22), the Civil Disobedience Movement (1930-31, 1932-34) and the Quit India Movement (1942) are recorded well in history and Gandhi's role is amply recognized. However, Gandhi himself gave importance to his 'Constructive Programme'. The principal points in this programme were: the adoption of Charkha and Khadi, and the Removal of Untouchability and Alcoholism. These had important socioeconomic implications, though Gandhi's resistance to the application of the methods of satyagraha to achieve the latter goals made him suspect in the eyes of B.R. Ambedkar and led to the Gandhi-Ambedkar debate when Gandhi opposed the proposal for a separate electorate for the Harijans in the Communal Award of 1932. Gandhi is also given credit for bringing women into the freedom struggle and into politics generally. On the 'national' question Gandhi worked for an inclusive concept of nationhood and pleaded for communal harmony. In the 1940s, when the Muslim League made a demand for partition of the country on the basis of the 'two-nation' theory, Gandhi corresponded with Jinnah for over a year in 1944 to persuade him to change his views and drop the demand for partition. On the eve of Independence, while the Nation celebrated its freedom, Gandhi spent his time in a remote area in Bengal applying the healing touch to a riot-torn people.

Gandhi's seminal work is *Hind Swaraj.* All his life he wrote on public issues and concepts to friends, followers and critics. The *Harijan, Navjivan* and *Young India* were important mouth pieces for public debate. Gandhi wrote prolifically on a wide range of subjects, including politics, religion, ethics, social reconstruction and even health and diet. His collected works have been compiled in a hundred volumes and the continuously growing body of commentary on and analysis of his life and works will fill many more volumes. A selection of his major works is given below.

1903 *Indian Opinion:* Gandhi launched this weekly newspaper in four languages – English, Gujarati, Hindi and Tamil.

1909 *Hind Swarajya* (written in Gujarati); translation of Tolstoy's *Letter to a Hindoo.*

1910 *Indian Home Rule* (the English translation of *Hind Swarajya* by Gandhi).

1919	Editor of the weeklies, *Young India* (in English) and *Navjivan* (in Gujarati).
1927	*The Story of .... Experiments with Truth:* Volume I.
1928	*Satyagraha in South Africa.*
1929	*The Story of my Experiments with Truth:* Volume II.
1933	Founds the English Weekly *Harijan.*
1941	*Constructive Programme: Its Meaning and Place.*
1948	*A Draft Constitution* for the Indian National Congress.

2

Hind Swaraj or Indian Home Rule

M.K. Gandhi

I

The Congress and Its Officials

M.K. Gandhi

Reader: Just at present there is a Home Rule wave passing over India. All our countrymen appear to be pining for National Independence. A similar spirit pervades them even in South Africa. Indians seem to be eager to acquire rights. Will you explain your views in this matter?

Editor: You have put the question well, but the answer is not easy. One of the objects of a newspaper is to understand popular feeling and to give expression to it; another is to arouse among the people certain desirable sentiments; and the third is fearlessly to expose popular defects. The exercise of all these three functions is involved in answering your question. To a certain extent the people's will have to be expressed; certain sentiments will need to be fostered, and defects will have to be brought to light. But, as you have asked the question, it is my duty to answer it.

Reader: Do you then consider that a desire for Home Rule has been created among us?

Editor: That desire gave rise to the National Congress. The choice of the word "National" implies it.

Reader: That surely, is not the case. Young India seems to ignore the Congress. It is considered to be an instrument for perpetuating British Rule.

Editor: That opinion is not justified. Had not the Grand Old Man of India prepared the soil, our young men could not have even spoken about Home Rule. How can we forget what Mr.

Reprinted with the permission of Navajivan Trust, Ahmedabad, from M.K. Gandhi, *Hind Swaraj,* seventeenth reprint (Ahmedabad: Navajivan Publishing House, 2005), pp. 17-90.

Hume has written, how he has lashed us into action, and with what effort he has awakened us, in order to achieve the objects of the Congress? Sir William Wedderburn has given his body, mind and money to the same cause. His writings are worthy of perusal to this day. Professor Gokhale in order to prepare the nation, embraced poverty and gave twenty years of his life. Even now, he is living in poverty. The late Justice Budruddin Tyebji was also one of those who, through the Congress, sowed the seed of Home Rule. Similarly, in Bengal, Madras, the Punjab and other places, there have been lovers of India and members of the Congress, both Indian and English.

Reader: Stay, stay; you are going too far, you are straying away from my question. I have asked you about Home - or Self-Rule; you are discussing foreign rule. I do not desire to hear English names, and you are giving me such names. In these circumstances, I do not think we can ever meet. I shall be pleased if you will confine yourself to Home Rule. All other talk will not satisfy me.

Editor: You are impatient. I cannot afford to be likewise. If you will bear with me for a while, I think you will find that you will obtain what you want. Remember the old proverb that the tree does not grow in one day. The fact that you have checked me and that you do not want to hear about the well-wishers of India shows that, for you at any rate, Home Rule is yet far away. If we had many like you, we would never make any advance. This thought is worthy of your attention.

Reader: It seems to me that you simply want to put me off by talking round and round. Those whom you consider to be well- wishers of India are not such in my estimation. Why, then, should I listen to your discourse on such people? What has he whom you consider to be the Father of the Nation done for it? He says that the English Governors will do justice and that we should co-operate with them.

Editor: I must tell you, with all gentleness, that it must be a matter of shame for us that you should speak about that great man in terms of disrespect. Just look at his work. He has dedicated his life to the service of India. We have learned what we know from him. It was the respected Dadabhai who taught us that the English, had sucked our life-blood. What does it matter that, today, his trust is still in the English nation? Is Dadabhai less to be honoured because, in the exuberance of youth, we are prepared to go a step further? Are we, on that account, wiser than he? It is a mark of wisdom not to kick away the very step from which we have risen higher. The removal of a step from a staircase brings down the whole of it. When, out of infancy, we grow into youth, we do not despise infancy, but, on the contrary, we recall with affection the days of our childhood. If, after many years of study, a teacher were to teach me something, and if I were to build a little more on the foundation laid by that teacher, I would not, on that account, be considered wiser than the teacher. He would always command my respect. Such is the case with the Grand Old Man of India. We must admit that he is the author of nationalism.

Reader: You have spoken well. I can now understand that we must look upon Mr. Dadabhai with respect. Without him and men like him, we should probably not have the spirit that fires us. How can the same be said of Professor Gokhale? He has constituted himself a great friend of the English; he says that we have to learn a great deal from them, that we have to learn their political wisdom, before we can talk of Home Rule. I am tired of reading his speeches.

Editor: If you are tired, it only betrays your impatience. We believe that those, who are discontented with the slowness of their parents and are angry because the parents would not run with their children, are considered disrespectful to their parents. Professor Gokhale occupies the place of a parent. What does it matter if he cannot run with us? A nation that is desirous of securing Home Rule cannot afford to despise its ancestors. We shall become useless, if we lack respect for our elders. Only men with mature thoughts are capable of ruling themselves and not the hasty-tempered. Moreover, how many Indians were there like Professor Gokhale, when he gave himself to Indian education? I verily believe that whatever Professor Gokhale does, he does with pure motives and with a view of serving India. His devotion to the Motherland is so great that he would give his life for it, if necessary. Whatever he says is said not to flatter anyone but because he believes it to be true. We are bound, therefore, to entertain the highest regard for him.

Reader: Are we, then, to follow him in every respect?

Editor: I never said any such thing. If we conscientiously differed from him, the learned Professor himself would advise us to follow the dictates of our conscience rather than him. Our chief purpose is not to decry his work, but to believe that he is infinitely greater than we are, and to feel assured that compared with his work for India, ours is infinitesimal. Several newspapers write disrespectfully of him. It is our duty to protest against such writings. We should consider men like Professor Gokhale to be the pillars of Home Rule. It is a bad habit to say that another man's thoughts are bad and ours only are good and that those holding different views from ours are the enemies of the country.

Reader: I now begin to understand somewhat your meaning. I shall have to think the matter over. But what you say about Mr. Hume and Sir William Wedderburn is beyond my comprehension.

Editor: The same rule holds good for the English as for the Indians. I can never subscribe to the statement that all Englishmen are bad. Many Englishmen desire Home Rule for India. That the English people are somewhat more selfish than others is true, but that does not prove that every Englishman is bad. We who seek justice will have to do justice to others. Sir William does not wish ill to India, — that should be enough for us. As we proceed, you will see that, if we act justly, India will be sooner free. You will see, too, that if we shun every Englishman as an enemy, Home Rule will be delayed. But if we are just to them, we shall receive their support in our progress towards the goal.

Reader: All this seems to me at present to be simply nonsensical. English support and the obtaining of Home Rule are two contradictory things. How can the English people tolerate Home Rule for us? But I do not want you to decide this question for me just yet. To spend time over it is useless. When you have shown how we can have Home Rule, perhaps I shall understand your views. You have prejudiced me against you by discoursing on English help. I would, therefore, beseech you not to continue this subject.

Editor: I have no desire to do so. That you are prejudiced against me is not a matter for much anxiety. It is well that I should say unpleasant things at the commencement. It is my duty patiently to try to remove your prejudice.

Reader: I like that last statement. It emboldens me to say what I like. One thing still puzzles me. I do not understand how the Congress laid the foundation of Home Rule.

Editor: Let us see. The Congress brought together Indians from different parts of India, and enthused us with the idea of nationality. The Government used to look upon it with disfavour. The Congress has always insisted that the Nation should control revenue and expenditure. It has always desired self-government after the Canadian model. Whether we can get it or not, whether we desire it or not, and whether there is not something more desirable, are different questions. All I have to show is that the Congress gave us a foretaste of Home Rule. To deprive it of the honour is not proper, and for us to do so would not only be ungrateful, but retard the fulfillment of our object. To treat the Congress as an institution inimical to our growth as a nation would disable us from using that body.

II
The Partition of Bengal

Reader: Considering the matter as you put it, it seems proper to say that the foundation of Home Rule was laid by the Congress. But you will admit that this cannot be considered a real awakening. When and how did the real awakening take place?

Editor: The seed is never seen. It works underneath the ground, is itself destroyed, and the tree which rises above the ground is alone seen. Such is the case with the Congress. Yet, what you call the real awakening took place after the Partition of Bengal. For this we have to be thankful to Lord Curzon. At the time of the Partition, the people of Bengal reasoned with Lord Curzon, but in the pride of power he disregarded all their prayers. He took it for granted that Indians could only prattle, that they could never take any effective steps. He used insulting language, and in the teeth of all opposition partitioned Bengal. That day may be considered to be the day of the partition of the British Empire. The shock the British power received through the Partition has never been equalled by any other act. This does not mean that the other injustices done to India are less glaring than that done by the Partition. The salt-tax is not a small injustice. We shall see many such things later on. But the people were ready to resist the Partition. At that time feeling ran high. Many leading Bengalis were ready to lose their all. They knew their power; hence the conflagration. It is now well-nigh un-quenchable; it is not necessary to quench it either. The Partition will go, Bengal will be reunited, but the rift in the English barque will remain; it must daily widen. India awakened is not likely to fall asleep. The demand for the abrogation of the Partition is tantamount to a demand for Home Rule. Leaders in Bengal know this. British officials realize it. That is why the Partition still remains. As time passes, the Nation is being forged. Nations are not formed in a day; the formation requires years.

Reader: What, in your opinion, are the results of the Partition?

Editor: Hitherto we have considered that for redress of grievances we must approach the throne, and if we get no redress we must sit still, except that we may still petition. After the Partition, people saw that petitions must be backed up by force, and that they must be capable of suffering. This new spirit must be considered to be the chief result of the Partition. That spirit was seen in the outspoken writings in the Press. That which the people said tremblingly and in secret began to be said and to be written publicly. The Swadeshi movement was inaugurated. People, young and old, used to run away at the sight of an English face; it now no longer awes them. They do not fear even a row, or being imprisoned. Some of the best sons of India are at present in banishment. This is something different from mere petitioning. Thus are the people moved. The spirit generated in Bengal has spread in the north to the Punjab, and in the south to Cape Comorin.

Reader: Do you suggest any other striking result?

Editor: The Partition has not only made a rift in the English ship but has made it in ours also: Great events always produce great results. Our leaders are divided into two parties: the Moderates and the Extremists. These may be considered as the slow party and the impatient party. Some call the Moderates the timid party, and the Extremists the bold party. All interpret the two words according to their preconceptions. This much is certain — that there has arisen an enmity between the two. The one distrusts the other and imputes motives. At the time of the Surat Congress there was almost a fight. I think that this division is not a good thing for the country, but I think also that such divisions will not last long. It all depends upon the leaders how long they will last.

III
Discontent and Unrest

Reader: Then you consider the Partition to be a cause of the awakening? Do you welcome the unrest which has resulted from it?

Editor: When a man rises from sleep, he twists his limbs and is restless. It takes some time before he is entirely awakened. Similarly, although the Partition has caused an awakening, the comatose condition has not yet disappeared. We are still twisting our limbs and are still restless, and just as the state between sleep and awakening must be considered to be necessary, so may the present unrest in India be considered a necessary and, therefore, a proper state. The knowledge that there is unrest will, it is highly probable, enable us to outgrow it. Rising from sleep, we do not continue in a comatose state, but according to our ability, sooner or later, we are completely restored to our senses. So shall we be free from the present unrest which no one likes.

Reader: What is the other form of unrest?

Editor: Unrest is, in reality, discontent. The latter is only now described as unrest. During the Congress period it was labelled discontent. Mr. Hume always said that the spread of discontent in India was necessary. This discontent is a very useful thing. As long as a man is contented with his present lot, so long is it difficult to persuade him to come out of it. Therefore it is that every reform must be preceded by discontent. We throw away things we have, only when we cease to like them. Such discontent has been produced among us after reading the great works of Indians and Englishmen. Discontent has led to unrest, and the latter has brought about many deaths, many imprisonments, many banishments. Such a state of things will still continue. It must be so. All these may be considered good signs but they may also lead to bad results.

IV

What is Swaraj?

Reader: I have now learnt what the Congress has done to make India one nation, how the Partition has caused an awakening, and how discontent and unrest have spread through the land. I would now like to know your views on Swaraj. I fear that our interpretation is not the same as yours.

Editor: It is quite possible that we do not attach the same meaning to the term. You and I and all Indians are impatient to obtain Swaraj, but we are certainly not decided as to what it is. To drive the English out of India is a thought heard from many mouths, but it does not seem that many have properly considered why it should be so. I must ask you a question. Do you think that it is necessary to drive away the English, if we get all we want?

Reader: I should ask of them only one thing, that is: "Please leave our country." If, after they have complied with this request, their withdrawal from India means that they are still in India. I should have no objection. Then we would understand that, in their language, the word "gone" is equivalent to "remained".

Editor: Well then, let us suppose that the English have retired. What will you do then?

Reader: That question cannot be answered at this stage. The state after withdrawal will depend largely upon the manner of it. If, as you assume, they retire, it seems to me we shall still keep their constitution and shall carry on the Government. If they simply retire for the asking we should have an army, etc., ready at hand. We should, therefore, have no difficulty in carrying on the Government.

Editor: You may think so; I do not. But I will not discuss the matter just now. I have to answer your question, and that I can do well by asking you several questions. Why do you want to drive away the English?

Reader: Because India has become impoverished by their Government. They take away our money from year to year. The most important posts are reserved for themselves. We are kept in a state of slavery. They behave insolently towards us and disregard our feelings.

Editor: If they do not take our money away, become gentle, and give us responsible posts, would you still consider their presence to be harmful?

Reader: That question is useless. It is similar to the question whether there is any harm in associating with a tiger if he changes his nature. Such a question is sheer waste of time. When a tiger changes his nature, Englishmen will change theirs. This is not possible, and to believe it to be possible is contrary to human experience.

Editor: Supposing we get Self-Government similar to what the Canadians and the South Africans have, will it be good enough?

Reader: That question also is useless. We may get it when we have the same powers; we shall then hoist our own flag. As is Japan, so must India be. We must own our navy, our army, and we must have our own splendour, and then will India's voice ring through the world.

Editor: You have drawn the picture well. In effect it means this: that we want English rule without the Englishman. You want the tiger's nature, but not the tiger; that is to say, you would make India English. And when it becomes English, it will be called not Hindustan but *Englistan.* This is not the Swaraj that I want.

Reader: I have placed before you my idea of Swaraj as I think it should be. If the education we have received be of any use, if the works of Spencer, Mill and others be of any importance, and if the English Parliament be the Mother of Parliaments, I certainly think that we should copy the English people, and this to such an extent that, just as they do not allow others to obtain a footing in their country, so we should not allow them or others to obtain it in ours. What they have done in their own country has not been done in any other country. It is, therefore, proper for us to import their institutions. But now I want to know your views.

Editor: There is need for patience. My views will develop of themselves in the course of this discourse. It is as difficult for me to understand the true nature of Swaraj as it seems to you to be easy. I shall, therefore, for the time being, content myself with endeavouring to show that what you call Swaraj is not truly Swaraj.

V

The Condition of England

Reader: Then from your statement I deduce that the Government of England is not desirable and not worth copying by us.

Editor: Your deduction is justified. The condition of England at present is pitiable. I pray to God that India may never be in that plight. That which you consider to be the Mother of Parliaments is like a sterile woman and a prostitute. Both these are harsh terms, but exactly fit the case. That Parliament has not yet, of its own accord, done a single good thing. Hence I have compared it to a sterile woman. The natural condition of that Parliament is such that, without outside pressure, it can do nothing. It is like a prostitute because it is under the control of ministers who change from time to time. Today it is under Mr. Asquith, tomorrow it may be under Mr. Balfour.

Reader: You have said this sarcastically. The term "sterile woman" is not applicable. The Parliament, being elected by the people, must work under public pressure. This is its quality.

Editor: You are mistaken. Let us examine it a little more closely. The best men are supposed to be elected by the people. The members serve without pay and therefore, it must be assumed, only for the public weal. The electors are considered to be educated and therefore we should assume that they would not generally make mistakes in their choice. Such a Parliament should not need the spur of petitions or any other pressure. Its work should be so smooth that its effects would be more apparent day by day. But, as a matter of fact, it is generally acknowledged that the members are hypocritical and selfish. Each thinks of his own little interest. It is fear that is the guiding motive. What is done today may be undone tomorrow. It is not possible to recall a single instance in which finality can be predicted for its work. When the greatest questions are debated, its members have been seen to stretch themselves and to doze. Sometimes the members talk away until the listeners are disgusted. Carlyle has called it the "talking shop of the world". Members vote for their party without a thought. Their so-called, discipline binds them to it. If any member, by way of exception, gives an independent vote, he is considered a renegade. If the money and the time wasted by Parliament were entrusted to a few good men, the English nation would be occupying today a much higher platform. Parliament is simply a costly toy of the nation. These views are by no means peculiar to me. Some great English thinkers have expressed them. One of the members of that Parliament recently said that a true Christian could not become a member of it. Another said that it was a baby. And if it has remained a baby after an existence of seven hundred years, when will it outgrow its babyhood ?

Reader: You have set me thinking; you do not expect me to accept at once all you say. You give me entirely novel views. I shall have to digest them. Will you now explain the epithet "prostitute"?

Editor: That you cannot accept my views at once is only right. If you will read the literature on this subject, you will have some idea of it. Parliament is without a real master? Under the Prime Minister, its movement is not steady but it is buffeted about like a prostitute. The Prime Minister is more concerned about his power than about the welfare of Parliament. His energy is concentrated upon securing the success of his party. His care is not always that Parliament shall do right. Prime Ministers are known to have made Parliament do things merely for party advantage. All this is worth thinking over.

Reader: Then you are really attacking the very men whom we have hitherto considered to be patriotic and honest?

Editor: Yes, that is true; I can have nothing against Prime Ministers, but what I have seen leads me to think that they cannot be considered really patriotic. If they are to be considered honest because they do not take what are generally known as bribes, let them be so considered, but they are open to subtler influences. In order to gain their ends, they certainly bribe people with honours. I do not hesitate to say that they have neither real honesty nor a living conscience.

Reader: As you express these views about Parliament, I would like to hear you on the English people, so that I may have your view of their Government.

Editor: To the English voters their newspaper is their Bible. They take their cue from their newspapers which are often dishonest. The same fact is differently interpreted by different newspapers, according to the party in whose interests they are edited. One newspaper would consider a great Englishman to be a paragon of honesty, another would consider him dishonest. What must be the condition of the people whose newspapers are of this type?

Reader: You shall describe it.

Editor: These people change their views frequently. It is said that they change them every seven years. These views swing like the pendulum of a clock and are never steadfast. The people would follow a powerful orator or a man who gives them parties, receptions, etc. As are the people, so is their Parliament. They have certainly one quality very strongly developed. They will never allow their country to be lost. If any person were to cast an evil eye on it, they would pluck out his eyes. But that does not mean that the nation possesses every other virtue or that it should be imitated. If India copies England, it is my firm conviction that she will be ruined.

Reader: To what do you ascribe this state of England?

Editor: It is not due to any peculiar fault of the English people, but the condition is due to modern civilization. It is a civilization only in name. Under it the nations of Europe are becoming degraded and ruined day by day.

VI
Civilization

Reader: Now you will have to explain what you mean by civilization.

Editor: It is not a question of what I mean. Several English writers refuse to call that civilization which passes under that name. Many books have been written upon that subject. Societies have been formed to cure the nation of the evils of civilization. A great English writer has written a work called *Civilization: Its Cause and Cure.* Therein he has called it a disease.

Reader: Why do we not know this generally?

Editor: The answer is very simple. We rarely find people arguing against themselves. Those who are intoxicated by modern civilization are not likely to write against it. Their care will be to find out facts and arguments in support of it, and this they do unconsciously, believing it to be true. A man whilst he is dreaming, believes in his dream; he is undeceived only when he is awakened from his sleep. A man labouring under the bane of civilization is like a dreaming man. What we usually read are the works of defenders of modern civilization, which undoubtedly claims among its votaries very brilliant and even some very good men. Their writings hypnotize us. And so, one by one, we are drawn into the vortex.

Reader: This seems to be very plausible. Now will you tell me something of what you have read and thought of this civilization?

Editor: Let us first consider what state of things is described by the word "civilization". Its true test lies in the fact that people living in it make bodily welfare the object of life. We will take some examples. The people of Europe today live in better-built houses than they did a hundred years ago. This is considered an emblem of civilization, and this is also a matter to promote bodily happiness. Formerly, they wore skins, and used spears as their weapons. Now, they wear long trousers, and, for embelishing their bodies, they wear a variety of clothing, and, instead of spears, they carry with them revolvers containing five or more chambers. If people of a certain country, who have hitherto not been in the habit of wearing much clothing, boots, etc., adopt European clothing, they are supposed to have become civilized out of savagery. Formerly, in Europe, people ploughed; their lands mainly by manual labour. Now, one man can plough a vast tract by means of steam engines and can thus amass great wealth. This is called a sign of civilization. Formerly, only a few men wrote valuable books. Now, anybody writes and prints anything he likes and poisons people's minds. Formerly, men travelled in waggons. Now, they fly through the air in trains at the rate of four hundred and more miles per day. This is considered the height of civilization. It has been stated that, as men progress, they shall be able to travel in airship and reach any part of the world in a few hours. Men will not need the use of their hands and feet. They will press a button, and they will have their clothing by their side. They will press another button, and they will have their newspaper. A third, and a motor-car will be in waiting for them. They will have a variety of delicately dished up food. Everything will be done by machinery. Formerly, when people wanted to fight with one another, they measured between them their bodily strength; now it is possible to take away thousands of lives by one man working behind a gun from a hill. This is civilization. Formerly, men worked in the open air only as much as they liked. Now thousands of workmen meet together and for the sake of maintenance work in factories or mines. Their condition is worse than that of beasts. They are obliged to work, at the risk of their lives, at most dangerous occupations, for the sake of millionaires. Formerly, men were made slaves under physical compulsion. Now they are enslaved by temptation of money and of the luxuries that money can buy. There are now diseases of which people never dreamt before, and an army of doctors are engaged in finding out their cures, and so hospitals have increased. This is a test of civilization. Formerly, special messengers were required and much expense was incurred in order to send letters; today, anyone can abuse his fellow by means of a letter for one penny. True, at the same cost, one can send one's thanks also. Formerly, people had two or three meals consisting of home-made bread and vegetables; now, they require something to eat every two hours so that they have hardly leisure for anything else. What more need I say? All this you can ascertain from several authoritative books. These are all true tests of civilization. And if anyone speaks to the contrary know that he is ignorant. This civilization takes note neither of morality nor of religion. Its votaries calmly state that their business is not to teach religion. Some even consider it to be a superstitious growth. Others put on the clock of religion, and prate about morality. But, after twenty years' experience, 1 have come to the conclusion that immorality is often taught in the name of morality. Even a child can understand that in all I have described above there can be no inducement to morality. Civilization seeks to increase bodily comforts, and it fails miserably even in doing so.

This civilization is irreligion, and it has taken such a hold on the people in Europe that those who are in it appear to be half mad. They lack real physical strength or courage. They keep up their energy by intoxication. They can hardly be happy in solitude. Women, who should be the queens of households, wander in the streets or they slave away in factories. For the sake of a pittance, half a million women in England alone are labouring under trying circumstances in factories or similar institutions. This awful fact is one of the causes of the daily growing suffragette movement.

This civilization is such that one has only to be patient and it will be self-destroyed. According to the teaching of Mahommed this would be considered a Satanic Civilization. Hinduism calls it the Black Age. I cannot give you an adequate conception of it. It is eating into the vitals of the English nation. It must be shunned. Parliaments are really emblems of slavery. If you will sufficiently think over this, you will entertain the same opinion and cease to blame the English. They rather deserve our sympathy. They are a shrewd nation and I therefore believe that they will cast off the evil. They are enterprising and industrious, and their mode of thought is not inherently immoral.

Neither are they bad at heart. I therefore respect them. Civilization is not an incurable disease, but it should never be forgotten that the English people are at present afflicted by it.

VII
Why was India Lost?

Reader: You have said much about civilization — enough to make me ponder over it. I do not now know what I should adopt and what I should avoid from the nations of Europe, but one question comes to my lips immediately. If civilization is a disease and if it has attacked England, why has she been able to take India, and why is she able to retain it?

Editor: Your question is not very difficult to answer, and we shall presently be able to examine the true nature of Swaraj; for I am aware that I have still to answer that question. I will, however, take up your previous question. The English have not taken India; we have given it to them. They are not in India because of their strength, but because we keep them. Let us now see whether these propositions can be sustained. They came to our country originally for purposes of trade. Recall the Company Bahadur. Who made it Bahadur? They had not the slightest intention at the time of establishing a kingdom. Who assisted the Company's officers? Who was tempted at the sight of their silver? Who bought their goods? History testifies that we did all this. In order to become rich all at once we welcomed the Company's officers with open arms. We assisted them. If I am in the habit of drinking *bhang* and a seller thereof sells it to me, am 1 to blame him or myself? By blaming the seller, shall I be able to avoid the habit? And, if a particular retailer is driven away will not another take his place? A true servant of India will have to go to the root of the matter. If an excess of food has caused me indigestion, I shall certainly not avoid it by blaming water. He is a true physician who probes the cause of disease, and if you pose as a physician for the disease of India, you will have to find out its true cause.

Reader: You are right. Now I think you will not have to argue much with me to drive your conclusions home. I am impatient to know your further views. We are now on a most interesting topic. I shall, therefore, endeavour to follow your thought, and stop you when I am in doubt.

Editor: 1 am afraid that, in spite of your enthusiasm, as we proceed further, we shall have differences of opinion. Never-the less 1 shall argue only when you stop me. We have already seen that the English merchants were able to get a footing in India because we encouraged them. When our Princes fought among themselves, they sought the assistance of Company Bahadur. That corporation was versed alike in commerce and war. It was unhampered by questions of morality. Its object was to increase its commerce and to make money. It accepted our assistance, and increased the number of its warehouses. To protect the latter it employed an army which was utilized by us also. Is it not then useless to blame the English for what we did at that time? The Hindus and the Mahomedans were at daggers drawn. This, too, gave the Company its opportunity and thus we created the circumstances that gave the Company its control over India. Hence it is truer to say that we gave India to the English than that India was lost.

Reader: Will you now tell me how they are able to return India?

Editor: The causes that gave them India enable them to retain it. Some Englishmen state that they took and they hold India by the sword. Both these statements are wrong. The sword is entirely useless for holding India. We alone keep them. Napolean is said to have described the English as a nation of shopkeepers. It is a fitting description. They hold whatever dominions they have for the sake of their commerce. Their army and their navy are intended to protect it. When the Transvaal offered no such attractions, the late Mr. Gladstone discovered that it was not right for the English to hold it. When it became a paying proposition, resistance led to war. Mr. Chamberlain soon discovered that England enjoyed a suzerainty over the Transvaal. It is related that someone asked the late President Kruger whether there was gold in the moon. He replied that it was highly unlikely because, if there were, the English would have annexed it. Many problems can be solved by remembering that money is their God. Then it follows that we keep the English in India for our base self-interest. We like their commerce; they please us by their subtle methods and get what they want from us. To blame them for this is to perpetuate their power. We further strengthen their hold by quarrelling amongst ourselves. If you accept the above statements, it is proved that the English entered India for the purposes of trade. They remain in it for the same purpose and we help them to do so. Their arms and ammunition are perfectly useless. In this connection I remind you that it is the British flag which is waving in Japan and not the Japanese. The English have a treaty with Japan for the sake of their commerce, and you will see that if they can manage it their commerce will greatly expand in that country. They wish to convert the whole world into a vast market for their goods. That they cannot do so is true, but the blame will not be theirs. They will leave no stone unturned to reach the goal.

VIII
The Condition of India

Reader: I now understand why the English hold India. I should like to know your views about the condition of our country.

Editor: It is a sad condition. In thinking of it my eyes water and my throat gets parched. I have grave doubts whether I shall be able sufficiently to explain what is in my heart. It is my deliberate opinion that India is being ground down, not under the English heel, but under that of modern civilization. It is groaning under the monster's terrible weight. There is yet time to escape it, but every day makes it more and more difficult. Religion is dear to me and my first complaint is that India is becoming irreligious. Here I am not thinking of the Hindu or the Mahomedan or the Zoroastrian religion but of that religion underlies all religions. We are turning away from God.

Reader: How so?

Editor: There is a charge laid against us that we are a lazy people and that Europeans are industrious and enterprizing. We have accepted the charge and we therefore wish to change our condition. Hinduism, Islam, Zoroastrianism, Christianity and all other religions teach that we should remain passive about worldly pursuits and active about godly pursuits, that we should set a limit to our worldly ambition and that our religious ambition should be illimitable. Our activity should be directed into the latter channel.

Reader: You seem to be encouraging religious charlatanism. Many a cheat has, by talking in a similar strain, led the people astray.

Editor: You are bringing an unlawful charge against religion. Humbug there undoubtedly is about all religions. Where there is light, there is also shadow. I am prepared to maintain that humbugs in worldly matters are far worse than the humbugs in religion. The humbug of civilization that I am endeavouring to show to you is not to be found in religion.

Reader: How can you say that? In the name of religion Hindus and Mahomedans fought against one another. For the same cause Christians fought Christians. Thousands of innocent men have been murdered, thousands have been burned and tortured in its name. Surely, this is much worse than any civilization.

Editor: I certainly submit that the above hardships are far more bearable than those of civilization. Everybody understands that the cruelties you have named are not part of religion although they have been practised in its name; therefore there is no aftermath to these cruelties. They will always happen so long as there are to be found ignorant and credulous people. But there is no end to the victims destroyed in the fire of civilization. Its deadly effect is that people come under its scorching flames believing it to be all good. They become utterly irreligious and, in reality, derive little advantage from the world. Civilization is like a mouse gnawing while it is soothing us. When its full effect is realized, we shall see that religious superstition is harmless compared to that of modern civilization. I am not pleading for a continuance of religious superstitions. We shall certainly fight them tooth and nail, but we can never do so by disregarding religion. We can only do so by appreciating and conserving the latter.

Reader: Then you will contend that the Pax Britannica is a useless encumbrance?

Editor: You may see peace if you like; I see none.

Reader: You make light of the terror that the Thugs, the Pindaris and the Bhils were to the country.

Editor: If you give the matter some thought, you will see that the terror was by no means such a mighty thing. If it had been a very substantial thing, the other people would have died away before the English advent. Moreover, the present peace is only nominal, for by it we have become emasculated and cowardly.

We are not to assume that the English have changed the nature of the Pindaris and the Bhils. It is therefore, better to suffer the Pindari peril than that someone else should protect us from it and thus render us effeminate. I should prefer to be killed by the arrow of a Bhil than to seek unmanly protection. India without such protection was an India full of valour. Macaulay betrayed gross ignorance when he libelled Indians as being practically cowards. They never merited the charge. Cowards living in a country inhabited by hardy mountaineers and infested by wolves and tigers must surely find an early grave. Have you ever visited our fields? I assure you that our agriculturists sleep fearlessly on their farms even today; but the English and you and I would hesitate to sleep where they sleep. Strength lies in absence of fear, not in the quantity of flesh and muscle we may have on our bodies. Moreover, I must remind you who desire Home Rule that, after all, the Bhils, the Pindaris, and the Thugs are our own countrymen. To conquer them is your and my work. So long as we fear our own brethren, we are unfit to reach the goal.

IX
The Condition of India (Continued): Railways

Reader: You have deprived me of the consolation I used to have regarding peace in India.

Editor: I have merely given you my opinion on the religious aspect, but when I give you my views as to the poverty of India, you will perhaps begin to dislike me because what you and I have hitherto considered beneficial for India no longer appears to me to be so.

Reader: What may that be?

Editor: Railways, lawyers and doctors have impoverished the country so much so that, if we do not wake up in time, we shall be ruined.

Reader: I do now, indeed, fear that we are not likely to agree at all. You are attacking the very institutions which we have hitherto considered to be good.

Editor: It is necessary to exercise patience. The true inwardness of the evils of civilization you will understand with difficulty. Doctors assure us that a consumptive clings to life even when he is about to die. Consumption does not produce apparent hurt – it even produces a seductive colour about a patient's face so as to induce the belief that all is well. Civilization is such a disease and we have to be very wary.

Reader: Very well, then. I shall hear you on the railways.

Editor: It must be manifest to you that, but for the railways, the English could not have such a hold on India as they have. The railways, too, have spread the bubonic plague. Without them, the masses could not move from place to place. They are the carriers of plague germs. Formerly we had natural segregation.

Railways have also increased the frequency of famines because, owing to facility of means of locomotion, people sell out their grain and it is sent to the dearest markets. People become careless and so the pressure of famine increases. Railways accentuate the evil nature of man. Bad men fulfil their evil designs with greater rapidity. The holy places of India have become unholy. Formerly, people went to these places with very great difficulty. Generally, therefore, only the real devotees visited such places. Nowadays rogues visit them in order to practise their roguery.

Reader: You have given a one-sided account. Good men can visit these places as well as bad men. Why do they not take the fullest advantage of the railways?

Editor: Good travels at a snail's pace – it can, therefore, have little to do with the railways. Those who want to do good are not selfish, they are not in a hurry, they know that to impregnate people with good requires a long time. But evil has wings. To build a house takes time. Its destruction takes none. So the railways can become a distributing agency for the evil one only. It may be a debatable matter whether railways spread famines, but it is beyond dispute that they propagate evil.

Reader: Be that as it may, all the disadvantages of railways are more than counterbalanced by the fact that it is due to them that we see in India the new spirit of nationalism.

Editor: I hold this to be a mistake. The English have taught us that we were not one nation before and that it will require centuries before we become one nation. This is without foundation. We were one nation before they came to India. One thought inspired us. Our mode of life was the same. It was because we were one nation that they were able to establish one kingdom. Subsequently they divided us.

Reader: This requires an explanation.

Editor: I do not wish to suggest that because we were one nation we had no differences, but it is submitted that our leading men travelled throughout India either on foot or in bullock-carts.

They learned one another's languages and there was no aloofness between them. What do you think could have been the intention of those farseeing ancestors of ours who established Setubandha (Rameshwar) in the South, Jagannath in the East and Hardwar in the North as places of pilgrimage? You will admit they were no fools. They knew that worship of God could have been performed just as well at home. They taught us that those whose hearts were aglow with righteousness had the Ganges in their own homes. But they saw that India was one undivided land so made by nature. They, therefore, argued that it must be one nation. Arguing thus, they established holy places in various parts of India, and fired the people with an idea of nationality in a manner unknown in other parts of the world. And we Indians are one as no two Englishmen are. Only you and I and others who consider ourselves civilized and superior persons imagine that we are many nations. It was after the advent of railways that we began to believe in distinctions, and you are at liberty now to say that it is through the railways that we are beginning to abolish those distinctions. An opium-eater may argue the advantage of opium-eating from the fact that he began to understand the evil of the opium habit after having eaten it. I would ask you to consider well what I had said on the railways.

Reader: I will gladly do so, but one question occurs to me even now. You have described to me the India of the pre-Mahomedan period, but now we have Mahomedans, Parsis and Christians. How can they be one nation? Hindus and Mahomedans are old enemies. Our very proverbs prove it. Mahomedans turn to the West for worship, whilst Hindus turn to the East. The former look down on the Hindus as idolaters. The Hindus worship the cow, the Mahomedans kill her. The Hindus believe in the doctrine of non-killing, the Mahomedans do not. We thus meet with differences at every step. How can India be one nation?

X
The Condition of India (Continued): The Hindus and The Mahomedans

Editor: Your last question is a serious one and yet, on careful consideration, it will be found to be easy of solution. The question arises because of the presence of the railways, of the lawyers and of the doctors. We shall presently examine the last two. We have already considered the railways. I should, however, like to add that man is so made by nature as to require him to restrict his movements as far as his hands and feet will take him. If we did not rush about from place to place by means of railways and such other maddening conveniences, much of the confusion that arises would be obviated. Our difficulties are of our own creation. God set a limit to a man's locomotive ambition in the construction of his body. Man immediately proceeded to discover means of overriding the limit. God gifted man with intellect that he might know his Maker. Man abused it so that he might forget his Maker. I am so constructed that I can only serve my immediate neighbours, but in my conceit I pretend to have discovered that I must with my body serve every individual in the Universe. In thus attempting the impossible, man comes in contact with different natures, different religions, and is utterly confounded. According to this reasoning, it must be apparent to you that railways are a most dangerous institution. Owing to them, man has gone further away from his Maker.

Reader: But I am impatient to hear your answer to my question. Has the introduction of Mahomedanism not unmade the nation?

Editor: India cannot cease to be one nation because people belonging to different religions live in it. The introduction of foreigners does not necessarily destroy the nation; they merge in it. A country is one nation only when such a condition obtains in it. That country must have a faculty for assimilation. India has ever been such a country. In reality there are as many religions as there are individuals; but those who are conscious of the spirit of nationality do not interfere with one another's religion. If they do, they are not fit to be considered a nation. If the Hindus believe that India should be peopled only by Hindus, they are living in dreamland. The Hindus, the Mahomedans, the Parsis and the Christians who have made India their country are fellow-countrymen, and they will have to live in unity, if only for their own interest. In no part of the world are one nationality and one religion synonymous terms; nor has it ever been so in India.

Reader: But what about the inborn enmity between Hindus and Mahomedans ?

Editor: That phrase has been invented by our mutual enemy. When the Hindus and Mahomedans fought against one another, they certainly spoke in that strain. They have long since ceased to fight. How, then, can there be any inborn enmity? Pray remember this too, that we did not cease to fight only after British occupation. The Hindus flourished under Moslem sovereigns and Moslems under the Hindu. Each party recognized that mutual fighting was suicidal, and that neither party would abandon its religion by force of arms. Both parties, therefore, decided to live in peace. With the English advent quarrels recommenced.

The proverbs you have quoted were coined when both were fighting; to quote them now is obviously harmful. Should we not remember that many Hindus and Mahomedans own the same ancestors and the same blood runs through their veins? Do people become enemies because they change their religion? Is the God of the Mahomedan different from the God of the Hindu? Religions are different roads converging to the same point. What does it matter that we take different roads so long as we reach the same goal? Wherein is the cause for quarrelling?

Moreover, there are deadly proverbs as between the followers of Shiva and those of Vishnu, yet nobody suggests that these two do not belong to the same nation. It is said that the Vedic religion is different from Jainism, but the followers of the respective faiths are not different nations. The fact is that we have become enslaved and, therefore, quarrel and like to have our quarrels decided by a third party. There are Hindu iconoclasts as there are Mahomedan. The more we advance in true knowledge, the better we shall understand that we need not be at war with those whose religion we may not follow.

Reader: Now I would like to know your views about cow-protection.

Editor: I myself respect the cow, that is, I look upon her with affectionate reverence. The cow is the protector of India because, being an agricultural country, she is dependent on the cow. The cow is a most useful animal in hundreds of ways. Our Mahomedan brethren will admit this.

But, just as I respect the cow, so do I respect my fellow-men. A man is just as useful as a cow no matter whether he be a Mahomedan or a Hindu. Am I, then, to fight with or kill a Mahomedan in order to save a cow? In doing so, I would become an enemy of the Mahomedan as well as of the cow. Therefore, the only method I know of protecting the cow is that I should approach my Mahomedan brother and urge him for the sake of the country to join me in protecting her. If he would not listen to me I should let the cow go for the simple reason that the matter is beyond my ability. If I were overfull of pity for the cow, I should sacrifice my life to save her but not take my brother's. This, I hold, is the law of our religion.

When men become obstinate, it is a difficult thing. If I pull one way my Moslem brother will pull another. If I put on a superior air, he will return the compliment. If I bow to him gently, he will do it much more so; and if he does not, I shall not be considered to have done wrong in having bowed. When the Hindus became insistent, the killing of cows increased. In my opinion, cow-protection societies may be considered cow-killing societies. It is a disgrace to us that we should need such societies. When we forgot how to protect cows, I suppose we needed such societies.

What am I to do when a blood-brother is on the point of killing a cow? Am I to kill him, or to fall down at his feet and implore him? If you admit that I should adopt the latter course, I must do the same to my Moslem brother.

Who protects the cow from destruction by Hindus when they cruelly ill-treat her? Whoever reasons with the Hindus when they mercilessly belabour the progeny of the cow with their sticks? But this has not prevented us from remaining one nation.

Lastly, if it is be true that the Hindus believe in the doctrine of non-killing and the Mahomedans do not, what, pray, is the duty of the former? It is not written that a follower of the religion of Ahimsa (non-killing) may kill a fellow-man. For him the way is straight. In order to save one being, he may not kill another. He can only plead – therein lies his sole duty.

But does every Hindu believe in Ahimsa? Going to the root of the matter, not one man really practises such a religion because we do destroy life. We are said to follow that religion because we want to obtain freedom from liability to kill any kind of life. Generally speaking, we may observe that many Hindus partake of meat and are not, therefore, followers of Ahimsa. It is, therefore, preposterous to suggest that the two cannot live together amicably because the Hindus believe in Ahimsa and the Mahomedans do not.

These thoughts are put into our minds by selfish and false religious teachers. The English put the finishing touch. They have habit of writing history; they pretend to study the manners and customs of all peoples. God has given us a limited mental capacity, but they usurp the function of the Godhead and indulge in novel experiments. They write about their own researches in most laudatory terms and hypnotize us into believing them. We in our ignorance then fall at their feet.

Those who do not wish to misunderstand things may read up the Koran, and they will find therein hundreds of passages acceptable to the Hindus; and the Bhagavadgita contains passages to which not a Mahomedan can take exception. Am I to dislike a

Mahomedan because there are passages in the Koran I do not understand or like? It takes two to make a quarrel. If I do not want to quarrel with a Mahomedan, the latter will be powerless to foist a quarrel on me; and, similarly, I should be powerless if a Mahomedan refuses his assistance to quarrel with me. An arm striking the air will become disjointed. If everyone will try to understand the core of his own religion and adhere to it, and will not allow false teachers to dictate to him, there will be no room left for quarrelling.

Reader: But will the English ever allow the two bodies to join hands?

Editor: This question arises out of your timidity. It betrays our shallowness. If two brothers want to live in peace, is it possible for a third party to separate them? If they were to listen to evil counsels we would consider them to be foolish. Similarly, we Hindus and Mahomedans would have to blame our folly rather than the English, if we allowed them to put us asunder. A clay pot would break through impact, if not with one stone, then with another. The way to save the pot is not to keep it away from the danger point but to bake it so that no stone would break it. We have then to make our hearts of perfectly baked clay. Then we shall be steeled against all danger. This can be easily done by the Hindus. They are superior in numbers; they pretend that they are more educated; they are, therefore, better able to shield themselves from attack on their amicable relations with the Mahomedans.

There is mutual distrust between the two communities. The Mahomedans, therefore, ask for certain concessions from Lord Morley. Why should the Hindus oppose this? If the Hindus desisted, the English would notice it, the Mahomedans would gradually begin to trust the Hindus, and brotherliness would be the outcome. We should be ashamed to take our quarrels to the English. Everyone can find out for himself that the Hindus can lose nothing by desisting. That man who has inspired confidence in another has never lost anything in this world.

I do not suggest that the Hindus and the Mahomedans will never fight. Two brothers living together often do so. We shall sometimes have our heads broken. Such a thing ought not to be necessary, but all men are not equitable. When people are in a rage, they do many foolish things. These we have to put up with. But when we do quarrel, we certainly do not want to engage counsel and resort to English or any law-courts. Two men fight; both have their heads broken, or one only. How shall a third party distribute justice amongst them? Those who fight may expect to be injured.

XI
The Condition of India (Continued): Lawyers

Reader: You tell me that when two men quarrel they should not go to a law-court. This is astonishing.

Editor: Whether you call it astonishing or not, it is the truth. And your question introduces us to the lawyers and the doctors. My firm opinion is that the lawyers have enslaved India, have accentuated Hindu-Mahomedan dissensions and have confirmed English authority.

Reader: It is easy enough to bring these charges, but it will be difficult for you to prove them. But for the lawyers, who would have shown us the road to independence? Who would have protected the poor? Who would have secured justice? For instance, the late Manomohan Ghose defended many a poor man free of charge. The Congress, which you have praised so much is dependent for its existence and activity upon the work of the lawyers. To denounce such an estimable class of men is to spell injustice, and you are abusing the liberty of the Press by decrying lawyers.

Editor: At one time I used to think exactly like you. I have no desire to convince you that they have never done a single good thing. I honour Mr. Ghose's memory, it is quite true that he helped the poor. That the Congress owes the lawyers something is believable. Lawyers are also men, and there is something good in every man. Whenever instances of lawyers having done good can be brought forward, it will be found that the good is due to them as men rather than as lawyers. All I am concerned with is to show you that the profession teaches immorality; it is exposed to temptation from which few are saved.

The Hindus and the Mahomedans have quarrelled. An ordinary man will ask them to forget all about it; he will tell them that both must be more or less at fault, and will advise them no longer to quarrel. But they go to lawyers. The latter's duty is to side with their clients and to find out ways and arguments in favour of the clients, to which they (the clients) are often strangers. If they do not do so, they will be considered to have degraded their profession. The lawyers, therefore, will, as a rule, advance quarrel instead of repressing them. Moreover, men take up that profession, not in order to help others out of their miseries, but to enrich themselves. It is one of the avenues of becoming wealthy and their interest exists in multiplying disputes. It is within my knowledge that they are glad when men have disputes. Petty pleaders actually manufacture them. Their touts, like so many leeches, suck the blood of the poor people. Lawyers are men who have little to do. Lazy people, in order to indulge in luxuries, take up such professions. This is a true statement. Any other argument is a mere pretension. It is the lawyers who have discovered that theirs is an honourable profession. They frame laws as they frame their own praises. They decide what fees they will charge and they put on so much side that poor people almost consider them to be heaven-born.

Why do they want more fees than common labourers? Why are their requirements greater? In what way are they more profitable to the country than the labourers? Are those who do good entitled to greater payment? And, if they have done anything for the country for the sake of money, how shall it be counted as good?

Those who know anything of the Hindu-Mahomedan quarrels know that they have been often due to the intervention of lawyers. Some families have been ruined through them; they have made brothers enemies. Principalities, having come under the lawyers' power, have become loaded with debt. Many have been robbed of their all. Such instances can be multiplied.

But the greatest injury they have done to the country is that they have tightened the English grip. Do you think that it would be possible for the English to carry on their Government without law courts? It is wrong to consider that courts are established for the benefit of the people. Those who want to perpetuate their power do so through the courts. If people were to settle their own quarrels, a third party would not be able to exercise any authority over them. Truly, men were less unmanly when they settled their disputes either by fighting or by asking their relatives to decide for them. They became more unmanly and cowardly when they resorted to the courts of law. It was certainly a sign of savagery when they settled their disputes by fighting. Is it any the less so, if I ask a third party to decide between you and me? Surely, the decision of a third party is not always right. The parties alone know who is right. We, in our simplicity and ignorance, imagine that a stranger, by taking our money, gives us justice.

The chief thing, however, to be remembered is that without lawyers courts could not have been established or conducted and without the latter the English could not rule. Supposing that there were only English judges, English pleaders and English police, they could only rule over the English. The English could not do without Indian judges and Indian pleaders. How the pleaders were made in the first instance and how they were favoured you should understand well. Then you will have the same abhorrence for the profession that I have. If pleaders were to abandon their profession, and consider it just as degrading as prostitution, English rule would break up in a day. They have been instrumental in having the charge laid against us that we love quarrels and courts as fish love water. What I have said with reference to the pleaders necessarily applies to the judges; they are first cousins; and the one gives strength to the other.

XII
The Condition of India (Continued): Doctors

Reader: I now understand the lawyers; the good they may have done is accidental. I feel that profession is certainly hateful. You, however, drag in the doctors also, how is that?

Editor: The views I submit to you are those I have adopted. They are not original. Western writers have used stronger terms regarding both lawyers and doctors. One writer has linked the whole modern system to the Upas tree. Its branches are represented by parasitical professions, including those of law and medicine and over the trunk has been raised the axe of true religion. Immorality is the root of the tree. So you will see that the views do not come right out of my mind but represent the combined experiences of many. I was at one time a great lover of the medical profession. It was my intention to become a doctor for the sake of the country. I no longer hold that opinion. I now understand why the medicine men (the vaids) among us have not occupied a very honourable status.

The English have certainly effectively used the medical profession for holding us. English physicians are known to have used their profession with several Asiatic potentates for political gain.

Doctors have almost unhinged us. Sometimes I think that quacks are better than highly qualified doctors. Let us consider: the business of a doctor is to take care of the body, or, properly speaking, not even that. Their business is really to rid the body of diseases that may afflict it. How do these diseases arise? Surely by our negligence or indulgence. I overeat, I have indigestion, I go to a doctor, he gives me medicine, I am cured. I overeat again, I take his pills again. Had I not taken the pills in the first instance, I would not have suffered the punishment deserved by me and I would not have overeaten again. The doctor intervened and helped me to indulge myself. My body thereby certainly felt more at ease; but my mind became weakened. A continuance of a course of medicine must, therefore, result in loss of control over the mind.

I have indulged in vice, I contract a disease, a doctor cures me, the odds are that I shall repeat the vice. Had the doctor not intervened, nature would have done its work, and I would have acquired mastery over myself, would have been freed from vice and would have become happy.

Hospitals are institutions for propagating sin. Men take less care of their bodies and immorality increases. European doctors are the worst of all. For the sake of a mistaken care of the human body, they kill annually thousands of animals. They practice vivisection. No religion sanctions this. All say that it is not necessary to take so many lives for the sake of our bodies.

These doctors violate our religious instinct. Most of their medical preparations contain either animal fat or spirituous liquors; both of these are tabooed by Hindus and Mahomedans. We may pretend to be civilized, call religious prohibitions a superstition and want only indulge in what we like. The fact remains that the doctors induce us to indulge, and the result is that we have become deprived of self-control and have become effeminate. In these circumstances, we are unfit to serve the country. To study European medicine is to deepen our slavery.

It is worth considering why we take up the profession of medicine. It is certainly not taken up for the purpose of serving humanity. We become doctors so that we may obtain honours and riches. I have endeavoured to show that there is no real service of humanity in the profession, and that it is injurious to mankind. Doctors make a show of their knowledge, and charge exorbitant fees. Their preparations, which are intrinsically worth a few pence, cost shillings. The populace, in its credulity and in the hope of ridding itself of some disease, allows itself to be cheated. Are not quacks then, whom we know, better than the doctors who put on an air of humaneness?

XIII
What is True Civilization?

Reader: You have denounced railways, lawyers and doctors. I can see that you will discard all machinery. What, then, is civilization?

Editor: The answer to that question is not difficult. I believe that the civilization India has evolved is not to be beaten in the world. Nothing can equal the seeds sown by our ancestors. Rome went, Greece shared the same fate; the might of the Pharaohs was broken; Japan has become Westernized; of China nothing can be said; but India is still, somehow or other, sound at the foundation. The people of Europe learn their lessons from the writings of the men of Greece or Rome, which exist no longer in their former glory. In trying to learn from them, the Europeans imagine that they will avoid the mistakes of Greece and Rome. Such is their pitiable condition. In the midst of all this India remains immovable and that is her glory. It is a charge against India that her people are so uncivilized, ignorant and stolid, that it is not possible to induce them to adopt any changes. It is a charge really against our merit. What we have tested and found true on the anvil of experience, we dare not change. Many thrust their advice upon India, and she remains steady. This is her beauty; it is the sheet-anchor of our hope.

Civilization is that mode of conduct which points out to man the path of duty. Performance of duty and observance of morality are convertible terms. To observe morality is to attain mastery over our mind and our passions. So doing, we know ourselves. The Gujarati equivalent for civilization means "good conduct".

If this definition be correct, then India, as so many writers have shown, has nothing to learn from anybody else, and this is as it should be. We notice that the mind is a restless bird; the more it gets the more it wants, and still remains unsatisfied. The more we indulge our passions the more unbridled they become. Our ancestors, therefore, set a limit to our indulgences. They saw that happiness was largely a mental condition. A man is not necessarily happy because he is rich, or unhappy because he is poor. The rich are often seen to be unhappy, the poor to be happy. Millions will always remain poor. Observing all this, our ancestors dissuaded us from luxuries and pleasures. We have managed with the same kind of plough as existed thousands of years ago. We have retained the same kind of cottages that we had in former times and our indigenous education remains the same as before. We have had no system of life-corroding competition. Each followed his own occupation or trade and charged a regulation wage. It was not that we did not know how to invent machinery, but our forefathers knew that, if we set our hearts after such things, we would become slaves and lose our moral fibre. They, therefore, after due deliberation decided that we should only do what we could with our hands and feet. They saw that our real happiness and health consisted in a proper use of our hands and feet. They further reasoned that large cities were a snare and a useless encumbrance and that people would not be happy in them, that there would be gangs of thieves and robbers, prostitution and vice flourishing in them and that poor men would be robbed by rich men. They were, therefore, satisfied with small villages. They saw that kings and their swords were inferior to the sword of ethics, and they, therefore, held the sovereigns of the earth to be inferior to the Rishis and the Fakirs. A nation with a constitution like this is fitter to teach others than to learn from others. This nation had courts, lawyers and doctors, but they were all within bounds. Everybody knew that these professions were not particularly superior; moreover, these vakils and vaids did not rob people; they were considered people's dependants, not their masters. Justice was tolerably fair. The ordinary rule was to avoid courts. There were no touts to lure people into them. This evil, too, was noticeable only in and around capitals. The common people lived independently and followed their agricultural occupation. They enjoyed true Home Rule.

And where this cursed modern civilization has not reached, India remains as it was before. The inhabitants of that part of

India will very properly laugh at your new-fangled notions. The English do not rule over them, nor will you ever rule over them. Those in whose name we speak we do not know, nor do they know us. I would certainly advise you and those like you who love the motherland to go into the interior that has yet been not polluted by the railways and to live there for six months; you might then be patriotic and speak of Home Rule.

Now you see what I consider to be real civilization. Those who, want to change conditions such as I have described are enemies of the country and are sinners.

Reader: It would be all right if India were exactly as you have described it, but it is also India where there are hundreds of child widows, where two-year old babies are married, where twelve-year old girls are mothers and housewives, where women practise polyandry, where the practice of Niyoga obtains, where, in the name of religion, girls dedicate themselves to prostitution, and in the name of religion sheep and goats are killed. Do you consider these also symbols of the civilization that you have described?

Editor: You make a mistake. The defects that you have shown are defects. Nobody mistakes them for ancient civilization. They remain in spite of it. Attempts have always been made and will be made to remove them. We may utilize the new spirit that is born in us for purging ourselves of these evils. But what I have described to you as emblems of modern civilization are accepted as such by its votaries. The Indian civilization, as described by me, has been so described by its votaries. In no part of the world, and under no civilization, have all men attained perfection. The tendency of the Indian civilization is to elevate the moral being, that of the Western civilization is to propagate immorality. The latter is godless, the former is based on a belief in God. So understanding and so believing, it behoves every lover of India to cling to the old Indian civilization even as a child clings to the mother's breast.

XIV
How Can India Become Free?

Reader: I appreciate your views about civilization. I will have to think over them. I cannot take them in all at once. What, then, holding the views you do, would you suggest for freeing India?

Editor: I do not expect my views to be accepted all of a sudden. My duty is to place them before readers like yourself. Time can be trusted to do the rest. We have already examined the conditions for freeing India, but we have done so indirectly; we will now do so directly. It is a world-known maxim that the removal of the cause of a disease results in the removal of the disease itself. Similarly if the cause of India's slavery be removed, India can become free.

Reader: If Indian civilization is, as you say, the best of all, how do you account for India's slavery?

Editor: This civilization is unquestionably the best, but it is to be observed that all civilizations have been on their trial. That civilization which is permanent outlives it. Because the sons of India were found wanting, its civilization has been placed in jeopardy. But its strength is to be seen in its ability to survive the shock. Moreover, the whole of India is not touched. Those alone who have been affected by Western civilization have become enslaved. We measure the universe by our own miserable foot-rule. When we are slaves, we think that the whole universe is enslaved. Because we are in an abject condition, we think that the whole of India is in that condition. As a matter of fact, it is not so, yet it is as well to impute our slavery to the whole of India. But if we bear in mind the above fact, we can see that if we become free, India is free. And in this thought you have a definition of Swaraj. It is Swaraj when we learn to rule ourselves. It is, therefore, in the palm of our hands. Do not consider this Swaraj to be like a dream. There is no idea of sitting still. The Swaraj that I wish to picture is such that, after we have once realized it, we shall endeavour to the end of our life time to persuade others to do likewise. But such Swaraj has to be experienced, by each one for himself. One drowning man will never save another. Slaves ourselves, it would be a mere pretension to think of freeing others. Now you will have seen that it is not necessary for us to have as our goal the expulsion of the English. If the English become Indianized, we can accommodate them. If they wish to remain in India along with their civilization, there is no room for them. It lies with us to bring about such a state of things.

Reader: It is impossible that Englishmen should ever become Indianized.

Editor: To say that is equivalent to saying that the English have no humanity in them. And it is really beside the point whether they become so or not. If we keep our own house in order, only those who are fit to live in it will remain. Others will leave of their own accord. Such things occur within the experience of all of us.

Reader: But it has not occurred in history.

Editor: To believe that what has not occurred in history will not occur at all is to argue disbelief in the dignity of man. At any rate, it behoves us to try what appeals to our reason. All countries are not similarly conditioned. The condition of India is unique. Its strength is immeasurable. We need not, therefore, refer to the history of other countries. I have drawn attention to the fact that, when other civilizations have succumbed, the Indian has survived many a shock.

Reader: I cannot follow this. There seems little doubt that we shall have to expel the English by force of arms. So long as they are in the country we cannot rest. One of our poets says that slaves cannot even dream of happiness. We are day by day becoming weakened owing to the presence of the English. Our greatness is gone; our people look like terrified men. The English are in the country like a blight which we must remove by every means.

Editor: In your excitement, you have forgotten all we have been considering. We brought the English, and we keep them. Why do you forget that our adoption of their civilization makes their presence in India at all possible? Your hatred against them ought to be transferred to their civilization. But let us assume that we have to drive away the English by fighting, how is that to be done?

Reader: In the same way as Italy did it. What was possible for Mazzini and Garibaldi is possible for us. You cannot deny that they were very great men.

XV
Italy and India

Editor: It is well that you have instanced Italy. Mazzini was a great and good man; Garibaldi was a great warrior. Both are adorable; from their lives we can learn much. But the condition of Italy was different from that of India. In the first instance, the difference between Mazzini and Garibaldi is worth noting. Mazzini's ambition was not and has not yet been realized regarding Italy. Mazzini has shown in his writings on the duty of man that every man must learn how to rule himself. This has not happened in Italy. Garibaldi did not hold this view of Mazzini's, Garibaldi gave, and every Italian took arms. Italy and Austria had the same civilization; they were cousins in this respect. It was a matter of tit for tat. Garibaldi simply wanted Italy to be free from the Austrian yoke. The machinations of Minister Cavour disgrace that portion of the history of Italy. And what has been the result? If you believe that because Italians rule Italy the Italian nation is happy, you are groping in darkness. Mazzini has shown conclusively that Italy did not become free. Victor Emanuel gave one meaning to the expression; Mazzini gave another. According to Emanuel, Cavour and even Garibaldi, Italy meant the King of Italy and his henchmen. According to Mazzini, it meant the whole of the Italian people, that is, its agriculturists. Emanuel was only its servant. The Italy of Mazzini still remains in a state of slavery. At the time of the so-called national war, it was a game of chess between two rival kings with the people of Italy as pawns. The working classes in that land are still unhappy. They, therefore, indulge in assassination, rise in revolt, and rebellion on their part is always expected. What substantial gain did Italy obtain after the with-drawal of the Austrian troops? The gain was only nominal. The reforms for the sake of which the war was supposed to have been undertaken have not yet been granted. The condition of the people in general still remains the same. I am sure you do not wish to reproduce such a condition in India. I believe that you want the millions of India to be happy, not that you want the reins of Government in your hands. If that be so, we have to consider only one thing how can the millions obtain self-rule? You will admit that people under several Indian princes are being ground down. The latter mercilessly crush them. Their tyranny is greater than that of the English, and if you want such tyranny in India, then we shall never agree. My patriotism does not teach me that I am to allow people to be crushed under the heel of Indian princes if only the English retire. If I have the power, I should resist the tyranny of Indian princes just as much as that of the English. By patriotism I mean the welfare of the whole people, and if I could secure it at the hands of the English, I should bow down my head to them. If any Englishman dedicated his life to securing the freedom of India, resisting tyranny and serving the land, I should welcome that Englishman as an Indian.

Again, India can fight like Italy only when she has arms. You have not considered this problem at all. The English are splendidly armed; that does not frighten me, but it is clear that, to pit ourselves against them in arms, thousands of Indians must be armed. If such a thing be possible, how many years will it take? Moreover, to arm India on a large scale is to Europeanize it. Then her condition will be just as pitiable as that of Europe. This means, in short, that India must accept European civilization, and if that is what we want, the best thing is that we have among us those who are so well trained in that civilization. We will then fight for a few rights, will get what we can and so pass our days. But the fact is that the Indian nation will not adopt arms, and it is well that it does not.

Reader: You are over-stating the facts. All need not be armed. At first, we shall assassinate a few Englishmen and strike terror; then, a few men who will have been armed will fight openly. We may have to lose a quarter of a million men, more or less, but *we* shall regain our land. We shall undertake guerilla warfare, and defeat the English.

Editor: That is to say, you want to make the holy land of India unholy. Do you not tremble to think of freeing India by assassination? What we need to do is to sacrifice ourselves. It is a cowardly thought, that of killing others. Whom do you suppose to free by assassination? The millions of India do not desire it. Those who are intoxicated by the wretched modern civilization think these things. Those who will rise to power by murder will certainly not make the nation happy. Those who believe that India has gained by Dhingra's act and other similar acts in India make a serious mistake. Dhingra was a patriot, but his love was blind. He gave his body in a wrong way; its ultimate result can only be mischievous.

Reader: But you will admit that the English have been frightened by these murders, and that Lord Morley's reforms are due to fear.

Editor: The English are both a timid and a brave nation. England is, I believe, easily influenced by the use of gunpowder. It is possible that Lord Morley has granted the reforms through fear, but what is granted under fear can be retained only so long as the fear lasts.

XVI
Brute Force

Reader: This is a new doctrine, that what is gained through fear is retained only while the fear lasts. Surely, what is given will not be withdrawn?

Editor: Not so. The Proclamation of 1857 was given at the end of a revolt, and for the purpose of preserving peace. When peace was secured and people became simple-minded its full effect was toned down. If I cease stealing for fear of punishment, I would recommence the operation as soon as the fear is withdrawn from me. This is almost a universal experience. We have assumed that we can get men to do things by force and, therefore, we use force.

Reader: Will you not admit that you are arguing against yourself? You know that what the English obtained in their own country they obtained by using brute force. I know you have argued that what they have obtained is useless, but that does not affect my argument. They wanted useless things and they got them. My point is that their desire was fulfilled. What does it matter what means they adopted? Why should we not obtain our goal, which is good, by any means whatsoever, even by using violence? Shall I think of the means when I have to deal with a thief in the house? My duty is to drive him out anyhow. You seem to admit that we have received nothing, and that we shall receive nothing by petitioning. Why, then, may we not do so by using brute force? And, to retain what we may receive we shall keep up the fear by using the same force to the extent that it may be necessary. You will not find fault with a continuance of force to prevent a child from thrusting its foot into fire. Somehow or other we have to gain our end.

Editor: Your reasoning is plausible. It has deluded many. I have used similar arguments before now. But I think I know better now, and I shall endeavour to undeceive you. Let us first take the agrument that we are justified in gaining our end by using brute force because the English gained theirs by using similar means. It is perfectly true that they used brute force and that it is possible for us to do likewise, but by using similar means we can get only the same thing that they got. You will admit that we do not want that. Your belief that there is no connection between the means and the end is a great mistake.

Through that mistake even men who have been considered religious have committed grievous crimes. Your reasoning is the same as saying that we can get a rose through planting a noxious weed. If I want to cross the ocean, I can do so only by means of a vessel; if I were to use a cart for that purpose, both the cart and I would soon find the bottom. "As is the God, so is the votary", is a maxim worth considering. Its meaning has been distorted and men have gone astray. The means may be likened to a seed, the end to a tree; and there is just the same inviolable connection between the means and the end as there is between the seed and the tree. I am not likely to obtain the result flowing from the worship of God by laying myself prostrate before Satan. If, therefore, anyone were to say: "I want to worship God; it does not matter that I do so by means of Satan," it would be set down as ignorant folly. We reap exactly as we sow. The English in 1833 obtained greater voting power by violence. Did they by using brute force better appreciate their duty? They wanted the right of voting, which they obtained by using physical force. But real rights are a result of performance of duty; these rights they have not obtained. We, therefore, have before us in England the force of everybody wanting and insisting on his rights, nobody thinking of his duty. And, where everybody wants rights, who shall give them to whom? I do not wish to imply that they do no duties. They don't perform the duties corresponding to those rights; and as they do not perform that particular duty, namely, acquire fitness, their rights have proved a burden to them. In other words, what they have obtained is an exact result of the means they adopted. They used the means corresponding to the end. If I want to deprive you of your watch, I shall certainly have to fight for it; if I want to buy your watch, I shall have to pay you for it; and if I want a gift, I shall have to plead for it; and, according to the means I employ, the watch is stolen property, my own property, or a donation. Thus we see three different results from three different means. Will you still say that means do not matter?

Now we shall take the example given by you of the thief to be driven out. I do not agree with you that the thief may be driven out by any means. If it is my father who has come to steal I shall use one kind of means. If it is an acquaintance I shall use another, and in the case of a perfect stranger I shall use a third. If it is a white man, you will perhaps say you will use means different from those you will adopt with an Indian thief. If it is a weakling, the means will be different from those to be adopted for dealing with an equal in physical strength; and if the thief is armed from top to toe, I shall simply remain quiet. Thus we have a variety of means between the father and the armed man. Again, I fancy that I should pretend to be sleeping whether the thief was my father or that strong armed man. The reason for this is that my father would also be armed and I should succumb to the strength possessed by either and allow my things to be stolen. The strength of my father would make me weep with pity; the strength of the armed man would rouse in me anger and we should become enemies. Such is the curious situation. From these examples we may not be able to agree as to the means to be adopted in each case. I myself seem clearly to see what should be done in all these cases, but the remedy may frighten you. I therefore hesitate to place it before you. For the time being I will leave you to guess it, and if you cannot, it is clear you will have to adopt different means in each case. You will also have seen that any means will not avail to drive away the thief. You will have to adopt means to fit each case. Hence it follows that your duty is not to drive away the thief by any means you like.

Let us proceed a little further. That well-armed man has stolen your property; you have harboured the thought of his act; you are filled with anger; you argue that you want to punish that rogue, not for your own sake, but for the good of your neighbours; you have collected a number of armed men, you want to take his house by assault; he is duly informed of it, he runs away; he too is incensed. He collects his brother robbers, and sends you a defiant message that he will commit robbery in broad daylight. You are strong, you do not fear him, you are prepared to receive him. Meanwhile, the robber pesters your neighbours. They complain before you. You reply that you are doing all for their sake, you do not mind that your own goods have been stolen. Your neighbours reply that the robber never pestered them before, and that he commenced his depredations only after you declared hostilities against him. You are between Scylla and Charybdis. You are full of pity for the poor men. What they say is true. What are you to do? You will be disgraced if you now leave the robber alone. You, therefore, tell the poor men: "Never mind. Come, my wealth is yours, I will give you arms, I will teach you how to use them; you should belabour the rogue; don't you leave him alone." And so the battle grows; the robbers increase in numbers; your neighbours have deliberately put themselves to inconvenience. Thus the result of wanting to take revenge upon the robber is that you have disturbed your own peace; you are in perpetual fear of being robbed and assaulted; your courage has given place to cowardice. If you will patiently examine the argument, you will see that I have not overdrawn the picture. This is one of the means. Now let us examine the other. You set this armed robber down as an ignorant brother; you intend to reason with him at a suitable opportunity; you argue that he is, after all, a fellow-man; you do not know what prompted him to steal. You, therefore, decide that, when you can, you will destroy the man's motive for stealing. Whilst you are thus reasoning with yourself, the man comes again to steal. Instead of being angry with him you take pity on him. You think that this stealing habit must be a disease with him. Henceforth, you therefore, keep your doors and windows open, you change your sleeping-place, and you keep your things in a manner most accessible to him. The robber comes again and is confused as all this is new to him; nevertheless, he takes away your things. But his mind is agitated. He inquires about you in the village, he comes to learn about your broad and loving heart, he repents, he begs your pardon, returns you your things, and leaves off the stealing habit. He becomes your servant, and you find for him honourable employment. This is the second method. Thus, you see, different means have brought about totally different results. I do not wish to deduce from this that robbers will act in the above manner or that all will have the same pity and love like you, but I only wish to show that fair means alone can produce fair results, and that, at least in the majority of cases, if not indeed in all, the force of love and pity is infinitely greater than the force of arms. There is harm in the exercise of brute force, never in that of pity.

Now we will take the question of petitioning. It is a fact beyond dispute that a petition, without the backing of force is useless. However, the late Justice Ranade used to say that petitions served a useful purpose because they were a means of educating people. They give the latter an idea of their condition and warn the rulers. From this point of view, they are not altogether useless. A petition of an equal is a sign of courtesy; a petition from a slave is a symbol of his slavery. A petition backed by force is a petition from an equal and, when he transmits his demand in the form of a petition, it testifies to his nobility. Two kinds of force can back petitions. "We shall hurt you if you do not give this," is one kind of force; it is the force of arms, whose evil results we have already examined. The second kind of force can thus be stated: "If you do not concede our demand, we shall be no longer your petitioners. You can govern us only so long as we remain the governed; we shall no longer have any dealings with you." The force implied in this may be described as love-force, soul-force, or, more popularly but less accurately, passive resistance. This force is indestructible. He who uses it perfectly understands his position. We have an ancient proverb which literally means: " One negative cures thirty-six diseases." The force of arms is powerless when matched against the force of love or the soul.

Now we shall take your last illustration, that of the child thrusting its foot into fire. It will not avail you. What do you really do to the child? Supposing that it can exert so much physical force that it renders you powerless and rushes into fire, then you cannot prevent it. There are only two remedies open to you — either you must kill it in order to prevent it from perishing in the flames, or you must give your own life because you do not wish to see it perish before your very eyes. You will not kill it. If your heart is not quite full of pity, it is possible that you will not surrender yourself by preceding the child and going into the fire yourself. You, therefore, helplessly allow it to go into the flames. Thus, at any rate, you are not using physical force. I hope you will not consider that it is still physical force, though of a low order, when you would forcibly prevent the child from rushing towards the fire if you could. That force is of a different order and we have to understand what it is.

Remember that, in thus preventing the child, you are minding entirely its own interest, you are exercising authority for its sole benefit. Your example does not apply to the English. In using brute force against the English you consult entirely your own, that is the national interest. There is no question here either of pity or of love. If you say that the actions of the English, being evil, represent fire, and that they proceed to their actions through ignorance, and that therefore they occupy the position of a child and that you want to protect such a child, then you will have to overtake every evil action of that kind by whomsoever committed and, as in the case of the evil child, you will have to sacrifice yourself. If you are capable of such immeasurable pity, I wish you well in its exercise.

XVII
Passive Resistance

Reader: Is there any historical evidence as to the success of what you have called soul-force or truth-force? No instance seems to have happened of any nation having risen through soul-force. I still think that the evil-doers will not cease doing evil without physical punishment.

Editor: The poet Tulsidas has said: "Of religion, pity, or love, is the root, as egotism of the body. Therefore, we should not abandon pity so long as we are alive." This appears to me to be a scientific truth. I believe in it as much as I believe in two and two being four. The force of love is the same as the force of the soul or truth. We have evidence of its working at every step. The universe would disappear without the existence of that force. But you ask for historical evidence. It is, therefore, necessary to know what history means. The Gujarati equivalent means: "It so happened." If that is the meaning of history, it is possible to give copious evidence. But, if it means the doings of the kings and emperors, there can be no evidence of soul-force or passive resistance in such history. You cannot expect silver ore in a tin mine. History, as we know it, is a record of the wars of the world, and so there is a proverb among Englishmen that a nation which has no history, that is, no wars, is a happy nation. How kings played, how they became enemies of one another, how they murdered one another, is found accurately recorded in history, and if this were all that had happened in the world, it would have been ended long ago. If the story of the universe had commenced with wars, not a man would have been found alive today. Those people who have been warred against have disappeared as, for instance, the natives of Australia of whom hardly a man was left alive by the intruders. Mark, please, that these natives did not use soul-force in self-defence, and it does not require much foresight to know that the Australians will share the same fate as their victims. "Those that take the sword shall perish by the sword." With us the proverb is that professional swimmers will find a watery grave.

The fact that there are so many men still alive in the world shows that it is based not on the force of arms but on the force of truth or love. Therefore, the greatest and most unimpeachable evidence of the success of this force is to be found in the fact that, in spite of the wars of the world, it still lives on.

Thousands, indeed tens of thousands, depend for their existence on a very active working of this force. Little quarrels of millions of families in their daily lives disappear before the exercise of this force. Hundreds of nations live in peace. History does not and cannot take note of this fact. History is really a record of every interruption of the even working of the force of love or of the soul. Two brothers quarrel; one of them repents and re-awakens the love that was lying dormant in him; the two again begin to live in peace; nobody takes note of this. But if the two brothers, through the intervention of solicitors or some other reason take up arms or go to law — which is another form of the exhibition of brute force, — their doings would be immediately noticed in the Press, they would be the talk of their neighbours and would probably go down to history. And what is true of families and communities is true of nations. There is no reason to believe that there is one law for families and another for nations. History, then, is a record of an interruption of the course of nature. Soul-force, being natural, is not noted in history.

Reader: According to what you say, it is plain that instances of this kind of passive resistance are not to be found in history. It is necessary to understand this passive resistance more fully. It will be better, therefore, if you enlarge upon it.

Editor: Passive resistance is a method of securing rights by personal suffering; it is the reverse of resistance by arms. When I refuse to do a thing that is repugnant to my conscience, I use soul-force. For instance, the Government of the day has passed a law which is applicable to me. I do not like it. If by using violence I force the Government to repeal the law, I am employing what may be termed body-force. If I do not obey the law and accept the penalty for its breach, I use soul-force. It involves sacrifice of self.

Everybody admits that sacrifice of self is infinitely superior to sacrifice of others. Moreover, if this kind of force is used in a cause that is unjust, only the person using it suffers. He does not make others suffer for his mistakes. Men have before now done many things which were subsequently found to have been wrong. No man can claim that he is absolutely in the right or that a particular thing is wrong because he thinks so, but it is wrong for him so long as that is his deliberate judgment. It is therefore meet that he should not do that which he knows to be wrong, and suffer the consequence whatever it may be. This is the key to the use of soul-force.

Reader: You would then disregard laws — this is rank disloyalty. We have always been considered a law-abiding nation. You seem to be going even beyond the extremists. They say that we must obey the laws that have been passed, but that if the laws be bad, we must drive out the law-givers even by force.

Editor: Whether I go beyond them or whether I do not is a matter of no consequence to either of us. We simply want to find out what is right and to act accordingly. The real meaning of the statement that we are a law-abiding nation is that we are passive resisters. When we do not like certain laws, we do not break the heads of law-givers but we suffer and do not submit to the laws. That we should obey laws whether good or bad is a newfangled notion. There was no such thing in former days. The people disregarded those laws they did not like and suffered the penalties for their breach. It is contrary to our manhood if we obey laws repugnant to our conscience. Such teaching is opposed to a religion and means slavery. If the Government were to ask us to go about without any clothing, should we do so? If I were a passive resister, I would say to them that I would have nothing to do with their law. But we have so forgotten ourselves and become so compliant that we do not mind any degrading law.

A man who has realized his manhood, who fears only God, will fear no one else. Man-made laws are not necessarily binding on him. Even the Government does not expect any such thing from us. They do not say: "You must do such and such a thing," but they say: "If you do not do it, we will punish you." We are sunk so low that we fancy that it is our duty and our religion to do what the law lays down. If man will only realize that it is unmanly to obey laws that are unjust, no man's tyranny will enslave him. This is the key to self-rule or home-rule.

It is a superstition and ungodly thing to believe that an act of a majority binds a minority. Many examples can be given in which acts of majorities will be found to have been wrong and those of minorities to have been right. All reforms owe their origin to the initiation of minorities in opposition to majorities. If among a band of robbers a knowledge of robbing is obligatory, is a pious man to accept the obligation? So long as the superstition that men should obey unjust laws exists, so long will their slavery exist. And a passive resister alone can remove such a superstition.

To use brute-force, to use gunpowder, is contrary to passive resistancc, for it means that we want our opponent to do by force that which we desire but he does not. And if such a use of force is justifiable, surely he is entitled to do likewise by us. And so we should never come to an agreement. We may simply fancy, like the blind horse moving in a circle round a mill, that we are making progress. Those who believe that they are not bound to obey law which are repugnant to their conscience have only the remedy of passive resistance open to them. Any other must lead to disaster.

Reader: From what you say I deduce that passive resistance is a splendid weapon of the weak, but that when they are strong they may take up arms.

Editor: This is gross ignorance. Passive resistance that is, soul-force, is matchless. It is superior to the force of arms. How, then, can it be considered only a weapon of the weak? Physical-force men are strangers to the courage that is requisite in a passive resister. Do you believe that a coward can ever disobey a law that he dislikes? Extremists are considered to be advocates of brute force. Why do they, then, talk about obeying laws? I do not blame them. They can say nothing else. When they succeed in driving out the English and they themselves become governors, they will want you and me to obey their laws. And that is a fitting thing for their constitution. But a passive resister will say he will not obey a law that is against his conscience, even though he may be blown to pieces at the mouth of a cannon.

What do you think? Wherein is courage required — in blowing others to pieces from behind a cannon, or with a smiling face to approach a cannon and be blown to pieces? Who is the true warrior — he who keeps death always as a bosom-friend, or he who controls the death of others? Believe me that a man devoid of courage and manhood can never be a passive resister.

This however, I will admit: that even a man weak in body is capable of offering this resistance. One man can offer it just as well as millions. Both men and women can indulge in it. It does not require the training of an army; it needs no jiu-jitsu. Control over the mind is alone necessary, and when that is attained, man is free like the king of the forest and his very glance withers the enemy.

Passive resistance is an all-sided sword, it can be used anyhow; it blesses him who uses it and him against whom it is used. Without drawing a drop of blood it produces far-reaching results. It never rusts and cannot be stolen. Competition between passive resisters does not exhaust. The sword of passive resistance does not require a scabbard. It is strange indeed that you should consider such a weapon to be a weapon merely of the weak.

Reader: You have said that passive resistance is a speciality of India. Have cannons never been used in India?

Editor: Evidently, in your opinion, India means its few princes. To me it means its teeming millions on whom depends the existence of its princes and our own.

Kings will always use their kingly weapons. To use force is bred in them. They want to command, but those who have to obey commands do not want guns; and these are in a majority throughout the world. They have to learn either body-force or soul-force. Where they learn the former, both the rulers and the ruled become like so many madmen; but where they learn soul-force, the commands of the rulers do not go beyond the point of their swords, for true men disregard unjust commands. Peasants have never been subdued by the sword, and never will be. They do not know the use of the sword, and they are not frightened by the use of it by others. That nation is great which rests its head upon death as its pillow. Those who defy death are free from all fear. For those who are labouring under the delusive charms of brute-force, this picture is not overdrawn. The fact is that, in India, the nation at large has generally used passive resistance in all departments of life. We cease to co-operate with our rulers when they displease us. This is passive resistance.

I remember an instance when, in a small principality, the villagers were offended by some command issued by the prince. The former immediately began vacating the village. The prince became, nervous, apologized to his subjects and withdrew his command. Many such instances can be found in India. Real Home Rule is possible only where passive resistance is the guiding force of the people. Any other rule is foreign rule.

Reader: Then you will say that it is not at all necessary for us to train the body?

Editor: I will certainly not say any such thing. It is difficult to become a passive resister unless the body is trained. As a rule, the mind, residing in a body that has become weakened by pampering, is also weak, and where there is no strength of mind there can be no strength of soul. We shall have to improve our physique by getting rid of infant marriages and luxurious living. If I were to ask a man with a shattered body to face a cannon's mouth I should make a laughing-stock of myself.

Reader: From what you say, then, it would appear that it is not a small thing to become a passive resister, and, if that is so, I should like you to explain how a man may become one.

Editor: To become a passive resister is easy enough but it is also equally difficult. I have known a lad of fourteen years become a passive resister; I have known also sick people do likewise; and I have also known physically strong and otherwise happy people unable to take up passive resistance. After a great deal of experience it seems to me that those who want to become passive resisters for the service of the country have to observe perfect chastity, adopt poverty, follow truth, and cultivate fearlessness.

Chastity is one of the greatest disciplines without which the mind cannot attain requisite firmness. A man who is unchaste loses stamina, becomes emasculated and cowardly. He whose mind is given over to animal passions is not capable of any great effort. This can be proved by innumerable instances. What then, is a married person to do is the question that arises naturally; and yet it need not. When a husband and wife gratify the passions, it is no less an animal indulgence on that account. Such an indulgence, except for perpetuating the race, is strictly prohibited. But a passive resister has to avoid even that very limited indulgence because he can have no desire for progeny. A married man, therefore, can observe perfect chastity. This subject is not capable of being treated at greater length. Several questions arise: How is one to carry one's wife with one, what are her rights, and other similar questions. Yet those who wish to take part in a great work are bound to solve these puzzles.

Just as there is necessity for chastity, so is there for poverty. Pecuniary ambition and passive resistance cannot well go together. Those who have money are not expected to throw it away, but they *are* expected to be indifferent about it. They must be prepared to lose every penny rather than give up passive resistance.

Passive resistance has been described in the course of our discussion as truth-force. Truth, therefore, has necessarily to be followed and that at any cost. In this connection, academic questions such as whether a man may not lie in order to save a life, etc., arise, but these questions occur only to those who wish to justify lying. Those who want to follow truth every time are not placed in such a quandary; and if they are, they are still saved from a false position.

Passive resistance cannot proceed a step without

fearlessness. Those alone can follow the path of passive resistance who are free from fear, whether as to their possessions, false honour, their relatives, the government, bodily injuries or death.

These observances are not to be abandoned in the belief that they are difficult. Nature has implanted in the human breast ability to cope with any difficulty or suffering that may come to man unprovoked. These qualities are worth having, even for those who do not wish to serve the country. Let there be no mistake, as those who want to train themselves in the use of arms are also obliged to have these qualities more or less. Everybody does not become a warrior for the wish. A would-be warrior will have to observe chastity and to be satisfied with poverty as his lot. A warrior without fearlessness cannot be conceived of. It may be thought that he would not need to be exactly truthful, but that quality follows real fearlessness. When a man abandons truth, he does so owing to fear in some shape or form. The above four attributes, then, need not frighten anyone. It may be as well here to note that a physical-force man has to have many other useless qualities which a passive resister never needs. And you will find that whatever extra effort a swordsman needs is due to lack of fearlessness. If he is an embodiment of the latter, the sword will drop from his hand that very moment. He does not need its support. One who is free from hatred requires no sword. A man with a stick suddenly came face to face with a lion and instinctively raised his weapon in self-defence. The man saw that he had only prated about fearlessness when there was none in him. That moment he dropped the stick and found himself free from all fear.

XVIII
Education

Reader: In the whole of our discussion, you have not demonstrated the necessity for education; we always complain of its absence among us. We notice a movement for compulsory education in our country. The Maharaja Gaekwar has introduced it in his territories. Every eye is directed towards them. We bless the Maharaja for it. Is all this effort then of no use?

Editor: If we consider our civilization to be the highest, I have regretfully to say that much of the effort you have described is of no use. The motive of the Maharaja and other great leaders who have been working in this direction is perfectly pure. They, therefore, undoubtedly deserve great praise. But we cannot conceal from ourselves the result that is likely to flow from their effort.

What is the meaning of education? It simply means a knowledge of letters. It is merely an instrument, and an instrument may be well used or abused. The same instrument that may be used to cure a patient may be used to take his life, and so may a knowledge of letters. We daily observe that many men abuse it and very few make good use of it; and if this is a correct statement, we have proved that more harm has been done by it than good.

The ordinary meaning of education is a knowledge of letters. To teach boys reading, writing and arithmetic is called primary education. A peasant earns his bread honestly. He has ordinary knowledge of the world. He knows fairly well how he should behave towards his parents, his wife, his children and his fellow villagers. He understands and observes the rules of morality. But he cannot write his own name. What do you propose to do by giving him a knowledge of letters? Will you add an inch to his happiness? Do you wish to make him discontented with his cottage or his lot? And even if you want to do that, he will not need such an education. Carried away by the flood of western thought we came to the conclusion, without weighing pros and cons that we should give this kind of education to the people.

Now let us take higher education. I have learned Geography, Astronomy, Algebra, Geometry, etc. What of that? In what way have I benefited myself or those around me? Why have I learned these things? Professor Huxley has thus defined education: "That man I think has had a liberal education who has been so trained in youth that his body is the ready servant of his will and does with ease and pleasure all the work that as a mechanism it is capable of; whose intellect is a clear, cold, logic engine with all its parts of equal strength and in smooth working order—whose mind is stored with a knowledge of the fundamental truths of nature ... whose passions are trained to come to heel by a vigorous will, the servant of a tender conscience...who has learnt to hate all vileness and to respect others as himself. Such a one and no other, I conceive, has had a liberal education, for he is in harmony with nature. He will make the best of her and she of him."

If this is true education, I must emphatically say that the sciences I have enumerated above I have never been able to use for controlling my senses. Therefore, whether you take elementary education or higher education, it is not required for the main thing. It does not make men of us. It does not enable us to do our duty.

Reader: If that is so, I shall have to ask you another question. What enables you to tell all these things to me? If you had not received higher education, how would you have been able to explain to me the things that you have?

Editor: You have spoken well. But my answer is simple: I do not for one moment believe that my life would have been wasted, had I not received higher or lower education. Nor do I consider that I necessarily serve because I speak. But I do desire to serve and in endeavouring to fulfil that desire, I make use of the education I have received. And, if I am making good use of it, even then it is not for the millions, but I can use it only for such as you, and this supports my contention. Both you and I have come under the bane of what is mainly false education. I claim to have become free from its ill effect, and I am trying to give you the benefit of my experience and in doing so, I am demonstrating the rottenness of this education.

Moreover, I have not run down a knowledge of letters in all circumstances. All I have now shown is that we must not make of it a fetish. It is not our *Kamadhuk*. In its place it can be of use and it has its place when we have brought our senses under subjection and put our ethics on a firm foundation. And then, if we feel inclined to receive that education, we may make good use of it. As an ornament it is likely to sit well on us. It now follows that it is not necessary to make this education compulsory. Our ancient school system is enough. Character-building has the first place in it and that is primary education. A building erected on that foundation will last.

Reader: Do I then understand that you do not consider English education necessary for obtaining Home Rule?

Editor: My answer is yes and no. To give millions a knowledge of English is to enslave them. The foundation that Macaulay laid of education has enslaved us. I do not suggest that he has any such intention, but that has been the result. Is it not a sad commentary that we should have to speak of Home Rule in a foreign tongue?

And it is worthy of note that the systems which the Europeans have discarded are the systems in vogue among us. Their learned men continually make changes. We ignorantly adhere to their cast-off systems. They are trying each division to improve its own status. Wales is a small portion of England. Great efforts are being made to revive a knowledge of Welsh among Welshmen. The English Chancellor, Mr. Lloyd George is taking a leading part in the movement to make Welsh children speak Welsh. And what is our condition? We write to each other in faulty English, and from this even our M.A.s are not free; our best thoughts are expressed in English; the proceedings of our Congress are conducted in English; our best newspapers are printed in English. If this state of things continues for a long time, posterity will — it is my firm opinion — condemn and curse us.

It is worth noting that, by receiving English education, we have enslaved the nation. Hypocrisy, tyranny, etc. have increased; English-knowing Indians have not hesitated to cheat and strike terror into the people. Now, if we are doing anything for the people at all, we are paying only a portion of the debt due to them.

Is it not a painful thing that, if I want to go to a court of justice, I must employ the English language as a medium, that when I become a barrister, I may not speak my mother tongue and that someone else should have to translate to me from my own language? Is not this absolutely absurd? Is it not a sign of slavery? Am I to blame the English for it or myself? It is we, the English-knowing Indians, that have enslaved India. The curse of the nation will rest not upon the English but upon us.

I have told you that my answer to your last question is both yes and no. I have explained to you why it is yes. I shall now explain why it is no.

We are so much beset by the disease of civilization, that we cannot altogether do without English-education. Those who have already received it may make good use of it wherever necessary. In our dealings with the English people, in our dealings with our own people, when we can only correspond with them through that language, and for the purpose of knowing how disgusted they (the English) have themselves become with their civilization, we may use or learn English, as the case may be. Those who have studied English will have to teach morality to their progeny through their mother tongue and to teach them another Indian language; but when they have grown up, they may learn English, the ultimate aim being that we should not need it. The object of making money thereby should be eschewed. Even in learning English to such a limited extent we shall have to consider what we should learn through it and what we should not. It will be necessary to know what sciences we should learn. A little thought should show you that immediately we cease to care for English degrees, the rulers will prick up their ears.

Reader: Then what education shall we give?

Editor: This has been somewhat considered above, but we will consider it a little more. I think that we have to improve all our languages. What subjects we should learn through them need not be elaborated here. Those English books which are valuable, we should translate into the various Indian languages. We should abandon the pretension of learning many sciences. Religious, that is ethical, education will occupy the first place. Every cultured Indian will know in addition to his own provincial language, if a Hindu, Sanskrit; if a Mahomedan, Arabic; if a Parsee, Persian; and all, Hindi. Some Hindus should know Arabic and Persian; some Mahomedans and Parsees, Sanskrit. Several Northerners and Westerners should learn Tamil. A universal language for India should be Hindi, with the option of writing it in Persian or Nagari characters. In order that the Hindus and the Mahomedans may have closer relations, it is necessary to know both the characters. And, if we can do this, we can drive the English language out of the field in a short time. All this is necessary for us, slaves. Through our slavery the nation has been, enslaved, and it will be free with our freedom.

Reader: The question of religious education is very difficult.

Editor: Yet we cannot do without it. India will never be godless. Rank atheism cannot flourish in this land. The task is indeed difficult. My head begins to turn as I think of religious education. Our religious teachers are hypocritical and selfish; they will have to be approached. The Mullas, the Dasturs and the Brahmins; hold the key in their hands, but if they will not have the good sense, the energy that we have derived from English education will have to be devoted to religious education. This is not very difficult. Only the fringe of the ocean has been polluted and it is those who are within the fringe who alone need cleansing. We who come under this category can even cleanse ourselves because my remarks do not apply to the millions. In order to restore India to its pristine condition, we have to return to it. In our own civilization there will naturally be progress, retrogression, reforms, and reactions; but one effort is required, and that is to drive out Western civilization. All else will follow.

XIX
Machinery

Reader: When you speak of driving out Western civilization, I suppose you will also say that we want no machinery.

Editor: By raising this question, you have opened the wound I have received. When I read Mr. Dutt's *Economic History of India*, I wept; and as I think of it again my heart sickens. It is machinery that has impoverished India. It is difficult to measure the harm that Manchester has done to us. It is due to Manchester that Indian handicraft has all but disappeared.

But I make a mistake. How can Manchester be blamed? We wore Manchester cloth and this is why Manchester wove it. I was delighted when I read about the bravery of Bengal. There were no cloth mills in that presidency. They were, therefore, able to restore the original hand-weaving occupation. It is true Bengal encourages the mill-industry of Bombay. If Bengal had proclaimed a boycott of all machine made goods, it would have been much better.

Machinery has begun to desolate Europe. Ruination is now knocking at the English gates. Machinery is the chief symbol of modern civilization; it represents a great sin.

The workers in the mills of Bombay have become slaves. The condition of the women working in the mills is shocking. When there were no mills, these women were not starving. If the machinery craze grows in our country, it will become an unhappy land. It may be considered a heresy, but I am bound to say that it were better for us to send money to Manchester and to use flimsy Manchester cloth than to multiply mills in India. By using Manchester cloth we only waste our money; but by reproducing Manchester in India, we shall keep our money at the price of our blood, because our very moral being will be sapped, and I call in support of my statement the very mill-hands as witnesses. And those who have amassed wealth out of factories are not likely to be better than other rich men. It would be folly to assume that an Indian Rockefeller would be better than the American Rockefeller. Impoverished India can become free, but it will be hard for any India made rich through immorality to regain its freedom. I fear we shall have to admit that moneyed men support British rule; their interest is bound up with its stability. Money renders a man helpless. The other thing which is equally harmful is sexual vice. Both are poison. A snake-bite is a lesser poison than these two, because the former merely destroys the body but the latter destroy body, mind and soul. We need not, therefore, be pleased with the prospect of the growth of the mill-industry.

Reader: Are the mills, then, to be closed down?

Editor: That is difficult. It is no easy task to do away with a thing that is established. We, therefore, say that the non-beginning of a thing is supreme wisdom. We cannot condemn mill-owners; we can but pity them. It would be too much to expect them to give up their mills, but we may implore them not to increase them. If they would be good they would gradually contract their business. They can establish in thousands of households the ancient and sacred handlooms and they can buy out the cloth that may be thus woven. Whether the mill-owners do this or not, people can cease to use machine-made goods.

Reader: You have so far spoken about machine-made cloth, but there are innumerable machine-made things. We have either to import them or to introduce machinery into our country.

Editor:Indeed, our gods even are made in Germany. What need, then, to speak of matches, pins and glassware? My answer can be only one. What did India do before these articles were introduced? Precisely the same should be done today. As long as we cannot make pins without machinery so long will we do without them. The tinsel splendour of glassware we will have nothing to do with, and we will make wicks, as of old, with home-grown cotton and use handmade earthen saucers for lamps. So doing, we shall save our eyes and money and support Swadeshi and so shall we attain Home Rule.

It is not to be conceived that all men will do all these things at one time or that some men will give up all machine-made things at once. But, if the thought is sound, we shall always find out what we can give up and gradually cease to use it. What a few may do, others will copy; and the movement will grow like the coconut of the mathematical problem. What the leaders do, the populace will gladly do in turn. The matter is neither complicated nor difficult. You and I need not wait until we can carry others with us. Those will be the losers who will not do it, and those who will not do it, although they appreciate the truth, will deserve to be called cowards.

Reader: What, then, of the tram-cars and electricity?

Editor: This question is now too late. It signifies nothing. If we are to do without the railways we shall have to do without the tram-cars. Machinery is like a snake-hole which may contain from one to a hundred snakes. Where there is machinery there are large cities; and where there are large cities, there are tram-cars and railways; and there only does one see electric light. English villages do not boast of any of these things. Honest physicians will tell you that where means of artificial locomotion have increased, the health of the people has suffered. I remember that when in a European town there was a scarcity of money, the receipts of the tramway company, of the lawyers and of the doctors went down and people were less unhealthy. I cannot recall a single good point in connection with machinery. Books can be written to demonstrate its evils.

Reader: Is it a good point or a bad one that all you are saying will be printed through machinery?

Editor: This is one of those instances which demonstrate that sometimes poison is used to kill poison. This, then, will not be a good point regarding machinery. As it expires, the machinery, as it were, says to us: "Beware and avoid me. You will derive no benefits from me and the benefit that may accrue from printing will avail only those who are infected with the machinery-craze."

Do not, therefore, forget the main thing. It is necessary to realize that machinery is bad. We shall then be able gradually to do away with it. Nature has not provided any way whereby we may reach a desired goal all of a sudden. If, instead of welcoming machinery as a boon, we should look upon it as an evil, it would ultimately go.

XX
Conclusion

Reader: From your views I gather that you would form a third party. You are neither an extremist nor a moderate.

Editor: That is a mistake. I do not think of a third party at all. We do not all think alike. We cannot say that all the moderates hold identical views. And how can those who want only to serve have a party? I would serve both the moderates and the extremists. Where I differ from them, I would respectfully place my position before them and continue my service.

Reader: What, then, would you say to both the parties?

Editor: I would say to the extremists: "I know that you want Home Rule for India; it is not to be had for your asking. Everyone will have to take it for himself. What others get for me is not Home Rule but foreign rule; therefore, it would not be proper for you to say that you have obtained Home Rule if you have merely expelled the English. I have already described the true nature of Home Rule. This you would never obtain by force of arms. Brute-force is not natural to Indian soil. You will have, therefore, to rely wholly on soul-force. You must not consider that violence is necessary at any stage for reaching our goal."

I would say to the moderates: "Mere petitioning is derogatory; we thereby confess inferiority. To say that British rule is indispensable, is almost a denial of the Godhead. We cannot say that anybody or anything is indispensable except God. Moreover, commonsense should tell us that to state that, for the time being, the presence of the English in India is a necessity, is to make them conceited.

"If the English vacated India, bag and baggage, it must not be supposed that she would be widowed. It is possible that those who are forced to observe peace under their pressure would fight after their withdrawal. There can be no advantage in suppressing an eruption; it must have its vent. If, therefore, before we can remain at peace, we must fight amongst ourselves, it is better that we do so. There is no occasion for a third party to protect the weak. It is this so-called protection which has unnerved us. Such protection can only make the weak weaker. Unless we realize this, we cannot have Home Rule. I would paraphrase the thought of an English divine and say that anarchy under Home Rule were better than orderly foreign rule. Only, the meaning that the learned divine attached to Home Rule is different from Indian Home Rule according to my conception. We have to learn, and to teach others, that we do not want the tyranny of either English rule or Indian rule."

If this idea were carried out, both the extremists and the moderates could join hands. There is no occasion to fear or distrust one another.

Reader: What, then, would you say to the English?

Editor: To them I would respectfully say: "I admit you are my rulers. It is not necessary to debate the question whether, you hold India by the sword or by my consent. I have no objection to your remaining in my country, but although you are the rulers, you will have to remain as servants of the people. It is not we who have to do as you wish, but it is you who have to do as we wish. You may keep the riches that you have drained away from this land, but you may not drain riches henceforth. Your function will be, if you so wish, to police India; you must abandon the idea of deriving any commercial benefit from us. We hold the civilization that you support to be the reverse of civilization. We consider our civilization to be far superior to yours. If you realize this truth, it will be to your advantage and, if you do not, according to your own proverb, you should only live in our country in the same manner as we do. You must not do anything that is contrary to our religions. It is your duty as rulers that for the sake of the Hindus you should eschew beef, and for the sake of Mahomedans you should avoid bacon and ham. We have hitherto said nothing because we have been cowed down, but you need not consider that you have not hurt our feelings by your conduct. We are not expressing our sentiments either through base selfishness or fear, but because it is our duty, now to speak out boldly. We consider your school and law courts to be useless. We want our own ancient schools and courts to be restored. The common language of India is not English but Hindi. You should, therefore, learn it. We can hold communication with you only in our national language.

"We cannot tolerate the idea of your spending money on railways and the military. We see no occasion for either. You may fear Russia; we do not. When she comes we shall look after her. If you are with us, we may then receive her jointly. We do not need any European cloth. We shall manage with articles produced and manufactured at home. You may not keep one eye on Manchester and the other on India. We can work together only if our interests are identical.

"This has not been said to you in arrogance. You have great military resources. Your naval power is matchless. If we wanted to fight with you on your own ground, we should be unable to do so, but if the above submissions be not acceptable to you, we cease to play the part of the ruled. You may, if you like, cut us to pieces. You may shatter us at the cannon's mouth. If you act contrary to our will, we shall not help you; and without our help, we know that you cannot move one step forward.

"It is likely that you will laugh at all this in the intoxication of your power. We may not be able to disillusion you at once; but if there be any manliness in us, you will see shortly that your intoxication is suicidal and that your laugh at our expense is an aberration of intellect. We believe that at heart you belong to a religious nation. We are living in a land which is the source of religions. How we came together need not be considered, but we can make mutual good use of our relations.

"You, English, who have come to India are not good specimens of the English nation, nor can we, almost half-Anglicized Indians, be considered good specimens of the real Indian nation. If the English nation were to know all you have done, it would oppose many of your actions. The mass of the Indians have had few dealings with you. If you will abandon your so-called civilization and search into your own scriptures, you will find that our demands are just. Only on condition of our demands being fully satisfied may you remain in India; and if you remain under those conditions, we shall learn several things from you and you will learn many from us. So doing we shall benefit each other and the world. But that will happen only when the root of our relationship is sunk in a religious soil."

Reader: What will you say to the nation?

Editor: Who is the nation?

Reader: For our purposes it is the nation that you and I have been thinking of, that is those of us who are affected by European civilization, and who are eager to have Home Rule.

Editor: To these I would say, "It is only those Indians who are imbued with real love who will be able to speak to the English in the above strain without being frightened, and only those can be said to be so imbued who conscientiously believe that Indian civilization is the best and that the European is a nine day's wonder. Such ephemeral civilizations have often come and gone and will continue to do so. Those only can be considered to be so imbued who, having experienced the force of the soul within themselves, will not cower before brute-force, and will not, on any account, desire to use brute-force. Those only can be considered to have been so imbued who are intensely dissatisfied with the present pitiable condition, having already drunk the cup of poison.

"If there be only one such Indian, he will speak as above to the English and the English will have to listen to him.

"These are not demands, but they show our mental state. We shall get nothing by asking; we shall have to take what we want, and we need the requisite strength for the effort and that strength will be available to him only who will act thus :

1. He will only on rare occasions make use of the English language;

2. If a lawyer, he will give up his profession, and take up a hand-loom;
3. If a lawyer, he will devote his knowledge to enlightening both his people and the English;
4. If a lawyer, he will not meddle with the quarrels between parties but will give up the courts and from his experience induce the people to do likewise;
5. If a lawyer, he will refuse to be a judge, as he will give up his profession;
6. If a doctor, he will give up medicine, and understand that rather than mending bodies, he should mend souls;
7. If a doctor, he will understand that no matter to what religion he belongs, it is better that bodies remain diseased rather than that they are cured through the instrumentality of the diabolical vivisection that is practiced in European schools of medicine;
8. Although a doctor, he will take up a hand-loom, and if any patients come to him will tell them the cause of their diseases, and will advise them to remove the cause rather than pamper them by giving useless drugs; he will understand that if by not taking drugs, perchance the patient dies, the world will not come to grief and that he will have been really merciful to him;
9. Although a wealthy man, yet regardless of his wealth, he will speak out his mind and fear no one;
10. If a wealthy man, he will devote his money to establishing hand-looms, and encourage others to use hand-made goods by wearing them himself;
11. Like every other Indian, he will know that this is a time for repentance, expiation and mourning;
12. Like every other Indian, he will know that to blame the English is useless, that they came because of us, and remain also for the same reason, and that they will either go or change their nature only when we reform ourselves;

13. Like others, he will understand that at a time of mourning, there can be no indulgence, and that, whilst we are in a fallen state, to be in gaol or in banishment is much the best;
14. Like others, he will know that it is superstition to imagine it necessary that we should guard against being imprisoned in order that we may deal with the people;
15. Like others, he will know that action is much better than speech; that it is our duty to say exactly what we think and face the consequences and that it will be only then that we shall be able to impress anybody with our speech;
16. Like others, he will understand that we shall become free only through suffering;
17. Like others, he will understand that deportation for life to the Andamans is not enough expiation for the sin of encouraging European civilization;
18. Like others, he will know that no nation has risen without suffering, that, even in physical warfare, the true test is suffering and not the killing of others, much more so in the warfare of passive resistance;
19. Like others, he will know that it is an idle excuse to say that we shall do a thing when the others also do it: that we should do what we know to be right, and that others will do it when they see the way; that when I fancy a particular delicacy, I do not wait till others taste it; that to make a national effort and to suffer are in the nature of delicacies; and that to suffer under pressure is no suffering."

Reader: This is a large order. When will all carry it out?

Editor: You make a mistake. You and I have nothing to do with the others. Let each do his duty. If I do my duty, that is, serve myself, I shall be able to serve others. Before I leave you, I will take the liberty of repeating:

1. Real home-rule is self-rule or self-control.
2. The way to it is passive resistance: that is soul-force or love-force.
3. In order to exert this force, Swadeshi in every sense is necessary.
4. What we want to do should be done, not because we object to the English or because we want to retaliate but because it is our duty to do so. Thus, supposing that the English remove the salt-tax, restore our money, give the highest posts to Indians, withdraw the English troops, we shall certainly not use their machine-made goods, nor use the English language, nor many of their industries. It is worth noting that these things are, in their nature, harmful; hence we do not want them. I bear no enmity towards the English but I do towards their civilization.

In my opinion, we have used the term "Swaraj" without understanding its real significance. I have endeavoured to explain it as I understand it, and my conscience testifies that my life henceforth is dedicated to its attainment.

3
Traditional Influences on the thought of Mahatma Gandhi

A. L. Basham

Introduction

It is not easy to say anything new about Mahatma Gandhi, for few men of the twentieth century have had so much written about them. I am no authority on the recent history of India in general, or on Gandhi in particular, and have read only a very small portion of the available material. Hence what I write can be only tentative, and based chiefly on my knowledge of early India.

Such knowledge is not very helpful for this task, for our problem is to assess Gandhi's debt not to ancient India in general, but to those aspects of Hindu culture which were preserved and emphasized in the Gujarat of the 1870s and 80s, and to those ancient Indian texts which he is known to have read and admired in his earlier years. Gandhi himself in many passages of his voluminous writings admits his debt to certain western sources, notably the Gospels (especially the Serman on the Mount), Tolstoy, Thoreau and Ruskin. There is no reason to minimize these influences. On the other hand, we may ask how far Gandhi accepted the doctrines of those sources in their own right, so to speak, and how far he looked on them as merely confirming and systematizing attitudes and values which he had obtained at home. Certain elements in the religious life of nineteenth-

* Reprinted with the permission of Oxford University Press, New Delhi from: R. Kumar (ed.), *Essays on Gandhian Politics: The Rowlatt Satyagragha of 1919* (London: OUP, 1971), pp. 17-42.

century Hinduism may have prepared the ground for some of Gandhi's ideas.

Gandhi's Youth

According to his autobiography, Gandhi's parents were in different degrees religious, as no doubt nearly everybody was in Porbandar and Rajkot at the time. His father, he says, had very little religious training, but he frequently visited temples and listened to pious discourses. In his last days he took to the *Bhagavad Gita,* and repeated verses of it aloud every day at prayer.[1] As is commonly the case in the Hindu household, Gandhi's mother was more earnest than his father in religious observance. She prayed before every meal, and visited the temple every day. She regularly performed the annual *Caturmãsa* fast in the rainy season, with numerous work of supererogation in the form of additional fasts and views. Yet she had 'strong common sense', and kept in touch with matters of state. Thus Gandhi grew up in an orthodox *Vaishnava* home.

It would seem that the influence of his parents affected rather his moral than his mystical sense. He tells us nothing about deep religious feelings or mystical experiences and visions, such as sometimes occur to intensely pious children in India and elsewhere. He mentions being greatly inspired by religious dramas, but rather than inciting mystical awe they merely confirmed his resolution to remain devoted to his parents and to speak the truth in all circumstances. He did not remember ever having told a lie at school, either to his teachers or to his classmates.[2]

As a boy he hated sports and gymnastics, and loved to serve as nurse to his father. He would hurry home from school for this purpose.[3] His education was also interrupted by his passionate love for his wife, Kasturbai, and he would think of her while at his lessons and long for nightfall.[4] In his autobiography he makes no pretence that he was a good student, and one suspects that he is over-modest. He learnt a little Sanskrit, without which he would have found it difficult to take any interest in the sacred books of Hinduism.[5]

He was a timid boy, 'haunted by the fear of thieves, ghosts and serpents'. He was ashamed of the fact that Kasturbai appeared to have more courage than he. For this and other reasons he was lured by an unnamed classmate to take up meat-eating. It was widely thought at the time by the reforming youth of India that meat-eating had a psychological or physiological effect on the character of the eater, and would make him strong and brave. The young Indian could thus excuse himself if he broke the cherished taboos of his community by appeals to the patriotic desire to expel the occupying power and to make India a free nation. Gandhi took to meat-eating as a duty. In the course of a year he seems to have eaten meat half a dozen times, and to have acquired a liking for it. He gave up his secret meat-eating feasts not because he thought them intrinsically wrong, but because they involved telling lies to his mother.[6]

Later the boy Gandhi also expressed a mild revolt against parental authority by taking to smoking cigarettes. Apparently he was not allowed pocket money and stole coppers from the servants in order to buy them. After a while he and the other boy who shared this secret vice grew so exasperated at the thought of being under such tight parental control that they resolved to commit suicide. They ate one or two *dhãturã* seeds and then decided to remain alive after all. The suicide was planned in the best Hindu tradition. The two worshipped in a temple before the attempt, and went to another one after they had given it up, in order to compose their minds. Later Gandhi confessed this and another theft to his ailing father and was freely forgiven.[7] The account of this incident, which most great men would have thought too trivial to record, shows clearly what an important effect it had on the boy.

Soon afterwards Gandhi's father died. In a memorable passage of his autobiography he tells us how, at the age of sixteen, passion for his wife took him away from his father's bedside a few minutes before the latter's death—an incident which left him with a sense of shame that he was never able to efface or forget.[8] While Gandhi's mistrust of sex evidently owes much to other sources, this traumatic event no doubt had an immense effect on his later attitude.

The *Vaisnava* temple where his mother worshipped had no appeal for him. His old nurse, Rambha, whom he recalls with respect and affection, taught him to call on the name of Ram as an antidote to his fear of the dark. 'The good seed sown in childhood was not sown in vain', he tells us, and records that this calling on the name of God in trouble was in later life 'an infallible remedy'.[9] In fact in his last moments it was not the profound mysticism of the *Bhagavad Gitã* which gave him strength, far less the Sermon on the Mount, but the simple formula taught him by his nurse.

When Gandhi was thirteen a locally famous devotee visited his father every evening to recite the *Rãmãyan* in Tulsi Das's Hindu version. The boy was 'enraptured at his reading', and in his maturity he regarded the Tulsi *Rãmãyan* as 'the greatest book in all devotional literature'. However, it is not clear whether at that time he more enjoyed the religious and moral content of the poem or the poetry itself and the exciting narrative. He was not then impressed by the *Bhãgavata Purãna* and his reading of *Manusmrti* made him 'incline somewhat towards atheism'. Jaina monks often visited his father and talked with him 'on subjects religious and mundane', but at that time Jainism, which is characterized by extreme *ahimsa,* seems to have had little or no influence on him, since he infringed this principle by eating meat, and confesses to having killed 'bugs and such other insects, regarding it as a duty'. If we are to believe his recollections, his boyhood, though not particularly religious, was characterized by intense conscientiousness and moral fervour. He quotes a Gujarati stanza by the poet Shyãmal Bhatt as having 'gripped his mind and heart' in his boyhood:

For a bowl of water give a goodly meal;
For a kindly greeting bow thou down with zeal;
For a simple penny pay thou back with gold;
If thy life be rescued, life do not withhold.
Thus the words and actions of the wise regard;
Every little service tenfold they reward.
But the truly noble know all men as one,

And return with gladness good for evil done.[10]

I am unable to obtain a better translation of these verses, which are quoted from the *Autobiography*. No doubt they are much more impressive in the original.

Thus when he first read the doctrines of the Sermon on the Mount and of Tolstoy his mind had already been prepared by the ethical teachings which he had absorbed in his childhood.

In general the boy seems to have favoured reform, and to have been anxious to throw off the shackles of tradition. His half-hearted attempt at suicide is evidence of the conflict, felt in some measure by all adolescent boys, between the urge towards freedom from parental restraints and love for the parents and the sense of security which they bestow. Such conflicts must have been particularly common among the educated Indian boys of Gandhi's generation. It would appear that on his father's death the rebel in him gained the upper hand, for his eagerness to go to England triumphed over his cowardice.[11] The fact that the Modh Baniya caste council of Bombay outcasted him before his departure had no effect on him and only made him more eager to go.[12]

Gandhi's years in England were perhaps the most formative of his life. Despite his shyness and immaturity, he evidently adapted himself better to his circumstances than do many Indian students in London at the present day. He seems to have been well supplied with funds, and at first tried to become as Western as possible, taking lessons in elocution, dancing, and the violin. He even had an English girl friend, whom he met and talked to every Sunday, only confessing that he was already married when he felt that the girl's interest in him was growing and that her guardian, an elderly widow, might be contemplating a formal engagement between the two. The exact chronology of these event is not quite clear, but it is evident that the incident took place before that meeting of his with the theosophists which turned his attention to the things of the spirit. He admits that he found the letter, confessing that he was a married man, very difficult to write, and we suspect that Gandhi's feelings for this unnamed and unidentified girl were much stronger than at first appears from the pages of the autobiography. It is only after describing this incident that he tells us of his religious life in England, which began to develop towards the end of his second year there.

It was in London that he became a convinced vegetarian, chiefly from reading English vegetarian propaganda. And here he came in touch with theosophists, through whom he was introduced to Sir Edwin Arnold's verse translation of the *Bhagavad Gita,* called *The Song Celestial.* He had heard this great Hindu text before, but previously it made little impression on him. Arnold's then famous poem on the life of Buddha, *The Light of Asia,* also appears to have affected his outlook. From Arnold and Mme Blavatsky he turned to the Bible. The Old Testament he found dull, but the Sermon on the Mount 'went straight to his heart', and put him in mind of the Gujarati verses he had learnt as a child.[13]

This, we believe, gives the key to the influences which worked on Gandhi. The Western source of inspiration served to remind him of the verses he had heard in his childhood, which expressed roughly the same ideas, and to confirm his faith in the teaching of both. We can find partial prototypes for most of his ideas in Indian tradition, but the stimulus for their reformulation along Gandhian lines came chiefly from the West, either through personal contact or from reading.

'Truth'

The dominant concept of Gandhi's ideology is 'Truth', *Satya* or its derivative in all north Indian languages. It is quite clear from his use of the word in many contexts that Gandhi's *Satya* is not the bare logical truth of modern scientific usage, merely the function or attribute of a proposition which corresponds to an event or fact. He tells us that in his boyhood the metaphysical aspects of religion did not greatly interest him.

> But one thing took deep root in me—the conviction that morality is the basis of things, and that truth is the

> substance of all morality. Truth became my sole objective. It began to grow in magnitude every day, and my definition of it also has been ever widening.[14]

He here admits that he uses the word with special overtones and connotations. It has been suggested that we can understand Gandhi's concept of truth if we substitute the word 'Reality' for it,[15] but this evidently does not fit his sense of the term in many passages, for instance the one quoted above. His slogans 'God is Truth' or 'Truth is God', if interpreted in this way, suggest a Spinozan or Hegelian natural monism, with no great ethical content. But Truth, for Gandhi, was the focal point of all his moral ideas.

Often he describes himself as 'a humble searcher after Truth'[16] or something similar. Self-claimed 'seekers after truth' are legion, both in East and West, and the term here can be taken in its literal English sense. The same is the case when Gandhi says: 'I have no policy... save the policy of truth and *ahimsa*'.[17] But a statement like 'to find Truth completely is to realize oneself and one's destiny'[18] suggests that his concept approaches that of ultimate reality, the *Brahman* of *Advaita* philosophy, the single entity underlying all things. Gandhi's own definitions of Truth are often far from clear. 'What is Truth? A difficult question, but I have solved it for myself by saying that it is what the voice within tells you.'[19] Here he seems to identify Truth with conscience. In another definition we are told:

> For me truth is the sovereign principle ... This Truth is not only truthfulness in word, but truthfulness in thought also, and not only the relative truth of our conception, but the Absolute Truth, the Eternal Principle, that is God ... I worship God as Truth only. I have not yet found Him, but I am seeking after Him. Often in my progress I have had faint glimpses of the Absolute Truth, God, and daily the conviction is growing upon me that He alone is real and all else is unreal....
>
> The world crushes the dust under its feet, but the seeker after Truth should be so humble himself that even the dust

> could crush him. Only then, and, not until then, will he have a glimpse of Truth.[20]

Often Gandhi makes a complete identification of God and Truth:

> The little fleeting glimpses... that I have been able to have of Truth can hardly convey an idea of the indescribable lustre of Truth, a million times more intense than that of the sun... A perfect vision of Truth can only follow a complete realization of *ahimsa.*[20]

> To see the universal and all-pervading spirit of Truth face to face one must be able to love the meanest of creation as oneself.[21]

But in his writings we also find references to Truth which emphasize its moral or ethical character.[22] In the introduction to his autobiography he states that his 'Experiments with Truth' include 'experiments with non-violence, celibacy and other principles of conduct believed to be distinct from truth'. But for him 'Truth is the sovereign principle, which includes numerous other principles'.

The passages which we have quoted are sufficient to show the very wide range of connotations which Truth possessed for Gandhi. We can perhaps find passages in Western literature in various languages where the word is given so many meanings, but in fact Gandhi's concept of Truth, implying not only factual truth, truthful speech, honesty, and the resolute carrying out of vows, promises, and plans, but also ultimate reality, can scarcely be parallelled outside India. On reading these quotations the mind turns to the *Upanisads:*

> This Self (the Absolute *Brahman*) is obtained through Truth and penance. ... Truth only conquers,[23] not falsehood. By Truth the divine road was made whereby the sages, their wishes fulfilled, ascend to the supreme abode of Truth.[24]

> Here is instruction — 'No No' *(Neti, neti).* There is nothing higher than that and its name is 'The Truth of Truth', for the breaths [i.e. life] are Truth, and he is the Truth of them.[25]

> In that which is so minute all things have their soul. 'That is Truth, that is the Self.' And that thou art, Svetaketu.[26]

We have no evidence that passages such as these had made any impression on the young Gandhi when he left for London, and it is probable that at that time he had never heard or read them, for the *Upanishads* were not the usual religious literature of the Indian *vaisya* classes of those days. But his concept of Truth did not need the *Upanishads* to inspire it. Gandhi's nurse, as we have seen, taught him to call on the name of God, in the form of Rama. One of the commonest ejaculations of popular north Indian Vaisnavism is *Ram-nam sac hai,* 'The Name of Ram is true' (or 'is Truth', since modern Indian *sac,* like the Sanskrit *satya,* may be either an adjective or a noun). Here we have already the possible source of the Gandhian emphasis on Truth, and of the special and un-Western usage of the word in Gandhi's speeches and writings. The implication of the phrase to the believer is not simply that God exists; it must also connote that the essence *(nam,* name) of divinity is ultimate reality, and that God carries out his promises without swerving and expects his followers to do likewise. The use of the word *sac* with this extended connotation can also be found in the Hindi *Ramayan* of Tulsi Das, the one religious text which made a great impression on Gandhi in his childhood; for instance, Dasaratha replies to the accusations of his wicked wife Kaikeyi in the following terms:

> Don't accuse me of lying!... It has always been the custom in the clan of Raghu to keep one's word even at the cost of one's life.
>
> All sins together are not as bad as untruth ... for in Truth all good deeds are rooted. This the *Vedas,* the *Puranas* and the *Laws of Manu* all declare.[27]

Here the question is not one of simply speaking the truth. The argument revolves around whether Dasaratha shall bestow a promised boon, keeping his word at great cost to himself and his family. We have no access to a concordance of the Tulsi *Ramayan,* but many similar usages of the word *satya* or *sac* must occur throughout the poem.

Unlike the English 'truth', which is related to such words as 'trust' and 'troth', *satya* is semantically akin to the word *sat,* 'existence', 'being', the first property of the Absolute Essence *(Sac-cid-ananda)* or Brahman according to Vedãnta philosophy. Its overtones are therefore more metaphysical than those of the corresponding English word, and in both Sanskrit and modern Indian languages its range of meaning is wider. The standard Sanskrit-English dictionary gives the following equivalents of *satya* as an adjective: 'true, real, actual, genuine, sincere, honest, truthful, faithful, pure, virtuous, successful effectual, valid'. As a noun it has an even wider range: 'truth, reality,.. speaking the truth, sincerity, veracity,... a solemn asseveration, vow, promise, oath,.... demonstrated conclusion, dogma,.... the quality of goodness of purity or knowledge....'[28] Many of these meanings were carried over into modern Indian languages.

Thus the fundamental concept of Gandhi's philosophy owes nothing to Western sources. It was developed from the Hindu tradition in which he was brought up. Truth for Gandhi seems to incorporate some of the content of the pregnant Indian word *Dharma,* especially in its Buddhist usage, as the eternal moral law by following which a man may achieve bliss. His knowledge of Buddhism does not appear to have been very profound, and he acquired what knowledge he had from his London days onwards. The coincidence is striking, however, for Buddhism tends to exalt *Dharma* to the status of divinity, and in Mahayana Buddhism the Absolute is often called *Dharmakaya,* 'The Body of Dharma'. Another possible parallel to Gandhi's 'Truth' is the Vedic concept of *Rta,* the divinely ordained course of nature, which was associated in the minds of the Aryans with truth, honesty, regularity, and carrying out one's resolutions. The term is rare in classical Sanskrit, but its privative *anrta* came to possess the regular meaning of lying or dishonesty. It is hardly likely, however, that Gandhi was aware of this resemblance, or indeed of the Vedic doctrine of *Rta* itself, before his departure for England, and we can only look on it as an interesting example of the persistence and development of the concepts of Indian thought. While we have no positive evidence that the one influenced the other, the chronological sequence: *Rta— Dharma—* 'Truth' is impressive.

Gandhi's frequent use of the slogan 'Truth is God' and certain passages from his speeches and writings taken out of their context might be used to suggest that he was at heart a rationalist or at least an *advaitin,* believing only in an impersonal Absolute. In one well-known passage he declares: 'I am a part and parcel of the whole and cannot find him [i.e. God] apart from the rest of humanity.'[29] He read something of Hindu and Buddhist philosophy, and of Western humanist and rationalist literature no doubt, and with typically Indian catholicity he tried to make room for the attitudes of other schools of thought. In a remarkable passage he admitted the influence of the typically Jain doctrine of *anekantavada,* which, in its original form, implied that a proposition might at the same time be true and false from two relative points of view:

> I am advaitist and yet I can support dvaitism [dualism]. The world is changing every moment, and is therefore unreal, it has no permanent existence. But though it is constantly changing, it has a something about it which persists and it is therefore to that extent real. I have therefore no objection to calling it real and unreal, and thus being called an *anekantavad* or *syadvadi*. But my syadvada is not the syadvada of the learned, it is peculiarly my own.[30]

This aspect of Gandhi's thought is typical of Indian philosophy, which admits relative truth and degrees of truth, without references to Aristotelian logic, according to which truth is an absolute quality and a proposition must be either true or false. The same typically Indian point of view is vividly exemplified in Rama- Krishna's famous slogan, 'All Religions are True'. This proposition, from the logical point of view, is obviously false, but nevertheless it has a definite significance and validity. More than once Gandhi himself repeated this phrase, though he qualified it by declaring that all religions had 'some error in them',[31] that they had 'fundamental truth',[32] or that they were true 'more or 'less'.[33] At the same time be proclaimed himself in word and action a Hindu. Such an attitude seems inconsistent by strictly logical standards, but it was one which many intelligent Indians would agree with, and is thoroughly in keeping with traditional Indian ways of thought.

Whatever intellectual theories he may have had, he was emotionally a simple theistic Hindu, with absolute faith in God. 'I am surer of His existence than of the fact that you and I are sitting in this room.'[34] His faith never wavered and was evidently strengthened by mystical experience, though he made no claim to be a *jivan-mukta,* or to any special revelation. His references to his own spiritual life are in terms of the utmost humility, and are in this respect very different from those of a certain Indian contemporary who gave up a promising career as a national leader for a very successful one as mystical teacher. The activity which Gandhi called 'prayer' was in fact mystical communion, and he describes it as such.[35] Yet he never suggests that he is more than an imperfect seeker, rather than a finder. This attitude is possibly to some extent influenced by Western religious ideas, since for the Hindu *sannyasi* humility in the face of his devotees is not always accounted a virtue.

Gandhi's willingness to compromise on matters which he considered inessential, and his admitted inconsistencies,[36] hardly invalidate his sincerity. He believed firmly in the doctrine of rebirth,[37] which is the hallmark of the religions which originated in India, and sharply distinguishes them from those of the West; and he even justified such difficult aspects of Hinduism as cow worship: 'It is for me a poem of pity. I worship it and I shall defend its worship against the whole world.'[38] As a Hindu he might legitimately ignore or interpret figuratively aspects of the religion which appeared irrelevant to the contemporary situation, and he might legitimately derive inspiration from the teachings of other religions. This he did in large measure, but throughout his life, at least from his student days onwards, he was impelled by an intense theistic faith, rooted in the *Ramayan* which he heard as a child, and thoroughly Hindu in character.

Ahimsã

Non-violence for Gandhi was a principle second only to 'Truth' in importance. Indeed, sometimes it even appears to transcend Truth. 'Non-violence', he wrote in 1922, 'is the first article of my faith. It is also the last article of my creed.'[39] *Ahimsã* is a common enough word in ancient Indian literature and Gandhi claimed to be following in up-to-date form an ancient Indian ideal, which he had also read in 'the teachings of all the greatest teachers of the World —Zoroaster, Mahavir *[sic],* Daniel, Jesus, Muhammad, Nanak, and a host of others'.[40]

The classical doctrine of *ahimsã* was interpreted differently in the light of *varna* and *ãsrama,* class and stage of life. It involved, not only such considerations as participation in warfare and meat eating, but also the forcible apprehension and punishment of criminals and self-defence.

Warfare was rarely condemned in ancient India. The *Bhagavad Gitã,* with was one of Gandhi's chief sources of inspiration, was composed partly with a view to justifying participation in righteous war, even when the war was waged against one's own kith and kin. The *ksatriya,* or member of the warrior class, had the positive duty to fight, loyally serving his king in all circumstances. Similarly the policeman or other officer of the king was justified in using force in apprehending a suspected criminal, the judge in sentencing him to mutilation or death, and the executioner in putting the sentence into effect. Only in a few Buddhist texts and in the edicts of Asoka do we find explicit condemnation of war.

Ideally, however, war was an affair of the *ksatriya* class, the fighters and rulers *par excellence.* Though the members of other castes often took part in fighting or served as non-combatants, it was not their caste duty to do so. The priesthood in particular should ideally remain 'above the battle', though there are many examples of martial brahmans. The right of self-defence was generally conceded to the Ramayan. If a learned brahman of the highest sanctity made a violent attack on a man of lower class and the latter could only save his life by killing the brahman, he incurred no sin and was not liable to punishment.[41] In the realm of politics it was generally conceded that the subjects had the moral right to rise in revolt and put a tyrannical king to death, though there was some contrary opinion.

In classical Hinduism the most significant aspect of *ahimsa* was in respect of killing animals for food and meat-eating. Many injunctions in the *Smrti* and other literature led to the spread of vegetarianism among the higher castes. It was by no means universal, however. The low castes were never averse to eating meat. At the other end of the scale the warriors traditionally hunted, and ate the game they killed. In Bengal and some other regions fish was by convention looked on as an aquatic vegetable. The Tantrists ate meat as part of their ritual. However, the general sentiments of classical Hinduism were much in favour of vegetarianism and the preservation of animal life. The Jains were particularly emphatic in this respect.

It must be remembered that the *ahimsa* described in the foregoing paragraph refers to the ordinary layman, the *grhastha*. The ascetic was bound by much more stringent rules. There were many cases of hypocrisy and laxity, but the ideals set before the forest hermits and wandering ascetics, for instance in the Lawbook of Manu (Book VI), were rigid in their insistence on absolute *ahimsa*. The hermit must be a complete vegetarian and, moreover, should eat only food which he had collected from wild plants and trees, avoiding all cultivated food, presumably because this involved injury to life in the process of ploughing, reaping, and so on. The wandering ascetic might only eat what was given to him, and it is not expressly stated that he should always be a vegetarian, though this seems to have been usual. He should be absolutely non-violent, even carefully scanning the ground on which he walks to avoid treading on insects.[42] And in the face of threatening violence he should always remain calm, unruffled, and benevolent:

> He should be patient when insulted
> nor should he insult anyone;
> nor should he feel enmity towards anyone
> for the sake of this (mortal) body.
> He should not feel anger towards one who is angry.
> He should bless the man who curses him.[43]

The ascetic ideal was even more strongly emphasized in Jainism, which so deeply influenced the life of Gujarat. The hylozoistic philosophy of Jainism resulted in regulations verging on the fantastic, calculated to avoid injury to the minute and humble forms of life in air, water, metal and fire. Even the eating of vegetable food was looked on as an unfortunate necessity. And unconscious injury to life, such as accidentally treading on an ant, was almost as dangerous to the soul as an act of violence consciously committed. The discipline of strict *ahimsã* applied in its full force to the Jain monk, and even the layman was encouraged to follow the monks' example as far as possible, and to undertake retreats, accepting monastic discipline for limited periods. In any case no Jain layman could legitimately eat meat or kill a flea, though even the Jains in earlier times made exceptions in the case of rulers and their servants, who were permitted in this degenerate age to take part in war and to punish criminals.

The period of the Delhi Sultanate witnessed the rise of schools of popular devotional Hinduism in the Indo-Aryan-speaking regions of India. Most of these originated from teachers who composed hymns (chiefly addressed to Visnu in the *avataras* of Krishna or Rama) in the current languages of the time. They much stimulated the religious life of the Hindus, especially of the non-brahmans. The *bhakta* hymnodists taught intense devotion to a personal deity; in the realm of morals they encouraged brotherly love and integrity in thought, speech, and deed, and they deprecated ritualism. The general tendency of their message was to encourage the layman to raise his standards of behaviour, and they set something approaching the ascetic ideal before all and sundry. The Gujarati verses quoted above and the *Rãmãyan* of Tulsi Das, both of which Gandhi knew and loved as a boy, are products of the great *bhakti* movement, which encouraged non-violence towards all living things, with its corollary of vegetarianism.

Thus in nineteenth-century Gujarat, so strongly influenced both by later devotional Hinduism and by Jainism, ideas of strict non-violence and vegetarianism dominated the ethical systems of the middle classes. The boy Mohandas Gandhi rebelled against them. He ate meat secretly and only gave up his vice through his devotion to 'Truth' and his shame at having to tell lies. When he arrived in England he did not really believe in *ahimsa,* but he remained a vegetarian because he had given his word to his mother to do so. It was only after reading a now-forgotten English book on the subject that he became 'a vegetarian by choice'.[44] Later the Sermon on the Mount strengthened his belief in non-violence,[45] which was confirmed in South Africa by his study of Tolstoy.[46] Yet the foundations of Gandhi's non-violence were obviously laid in his childhood. He tells us that his first reading of certain verses of the Sermon on the Mount ('Whosoever shall smite thee on the right cheek, turn to him the other also. And if any man take away thy coat let him have thy cloak also') immediately reminded him of the Gujarati verses of Shyamal Bhatt, quoted above. These lines are echoed in the *bhakti* poetry of all the languages of India, and their more positive interpretation of *ahimsa,* as returning good for evil rather than refraining from definite physical violence, is to be found in much Hindu devotional literature. Thus the Sermon in St. Matthew's Gospel seems to have acted as a potent stimulus in reviving and developing in his mind ideas which had been implanted in early childhood, and which were based on the religious ideology of nineteenth-century Gujarat.

Gandhi's non-violence differs from the orthodox Indian concept of *ahimsā* in that it is conceived in positive terms, and can serve as a very effective political weapon. 'The self-sacrifice of one innocent man is a million times more potent than the sacrifice of a million men who die in the act of killing others.'[47] Non-violence does not involve running away from a violent situation, or turning a blind eye to cruelty and oppression. Where there is a choice between cowardice and violence, violence is to be preferred.[48] But far better than either is non-violence, which is the very antithesis of cowardice, 'the summit of bravery'.[49]

In many respects Gandhi's non-violence admits exceptions which the orthodox Hindu would not agree to. 'In fear and trembling, in humility and penance' he was willing to do injury to monkeys which damaged and destroyed the crops of Sabarmati *ãshram,* 'hoping some day to find a way out'.[50] On one occasion a calf which was incurably sick and in great pain was put to death on his instruction, and he vigorously defended his action.[51] He did much to help the British in the Boer War and the First World War. And he declared that those who sincerely believe that violence is right are morally justified in using force.[52]

Thus Gandhi's non-violence is an extension of the classical Hindu principle of *ahimsa,* which involves merely doing as little injury to living beings as possible, in the direction firstly of 'loving one's enemy' and secondly of positively inviting injury in a non-violent spirit, as a form of resisting evil. For the first, as we have seen, there are many Indian precedents in Hindu, Jain, and Buddhist sources. For the second these are less easy to find, though they are not wholly absent. Buddhism contains several stories of pious monks who suffered persecution and torture without resentment and with complete calm. The legends of Asoka tell that he was converted, by this means. A story certainly known to Gandhi in his childhood was that of Prahlãda, the son of the demon Hiranyakasipu. Prahlada's devotion to Visnu so enraged his father that he ordered his son's destruction. The boy endured torture and suffering of all kinds without complaint, and his spiritual power was such that steel, poison, and flames had no effect on him. He did not, however, bring about the conversion of his father, who continued in his evil courses until he was destroyed by the Narasimha incarnation of Visnu. On at least one occasion Gandhi referred to Prahlada in this connection, in the rules and regulations of the *satyagraha ashram* at Sabarmati.[53] But in a passage repeated in more than one anthology of Gandhi's writings he mentions only Jesus Christ, Daniel, and Socrates as 'the purest form of passive resistance or soul force', and Tolstoy as 'the best and brightest modern exponent of the doctrine'. 'In India', he goes on, 'the doctrine was understood and commonly practiced long before it came into vogue in Europe', but he gives no concrete examples.[54] Probably he was thinking in terms of the general ethical doctrine of *ahimsa,* as it was applied in classical Hinduism to the ascetic and in Jainism and medieval Hindu *bhakti* to the layman also.

Satyãgraha

Gandhi's boyhood experiences can have provided few precedents for his techniques of passive resistance, deliberate infringement of the law, and open invitation of arrest and imprisonment in order to bring about political or social change. Nevertheless some practices did exist which may have inspired him in his later career. One such, which has been often noted, was *dharna,* or in Sanskrit *prayopavesa,* the custom of recovering a debt through the creditor sitting doggedly, perhaps for days, at the debtor's door. This custom is very ancient, being referred to in the legal texts of Apastamba, Manu, and several others.[56] Since similar practice is attested in ancient Ireland the customs may go back to the days of the primitive Indo-Europeans, before their migrations. *Dharna* was generally accompanied by fasting on the part of the creditor, and it had a very potent effect upon the debtor. Not only was he publicly put to shame, but also, if he held the beliefs current in his time and place, he felt himself endangered by the spiritual power produced by the creditor's persistence. The performance of *dharna* by a creditor might be counteracted by a similar performance on the part of the debtor. Thus there would ensue a sort of contest in the display of will-power, which might result in a friendly compromise.[57]

The practice of *dharna* might be put to other uses, for it was even thought possible to influence the gods by this means. A supplicant, despairing of less drastic means of obtaining a boon, might sit and fast for days at the door of a temple or shrine, and thus virtually compel the divinity to favour him. The whole idea of *dharna* is closely linked with the widely held and very ancient Indian belief, not unknown elsewhere, that mental or physical concentration has a positive effect upon material things, and that self-inflicted suffering in the form of *tapas* or asceticism generates an immense power that may even shake the gods on their heavenly thrones.

Dharna-like picketing was sometimes carried out by groups. A man performing *dharna* might be accompanied by his family members. The Kashmir Chronicle contains several cases of *dharna* against the ruler on the part of aggrieved subjects. Thus the wife of a dead brahman performed a fast in order to compel King Candrapida to find her husband's murderer. The king then himself fasted for three days and nights in a temple of Visnu and was rewarded by a dream, which showed him the means of detecting the criminal.[58] In the tenth, eleventh, and twelfth centuries we have records of the brahman corporations of Srinagar and its environs performing *prayopavesa* in order to achieve political ends. The most outstanding example is that whereby the brahmans in a time of interregnum in the tenth century were able to enforce the accession of Yasaskara, a complete nonentity. This was done by a large body of temple priests who accompanied their solemn fast with the noise of drums and cymbals.[59] Yasaskara, and perhaps other kings also, appointed special officers who were deputed to look into all cases of *prayopavesa* throughout the kingdom.[60] Later the irreligious Harsa (1089-1101) was compelled to exempt brahmans from corvee duty as a result of a protest of this kind.[61]

In the twelfth century such practices became more frequent, as the power of the monarchy waned. The pious Uccala (1101-11) vowed that if anyone in his kingdom ever died as a result *prayopavesa* he would take his own life.[62] In the reign of Bhiksacara (1120-1) the corporations performed a mass fast in favour of the exiled king Sussala. Kalhana gives quite a vivid description of the event, of which he may have been an eye-witness. The scene has no suggestion of solemnity about it. The brahmans sat in the courtyard of a large temple, amid rows of sacred images brought from their various shrines, and their fasting was accompanied by the continuous playing of drums, cymbals, and other musical instruments. They were surrounded by throngs of admiring citizens, who were ready to resist with force any attack on the brahmans, and brahmans and lower castes alike boldly debated the politics of the day, speaking insultingly to the royal officers who tried to reason with them.[63] After the pretender had suffered a defeat, however, the brahmans gave up their fast and ran away in fright, taking their sacred images with them.[64] The last example of *prayopavesa* recorded by Kalhana took place in his own day against an oppressive minister of King Jayasinha (1128-49), who had unjustly raised the taxes.

The fast was ineffective, and many of the brahmans burned themselves to death as a final act of protest.[65] They succeeded, however, in so impressing another young brahman that he vowed that he would assassinate the minister, and in fact he managed to wound him so badly that he was compelled to give up his office.[66]

The Kashmir Chronicle also records two cases of troops performing fasts of this kind in protest against their low pay.[67] In the second instance, under Sussala (1112-20), the soldiers sat with drawn swords, blocking the gates of the palace. The brahmans also fasted at the same time, and both priests and soldiers refused the king's attempts to buy them off.[68] The situation became so difficult that Sussala was forced to quit his capital, to be succeeded by Bhiksacara, whose brief reign, as we have seen, was also marked by similar fasts on the part of the brahmans.

The above instances, which by no means exhaust the references in the Kashmir Chronicle to the practice of *prayopavesa,* show that it was a regular political tool in the hands of the brahmans of the region, and might also be practised by other classes. The performers of this early form of *satyagraha* seem sometimes to have been strongly supported by the masses. Though he was himself a brahman, the historian Kalhana, an aristocrat and an advocate of strong government, generally looks on *prayopavesa* with disfavour, as one of the greatest dangers to the state.[69]

We know of no record of similar mass protests in other parts of medieval Hindu India, but this may be merely due to the fact that no detailed chronicles exist for any region but Kashmir. One remarkable incident shows that the practice of mass *dharna* was known to the brahmans of north India at a somewhat later period. Sultan Firuz Shah decided to impose the *jizya* or poll-tax on his brahman subjects, who hitherto had not been expected to pay it. The brahmans of Delhi appeared before the Sultan and declared that rather than pay the tax they would collect dry wood and burn themselves to death. The Sultan refused to make any concession, telling them that they could burn themselves rather than expect him to let them off. They fasted outside his hunting lodge for several days, until they were near death. When the Hindu citizens of Delhi heard of their plight they offered to pay the *jizya* on the brahmans' behalf. Ultimately the Sultan agreed to a compromise, and accepted *jizya* from the brahmans at the lowest of the three rates fixed, ten *tankas* per head per annum.[70] It is to be noted that this case of mass *dharna* was partially successful, even though it was directly against a ruler antagonistic to Hinduism.

In later periods cases of mass *dharna* are not known to us, though they may have taken place. Peaceful demonstrations against the reimposition of the *jizya* certainly occured in the reign of Aurangzeb. In one of these, in 1679, the whole road between the Red Fort at Delhi and the Jama Mosque was blocked by an unarmed crowd of Hindus. They refused to disperse in order to allow the Emperor to go to prayer at the Mosque, and were trampled down by elephants.[71] There is thus enough evidence to show that the seeds of *satyagraha* were already present in the Indian soil before Gandhi nursed them into growth.

We have found no account of anything resembling *prayopavesa* of this type in Tulsi Das's *Ramayan,* and it is not likely that Gandhi knew of the Kashmiri prototype of *satyagraha* before his return from England. The *Rajatarangini* was first fully translated into English only in 1901, five years before his first passive resistance movement in South Africa. In that time it is unlikely that it would have come to his notice. The exploits of the Kashmiri brahman corporations must have been well known to Motilal Nehru, whose son-in-law made a complete translation of the Chronicle, but Gandhi and Nehru were not in contact at this time. It is probable that, while still a boy at school, he had read something of the protest fast of the brahmans under Firuz Tughluq, but we know of no definite evidence to this effect. On the other hand, the practice of *dharna* as a means of recovering debts must have been well known to a boy of a Gujarat mercantile community at this period. Similarly the Jain custom of *sallekhana,* or fasting to death by gradually reducing the daily amount of food eaten, must have been known to him. But this had little relevance to Gandhi's political techniques, for it was normally only practised by elderly Jain monks with the purpose of achieving salvation as quickly as possible.

However, certain events in the port of Surat, not very far from Gandhi's birthplace, may have had some influence in the formation of his policy of *satyagraha.* The merchants of Surat had always formed a compact and wealthy community, and the well-to-do Gujarati merchant had a tradition of participation in politics going back to Hindu times. We have several records of protests of a more or less non-violent type, mounted chiefly by the mercantile population, but with considerable support from the masses. Thus on 30 August 1844 a large gathering of 30,000 people met to protest against a rise in the salt tax. Vociferous demonstrations, accompanied by a hartal, continued for three days. At first the demonstrators were 'not disposed to commit violence', but ultimately the cry was raised – 'Kill or be killed'. The demonstrators were forcibly dispersed, but their protest was not unsuccessful, for certain local duties were abolished altogether and the hated salt-tax was reduced."[72]

In April 1848 Surat saw a wave of mass agitation against the introduction of Bengali weights and measures, which the East India Company wished to make standard throughout its possessions. There is no record of serious violence, but only of a hartal and a deputation to the collector. As a result of the hartal the poorer people, who had no stores of grain, were put to some difficulty, and the local merchants organized free distribution of rice to the needy. This act of mass passive resistance was completely successful, since after several days' hartal it was decided to abandon the proposal to introduce the new weights and measures.[73]

In November and December 1860 there were angry demonstration in many cities of India, directed against the newly introduced income tax. These sometimes resulted in violence and almost invariably were accompanied by the ceremonial tearing up of income tax forms. At Surat on 29 November there was a demonstration of some 2,000 people, accompanied by a hartal. Though the crowd was in 'a very excited state' there are no reports of violence. The demonstration was ultimately broken up by mounted police and was, of course, unsuccessful.[74]

A very serious hartal occurred in Surat, for several days beginning on 1 April 1878, against a newly imposed licence tax. At this time Gandhi was eight and a half years old, and news of the disturbances, must have reached his family. According to the Acting Collector's Report 'representatives from almost every class and caste were adjured in the most solemn way to keep all the shops in their neighbourhood closed and to resist Government to the uttermost'. The hartal lasted for some five days, and there were numerous vociferous gatherings. However, there seems to have been no violence until 5 April, when a mob attacked the local government buildings. This was quickly stopped by armed police, and the demonstrations came to an end without achieving their objective.[75]

It is hardly likely that Gandhi was unaware of these demonstrations, and it is very probable that they, and others like them in other parts of India, had a considerable effect on his later policy. Indeed it may be said that civil disobedience, in the form of the more or less non-violent protesting crowd which refuses to disperse when ordered to do so, is traditional in Indian life.

Belief in the power of the concentrated will, especially when accompanied by fasting and penance, was common to Hindu and Jain alike, and such ideas must have been known to the young Gandhi from his early boyhood, long before he began to read in the Gospels of mountains being moved by the power of faith. We need seek for no Western prototypes for his doctrine of 'soul force', which is derived from the Indian conceptions of *punya* or spiritual merit, and *tejas,* the supernatural power accumulated from asceticism and meditation. The concepts have much in common with the Muslim *barkat* and, in their more primitive forms, with the widespread belief in a sort of supernatural electricity inherent in powerful beings and objects, known to anthropologists as *mana.*

It must be recognized that *satyagraha* is ethically a great refinement of *dharna* or *prayopavesa.* The creditors performing *dharna* and the Kashmiri brahmans performing *mass prayopavesa* evidently had no sentiments of love or compassion towards the objects of their fasts and vigils. They pinned their hope of success rather on their wills than on their moral fervour, though no doubt they were usually convinced of the justice of their cause. On at least one occasion, in 1921, Gandhi wrote against the practice, and sharply distinguished it from his own methods, calling *dharna* 'barbarity' and 'a crude way of using coercion', since the practitioner of *dharna* knows that he will not be injured by the object of his fast.[76] But in fact the relationship of *dharna* and *prayopavesa* to the techniques of civil disobedience seems closer than he was willing to admit. Gandhi gave those old Indian practices a more moral content by insisting that civil disobedience volunteers should, as far as lay in their power, cherish thoughts of love and benevolence towards their persecutors. This high ethical tone is certainly in keeping with the Sermon on the Mount but it is equally consistent with Hindu *bhakti,* as exemplified in the Gujarati verses quoted by Gandhi himself in his *Autobiography.* Gandhi's techniques may have been learnt in part from the West, but the practice of *satyagraha,* dependent as it was on belief in 'soul force', was in no way un-Indian. If the activities of the Irish rent-strikers and British suffragettes and the writings of Thoreau, among other 'Western' factors, stimulated Gandhi to work out the policy of *satyagraha,* it must also have owed much to the influences of his boyhood.

Other Features of Gandhi's Thought

Gandhi's very puritanical attitude to sex no doubt also derives from his youth. The incident on the night of his father's death would be sufficient in itself to encourage any sensitive young Hindu, on reaching maturer years and producing a family, to resolve on a life of celibacy. Celibacy is prescribed for both the Christian monk and the Hindu *sannyasi,* but in the two religions the motives behind the taboo on sex differ somewhat. Christian ascetic thought looks on sex with suspicion as one of the most potent sources of infatuation, and a very serious distraction of a man from his true aim, which is the worship of God; hence the Catholic priest or monk may not marry. Hinduism, Jainism, and Buddhism agree with Christianity on this point, but the two former emphasize another important reason for celibacy, which is also not unknown in Christian circles—sex is believed to sap both vital and spiritual power.

India has many legends of saintly hermits who, as a result of a carnal lapse, lost all their supernatural power and were no longer able to perform miracles. Gandhi's vow of *brahmacarya,* significantly taken just before his first South African civil disobedience campaign in 1906,[77] was largely inspired by this motive, interpreted in modern terms. His insistence on the value of celibacy owes little or nothing to the West, and his Christian disciple C. F. Andrews disagreed strongly with him on that point.[78]

Gandhi's views on class distinction may be traced to earlier Indian sources, and they began even in his childhood. When his mother told him not to touch an outcaste boy, he answered 'Why not?', and he states that his revolt against caste began from that day.[79] His interpretation of the four *varnas* of classical Hinduism, as the perversion of an originally rational division of humanity into four classes not necessarily dependent on birth and not necessarily endogamous, is substantially that of nineteenth-century reformers such as Vivekananda. And from the days of the Buddha onwards an under current of equalitarianism may be traced in many parts of India. No doubt Gandhi's views on human equality were strengthened by contact with the West, but they originated, like most of his ideas, in his childhood, and are not incompatible with the doctrines of reformers of earlier ages; these doctrines were never quite forgotten in India, though they had little effect on its social structure.

One feature of Gandhi's teaching for which we can find no Indian prototype is his doctrine of the spiritual and moral value of manual labour. The idea behind the Christian proverb *Laborare est orare* seems hardly to have occurred to any Indian of older times, though there may be a few passages to that effect in early Tamil and Telugu literature. The warrior was expected to keep tough by constant exercise and hunting. The *hatha-yogi* might perform the most difficult exercises in the hope of spiritual gain; the *brahmacari,* the religious student living in his teacher's home, was expected to collect firewood and perform various menial duties for his master; but the man who habitually earned his living with his hands was nearly always low in the social scale. The prejudice against manual labour was no doubt very strong among the nineteenth-century mercantile classes of Gujarat, for it would be reinforced by the Jain objection to all vigorous movement, which was believed to injure the minute invisible beings of earth and air. Gandhi explicitly admitted that he owed his belief in the dignity of labour chiefly to Ruskin's *Unto this Last*, which inspired him to establish in 1994 the first of his *ashrams*, the Phoenix Settlement near Durban.[80]

Also essentially non-Indian is his championship of equal rights for women. The Indian tradition gives woman an honoured place in the home and in society, but in Hinduism, Jainism, and Buddhism alike she is subordinate to man in greater or lesser degree. Earlier nineteenth-century Indian reformers had also worked for the emancipation of women, but their inspiration came mainly from Western sources, and their ideas could have had little influence on the youthful Gandhi. He admits that as late as 1898 he 'thought that the wife was the object of the husband's lust, born to do her husband's behest, rather than a helpmate, a comrade and a partner...[81] We can safely attribute his views on the place of women in society to the influence of Western feminism.

Gandhi's objection to mechanized twentieth-century life also has no counterpart in the attitudes of ancient India, which was never averse to innovations of a practical kind. The literature of state-craft abounds in references to *yantras,* or mechanical contrivances of a simple type. As a boy Gandhi seems to have been something of a rebel against tradition, and to have had no objection to making use of all the Western inventions available to him. As a student in London he was apparently thoroughly modern in his attitudes. In 1890 he visited the Great Exhibition in Paris; his main recollections, writing over 30 years later, were of Notre Dame and the Eiffel Tower. He has little to say in favour of the latter, which was 'a good demonstration of the fact that we are all children attracted by trinkets',[82] and he refers to Tolstoy's criticism of it. But he admits that he ascended the Tower and had a meal in its restaurant, and it is quite probable that the disparaging remarks he makes about it are the effect of hindsight. His objections to mechanized life, and to urban life generally, seem to have developed after his return from England, mainly no doubt as a result of reading Ruskin, Tolstoy, and Thoreau. But in a measure they reflected the conservatism of nineteenth-century Gujarat, and feelings which must have been widespread in Gandhi's childhood. Possibly in this respect time and maturity implanted in him the attitudes against which he had reacted in his youth – a common enough feature in the biographies of men and women the world over.

Conclusion

We suggest that several of Gandhi's concepts are fully in keeping with Indian tradition, and were probably developed from ideas which he absorbed in his childhood and youth, fertilized and brought to fruition by his contact with the West. Only two major planks in his platform—the dignity of manual labour and the emancipation of women—seem to have had no prototypes in India's past. He was no doubt a great innovator, but he built firmly on the foundation of his own tradition. It is possible that if he had never read the Gospels, Tolstoy, Ruskin, and much Western literature, Gandhi would not have entered politics at all, or, if he had done so, would have devised techniques and policies different from those which he actually did devise. But if he had not been brought up in a middle-class Hindu-Jain environment of the type that was to be found in nineteenth-century Porbandar and Rajkot his techniques and policies would have been very different indeed. His genius was even more successful than that of earlier reformers in harmonizing non-Indian ideas with the Hindu *Dharma,* and giving them a thoroughly Indian character; and he did this only by relating them to earlier doctrines and concepts.

Notes and References

1. *Auto.*, I, i. The following abbreviations are used in this chapter:

Auto. M.K. Gandhi, *An autobiography. The story of my experiments with truth* Translated from the

Gujarati by Mahadev Desai. London, 1949. (References by part and chapter.)

H *Harijan*, Poona and Ahmedabad, 1933-42.

MMG R.K. Prabhar and U.R. Rao, *The mind of Mahatma Gandhi*, O.U.P. Indian Branch, 2nd edn., 1946.

YI *Young India*, Ahmedabad, 1919-32.

2. *Auto.*, I. ii.
3. *Ibid.*, v.
4. *Ibid.*, iv.
5. *Ibid.*, v.
6. *Ibid.*, vii.
7. *Ibid.*, viii.
8. *Ibid.*, ix.
9. *Ibid.*, x.
10. *Auto.*, I. x.
11. *Ibid.*, xi.
12. *Ibid.*, xii.
13. *Ibid.*, xx.
14. *Auto.*, I. x.
15. B.S. Sharma, *Gandhi as a political thinker* (Ahmedabad, n.d.), p. 20.
16. *YI*, 12 May 1920, p. 2; *MMG*, p. 1.
17. *YI*, 20 January 1927, p. 21; *MMG*, p. 1.
18. *YI*, 17 November 1921, p. 377; *MMG*, p. 15.
19. *YI*, 31 December 1931, p. 428; *MMG*, p. 20.
20. *Auto.*, Introduction.
21. *Ibid.*, Conclusion.
22. *Ibid.*, I. x.
23. *Satyam eva jayate*, the motto of the Indian Republic.
24. *Mundaka Upanishad*, iii. I. 5-6.

25. *Brhadaranyaka Upanisad,* ii. 3. 6.
26. *Chandogya Upanisad,* vi. 8. 7.
27. Tulsi Das, *Sri-Ram-carit-manas* (ed. H.P. Poddar. Gorakhpur, V.S. 2015), ii. 27. 2-3.
28. Sir M. Monier Williams, *A Sanskrit-English dictionary* (Oxford, 1899), s.v. *satya*.
29. *H*, 29 August 1936, p. 226; *MMG*, p. 30.
30. *YI*, 21 January 1926; D.M. Datta, *The philosophy of Mahatma Gandhi* (Madison, Wis., 1953), p. 25.
31. *YI*, 19 January 1928, p. 22; *MMG*, p. 96.
32. *H*, 2 February 1934, p. 8; *MMG*, p. 97.
33. *YI*, 22 September 1927, p. 319; *MMG*, p. 94.
34. *H*, 14 May 1938, p. 109; *MMG*, p. 31.
35. *Ibid.*, pp. 33 ff.
36. *Ibid.*, pp. 45 ff.
37. *YI*, 5 June 1924, p. 187; *MMG*, p. 194.
38. *YI*, 1 January 1925, p. 8, *MMG*, p. 187.
39. *YI*, 23 March 1922, p. 166; *MMG*, p. 49.
40. *YI*, 9 February 1922, p. 85; *MMG*, p. 49. The choice of teachers is interesting – no doubt the first names to enter the writer's head at the time. Surprisingly, Buddha is omitted, while Zoroaster and Muhammad, not particularly rigid in their non-violence, are included. The appearance of Mahavira in the list is indicative of what may be gathered from other writings of Gandhi – a deep sympathy for the Jainism which was widespread in his native Gujarat. The inclusion of Daniel shows that Gandhi revised his views about at least parts of the Old Testament, which he read as a student in London 'without the least interest or understanding'.
41. Manusmrti, viii. 349.
42. Manusmrti, vi. 68.
43. *Ibid.*, vi. 47-8.

44. *Auto.*, I. xiv.
45. *Ibid.*, xx.
46. *Ibid.*, II. xxii, etc.
47. *YI*, 12 February 1925, p. 60; *MMG*, p. 49.
48. *YI*, 11 August 1920, p. 3; *MMG*, p. 53.
49. *YI*, 29 May 1924, p. 176; *MMG*, p. 54.
50. *YI*, 13 September 1928, p. 308; *MMG*, pp. 64-5.
51. *All men are brothers. Life and thoughts of Mahatma Gandhi as told in his own words* (Unesco, Melbourne University Press, 1953), pp. 41 ff. C. F. Andrews, *Mahatma Gandhi's ideas* (3rd impression, London, 1949), pp. 132 ff.
52. *Times of India*, 8 May 1941; *MMG*, p. 57.
53. Andrews, op. cit., p. 102; *MMG*, p. 178.
54. *MMG*, p. 78; *All men are brothers*, p. 99.
55. For references see P. V. Kane, *History of Dharmasastra*, vol. iii (Poona, 1946), p. 438; also L. Renou, 'Le jeune du creancier dans 1'Inde ancienne', *Journal Asiatique*, ccxxiv, pp. 117-24.
56. Renou, op. cit., pp. 123-4.
57. J. A. Dubois, *Hindu manners, customs and ceremonies*, 3rd edn. (Oxford, 1906), p. 666.
58. *Rajatarangini* (ed. Stein), iv. 82-108.
59. *Ibid.*, v. 468-77.
60. *Ibid.*, vi. 14.
61. *Ibid.*, vii. 1088.
62. *Ibid.*, viii. 51.
63. *Ibid.*, viii. 898-908.
64. *Ibid.*, 939.
65. *Ibid.*, 2224-6.
66. *Ibid.*, 2227-59.
67. *Ibid.*, vii. 1156-7; viii. 807-8.

68. *Ibid.*, viii. 807-17.
69. *Ibid.*, vii. 1611; viii. 110, 709.
70. Afif, *Tarikh-i-Firuzshahi*, v. 4 (ed. Calcutta, 1890, pp. 382-4); trans. S. A. A. Rizvi, *Tughluk Kalin Bharat*, vol. ii (Aligarh, 1957), pp. 150-1.
71. Sir Jadunath Sarkar, *Short History of Aurangzeb* (London, 1930), p. 158.
72. *Source material for a history of the Freedom Movement (collected from Bombay Government Records)*, vol. i (Bombay, 1957), pp. 1-16.
73. *Ibid.*, pp. 17-18.
74. *Source material ... Freedom Movement*, vol. i (Bombay, 1957), pp. 19-22.
75. *Ibid.*, p. 29.
76. *YI*, 2 September 1921.
77. *Auto*, III. vii-viii.
78. Andrews, op. cit., pp. 111-12.
79. *H*, 24 December 1938, p. 393; *MMG*, p. 107.
80. *YI*, 4 June 1931, p. 129; *MMG*, pp. 108-9.
81. *Auto.*, IV. xviii-xix.
82. *Ibid.*, x.

4

Gandhi's Writings in *Harijan*: A Plan of Action or Mere Philosophical Moorings

Bidyut Chakrabarty

Gandhi is an enigma. Although he wrote extensively on various themes pertaining to India's socio-economic and political life,[1] it is difficult to search for a well-argued thesis in Gandhi, presumably because there are areas in his thought that often project a different Gandhi altogether.[2] In order to deconstruct Gandhian thought in the perpective in which he was involved in a gigantic nationalist struggle of the twentieth century, what is probably incumbent is to assess Gandhi in two different ways: first, relating Gandhian political ideas to the actual anti-British onslaught that began with the 1920-22 Non-Cooperation Movement and culminated in the 1942 Quit India campaign in which Gandhi reigned supreme. Secondly, there were events, more significant perhaps from the point of view of anti-imperial struggle which, though they drew upon Gandhian preaching, deviated from the well-established norm of "nonviolence." The implication of such a deviation appears disastrous to Gandhi himself. But for those who participated in political movements which ran counter to nonviolence, the means of political action seem to have been derived from Gandhi. This perhaps suggests for "autonomy of political movements" even in the context of an overarching influence of a major political ideology, like nonviolence, in a struggle against an imperial power. In other words, what is sought to be argued here is that the context needs

* Reprinted with the permission of Gandhi Peace Foundation and *Gandhi Marg* from *Gandhi Marg* (July-September, 2003), pp. 132-153.

to be analyzed to explain the transformation of an ideology that had, more or less, prevailed over other competing ideologies during the Gandhi-led freedom struggle. One should also be careful to underline that despite marginalization of non-violence as a guiding force on occasions the anti-imperial counter-offensives, with whatever ideological underpinning, were not at all, spontaneous; instead, they were preceded by the consistent Congress effort at mobilizing masses both at the national and local levels through either social work or direct political campaign.

Given the complexity of socio-political environment in British India in which Gandhi articulated his voice of opposition, it is difficult to ignore the importance of the context which unmistakably had a bearing on his views. One is, thus, confronted with a lot of inconsistencies in his views as a political activist, presumably because the Mahatma reacted differently at different times in response to the circumstances. Primarily a political activist, Gandhi was probably aware of the inconsistency in his thought when he himself admitted,

> At times of writing I never think what I have said before. My aim is not be consistent with my previous statements on a given question, but to be consistent with truth as it may present itself to me at a given moment. The result has been that I have grown from truth to truth. I have saved memory from an undue strain.[3]

Juxtaposed with the above confession, the following statement is more revealing since the Mahatma himself characterized his language as "apohistoric". In his discussion with one of his disciples, Dharmadeva, he categorically stated that "my language is apohistoric, it lacks precision. It is therefore open to several interpretations."[4] Although his confession of being inconsistent on various occasions has led the analysts to accuse the Mahatma of "displaying the inconsistency of the opportunist politicians,"[5] the above quotation nonetheless shows the extent to which Gandhi, above all, a man of action, was sensitive to the environment in which he articulated his political response and thus probably hinted at the autonomy of political action under specific circumstances.

In seeking to deconstruct Gandhian thought in a constantly changing socio-economic and political milieu, one is invariably drawn to a complex process of interpenetration of ideas and the contemporary scene. Hence the idea of a system of thought appears misfit to the Mahatma, the political leader who had intuitively responded to the demands of the day as "it contributed to his quest for truth."[6] In other words, since ideas are nothing but comments on political situations and are intended to shape the men, women, and events, Gandhian thought, despite apparent inconsistency on occasions, requires to be grasped both as a political guide and as a moral inspiration. Underlying this probably remains the cues to understand the outbreak of violence in the Congress-led nationalist struggle between 1920 and 1942 in areas where Gandhi appeared to have been accepted as the leader. What is perhaps remarkable is the effort of the local Congress volunteer to justify violence as a means of political action as perfectly in tune with the Gandhian preaching. Here probably lies the defence of the argument that Gandhi, by striving to fashion and develop a new instrument or weapon of political change, introduced various other dimensions of political action which had cropped up, independent of and/or apparently contradictory with Gandhian thought, in response to a complex interplay of socio-economic and political forces involving the Congress, the British and the inputs from the international scene. Moreover, the fact that Gandhi, unlike his predecessors, swayed the masses with well-entrenched Indianness in his lifestyle and political vocabulary, demonstrated his ability to translate popular grievances into political action in the face of imperial oppression and atrocity. Attributing the rise of the Mahatma as an invincible leader in the nationalist struggle against the British to his physical and mental affinity with the traditions and temperament of the Indian masses, Subhas Chandra Bose, who opposed Gandhi and Gandhism almost throughout his active political career within the National Congress, commented thus:

> ....when the Mahatma speaks, he does so in a language that [the people] comprehend, not in the language of

> Herbert Spencer and Edmund Burke, as for instance, Sir Surendra Nath Banerjee would have done, but in that of the *Bhagvat Gita* and the *Ramayana.* When he talks to them about Swaraj, he does not dilate on the virtues of provincial autonomy or federation, he reminds them of the glories of *Ramarajya* [the kingdom of the mythical king Rama] and they understand. And he talks of conquering through love and *ahimsa* (nonviolence), they are reminded of Buddha and Mahavir and they accept him.[7]

Why Harijan?

Harijan, the mouthpiece of the Servants of Untouchables Society, was a weekly, usually published on Saturdays. The weekly made its appearance in 1933 and continued its publication almost uninterruptedly even after 1947. R.V. Shastri,[8] the founder-editor held this responsibility so long as it was published from Poona. One of the reasons that contributed to its publication was the defence of the 1932 Poona Pact in which Gandhi forced the Congress to accept reservation of seats for the "untouchables" even within the quota of caste Hindus,[9] as suggested by the 1932 Communal Award. Gandhi began writing in this weekly with arguments in favour of the arrangement as the only solution to avoid "a caste war" at "a historical juncture"[10] when the nationalist movement should not lose sight of its principal goal. As a regular contributor (except when he was incarcerated), Gandhi commented on the major socio-economic and political issues in a clear and lucid language. Unlike the *Hind Swaraj* which articulated his vision of a good society, his contributions in *Harijan* are varied and dwelt on themes which he might not have dealt with in detail elsewhere. Since the weekly was popular and read by millions of Indians, the Mahatma, on occasions, preferred to be polemical to establish an argument in preference to what he considered the narrow one. So *Harijan* provided a forum where Gandhi interacted with his colleagues; and or contemporaries over issues affecting the anti-British political movement in particular and the nation in general.

Apart from long pieces by Gandhi, there was a regular section in *Harijan,* known as "the Question Box" where Gandhi responded to the questions on various issues with contemporary relevance. The questions were generally structured around what Gandhi wrote in the weekly and elsewhere. Since the question box ensured a dialogue with those seeking to grapple with his views, the Mahatma was always favourably disposed towards this.[11] *Harijan* was significant in another respect. That was the forum in which Gandhi generally dealt with the criticism of his views, published in this weekly or elsewhere. While defending his arguments concerning "the untouchables" and the reservation scheme, as enunciated in the 1932 Poona pact,[12] Gandhi, for instance, confronted with Ambedkar who declined to publish his views in *Harijan* simply because it was tilted in favour of caste Hindus.[13] Not only was Ambedkar critical of the inherent castist tendencies of the weekly, he was unhappy with the term "Harijan," to identify the untouchables. By designating the untouchables as "Harijan", Gandhi had, as Ambedkar argued, sought to shift our attention from the curse of untouchability. The new name, he further added,

> has not elevated them in the eyes of the Hindus. The new name has become completely identified with the subject-matter of the old. Everybody knows that Harijans are simply no other than the old untouchables. The new name [therefore] provides no escape to the untouchables from the curse of untouchability.[14]

A believer in Varna Vyavastha, Gandhi attributed the articulation of untouchability to "the distinction between high and low that has crept into Hinduism and is corroding it."[15] Despite being critical of untouchability as it was practised in Hinduism, was in favour of "untouchability of a healthy kind [since] it is a rule of sanitation."[16] He therefore emphatically declared,

> the moment untouchability [in its present form] goes, caste system itself will be purified, that is to say, according to my dream, it will resolve into the true *varnadharma,* the four division of society, each complementary of the other and none inferior or superior to the other, each is necessary for the whole body of Hinduism as any other.[17]

Apart from the Gandhi-Ambedkar debate on this issue, *Harijan* also published the views of Rabindranath Tagore which ran counter to those of Gandhi, especially after the 1932 Poona Pact. Reducing the seats of the caste Hindus both in the central and provincial legislatures to accommodate the "Depressed Classes", the pact, Tagore lamented, "will be a source of perpetual communal jealousy leading to a constant disturbance of peace and fatal break in the spirit of mutual cooperation in [Bengal]."[18] Gandhi addressed the points raised by Tagore regarding the alleged injustice to Bengal since no representatives from Bengal participated in the deliberations. Articulating the difference with Tagore as an outcome of the difference in their viewpoints, Gandhi did not seem to be persuaded though this exchange of views adds hitherto unknown dimensions to the debate on untouchability in which Ambedkar has so far been identified as the only nationalist figure opposing Gandhi in this regard.

Major Issues

Harijan is a reconfirmation of a particular point of view that the Mahatma began espousing, in a systematic manner in the *Hind Swaraj.* These themes also laid the foundation of political theory that informed what later came to be identified as "Gandhism." As a practitioner of what he preached, Gandhi's comments on these themes are very useful in grasping the context that underwent dramatic changes in the wake of colonial rule. Gandhi's intervention is useful in another respect. His views on the following themes contributed to a substantial text that lends itself to the study of comparative political thought. Seeking to integrate what was worth salvaging in modern civilization within the framework of Indian civilization, Gandhi went beyond the conventional approach to "nationalist" thought where the so-called Indian vision was always uncritically glorified to champion "a sectarian" political thought.

Nation, Nationalism, and National Identity

Harijan is also very useful in grasping Gandhi's views on nation, nationalism, and national identity. He elaborated his views on these in two different ways; on occasions, he made statements explaining these concepts in India's context. He, however, preferred to deal with them while responding to the question in the Question Box. Unlike Jinnah, Gandhi conceptualized the Indian struggle for independence in a non-nationalist and non-national language. He rarely used the term "nation" except when forced to do so under circumstances in which Jinnah defended the two-nation theory. In opposition to Jinnah, Gandhi argued that language of nationalism was both incompatible to India and inherently absurd. India was not a nation but a civilization which had over the centuries benefited from the contributions of different races and religions. Indians were, therefore, not "a motley collection of groups but shared common aspirations and interests and a vague but nonetheless deeply felt commitment to the historical civilization."[19] Challenging the basis of the two-nation theory, Gandhi therefore asked, is India composed of two nations? If it is, why only two? Are not Christians a third, Parsis a fourth, and so on? ... How are the Muslims of Punjab different from the Hindus and Sikhs? Are they not all Punjabis, drinking the same water, breathing the same air and deriving sustenance from the same soil?[20] On another occasion, he emphatically argued:

> I have never heard that are as many nations as there are religions on earth. If there are, it would follow that a man changes his nationality when he changes his faith. Thus [according to this logic], the English, Egyptians, Americans, Japanese, etc., are not nations, but Muslims, Parsis, Sikhs, Hindus, Christians, Jews, Buddhists are different nations no matter where born. I am afraid, the logic [on which the argument is being defended] is very weak in maintaining, that nations are or should be divided according to their religions'.[21]

As regards the texture of a composite nation like India, Tagore seems to be in agreement with Gandhi. A champion of composite culture, Tagore lamented that "[t]he Hindu-Moslem disunity is..... alarming because nothing is more difficult to bridge than the gulf created by religious differences. [The disunity between [the two principal] communities is owing to a lack of proper mutual understanding due to differences of habits and customs. Thus Religion and custom have between them usurped the throne of Reason, thereby destroying all clarity of minds."[22] Unlike Tagore, Ambedkar found the processes favouring the rise of Pakistan as a separate nation-state as perfectly in tune with logic and reason. Since "Pakistan is [a] manifestation of a cultural unit demanding freedom for the growth of its own distinctive culture", Jinnah's campaign, argued Ambedkar, was both logical and reasonable. He further added: "The Muslims have developed a will to live as a nation. For them, nature has found a territory which they can "occupy and make it a state as well as a cultural home for the new-born Muslim nation."[23]

The Communal Question

Harijan was a forum where Gandhi dealt with the Hindu-Muslim question at some length by publishing his views at regular intervals. There seem to be two definite ways in which the Mahatma sought to conceptualize the inter-communal relationship. On the one hand, Gandhi was disturbed by the rapid deterioration of Hindu-Muslim relations primarily because without Hindu-Muslim unity, there could be no swaraj. He thus argued: "I must be impatient for Hindu-Muslim unity because I am impatient for swaraj. [And] the present bickering and petty recrimination between communities are an unnatural aberration."[24] Attributing the continuity of the British power in India to "the Hindu-Muslim division"[25] Gandhi, on the other hand, argued that "the British established themselves by taking advantage of our mutual quarrels and have remained by keeping them alive".[26] What is striking and clear is that Gandhi appeared to have over-emphasized the divisive nature of the British rule and undermined the socio-economic dimension of the Hindu-Muslim schism largely due to the catholicism of Hinduism. It seems that Gandhi strove to analyze the issue on the basis of a surface reading of the problem. This is reflected in his statements seeking to show the apparent unanimity between Hindus and Muslims despite clinging to different religious faith. On one occasion, he, for instance, referred to Sir Ali Imam whose "dress, manners, and food were the same as of the majority of the Hindus". Even the name Jinnah, Gandhi argued, "could be that of any Hindu". He also mentioned "Sir Mahommed Iqbal [who] used to speak with [pride of his brahminical descent. Iqbal and

Kitchlew are names common to Hindus and Muslims." Hence Gandhi concluded that "Hindus and Muslims of India are not two nations."[27] What puzzled Gandhi was the 'radical transformation of his colleagues who became the members of the League later since "they were whole-heartedly with the Congress during the memorable Khilafat days. [He therefore] refused to think that these erstwhile comrades can be bitter in their heart towards their fellow-workers as their speeches and writings of today."[28] So emphatic was his faith in the underlying fraternity among the Hindus and Muslims that he declared:

> I have no doubt that if the British rule which divides us by favouring one or the other as it suits the Britishers, were withdrawn today, Hindus and Muslims would forget their quarrels and live like brothers which they are. But supposing the worst happened and we had a civil war, it would last for a few days or months and we would settle down to business. In status we are equal. Immediately the British rule is really ended, we shall grow as never before. You don't know how the [British] rule has stunted the nation.[29]

Critique of Industrialism / Western Civilization

Gandhi was an ardent critic of modern civilization as it emerged in the West and as it was imported to India in the wake of colonial rule. He attached the very notions of modernity and progress and challenged the central claim that modern civilization was a leveller in which the productive capacities of human labour rose exponentially creating increased wealth and prosperity for all and hence increased leisure, comfort, health, and happiness. Far from attaining these objectives modern civilization, Gandhi argued, contributed to unbridled competition among human beings and thereby the evils of poverty, disease, war and suffering. It is precisely because modern civilization "looks at man (sic) as a limitless consumer and thus sets out to open the floodgates of industrial production that it also becomes the source of inequality, oppression, and violence on a scale hitherto unknown to human history."[30] What the Mahatma argued in *The Hind Swaraj* regarding industrial civilization was further reiterated in *Harijan*.

There are articles, comments, and statements replete with his condemnation of industrialism and the articulation to an alternative to modern civilization.

For Gandhi, India's economic future lay in *Charkha* (spinning-wheel)[31] and *Khadi* (homespun cotton textile).[32] "If India's villages are to live and prosper, the charkha must become universal". Rural civilization, argued Gandhi, "is impossible without the Charkha and all it implies, i.e. revival of village crafts.[33] Similarly, *Khadi* "is the only true economic proposition in term of the millions of villagers until such time, if ever, when a better system of supplying work and adequate wages for every able-bodied person above the age of sixteen, male or female, is found for his field, cottage or even factory in every one village of India."[34] Since mechanization was "an evil when there more hands than required for the work, as is the case in India, [he recommended] that the way to take work to the villagers is not through mechanization but through revival of the industries they have hitherto followed."[35] He therefore suggested that

> an intelligent plan will find the cottage method fit into the scheme for our country. Any planning in our country that ignores the absorption of labour wealth will be misplaced. [T] he centralized method of production, whatever may be its capacity to produce, is incapable of finding employment for as large a number of persons as we have to provide for. Therefore it stands condemned in this country.[36]

Gandhi was thoroughly convinced that industrialization as it is manifested in the West was simply devastating in India. His alternative revolves around his concern for providing profitable employment to all those who are capable. Not only does industrialism undermine the foundation of India's village economy, it "will also lead to passive or active exploitation of the villagers as the problems of competition and marketing come in."[37] Critical of Jawaharlal Nehru's passion for industrialization as the most viable way of instantly improving India's economy, he reiterated his position with characteristic firmness by saying that "no amount of socialization can eradicate... the evils, inherent in industrialism."[38] His target was a particular type of mind-set, seduced by the glitter of industrialism, defending at any cost industrialization of the country on a mass scale.[39] His support for traditional crafts was based not on conservative reasoning, but on solid economic grounds, in the sense that by way of critiquing the Western civilization, he had articulated an alternative model of economic development that was suited to the Indian reality. In response to a question, raised by Rammonohar Lohia regarding the utility of industrialism as complementary to handicrafts, Gandhi came out with a vision of a future social order and the role of industrialism. The social order of the future, argued Gandhi:

> will be based predominantly on the Charkha and all it implies. It will include everything that promotes the well-being of the villagers and village life... I do visualize electricity, ship-building, ironworks, machine-making and the like existing side by side with village handicrafts. But the order of dependence will be reversed. Hitherto the industrialization has been planned as to destroy the villages and their crafts. I do not share the socialist belief that centralization of the necessaries of life will conduce to the common welfare when the centralized industries are planned and owned by the State.[40]

Nonviolence, Khadi, and Satyagraha

According to Gandhi, *Ahimsa* or nonviolence was a mode of constructive political and social action just as truth-seeking was the active aspect of *Satya* (Truth). Taken together, truth and nonviolence constituted the basis of an immutable soul force, an essential component of *Satyagraha*. Ahimsa was the rule for realizing the truth of Satyagraha. "Truth is a positive value, while nonviolence is a negative value. Truth affirms [while] nonviolence forbids something which is real enough."[41] Ahimsa is a fundamental concept in Gandhi's theory of politics that provided an ideology to the nationalist movement that he led.[41] Radically different from the prevalent ideas of politics that drew on violence, ahimsa was also a novel experiment, based on Gandhi's own assessment of the socio-political situation in India. Satyagraha was not mere passive resistance. It denoted "intense activity" involving large mass of people. It was a legitimate, moral, and truthful form of political activity of the people against an unjust rule. A form of mass resistance to "free ourselves of the unjust rule of the Government by defying the unjust rule and accepting the punishment that goes with it."[43] Satyagraha is a universal principle of which civil disobedience is one of the many applications... [W]hat is essential is that we should not embarass an opponent who is in difficulty and make his difficulty our opportunity.[44]

Satyagraha is "a science of political struggle, in the sense that a *Satyagrahee,* endowed with highest moral values, is trained to fight the most ruthless state machinery in accordance with the canons of nonviolence. Just like an army." [I]t is enough if the *[Satyagrahee]* trusts his commander and honestly follows his instructions and is ready to suffer unto death without bearing malice against the so-called enemy... [The *Satyagrahee*] must render heart discipline to their commander. There should be no mental reservation'.[45] The commander was Gandhi, himself and he thus pronounced, "[j]ust as the General must insist on your taking to the Charkha which will be [your] uniform. Without full faith in truth, nonviolence and the Charkha, you cannot be my soldiers.'[46] According to the Mahatma, Khadi, purity, and the readiness to sacrifice oneself were three essential conditions for a *Satyagrahee.* Of these, Khadi was probably an instrument with both economic and political underpinnings. He thus confidently argued that "[t]he wheel is one thing that can become universal and replace the use of arms. If the millions cooperate in plying the Charkha for the sake of their economic liberation, the mere fact will give them an invincible power to achieve political liberation."[47]

The Future State

Harijan is a tract in which Gandhi documented his views on the future state of India. Although Gandhi declined to comment on the nature of government in a society based deliberately on nonviolence, he nonetheless mentioned that the structure of a state, "constructed in accordance with the law of nonviolence will be different in material particulars from what it is today."[48] Holding the federal structure, as conceived by the 1935 Government of India Act, as "an utter impossibility [since] it contemplates a partnership, however loose, among dissimilars,"[49] he argued that

> [i]mposed federation is likely to divide India more than it is today. It would be a great step if the British Government were to declare that they would not impose their federal structure on India. The Viceroy seems to be acting in that fashion if he is not saying so.... [A] clear declaration will... probably pave the way for real federation and therefore unity. That federation can naturally never be of the Government of India Act brand, whatever it is, it must be a product of the free choice of all India.[50]

Once a declaration to free India from bondage was made, the Mahatma was confident, it would not be difficult to defuse the fear of Minorities of being submerged by the majority since "[n]o charter of freedom will be worth looking at which does not ensure the same measure of freedom for the minorities as for the majority." He seemed to have applied the same logic while conceptualizing an alternative world order. Just like a "nation" state where the distinction between the majority and minority appear redundant, "an International League of nations [in which] all nations, big or small.... are fully independent", Gandhi argued, "the smallest nation will feel as tall as the tallest. The idea of superiority and inferiority will be wholly obliterated."[52]

Aware of the difficulties of bringing together disparate units under one central authority, Gandhi therefore suggested "cooperative federalism" as probably the most appropriate scheme for a multicultural, multi-lingual, and multi-religious state like India. Confronting a famine in Kathiawar (part of present Gujarat) Gandhi realized the importance of what he described as a "voluntary federation." By simply controlling the movement and prices of grain and fodder during the famine and scarcity, the government of India also prevented hoarding in speculators' hands or disposal to the extent of starving the places where they were grown and stored. Futhermore, the government decision to collect grain and fodder from outside the province and distribute in the famine areas also demonstrated the utility of a federal authority in grave circumstances like this. So, federation in Gandhi's conceptualization, is nothing but another way of attaining his "humanitarian" goal. Seeking to substantiate his contention, Gandhi further elaborated,

> [i]f the Kathiwar States would voluntarily federate, say, for water, forests and roads, purely for saving life, there would be no danger of a water famine such as threatens that cluster of States. There are States rich enough who can provide water for the whole of Kathiwar. I know it cannot be done in a day... Kathiwar has fairly good rivers and hills. There is no limit to the possibility of artesian wells. If all the States combine and the rich ones use their riches for the common good, they will be saved the awful prospect of people and cattle having to die of thirst.... This cannot be done unless States and the people regard the whole of Kathiwar as their joint and common land and have wisdom enough to desire to live on their land without perpetual dread of having to die of thirst when the God of rain stops supplies.[53]

A voluntary federation draws its sustenance from a constitutional arrangement dispelling the fear of majoritarianism. Gandhi's suggestion regarding the proposed constituent assembly was therefore turned to protect the multicultural character of the country. As the assembly would be elected on the widest possible franchise, it would possibly be the most appropriate forum to sort out the majority-minority conundrum through discussion. Given the composition of the assembly "[t]he Muslims, the Scheduled Classes, and every other class will be fully represented in the constituent assembly and they will have to decide their own special rights. Even the princes and the zamindars have nothing to fear if they become, and appear, as representatives of the ryots. Independent India will not tolerate any interests in conflict with the true interests of the masses, whether the latter are known as Muslims, Scheduled Classes, Parsis, Jews, Sikhs, Brahmins and non-Brahmins, or any other.[54] In his comment on the Congress resolution of 4 September 1939 regarding the Constituent Assembly,[55] he upheld that "the Constituent Assembly alone can produce a constitution indigenous to the country and truly and fully representing the will of the people. Undoubtedly such a constitution will not be ideal, but it will be real, however imperfect it may be in the estimation of the theorists or legal luminaries.[56] Not only was the Constituent Assembly desirable because of its representative character, it was also a platform to "obviate all clash of communal and class interests"[57] Gandhi was thus candid when he stated that:

> [m]y hope in desiring a Constituent Assembly is that whether the Muslims are represented by the Muslim League mentality or any other, the representatives when they come face to face with the reality will not think of cutting up India according to religions but will regard India as an indivisible whole and discover a national, i.e. Indian solution of even specially Muslim questions.[58]

A careful study of his arguments in favour of the constituent assembly clearly shows a shift in his perception about the Muslim League. His confession that the Congress "does not represent every single interest irrespective of class, caste, colour, or creed ... [and also] it has not on its register as many Muslims as it would like"[59] is illustrative here. *Harijan* is thus a unique document because nowhere else the Mahatma articulated his views on the constituent assembly as clearly as he did in this weekly.

Primary education was another area Gandhi pondered over with ulmost seriousness since it was one of the basic ingredients of a non-violent state. Critical of the British system of primary education since it was "devised without any thought of the economic advancement," Gandhi's alternative was based on sound economics, for all education will be through the medium of a craft. It was not education plus training in a craft, "but it is education," he underlined, "by means of a craft".[60] On another occasion, he therefore emphasized that:

> [p]rimary education shall be given through some craft or the other. Real education and an all-round development of the child is not possible without it. And such education must be self-supporting. This does not mean that each class will

> be self-supporting. However, boys or girls who will go through the seven-year curriculum in a craft-based school will be able to pay all these years expenses through their earnings from the crafts.[61]

As regards the script for the Indian languages, Gandhi's comments are more indicative than substantial. Although the issue was regarded "as an impertinence" in view of "aggressive provincialism", Gandhi nonetheless argued that "every nationalist [is] duty-bound to master the two major scripts of *Devnagari* and *Urdu*".[62]

Gandhi's comments on the British police are illustrative of what he perceived as an ideal form of bureaucracy that was to emerge in the aftermath of colonialism. Drawn on and inspired by *ahimsa*, Gandhi perceived the police as conducive to radically different socio-economic and political order in which "the spirit of violence will have all but vanished and internal disorder will have come under control". Characteristically diffterent from the present-day force, its ranks

> will be composed of believers in non-violence. They will be servants, not masters, of the people. The people will instinctively render them every help, and through mutual cooperation they will easily deal with ever-decreasing disturbances. The police force will have some kind of arms, but they will be rarely used, if at all. In fact, the policemen will be reformers. Their police work will be confined to primarily robbers and dacoits. Quarrels between labour and capital and strikes will be few and far between in a nonviolent state, because the influence of their nonviolent majority will be so great as to command the respect of the principal elements in society.[63]

Gandhi's views on women and their role in the nationalist movement are rather cryptic. The epic heroines, Sita and Draupadi, have been discussed as examples of women's capacity to suffer in situations underlining the struggle between "absolute" and "relative" Dharma.[64] The Congress leadership effectively mediated women discontents so that they remained targeted against imperialism. Gandhi too recognized the power of women and contained it for the cause of independence uniting the nation behind the freedom struggle at the cost of injustice within caste, class, and gender relations. Women therefore appear in the history of nationalism only "in a contributive role".[65] In this perspective, Gandhi viewed the role of women as complementary to that of men. Like other nationalists, he also believed that since women were "naturally" constrained, their "vocations" must be different. Because "[s]he is passive, he is active. She is essentially mistress of the house,... [h]e is the bread-winner." Hence it is degrading that women should be called upon or induced

> to forsake the hearth and shoulder the rifle for the protection of that hearth. It is a reversion to barbarity and the beginning of the end. In trying to ride the horse that man rides, she brings herself and him dowm. The sin will be on man's head for tempting or compelling his companion to desert her special calling. There is as much bravery in keeping one's home in good order and condition as there is in defending it against attack from without.[66]

Given his clearly stipulated position, the contribution of women was articulated in such a way as to accomodate them in the well- defined nationalist agenda. Hence Gandhi specified "spinning" as the exclusive domain of women. Spinning, he argued, "will remain woman's speciality... [since it] is essentially a slow and comparatively silent process."[67] Since they suffer silently for the betterment of humanity, they "are the incarnation of *ahimsa* [that means] infinite love and infinite capacity for suffering. Who but woman, the mother of man, shows this capacity in the largest measure?"[68]

Concluding Observations

Harijan is both a plan of action and an articulation of a philosophical instance on the basis of what Gandhi sincerely believed. Unlike *Hind Swaraj* which the Mahatma wrote while travelling, *Harijan* is a well-argued response to those issues confronting the nationalist movement and its supreme leader. There is no doubt that the issues that figured prominently in his earlier writings appeared more sharply presumably because the

Mahatma was also engaged in social reconstruction that might have been peripheral in the period before the 1930s. While in *Hind Swaraj,* Gandhi sought to present a coherent argument on society, history, and politics as well, *Harijan* is a compilation of a series of arguments on those contemporary issues which, according to him, required immediate attention. What is clear now is that in the aftermath of the 1921-22 Non Cooperation-Khilafat Movement, Gandhi had fashioned his role more as a social reformer and less as a political leader. The most important task Gandhi appeared to have undertaken was to build an India that was not tormented by divisions due to prejudices which are essentially artificial."[69] Accordingly, Gandhi challenged religious, gender-based, national, racial, and other divisions. It is altogether a different story that the Congress finally accepted partition as the best available formula to avoid further bloodbath and Gandhi was absolutely peripheral in the last days of negotiations for the transfer of power.

Gandhi continues to remain as relevant as before. The historical Gandhi[70] was killed in 1948, but the civilizational Gandhi continues to flourish even in the twenty-first century through his "dreams and aspirations for a great evolutionary leap in human civilization"[71] His greatest contribution as a thinker comes with his invitation to think freshly about the future, and he does so "by reaching for both the past and the present."[72] By questioning the inevitability and intractability of modernity, he wants to expose it as a construction that can be resisted. Although it is impossible to return to an earlier cosmos, the Gandhian experiments are powerful endeavours to fill in some of the blank spaces left by modernity. And the Mahatma was aware that the experiment that he had undertaken was neither novel nor unique because "truth and nonviolence are as old as the hills." All he had done was to try experiments in both on as vast a scale as [he] could do.[73]

Notes and References

1. Gandhi wrote a partial biography *(My Experiments with Truth).* A political treatise *(Hind Swaraj),* a few pamphlets, a very large number of articles in two weeklies he edited,

namely *Indian Opinion* (South Africa) and *Young India* (India), and even a larger number of letters to Viceroys, fellow politicians and disciples. Besides, he delivered speeches at conferences, congresses, and at his regular prayer meetings:

2. While examining the role of Gandhi in galvanizing the masses into action in the 1920-22 Non-Cooperation Movement. Shahid Amin thus argues that "there was no single authorized version of the Mahatma to which [the participants] may be said to have subscribed in 1921. Indeed, their ideas about Gandhi's 'orders' and 'powers'were often at variance with those of the local Congress-Khilafat leadership and clashed with the basic tenets of Gandhism itself. The violence of Chauri Chaura was rooted in this paradox". See Shahid Amin, "Gandhi as Mahatma: Gorakhpur District. Eastern Uttar Pradesh," in Ranajit Guha, ed., *Subaltern Studies,* Delhi: 1984, Vol. 3, p. 55. The same pattern recurred in the content of the 1942 Quit India Movement in Midnapur (Bengal) where the location of the Mahatma image within the existing pattern of popular beliefs and the way it informed direct action was "often at variance with the standard interpretation of the Congrees creed." See my *Local Politics and Indian Nationalism: Midnapur 1919-1944,* Manohar Publications, New Delhi, 1997, p. 198.
3. *Harijan,* 30 September 1939.
4. Gandhi's interview with Dharmadeva on 17January 1933, *The Collected Works of Mahatma Gandhi (The CWMG* hereafter), Publications Division Ministry of Information and Broadcasting, Government of India, 1958, Vol. 53, Appendix HI, p. 485.
5. W.H. Morris-Jones, "Mahatma Gandhi: Political Philosopher," *Political Studies,* Vol. No. 3, No. 1,1960, p. 17. According to Morris-Jones, Gandhi joins the company of Burke and others who have not escaped the accusations of displaying the inconsistency of the opportunist politician.
6. "Response from Within," *The CWMG*, Vol. 51, p. 286.

7. Subhas Chandra Bose. *The Indian Struggle, 1920-42,* Asia Publishing House, London, 1964 (reprint), p. 293.
8. R.V. Shastri was a Poona-based social worker and a freedom fighter actively associated with the activities of The Servants of Untouchables Society. Drawn to Gandhi and his ideology in the wake of the 1920-22 Non-Cooperation Movement, he took the initiative in the publication of the *Harijan* on the advice of the Mahatma.
9. Apart from reservation which will ensure their political representation in the legislature, the Poona Pact, Gandhi believed, would also provide *Harijan* with an arrangement "to take stock of their contribution towards their own purification and therefore the purification of Hinduism. But there is no doubt that by far the greatest responsibility rests on the shoulders of caste Hindus. Reformers should make it a point of winning over the orthodox people to the movement by gentleness, humility, self-sacrifice and increasing purity of character." *Harijan.* 22 July 1933. One of the best literary works on both the social-political background and the consequences thereof is Mulk Raj Anand's *Untouchable,* a novel that defended Gandhi as against Ambedkar who, according to the novelist, sought to undermine the manifesto of political freedom on which the Indian nationalist movement was based. See *Untouchable* (preface by E.M. Foster). Penguin Books, London, 1940 (reprint). In her *Children of God,* Shanta Rameshwar Rao dealt with the Gandhi-Ambedkar controversy over the issues raised in the Poona Pact. See *Children of God,* Orient Longman, Calcutta, 1992 (reprint). The occlusion of Ambedkar in both these novels is consistent with a certain tradition of writing about "untouchability" that has its roots in the antagonistic rhetoric of the Indian National Congress which responded to Ambedkar's threat of splitting the leadership with disdain and fear. Apart from literary works, the Pact appears to be an under-researched subject. However, the following two articles are indicative of the potential it has as a research topic: (a) Ravinder Kumar, "Ambedkar, Gandhi and the Poona Pact,"

Occasional Paper in *Society and History,* No. 20, Nehru Memorial Museum and Library, New Delhi, 1985 and (b) Valerian Rodrigues. "Between Tradition and Modernity: The Gandhi-Ambedkar Debate" in A.K. Narain and D.C. Ahir. *Dr. Ambedkar, Buddhism and Social Change,* B.R. Publishing, Delhi, 1944, pp. 129-45

10. *Harijan,* 11 February 1933.

11. Gandhi's favourite format of articulation of views seems to be "dialogue." The *Hind Swaraj,* for instance, was written in the form of a dialogue between the editor and the reader. What is striking is that by combining the role of an editor and a reader, Gandhi addressed those significant issues which are not merely contextual but also transcendental since a large number of them continue to be relevant even after the expiry of ninety years of its first publication in *Gujarati in 1910.*

12. Since separating the Scheduled Castes from the Hindus would be detrimental to the interest of the nation, Gandhi persuaded the Congress to accept the reservation for them, albeit through a system of joint electorates which was articulated in the 1932 Poona Pact. As per the Pact, the election would be in two stages. The primary election would be through separate electorates: here the Scheduled Castes alone would elect their candidates. The result of this round would determine who was entitled to stand in the second and final election in constituencies reserved for the Scheduled Castes. Once the candidates had been chosen by the Scheduled Castes in the primary election, the winning candidate would be decided through joint electorates. Thus the winner who would represent the Scheduled Castes would be elected by the Scheduled Castes and Hindus from among the list of candidates chosen by the Scheduled Castes.

13. Gandhi thus argued: *"Harijan* is not my weekly. So far as the proprietary rights are concerned, it belongs to the *Servants of Untouchables Society* and therefore I would like him [Ambedkar] to feel that it is as much his as of any Hindus." Gandhi's statement in *Harijan,* 11 February 1933.

14. *Dr. Babasaheb Ambedkar: Writings and Speeches, [Untouchables* or the *Children of India's Ghetto and Other Essays on Untouchables and Untouchability: Social, Political and Religious* Education Department Government of Maharashtra, 1999, Vol. 5, p. 363.

15. *Harijan,* 11 February 1933.

16. *Ibid.*

17. *Ibid.* In fact, on one occasion, he urged that "there would be only one caste known by the beautiful name Bhangi, that is to say the reformer or remover of all dirt." *Harijan,* 7 July 1946.

18. *Harijan,* 28 July 1933. In his letter to Gandhi, Tagore, further elaborates his arguments opposing the Pact by stating, "if [the Pact] remains unaltered [it] will inflict a serious injury upon the social and political life in Bengal. Justice is an important aspect of truth and if it is allowed to be violated for the sake of immediate peace or speedy cutting of some political knots in the long run, it is sure to come back to those who are apparently benefited by it and will claim a very heavy price for the concession cheaply gained... I look upon the whole thing from the point of humanity, which will cruelly suffer when its claim to justice is ignored." Rabindranath Tagore to Gandhi, 8 August 1933, published in Sabyasachi Bhattacharya (edited and compiled). *The Mahatma and the Poet: Letters and Debates between Gandhi and Tagore,* 1915-1914, National Book Trust, New Delhi, 1997, p. 149.

19. This is how Bhikhu Parekh paraphrases Gandhi's notion. See his "Nationalism in a Comparative Perspective," 'Verlag J.B. Metzler' *Politisches Denken Jahrbuch.* (Stuttgart, 1994) p. 63. That Gandhi rejected the nationalist language was also underlined by Partha Chatterjee who argued that "Gandhi does not even think within the thematic of nationalism. He seldom writes or speaks in terms of the conceptual frameworks or the modes of reasoning and inference adopted by the nationalists of his day, and quite emphatically rejects their rationalism,

scientism and historicism." See his, "Gandhi and the Critique of Civil Society" in Ranajit Guha ed., *Subaltern Studies: Writings on South Asian History and Society,* Oxford University Press, Delhi, 1984, p. 167.

20. *Harijan,* 28 October 1939, *The CWMG,* Vol. 70, p. 283.
21. *Harijan,* 11 November 1939, *The CWMG,* Vol. 70, p. 335.
22. Rabindranath Tagore, "The Congress," *The Modern Review,* July 1939 Gandhi quoted excerpts from this article in defence of his arguments underlining weaknesses of Jinnah's two-nation theory. See *Harijan,* 11 November 1939, *The CWMG*, Vol. 70, p. 332.
23. B.R. Ambedkar, "A Nation Calling for a Home," in *Dr. Babasaheb Ambedkar Writings and Speeches, Education Department Government* of *Maharashtra,* Bombay 1990, Vol. 8, p. 39.
24. *Harijan,* 5 August 1939, *The CWMG,* Vol. 70, p. 23.
25. Gandhi thus categorically stated that "[c]ommunal differences have been used by the British Government to thwart India's aspirations. That the process is likely to have been unconscious does not make it less mischievous." *Harijan,* 11 November 1939.
26. *Harijan,* 2 December 1939. *The CWMG*, Vol. 70, p. 387.
27. *Harijan,* 6 April 1940.
28. *Ibid.,* 7 October 1939, *The CWMG*, Vol. 70, p. 212.
29. *Ibid.,* 4 May 1940.
30. Partha Chatterjee elaborates this argument with reference to his analysis of Gandhi on the basis of what he wrote in the *Hind Swaraj*. See his "Gandhi and Critique of Civil Society" in Ranajit Guha ed., *Subaltern Studies: Writings on South Asian History and Society*, Oxford University Press, Delhi, 1984, p. 158.
31. Charkha, as Gandhi described it, "is our ammunition-guns and artillery and so we cannot afford to forsake it." *Harijan,* 6 April 1940, *The CWMG*, Vol. 71, p. 383.
32. Khadi, as Gandhi characterized it, "is the chief village handicraft" and "is a symbol of identification with the

poorest in the land." *Harijan,* 20 January 1940, *The CWMG,* Vol. 71, p. 103: *Harijan,* 30 December 1939, *The CWMG,* Vol. 71, p. 52.

33. *Harijan,* 4 November, 1939, *The CWMG*, Vol. 70, p. 316.

34. "Is Khadi Economically Sound," *Harijan,* 20 June 1936, *The CWMG*, Vol. 63, pp. 77-8.

35. "Village Industries," *Harijan*; 16 November 1934, *The CWMG*, Vol. 59, p. 356. The opposition to machine stems from his genuine concern for providing 'profitable employment' to all. He thus argued on another occasion: "[w]e should not use machinery for producing things which we can produce without its aid and have got the capacity to do so. As machinery makes you slave, we want to be independent and self-supporting; so we should not take the help of machinery when we can do without it. We want to make our villages free and self-sufficient and through them achieve our goal—liberty—and also protect it. I have no interest in the machine nor [do] I oppose it. If I can produce my things myself, I become my master and so need no machinery." *Harijan,* 6 April 1940, *The CWMG,* Vol. 71, p. 383.

36. "Mills Vs. Charkha," *Harijan,* 12 August 1939, *The CWMG,* Vol. 70, p. 74.

37. *Harijan,* 29 August 1936, a discussion with Maurice Frydman on 25 August 1936, *The CWMG,* Vol. 63, p. 241. Maurice Frydman, a Polish engineer, interested in village reconstruction movement, had met Gandhi earlier and was given the name Bharatanand.

38. *Harijan,* 29 September 1940, Interview to Francis G. Hickman, 17 September 1940. *The CWMG,* Vol. 73, pp. 29-30. The differences between Nehru and Gandhi may have had their root in the former's insistence on the creation of a planning commission in the Soviet style as a mechanism to bring about radical changes in the economy. See my "Jawaharlal Nehru and Planning, 1937-40." *Modern Asian Studies,* Vol. 26, No. 2, 1922.

39. Condemning the blind supporters of industrialism, Gandhi thus sarcastically stated, "instead of giving [the villagers] employment, by way of compensation, [we] give them lectures, magic-lantern shows and tinned music all at their expense, and pat ourselves on the back that we are working for their welfare. Can anything be more absurd?" "Motor Vs Cart." *Harijan* 16 September 1939, *The CWMG*, Vol. 70, p. 118.
40. *Harijan,* 27 January 1940, *The CWMG*, Vol. 71, p. 130.
41. "Meaning of the Gita," *The CWMG,* Vol. 28, p. 317.
42. Gandhi was persuaded because, as he himself argued, "[w]e have also discovered through our progress that in the application of non-violence we have been able to reach the mass mind far more quickly and for more extensively than before." *Harijan,* 24 February 1946.
43. Gandhi wrote this piece entitled "Satyagraha not Passive Resistance" on 2 September 1917, *The CWMG*, Vol. 13, p. 523.
44. *Harijan,* 6 January 1940, *The CWMG,* Vol. 71. p. 62.
45. *Harijan,* "What are the Basic Assumptions?" *Harijan,* 22 October 1938, *The CWMG*, Vol. 67, p. 437.
46. *Harijan,* 30 March 1940, *The CWMG*, Vol. 71, p. 360. The analogy of army and its functioning is striking, given Gandhi's well-defined opposition to Western military. He was probably inspired by the organized strength of an army which he sought to instill in the *Satyagrahees.*
47. *Harijan, 6* April 1940, *The CWMG*, Vol. 71, p. 378.
48. *Harijan,* 11 February 1939.
49. *Ibid.*
50. *Harijan,* 2 September 1939.
51. *Harijan,* 11 November 1939.
52. *Harijan,* 11 February 1939.
53. *Harijan,* 2 September 1939, *The CWMG*, Vol. 70, pp. 118-19.

54. *Harijan,* 28 October 1939, *The CWMG*, Vol. 70, pp. 208.
55. *Harijan,* 23 September 1939, *The CWMG*, Vol. 70, pp. 409-13.
56. "The only Way." *Harijan,* 25 November 1939, *The CWMG*, Vol. 70, p. 363.
57. *Harijan,* 6 January 1940, *The CWMG.* Vol. 71, p. 63.
58. *Harijan,* 23 March, 1940, *The CWMG*, Vol. 71, p. 345.
59. "Hindu-Muslim," *Harijan,* 8 June 1940, *The CWMG,* Vol. 72, p. 133.
60. *Harijan,* 28 October 1939, *The CWMG*, Vol. 70, p. 274.
61. Gandhi's letter to Ravishankar Shukla, 19 October 1939, *The CWMG*, Vol. 70, pp. 46-47.
62. "One Script for Daughters of Sanskrit." *Harijan,* 5 August 1939, *The CWMG,* Vol. 70, pp. 46.
63. "My Idea of a Police Force." *Harijan,* 1 September 1940, *The CWMG*, Vol. 72, p. 403.
64. Taking the example of Sita, Gandhi thus argued, "[p]hysically she was a weakling before Ravana, but her purity was more than a match even for his giant might. He tried to win her with all kinds of allurements but could not carnally touch her without her consent." *Harijan,* 25 August 1940. *The CWMG*, Vol. 72, p. 392.
65. Kumari Jayawardene has developed this argument in her *Feminism and Nationalism in the Third World* (Zed Books, London 1986), pp. 260-82.
66. *Harijan*, 24 February 1940, *The CWMG,* Vol. 71, pp. 207-8.
67. "Swaraj through Women," *Harijan,* 2 December 1939, *The CWMG.* Vol. 70, p. 381.
68. "What is Woman's Role?" *Harijan,* 24 February 1940, *The CWMG*, Vol. 71, p. 208.
69. *Harijan,* 17 February 1940, *The CWMG,* Vol. 71, p. 197.
70. According to Rajni Bakshi, "the historical Gandhi was a finite being complete with common frailties and unique strengths.... His various political actions—during

negotiations with the British or on the formation of Pakistan—can be questioned, dissected, even condemned. This Gandhi is now only of academic historical interest." Rajni Bakshi, *Bapu Kuti: Journeys in Rediscovery of Gandhi,* Penguin, New Delhi, 1998, p. 10.

71. Rajni Bakshi, *Bapu Kuti: Journeys in Rediscovery of Gandhi,* p. 10.

72. Ronald J. Tarchek, *Gandhi: Struggling for Autonomy.* Vistaar Publications, New Delhi, 1998, p. 230.

73. *Harijan,* 28 March 1936, *The CWMG,* Vol. 67, p. 193.

5
Critique of Modern Civilization

Bhikhu Parekh

British rule in India was a relationship of economic and political domination between an imperial power and its colony. It was based on conquest, consolidated after several wars and followed economic policies designed to serve British interests. Both the parties knew it was unequal, exploitative and based on force. As such it raised moral questions and needed justification. Their self-respect, sense of morality and morale required the British to convince themselves that they were right to rule over India. In order to ensure its orderly and continued existence and secure the co-operation and support of the Indians without whom they simply could not run the country, they also needed to convince their subjects that British rule was in their 'real' interest. It was, of course, possible for them to justify it to themselves in one way and to their subjects in another. However, they knew that such a strategy was open to the charge of inconsistency, even hypocrisy, and inherently precarious.

In order to achieve the dual objective of justifying their rule to themselves and their subjects in a single and consistent language, the British needed to show that they had something to give to the Indians which the latter badly *needed,* were unable to acquire *unaided* and was so *precious* as to compensate for whatever economic and political price they were required to pay.

---

* Reprinted by kind permission of Professor Bhikhu Parekh from *Gandhi's Political Philosophy: A Critical Examination* (Delhi: Ajanta Publication, 1991; first pub. 1989), pp. 11-35.

The logic of justification required a perfect match between British gifts and Indian needs, the British strength and the Indian deficiency. Following the fashion of the time the British wrapped their gifts in the language of civilization, which had latterly replaced Christianity as the unifying principle in Europe, taken over its universalist and proselytising mission and built up an ambiguous and uneasy relationship with it. Although modern civilization was a cooperative European product, the British role in its creation and dissemination was considerable. They were one of the first to industrialise themselves, more or less to recast their religion, ways of life and thought and major political, economic and other institutions, in the light of the dominant liberal culture and to roam all over the world as if possessed by its inherently restless and universal spirit. They claimed to 'represent' or 'embody' it to a greater degree than any other country and saw themselves as its transcendentally or historically accredited 'vehicle'.[1]

Since their civilization had in their view attained the highest possible level of human existence and cultivated capacities which all men *qua* men ought to develop, they had no doubt that it was universally desirable. All societies had a common destiny and destination, namely to become civilized in the British way and were to achieve this destiny by the same route. Hence the more 'advanced' among them, that is, those whose journey had brought them closer to the universal destination, provided the models for and had the moral duty to guide those who had not yet started, become stuck, were proceeding in a wrong direction or at an extremely slow pace. The British could not show that they represented the highest level of civilization without so defining it that it broadly corresponded to their own ways of life and thought. Like all ideological systems they abstracted, reified and absolutised the distinctive features of their ways of life and thought and presented them as a universal norm for evaluating all societies, including their own. Their facts became values for others an illicit logical move lying at the heart of every ideology. Other societies were therefore *always* deficient whereas the British was *necessarily* more or less perfect.

The British argued that they had brought to India the unique and most precious gift of civilization.[2] Since this civilization was deemed to be universally desirable, India obviously needed it. All they had to do was show that India lacked it and was unable to acquire it unaided. Unlike some of the other British colonies India had a well-developed *literati* tradition, a long history of civic life and considerable philosophical, artistic, scientific and other achievements. Since these were supposed to be some of the indices of civilization, obviously it could not be contemptuously dismissed as uncivilised. Some British writers and leaders did so dismiss it; most, however, acknowledged its great achievements, but contended that they were all in the past and did not redeem its contemporary degeneration. Its social structure and practices were oppressive, unjust and sometimes inhuman; its religions were incomprehensible, replete with meaningless rituals, polytheist, lacking a single authoritative text, and not really religions in the 'proper' sense of the term; its modes of thought were 'mystical and mythological' and largely irrational; and its people were emotional, excitable, undisciplined, unambitious, lacking in self-control, unreliable and very like women and children. The British view of India did, of course, change over time, largely as a result of their increased knowledge of its past and the changes in their conceptions of themselves and the yardsticks they employed. Throughout their rule, however, they continued to think of it as neither wholly uncivilised nor fully civilised but 'semi-civilised' or 'only half-civilised', and of the Indians as a moderately talented people who needed to be disciplined, guided and trained in the ways of civilisation.

A civilisation consists of ways of life and thought, and initiating people into it is necessarily an educational enterprise. Following the logic of the language of civilisation, the British justified their rule in educational terms and used pedagogical and tutorial metaphors with great regularity in their descriptions of what they thought they were doing. They were not masters but headmasters; the Indians were their pupils; the whole of India was one big public school, almost an Eton writ large; they had carefully fashioned a comprehensive moral and political curriculum; and their stern rule was designed to create the necessary pedagogical climate and only meant to last until such time as their pupils had graduated into political manhood as judged by the periodic assessment of their performance. Accordingly the British introduced a new language and taught their pupils how to speak to each other and their rulers in a 'civilised' tongue. They taught them new subjects and introduced them to the writings of Hume, Locke, Berkeley, Bentham, J. S. Mill and Spencer more or less in that order and later to those of the European scientists. They set up schools, colleges and universities to train them how to 'think' and develop 'good character'. Over time they created a large university-trained, English-speaking and British-orientated middle class, and predictably looked upon it as one of their greatest achievements. At the economic level they established new industries, taught the 'lazy' Indians the virtues of hard work, enterprise, self-discipline, thrift and efficiency, and laid the foundations of a modern industrial society tied to and subserving British interests. At the political level they introduced the modern state standing outside and above Indian society, and established quasi-representative institutions at the local, provincial and national levels with a view to 'training' their subjects in how to run their collective affairs in a 'civilised' manner. In these and other ways the British set about recreating India in their own image, not always with the impatience and arrogance of the French but nevertheless just as effectively and comprehensively. Although honest enough to admit that their economic interests were never out of their mind, they insisted that at least since 1857 when they acquired direct control over India, the economic relations between the two countries were mutually beneficial and that their primary concern was to execute their 'great historical task' of bringing to India the 'benefits of civilisation'.

Although the basic theme of civilising the semi-civilised Indians remained at the centre of the colonial ideology, the latter was a highly complex structure of ideas articulated at different levels and in different idioms at different periods. Since we cannot here discuss it in detail, we shall highlight its four internal tensions and contradictions. First, the British ways of life and thought in which the colonial ideology was grounded were not monolithic. Since they encouraged the spirit of rational criticism, they threw up a large body of internal critics whose writings were often used by the Indians to deflate the moral pretensions of the colonial ideology. Even as the dominant British way of life never overwhelm all Britons its colonial extension did not overwhelm all its subjects either. Second, like all idologies the colonial ideology was necessarily articutated in terms of such general principles as liberty, justice, the rule of law, equality and Individual rights, and provided the Indians with the intellectual and moral weapons with which to criticise and counter its claims. Third, the civilisation of which the British saw themselves as missionaries contained a tension at yet another level. It was essentially secular, yet Christianity was an integral part of it. The British did not see themselves as civilisational missionaries until around the first two decades of the 19th century. It is striking and hardly a coincidence that they did not lift the earlier restrictions on the Christian missionaries until around that period. The secular and religious missions had different, at times conflicting, messages. Although both justified colonialism and claimed the divine privilege of narcissistically moulding the rest of mankind in their own image, their languages differed and their relations remained as uneasy as those between Christianity and modern civilisation in Europe. The muted but unmistakable tensions between the two enabled the Indians to use one to embarrass the other and to retain a critical perspective.[3] Finally, the British justification of their rule paradoxically entailed its eventual dissolution. Once the Indians were inducted into British civilization, the British had on their own admission no right to rule over them. What was more, the British had to prove their *bona fides* by accelerating the education of their pupils and thus their own eventual departure. From time to time they and the Indians bitterly disagreed about the pace of constitutional development, but they were agreed on the nature of the disagreement and the ultimate goal.

British rule in India was Gandhi's inescapable starting point and a constant frame of reference. Like the generations of leaders from Rammohun Roy onwards, he was deeply puzzled and troubled by it. He wondered why the British had come to India in the first instance, had been able to consolidate their rule and render it acceptable to their subjects with apparent ease, what it had done to them and how they should respond to it. These and related questions worried him even as a young boy and continued to exercise his mind during his years in England and especially in South Africa. His reflections led him to conclude that the answers to them were to be found in the character of modern civilization. The British had come to India because of the inner compulsions of modern civilisation; they had been able to consolidate their rule because of their ability to legitimise it in the ideological language of civilization; their rule was not merely political but also moral and cultural in nature; and India had to respond to it not only at the political but primarily at the moral and cultural levels.[4]

For Gandhi the British came to India not by accident, nor in the adventurous spirit of a political buccaneer, but in search of new markets for their goods. 'Many problems can be solved by remembering that money is their God.' They needed to trade because their economic life was geared to unlimited production and could not survive without turning the whole world into a vast market. 'Europeans pounce upon new territories like crows upon a piece of meat. I am inclined to think that this is due to their mass-production factories.[5] As to why their economic life was so geared, he gave two different answers. Sometimes he pointed to its capitalist character and attributed over-production to its search for profits. More often he argued that capitalism was itself a product of the 'materialist' view of man. It was because man was defined as a creature of infinite desires that the constant satisfaction of his apparently endless wants and the accumulation of wealth acquired moral legitimacy and capitalism as a distinct economic system struck roots. For Gandhi moral transformation always preceded the economic and it was man's conception of himself that ultimately underpinned and sustained the economic system. Once capitalism came into existence, it had an obvious vested interest in propagating the underlying view of man and perpetuating a materialist civilisation. Gandhi was convinced that imperialism in one form or another was inherent in materialist civilisation and that Britain would have looked for colonies even if it had had a non-capitalist economy.[6] He did not explain when and why the materialist view of man emerged and why it was able to replace the older 'spiritual' view with such ease.

As to why the British had been able to consolidate their rule Gandhi's answer was more complex. He rejected the widely held view that they had a superior army, for when they first came to India they not only had none worth talking about but also no intention of conquering it. He also rejected the view that the innocent and absent-minded Indians, ill-tutored in the ways of the world, had been outwitted by the wily foreigners for, while this might explain their conquest, it did not explain why the Indians had not only acquiesced in it but also extended their co-operation to their rulers, who were too few to run a vast country on their own. In Gandhi's view the explanation was two-fold. First, the Indians had long been in the habit of fighting among themselves, and some of them turned to the newly arrived East India Company for financial and military help. The Company began to play an increasingly important role in Indian political life and its interference came to be accepted as ligitimate and necessary.[7] Over time it played off one group against another, broadened and consolidated its support and, before the Indians realised what had happened, established its rule. 'The English have not taken India; we have given it to them', Gandhi argued. 'To blame them... is to perpetuare their rule.'[8]

Gandhi's second explanation went deeper and centered on the ideological role of the concept of civilisation. The British were able to consolidate their rule because the Indians had 'developed *moha* for their civilization'. *Moha,* an old and important concept Krishna had used to describe Arjuna's state of mind during the *Mahabharata* war, means being enamoured of, bewitched by or infatuated with something inherently illusory.[9] By British civilization Gandhi meant both its industrial products and moral and political values, practices and institutions. The two were inseparable and were informed by the 'materialist' spirit. Industrial goods were not neutral material products but embodiments of the spirit of British civilisation. To want them was to want its constitutive values and institutions. Since the Indians had become enamoured of British civilisation, they traded in its products, thereby making it profitable and worthwhile for the British to rule over their country. If they had shown no interest in trade such a commercially-minded people as the British would not have conquered, let alone stayed on in India. Since the Indians had also been bewitched by British moral and political values, they obviously needed the British to teach these to them. And rather than find their rule morally insulting and outrageous, they thought it highly desirable and in their long-term interest.

The Indians, of course, had their own civilization and distinct views on what constituted a civilised man and society. These had to be discredited and their self-confidence undermined if British civilisation was to strike roots. Accordingly the British embarked upon a programme of systematic 'scientific indoctrination' devised and enforced by the intellectuals all too ready to place their knowledge at the service of the empire.[10] British historians either denied that India had its own civilisation or dismissed it as degenerate and the chief cause of its decline. They argued that pre-British India was a disorderly and chaotic society that had never known peace and stability and that they alone stood as a shield against chaos in India. British anthropologists produced biased accounts of Indian customs and practices and contended that they were all primitive and needed to be changed. Gandhi observed, 'The English... have a habit of writing history; they pretend to know the customs and practices of every society. They beat their own drums, and hypnotise us into believing them. In our gullibility we believe all that.'[11] British social scientists argued that material progress was the necessary precondition of moral progress, that India's moral decline was a result of its low economic development and that its moral regeneration could only be effected by the British pattern of industrialisation. British philosophers and psychologists went further and argued that by his very nature man was a restless and desiring being and that the multiplication of wants was the only driving force of history. In these and other ways the Indians were 'brainwashed' into doubting the value of their ancestral civilization and brought to the verge of 'civil suicide'. Once the moral conquest of the Indian mind was complete, the way was cleared for its economic and political exploitation.

For Gandhi British imperialism dominated India at three related but different levels. At the political level the arrogant colonial government oppressed the Indian people and denied their right to run their affairs themselves. At the economic level it exploited and impoverished them, destroyed their indigenous industries and subordinated their interests to those of the British economy. In Gandhi's view this was far more disturbing than political oppression and could continue even if India became independent. At the most disturbing moral and cultural level, British imperialism destroyed the identity and integrity of Indian civilisation and turned the Indians into brown Englishmen. Gandhi was convinced that the 'rule' of British *civilisation* could continue even if the British *government* were to stop ruling over India and British *capital* to cease exploiting it. British imperialism was unacceptable not only because of its political and even economic but moral and cultural consequences. The struggle against it had therefore to be mounted and independence obtained at all three levels, especially the last. At the cultural level the anti-imperialist struggle had to be fought, on two fronts simultaneously. First, British civilisation, which so infatuated and blinded the Indians to the moral enormity of foreign rule and legitimised their economic and political domination must be subjected to a thorough-going critique. Second, the basic structure of Indian civilisation, which they largely saw through the biased British perspective, must be sensitively teased out and defended.

In interpreting British imperialism in this way, Gandhi integrated and went beyond the three different types of critique advanced by his predecessors. Broadly speaking, Dadabhai Naoroji, Surendra Nath Banerjee, Gokhale and the so-called liberals had welcomed the political and cultural advantages of British rule but attacked it on the grounds that it had drained India's wealth, ruined its industries, imposed unfair trading arrangements and subordinated its economic development to

British colonial interests. Although mindful of its economic and cultural consequences, the leaders of the terrorist movements in Bengal and Maharashtra attacked it on political grounds and were the first to develop a distinctive theory of political as distinct from cultural nationalism. They argued that the Indians had as much right to run their affairs as the British had to run theirs, that colonialism was a form of slavery and an outrage to Indian dignity and self-respect, and that the 'honour' of 'mother India' demanded that she should be freed of the 'foreign yoke'. In a culture which conceptualises energy in feminine terms and associates activity and restlessness with woman and passivity and detachment with man, it was not at all surprising that the votaries of violence should have idealised 'mother' India and drawn inspiration from the Goddess *Kali.* Finally Vivekananda, B. C. Pal, Tilak and the so-called conservative leaders concentrated on the need to preserve the integrity of traditional ways of life and thought. They introduced the concept of Indian civilisation to match the one championed by the British, sharply distinguished the two and attacked foreign rule not so much because it involved economic exploitation and violated Indian pride as because it imposed an alien materialist civilisation on India's essentially spiritual one.

Gandhi's critique of British rule encompassed all three. He was acutely aware of its economic motivation and highlighted the grave economic damage it had done and was doing to the country. He used the language of national honour, pride and dignity as freely as the terrorists and felt just as protective and reverential about 'mother' India. He was even more sensitive to the integrity of Indian civilisation than were the conservative leaders. Indeed he argued that most of them were more interested in the 'synthesis' of the two civilisations than in the integrity of their own, had unwittingly reinterpreted and anglicised it far more than they realised or cared to admit, and that their critique of British imperialism was half-hearted and lacked moral depth. Gandhi's critique not only included but also related and integrated the three earlier critiques into a comprehensive theoretical framework. He argued that political independence was important not only as an expression of India's pride and a necessary means to stop its economic exploitation but also to preserve its civilisation, without which political independence remained fragile. The economic exploitation had to be ended not only to sustain Indian independence and improve the living conditions of its people but also to preserve the social and economic basis of its civilisation. Thanks to its range and depth Gandhi's critique of British imperialism was able to provide a coherent theoretical platform on which Indians of different ideological persuasions could unite.

The extent to which Gandhi went beyond his predecessors, especially the so-called conservatives, was evident in the way he defined the nature of the cultural encounter between Britain and India. While they had argued that the conflict was between the Indian and European or between the Eastern and Western civilisations, Gandhi insisted that it was really between the ancient and modern. As he put it, there is 'no such thing as Western or European civilisation, but there is a modern civilisation'.[12] His apparently trivial redefinition was in fact intended to alter the terms of the debate in his favour and achieve several ideological and political advantages.[13] First, he was able to reject the currently fashionable view among many British and Indian writers that the East and the West were radically different and shared nothing in common. For Gandhi such a doctrine had no basis in facts, denied the fundamental unity of mankind and bred cultural parochialism. Second, he was able to attack modern civilization without attacking the West. He greatly admired Socrates and Christianity, such modern writers as Tolstoy, Ruskin and Thoreau and several Western values and practices, and wished to exclude them from his criticism. Third, the distinction enabled Gandhi to argue that modern civilisation was of relatively recent origin in the West and that its pre-modern counterpart was very different and more like the Indian. He hoped thereby to remind the West of its earlier traditions and values, evoke its temporarily suppressed historical memories and elicit its support for his fight against modern civilisation. He was able to argue that since Indian civilisation stood for values to which the West had itself for centuries subscribed and was only trying to preserve their common heritage, by attacking and undermining it the West not only betrayed its own great past but also damaged its chances of future redemption. Fourth, by arguing that industrial civilisation was modern and 'still very young', Gandhi intended to suggest that it lacked the wisdom and maturity conferred by age, an important argument in a country that revered age. Finally, Gandhi hoped to convince his countrymen that in fighting modern civilisation they were not being reactionary. They were only combating the arrogance and impetuosity of an historical upstart and helping to preserve the permanent values of the whole of mankind, including the West. The idea of saving the soul of their misguided masters tickled Indian pride and made Gandhi's harsh message more acceptable.

For Gandhi, then, India was a great battlefield, the modern *kurukshetra* on which modern and ancient civilisations, the past and the present, were locked in a momentous battle for the future. The British were the best representatives of modern civilisation and the Indians of the ancient. The former had fancied themselves as the missionaries of modern civilisation. Gandhi turned the Indians into missionaries of a universal civilisation based on the great ancient values enriched by some of the valid insights of the modern. The hold of the colonial ideology was such that even its shrewdest critic did not transcend but largely reinterpreted its terms of debate.

Gandhi's critique of modern civilisation was far more complex than is generally imagined and quite different from that of such other writers as Rousseau, Carlyle, Ruskin, Tolstoy and Thoreau, by the last three of whom he was deeply influenced. In his view modern civilisation was grounded in a fatally flawed theory of man. Unlike ancient civilisation which was soul-or-spirit-centred, the modern was body-centered and in that sense 'materialistic'. For Gandhi the body had two basic characteristics. First, it was distinct, self-enclosed and separated from and only capable of preserving its integrity by maintaining its separateness from other bodies. As such it was the ontological basis of the human sense of particularity, and the source of the illusion that each individual was an independent and self-centred ego only externally and contingently related to others and constantly concerned to preserve his identity by keeping the invasive others at a safe distance. Second, the body was the seat of the senses, and thus of wants and desires. By their very nature desires recurred with rhythmic regularity and were never satiated. They were also interrelated and one desire always gave rise to others. *Qua* sensual and desiring being, man was necessarily propelled by his inherently limitless desires and was always restless and dissatisfied.

A body-centred, or materialist view of man thus attributed two basic properties to him and regarded them as natural and legitimate, namely 'selfishness' and an 'infinite multiplicity of wants'.[14] A civilisation based on such a flawed view necessarily suffered from several basic and interrelated limitations. First, it lacked moral and spiritual depth. Second, since it had no guiding principles to decide what desires deserved to be satisfied and within what limits, it led to a way of life devoid of meaning and purpose. Third, it de-humanised man and had a profound anti-human bias. Fourth, it perverted the human psyche and was suffused with the spirit of violence. Finally, it reduced wisdom to knowledge and the latter to a form of power only useful as an instrument of control over nature and other men. It thereby not only perverted the pursuit of truth but also lacked a system of knowledge capable of critically evaluating its basic assumptions and objectives.

For Gandhi modern civilisation was propelled by the two interrelated principles of greed and want. It was controlled by 'a few capitalist owners' who had only one aim, to make profit, and only one means to do so, to produce goods that satisfied people's wants. They had a vital vested interest in constantly whetting jaded appetites, planting new wants and creating a moral climate in which not to want the goods daily pumped into the market and to keep pace with the latest fashions was to be abnormal and archaic. Indeed, since self-discipline or restriction of desires, the very emblem of human dignity, threatened to cause mass unemployment, throw the economic system out of gear and cause human suffering, it was seen as anti-social and immoral. Not surprisingly men saw themselves not as self-determining moral subjects but as consumers or vehicles for the satisfaction of externally-induced wants.

The capitalist search for profits led to mechanisation and 'industrialism'. For Gandhi machines relieved drudgery, created leisure, increased efficiency and were indispensable when there was a shortage of labour. Their use must therefore be guided by a well-considered moral theory indicating how men should live, spend their free time and relate to one another. Since the modern economy lacked such a theory and was only propelled by the search for profit, it mechanised production without any regard for its wider moral, cultural and other consequences. Machines were introduced even when there was no obvious need for them and were in fact likely to throw thousands out of work. This was justified either in the name of increased leisure without anyone asking why it was important and what to do with it, or of cheaper goods, as if man was only a passive consumer and not an active moral being for whose sanity, self-respect and dignity the right to work was far more important than the febrile gratification of trivial wants.[15] Treated with the veneration and awe accorded to the gods in primitive societies, machines had come to cast a magic spell on modern man and followed their own will. For Gandhi the mechanisation or fetishism of technology was closely tied up with the larger phenomenon of industrialism, another apparently self-propelling and endless process of creating larger and larger industries with no other purpose than to produce cheap consumer goods and maximise profit.[16] He argued that since modern economic life followed an inexorable momentum of its own, it reduced men to its helpless and passive victims and represented a new form of slavery, more comfortable and invidious and hence more dangerous than the earlier ones.

Based on the belief that life was continuous motion and movement, that unless one was constantly on the move one was not alive and that the faster the tempo of life the more alive one was, modern civilization was inherently restless and intolerant of stability. It aimed to conquer time and space and developed increasingly speedier modes of transport and communication. Cars were replaced by trains, and the latter by planes, but no one asked why one needed to travel so fast and what one intended to do with the time saved. Thanks to its restlessness and 'mindless activism' incorrectly equated with dynamism and energy, modern civilisation undermined man's unity with his environment and fellow men and destroyed stable and long-established communities. In the absence of natural and social roots and the stable and enduring landmarks, which alone gave man a sense of identity and continuity, modern man had become abstract, indeterminate and empty. He was not internally or organically related to others and his relations with them were not grounded in the sentiments of fellow feeling and good will. Everyone was a stranger to everyone else and no one cared for or knew how to behave towards others.[17]

As a result people's moral life suffered a profound distortion. First, it became as abstract as the men it was supposed to relate, and was reduced to a set of self-consciously followed and externally legislated and enforced impersonal rules. Other men mattered not because one cared for them but because the moral rules so required. Second, rather than an expression and fulfillment of man's nature, morality was seen as a necessary but painful and widely resented restriction of freedom, a kind of tax he had to pay in order to be able to enjoy his residual freedom unhindered. It was therefore reduced to the barest minimum, requiring little more than what was needed to prevent men from destroying one another. Third, a society of basically amoral and internally unrelated beings was characterised by a climate of suspicion, fear, hostility and tension. Each perceived the rest as actual or potential enemies who impinged on his consciousness only when and insofar as they posed a threat, and amongst whom he could hope to survive only by sheltering behind carefully planned and fiercely guarded physical, emotional and moral fortifications.

Fourth, since in the absence of the nourishing soil of the sentiments, of good will and mutual concern the moral life lacked roots and vitality, it had to depend on the non-moral motive of fear. Modern man took care not to harm others lest they should harm him, and he did a good turn to them as an investment for the future. Morality was reduced to reciprocal egoism or enlightened self-interest and was sustained by fear. Since self-interest was not a moral principle, Gandhi argued that enlightened self-interest was not one either. In modern civilization morality was a form of prudence, a more effective way of pursuing self-interest, and was virtually exorcised out of existence. Finally, modern civilisation denuded morality of its vital internal dimension or what he called the quality of the soul. Jealousy, hatred, meanness, ill-will, perverse pleasure at another's misfortunes and sordid thoughts and fantasies were moral impurities reflecting an ill-developed soul. Moral growth consisted in overcoming these deficiencies and developing a beautiful and noble soul. Although this had been long cherished by Christianity, modern man felt threatened by it. Being only concerned to get on in the world and lead a comfortable life, he not only saw no value in the purity of the soul and the quality of his motives but found such concerns a hindrance. Not an introspective, reflective, self-critical, sensitive and tender-hearted but a tough, aggressive, ambitious and suspicious man was the ideal and the necessary basis of modern civilisation.

Modern man, Gandhi went on, spent most of his energy trying to steady himself in a hostile and unsteady environment. He had neither the inclination nor the ability to slow down the tempo of his life, relax, compose himself, reflect on his pattern of life and nurture the inner springs of energy. He lived outside himself and exhausted himself physically and spiritually. Predictably he needed to depend on such ultimately debilitating sources of instant energy as intoxicating spirits, tea and coffee, in order constantly to whip himself into action. Inwardly empty and frightened to be alone with himself, he was always busy, turning to one activity after another, easily bored and feverishly looking for new sources of amusement. Gandhi thought that modern civilisation had a depressing air of 'futility' and 'madness' about it and was likely to destroy itself before long.[18]

In Gandhi's view the exploitation of one's fellow men was built into the very structure of modern civilisation. Consumers were constantly manipulated into desiring things they did not need and which were not in their long-term interest. Workers were made to do boring jobs at subsistence wages under inhuman conditions and given little opportunity or encouragement to develop their intellectual and moral potential. The poor were treated with contempt and held responsible for their own misfortunes. The weaker races were treated as if they were animals and bought and sold and brutally exploited. The weaker nations were conquered, mercilessly oppressed and used as dumping grounds for surplus goods and as sources of cheap raw material. For Gandhi imperialism was only an acute manifestation of the aggressive and exploitative impulse lying at the very heart of modern civilisation and at work in all areas of human relationships.

It was therefore hardly surprising that modern civilisation rested on and was sustained by massive violence. It involved violence against oneself, in a society of ambitions, competitive and mutually fearful men, no one could survive without developing a regimented and militant psyche, suppressing his tender feelings and doubts and becoming like a mobile weapon of destruction ready to hurt itself on the slightest provocation. It also involved violence against other men at both the personal and collective levels. Since each felt threatened by others and desperately sought to keep them at a manageable distance, he had to rely on the use or threat of verbal, emotional, moral and even physical violence ultimately backed up by the concentrated violence of the modern state. The relations between organized groups, classes and states were even more tense and aggressive and scarred by open or cold wars. Modern civilisation also involved an egregious amount of violence against nature, which was largely seen as man's property to do with it what he liked. Its resources were ruthlessly exploited and its rhythm and balance disturbed, and the animals were freely killed or tortured for food, sport, fancy clothes and medical experiments. In Gandhi's view violence 'oozed from every pore' of modern society and had so much become a way of life that modern man could not cope with his relations with himself or other men without translating them into the military language of conflict, struggle, mastery, subjugation, domination, victory and defeat. Deeply rooted in violence man felt suffocated in its absence.

For Gandhi a civilisation properly so-called placed man at its center and measured its greatness in terms of its ability to produce men and women possessing such distinctively human powers as self-determination, autonomy, self-knowledge, self-discipline and social co-operation. Modern civilisation did the opposite. By encouraging them to alienate their powers to large organisations run by experts, it rendered men passive, helpless and heteronomous. Gandhi took the example of medical science, the pride and glory of modern civilisation.[19] Ideally it should aim at two things. First, it should help people acquire a greater understanding and control of their bodies by explaining to them the causes and aetiology of their ailments, how to prevent them and how they were integrally related to their ways of life. Second, since the body was not an inert machine but a living organism with its own rhythm and built-in intelligence, medical science should mobilise its internal resources and wisely activate them where necessary by external help. Modern medicine did neither. Every time someone complained of an ailment, he was required to hand over the custody of his body to the experts to do what they liked with it, as if it was a contingently related appendage about which he needed to know nothing and for which he bore no responsibility. Predictably the patient learned nothing from his ailment, developed it again, was treated the same way the next time around, and the vicious cycle went on unabated. Thanks to their training the medical experts were unable effectively to deal with the body unless they enjoyed an unchallenged monopoly over it. For his part heteronomous modern man was only too willing to alienate his body and abdicate all control over it. The silent collaboration between the two spawned the huge medical establishment enjoying and closely guarding its monopoly of medical knowledge. It was as if all the bodies in a society were abstracted from their human bearers, nationalised and bureaucratically managed by this organised body of experts.

Medical science also showed little respect for the integrity of the body and was suffused with the spirit of violence characteristic of modern civilisation. It did not see the ailment as the overworked and undisciplined body's plea for rest and discipline, but rather as an unacceptable interference with its hectic routine, requiring an immediate and effective response.

The body was not allowed to cope with illness at its own pace and by means of its own judiciously activated resources; instead its sluggish rhythm was aggressively manipulated by bombarding it with powerful chemical agents which ended up doing it grave long-term harm. Like the other form of violence, medical violence too was subject to an inflationary spiral. Once the 'enemies' invading the body developed 'defences' against one set of drugs, more potent ones were invented doing yet greater violence to it and to the animals on whom they were first tried out. The poor body became a battlefield where powerful armies fought out a deadly contest in which it was itself often the first casualty.

Gandhi thought that the same dehumanising phenomenon was evident in the field of law.[20] Men were intelligent and moral beings capable of resolving their differences by discussing them in the spirit of charity and good will or by seeking the arbitration of widely respected men and women in their community. Instead, every time he failed to get what he thought was his due, modern man rushed to the court of law where trained experts in the esoteric body of legal knowledge conducted expensive and incomprehensible debates about him without his participation. Just as the medical establishment reduced him to a passive object, the legal establishment reduced him to a case to be discussed as if he were a child to be tutored into what to say about his own actions and incapable of participating in their evaluation. Even as medical science did little to develop the body's own resources, the legal system did little to develop and mobilise man's moral impulses and capacities for reflection and introspection. Instead it required him to alienate them to a central agency telling him how to run his life and conduct his relations with others, including his own neighbours, wife, ex-wife and children. Gandhi found it strange that modern man, who talked so much about his self-respect and dignity, did not find all this deeply humiliating.

Gandhi argued that the highly centralised and bureaucratic modern state enjoying and jealously guarding its monopoly of political power was a necessary product of modern civilisation. Competitive and aggressive men ruthlessly pursuing their own interests could only be held together by a well-armed state. Since they were all strangers to one another and lacked the bonds of good will and mutual concern, their relations could only be regulated by impersonal rules imposed and enforced by such a powerful external agency as the state. The centralisation of production in the modern economy created social and economic problems of national and international magnitude, and again required a centralised political agency to deal with them. Unemployment, poverty and the social and economic inequalities created by the modern economy led to acute and legitimate discontent and required a well-armed state to deter its desperate citizens from resorting to violence. 'Shorn of all the camouflage the exploitation of the masses of Europe is sustained by violence', Gandhi argued. The centralised modern state was also necessary to protect international markets and overseas investments.

For Gandhi the state dehumanised its citizens in more or less the same ways as the medical, legal and other institutions. It had a vested institutional interest in monopolising all initiative and fostering a state-centered political culture. The more its citizens became 'addicted' to it and the more they felt helpless without it, the safer it felt. Accordingly it systematically nurtured the illusion that the problems of society were too complex and intractable to be solved by ordinary citizens acting individually or collectively, and were best left to the state and its official agencies. It felt threatened by active and independent-minded citizens determined to participate in the conduct of their affairs and worried lest they should be morally compromised by what it did in their name. It therefore denied them access to vital information and opportunities for political participation, and discouraged independent and vibrant local communities capable of challenging its decisions.

Even as the state monopolised all political power, it tended to monopolise all morality. Since its atomic and morally depleted citizens lacked organic bonds and the capacity to organise and run their social relations themselves, the state was the sole source of moral order. It alone guaranteed civilised existence and saved society from total disintegration. As such it came to be seen as the highest moral institution, whose preservation was a supreme moral value. Whatever was prejudicial to its interests was immoral and whatever promoted them was moral.

All moral sentiments were sucked into it, all moral energies were appropriated by it, all moral norms were judged in terms of its interests, and its laws were deemed to be the sole determinants of collective morality. Dying for the state was a supreme virtue, and fighting in its wars the highest duty. Disobeying its laws was strongly disapproved of and all attempts to weigh them in the highest moral scale were discouraged on the ground that political life was either amoral or governed by its own distinct morality. The human being was thus reduced to the citizen, and the latter in turn to a passive and uncritical subject.

Gandhi argued that, although the state claimed to be a moral institution transcending narrow group interests and pursuing the well-being of the whole community, it was in fact little more than an arena of conflict between organised interests manipulated and controlled by the more powerful among them. Since men of independent spirit and honour generally avoided it, it was largely in the care of men and women forging convenient alliances with powerful interest groups and using it to serve their interests. Gandhi thought that in these respects the democratic governments were no better than the undemocratic and belonged to the 'same species'. They were just as vulnerable to the pressures of the dominant class and just as 'ruthless' and ready to use violence in the pursuit of its interests. In its actual practice a democracy was basically a form of government in which a 'few men capture power in the name of the people and abuse it', a 'game of chess' between rival parties with the people as 'pawns'.[21] Although the fact that democratic government was periodically elected by and accountable to ordinary people made a difference, it also served as a 'camouflage' hiding the basic fact that the masses were often 'exploited by the ruling class . . . under the sacred name of democracy.[22] Democracy thus veiled and conferred moral legitimacy on the reality of exploitation, and had only a marginal moral edge over fascism.

Gandhi contended that the British parliament, the mother of parliaments and the home of democracy, was not much better than its counterparts elsewhere.[23] It was largely a 'talking shop' capable neither of exercising much control over the government nor of pursuing the national interest. It was dominated by political parties whose sole concern was to capture and remain in power by manipulating public opinion and subserving powerful economic interests. Its members meekly followed the party line, rarely resigned on matters of principle and had 'neither real honesty nor a living conscience'. Although generally immune to crude forms of financial corruption and bribes, Gandhi thought that they were open to the 'subtler influences' of honours, offers of government posts and political patronage.[24] They claimed to be patriotic but had little real love of the country, which consisted not only of the privileged few but the 'whole people' the pursuit of whose well-being must therefore be the true test of patriotism. So long as the masses were exploited, confined to mindless and poorly-paid jobs, and felt impotent and powerless, Britain could not be called a democracy or its politicians patriotic.[25]

Gandhi did not think much of the British electorate either. Unable to look beyond their narrow self-interest, the voters cared little for the long-term interest of their country and the problems and suffering of their less privileged fellow citizens and joined and voted for the parties most likely to promote their interests. They took little interest in the way their country was governed and lazily accepted the biased information and opinions peddled by the newspapers. Gandhi observed :

> To the English voters their newspaper is their Bible. They take their cue from their newspapers which are often dishonest. The same fact is differently interpreted by different newspapers, according to the party in whose interests they are edited.[26]

In Gandhi's view the much-vaunted independence of the press was largely a myth. The press was owned by the capitalists who saw it as yet another industry for manufacturing and selling opinions and who had little regard for their grave moral responsibility. It was not concerned with truth but propaganda, not the education but manipulation of public opinion. Rather than strengthen democracy it corrupted and subverted its very basis.

Although convinced that the foundation of modern civilisation was 'rotten', Gandhi did not dismiss it altogether and praised what he took to be its three great achievements. First, he admired its scientific spirit of inquiry. He observed :

> I have been a sympathetic student of the Western social order, and I have discovered that underlying the fever that fills the soul of the West, there is a restless search for Truth. I value that spirit. Let us study our Eastern institutions in that spirit of scientific inquiry.[27]

Not that the scientific spirit was unknown in the pre-modern West or ancient India. Rather it was muted and denied the full scope it had received in the modern age. For Gandhi the scientific spirit meant the spirit of rational inquiry, 'the spirit of search for the truth in place of being satisfied with tradition without question', and implied intellectual curiosity, rigorous pursuit of truth and critical examination of established beliefs. Gandhi's admiration of the scientific *spirit,* however, did not extend to the scientific *culture.* In his view modern civilisation was right to give pride of place to reason, but wrong to make a 'fetish' of it and ignore its limitations. Such areas of human experience as religion raised matters transcending reason and requiring faith. In some other areas of life, such as morality and politics, reason was inherently inadequate and needed to be guided and supplemented by wisdom, conscience, intuition and moral insight. Since it was essentially an analytical and discursive faculty and its conclusions were necessarily tentative and liable to be subverted by superior arguments, it was inherently unstable and could never form the basis of human life. It certainly had an important role to play in social life, but a society that relied on it alone would not last a day. Gandhi thought that as in the other areas of life, modern civilisation had grasped an important truth but turned it into a falsehood by ignoring its limits.

For Gandhi the second great achievement of modern civilisation consisted in understanding and bringing the natural world under greater human control. Being body-centred it had concentrated most of its energies on improving the material conditions of life. It had developed the ability to anticipate and control natural calamities, eliminate diseases, improve health and public hygiene, prolong life and reduce or relieve human drudgery. It had also developed new means of transport and communication, brought the world closer, increased human comforts and improved the material quality of life. Gandhi contended that since these and other achievements were secured within a fundamentally flawed framework, they had suffered a profound distortion. It was important to preserve and prolong life, but modern civilisation had turned it into the highest value and cultivated a morbid fear of death. Medical science was a great human achievement, but it showed little respect for the human body, drained its indigenous resources, weakened self-discipline and treated the animals as mere means to human well-being. Machines had a place in life, but modern civilisation had turned them into autonomous agents following their own will. Industries were desirable, but modern civilisation had made them the very basis and centre of society. In short, since it lacked a balanced theory of man, many of the achievements of modern civilisation had become forces for evil and harmed rather than helped men.

Third, in Gandhi's view modern civilisation had greatly contributed to the organisational side of life. It had cultivated civic virtues, respect for rules, the capacity to subordinate the personal to the collective interest, public morality, mutual respect and punctuality, Gandhi argued that although he had 'thankfully copied' many of these 'great' qualities without which his personal and especially political life would have been poorer, modern civilisation had once again misinterpreted them and ignored their limits. It had reduced morality to enlightened self-interest and undermined its autonomy. It had rightly subordinated the individual to collective interest, but failed to provide sufficient room for diversity. It rightly stressed the value of organisation, but it over-institutionalised men and left no space for conscientious objection and the lonely dissenter. It was right to emphasise rules, but wrong not to realise that they could never exhaust moral life and were precarious unless grounded in finer human impulses.

For Gandhi, then, modern civilisation was a highly complex human achievement, and the response to it had to be equally complex. Its foundation was shaky but it had genuine achievements to its credit. Unlike his predecessors, Gandhi argued that its achievements could not be abstracted and promiscuously combined with those of Indian civilisation. Since they were secured within a fundamentally mistaken framework and vitiated by their provenance, they had to be purged of their distortions and 'purified' before they were fit to be incorporated into a different framework. For example, it was not enough to say that mechanisation was bad but the machines were good, or that rationalism should be rejected but the spirit of rational inquiry retained. Modern machines, invented within the context of the materialist civilisation that determined their nature, place in life and mode of operation, were not culturally neutral. A differently constituted civilisation had to use the available scientific knowledge to develop different kinds of machines and put them to different uses. The other achievements of modern civilisation had to be subjected to a similar critical and 'cleansing' process.

Before concluding the chapter we might make a few general comments on Gandhi's critique of modern civilisation. Although bearing a strong resemblance to the criticisms of such writers as Rousseau, Ruskin, Carlyle, Tolstoy, Nietzsche and Marx, Gandhi's critique contained original and important insights derived from the two great advantages he enjoyed over them. First, as a colonial native belonging to a despised race and an oppressed country, he experienced the darker side of modern civilisation not directly accessible to them. Second, as an heir to the rich and differently structured Indian civilisation, he brought to his critique an intellectual perspective and moral sensitivity not available to its Western critics.

Gandhi saw that despite all its egalitarian pretensions, modern civilisation was deeply racist and placed non-whites more or less outside the pale of common humanity. He saw too that despite its commitment to human dignity, it was inherently exploitative and had not the slightest hesitation in oppressing other countries and trading in human beings whether in the morally outrageous form of slavery or the slightly less inhuman form of indentured labour. Unlike its Western critics Gandhi saw that these and other evils were not mere aberrations but inherent in the structure of modern civilisation. Its flawed theory of man profoundly distorted its interpretations of such moral values as human dignity, liberty and equality and prevented it from appreciating their true nature and realising their full moral potential. It did not value the full range of human freedom but largely the freedom to pursue self-interest, not the equal development of all men but the equal right to pursue self-interest, not the dignity of all men but only of those satisfying a conveniently biased definition of man. Gandhi also saw that a civilisation that ill-treated outsiders could hardly avoid ill-treating its own people. He was thus able to link up the exploitation and degradation of its internal and external victims and locate them in a global perspective.

As one deeply grounded in another civilisation Gandhi brought to his critique of modern civilisation a fresh perspective. Thanks to his Indian background he was intensely sensitive to the fact that, although apparently civil and non-violent, modern civilisation was suffused with the spirit of aggression and violence which it had learned to contain but had not at all mastered. In his view the colonial, the European and the two world wars could not be conveniently dismissed as mere accidents or products of human folly and miscalculation. No civilization could launch, live with and periodically unleash such devastating and brutal wars without being able to justify them to itself, and Gandhi could not see how it could do so except on the basis of a distorted system of values and blunted moral sensibilities. Again, he saw that self-determination and autonomy remained fragile without moral self-discipline and that in the absence of an adequate moral basis the modern doctrines of liberty and equality provided flimsy defences against exploitation and oppression. The intense sense of moral responsibility which Gandhi derived from his culture alerted him to the way large organisations swallowed up modern man and stifled his individuality and capacity for dissent. As an outsider he saw too that modern civilisation contained a deep tension. At one level it claimed to be and was Christian; at another it was anthropocentric, obsessed with the satisfaction of material wants, propelled by greed and essentially irreligious. Its two conflicting tendencies naturally rendered it schizophrenic and unstable. No civilization could live with such a tension without trying to find ways of resolving it. Gandhi thought that for all practical purposes modern civilization had jettisoned Christianity and only used it to cover up and justify its aggressive pursuit of narrow self-interest. Although Tolstoy, Ruskin, Marx and others had highlighted this, few matched the clarity and penetration of Gandhi's criticism.

Gandhi's advantages were also his disadvantages. Since he largely concentrated on the darker side of modern civilisation, he overlooked some of its great achievements and strengths. And since he saw it from the outside he oversimplified it and did not fully understand its complex structure. As a colonial subject deeply sensitive to the economic damage it had caused in India, he concentrated on its exploitative tendencies and equated it with industrialization and capitalism. He was therefore unable to appreciate the full range and moral depth of the new vision of man inspiring and informing it. Although preoccupied with the satisfaction of ever-increasing wants, it was at a deeper level guided by the search for personal independence and autonomy, a non-hierarchical social structure, the passionate concern to understand the world and man's mastery over his own environment and destiny. It did foster selfishness and greed, but it also stressed human unity, individuality, equality, liberty, creativity, rationality and man's all-round development. And although it conveniently misdefined and restricted some of these values to the privileged few and failed to tap their full moral potential, that neither diminished their world-historical importance nor detracted from the fact that they represented a collective human heritage. Materialist at one level, modern civilisation also had a spiritual dimension.

Since Gandhi viewed it as an undifferentiated whole, he was unable to distinguish and analyse the complex pattern of relationship between its different components such as capitalism, imperialism, industrialisation, the egoistic view of man and modern science, all of which he regarded as part of the same general phenomenon. He was therefore unable to see that industrialisation need not be accompanied by either capitalism or the egoistic view of man, that imperialism, was not inherent in industrialisation, and that modern science was only contingently related to imperialism and the egoistic view of man. He could not provide a satisfactory theory of imperialism either, and naively imagined that every country embarking on large-scale industrialisation was bound to become imperialist. More importantly, his inadequate understanding of modern civilisation limited his intellectual options and compelled him to reject far more than he needed to. Since he thought that nearly all its evils sprang from large-scale industrialisation, he remained deeply hostile to it and neither appreciated the economic aspirations of his countrymen and the dynamics of the economic reality unfolding before him, not offered a viable alternative.

Gandhi's analysis of modern civilisation also made it difficult for him to give an adequate account of what he took to be its three major achievements. He could not explain the rise of the scientific spirit and the development of what he called the organisational side of life, and treated them as if they were accidental products of modern civilisation. He failed to notice that they were vital to the very existence of the modern industrial society and could not be developed outside it. Gandhi was thus caught up in the paradoxical position of wanting to appropriate part of the 'spirit' of modern civilisation while rejecting the very institutions and the social structure that embodied and, nurtured it. Like other religious thinkers he abstracted the spirit from the body and thought that the former could survive without the latter. As we shall see, this was one of the major sources of many of his difficulties.

Notes and References

1. For good discussions, see Eric Stokes, *The English Utilitarians in India* (Cambridge: 1964); Ashis Nandy, *The Intimate Enemy* (Delhi: Oxford University Press 1983); Bipan Chandra, *Nationalism and Colonialism in Modern India* (Delhi: 1979).
2. For useful information and analysis, see Francis Hutchins, *The Illusion of Permanence; British Imperialism in India*

(Princeton University Press, 1967); Northcote Parkinson, *East and West* (New York: Mentor 1965); Kenneth Ballhatchet, *Race, Sex and Class Under the Raj (London-Widenfeld and Nicholson* 1980); V. G. Kiernarr, *The Lords of Human Kind* (London: 1972), and James Morris, *Farewell to Trumpets: An Imperial Retreat* (London- Faber and Faber 1978).

3. For a good discussion, see Nandy, *op. cit.*, ch. 1.
4. For Gandhi's critique of modern civilization and the sources of the quotations in the chapter, see *Hind Swaraj* and Iyer, Vol. 1, Part IV.
5. *Unto This Last* - a Paraphrase, p. IX .
6. *Young India* (hereafter YI) 20 December 1928 and 21 November 1931.
7. *Hind Swaraj* (hereafter *HS*), p. 39.
8. *HS*, pp. 38 and 40.
9. Gandhi sometimes translated it as 'hypnotised'.
10. *HS*, pp. 43 and 46.
11. *Ibid.*, p. 52. Translation amended.
12. Iyer, Vol. 1, p. 293.
13. *Ibid.*, p. 298.
14. *Ibid.*, p. 328.
15. *YI*, 17 September 1925.
16. *YI*, 7 October 1926 and 12 November 1931; *HS*, pp. 93 f.
17. *HS*, p. 49.
18. *HS*, p. 37.
19. *Ibid.*, pp. 58 f.
20. *Ibid.*, pp. 55 f.
21. *Ibid.*, p. 67.
22. *YI*, 3 September 1925.
23. *HS*, pp. 31 f.
24. *Ibid.*, p. 33.

25. *Ibid.*, p. 68.
26. *Ibid.*, p. 33
27. *Collected Works* (hereafter CW), Vol. 32, p. 219.

6
Gandhi's Idea of Nation in *Hind Swaraj*

Anthony J. Parel

Hind Swaraj is recognized by all as being Gandhi's most fundamental work. In this article I propose to argue that a proper understanding of the idea of "nation" propounded therein is a necessary condition for a proper understanding of the teaching of that book taken as a whole. That teaching concerns, in the immediate instance, the nature of *swaraj* and the ways and means of attaining it. But the nature of *swaraj* cannot be fully understood unless it is also understood that the subjects enjoying it or going to enjoy it are the nation and the self. *Hind,* i.e., India considered as nation, and the self, i.e., each Indian considered as a member of that nation are the two subjects of *swaraj.* The originality of Gandhi's teaching in this book consists in arguing that there is a connection between the process by which the nation attains its independence and the process by which the self attains control over itself. The attainment of self-control, in Gandhi's view, ought not to be considered as a solipsist affair. Gandhi's most important contribution to Indian thought is that self-control and self-realization ought to lead simultaneously to the well-being of the nation as a whole. This is also Gandhi's distinct contribution to political theory. At the time of the writing of *Hind Swaraj,* Gandhi was painfully aware that those who cared for the nation, such as the apostles of violence, did not care for the soul; and that those who cared for the soul, did not care for the nation. Gandhi wanted to bridge

* Reprinted with the permission of Gandhi Peace Foundation and *Gandhi Marg* from *Gandhi Marg* (October-December 1991), pp. 261-281.

the gap between these two forms of human striving. That is to say, he sought to purge modern Indian nationalism of its reliance on brute force, and to instill in the minds of those who cared for the soul, the need to become civic minded as well as peace minded. Such is the complex meaning of *swaraj* in *Hind Swaraj.*

But that meaning can be fully appreciated only if we understand what Gandhi means by "nation" and the concepts associated with it, such as "nationalism," "nationality," and "national." And it is towards clarifying that meaning that this article is dedicated.

That in writing *Hind Swaraj* the idea of nation was uppermost in Gandhi's mind can be inferred from several sources. First, there is an important letter which he wrote to Lord Ampthill on the eve of writing the book. The letter in question gives a preview of what he was going to argue in the work. It would contain, he wrote, "the result of my observations on the nationalist movement among my countrymen. An awakening of the national consciousness is unmistakable. But among the majority it is in a crude shape and there is not a corresponding spirit of self-sacrifice."[1] The Indian nationalists he met in London in 1909 relied, he felt, on the presuned efficacy of violence. This was the chief defect of their nationalism. And the position that he would adopt in the book seeks to remove this defect. As he said: "I share the national spirit but I totally dissent from the methods whether of the extremists or of the moderates. For either party ultimately relies on violence.[2] Given these views, one is not surprised at what one finds in the Preface to the original Gujarati version of the book: "The only motive," in writing the book, it states, "was to serve my country, to find Truth and to follow it."[3] For him serving the country and finding and following the Truth were connected, inseparable processes. The Preface to the English version of the book also underlines the nationalist intent of the book: "Had I not been called upon by hundreds of my countrymen, and not a few English friends, to express my opinion on the Nationalist movement in India. I would even have refrained... from reducing my views in writing."[4]

How important the idea of nation is for the argument of *Hind Swaraj* may be gauged from the number of times the word "nation" and its cognates occur in the book: they occur 75 times; not an insignificant fact, considering that the text of the book is only 56 pages long in the *Collected Works of Mahatma Gandhi.* The frequency is eleven in each of chapters 1 and 9, and ten in each of chapters 10, 17, and 20.

An equally significant phenomenon is the Gujarati word he uses to express the idea of nation: the word is *praja.* One can only speculate as to what prompted Gandhi to think of nation in terms of *praja* rather than in those of ra*shtra.* The Hindi translation of *Hind Swaraj,* consistently renders *praja* as rashtra. The common usage in other Indian languages also seems to have been *rashtra.* Thus, for example, Aurobindo Ghose refers to the "Nationalist Committee" set up by the Extremist party at the Surat Congress as *Rashtriya* Mandali.[5] It could be that for Gandhi *praja* underlined the idea of "people" or "community," whereas *rashtra* underlined that of power. Whatever the reasons, for Gandhi Indians are in the first instance a *praja,* and only secondarily are they the speakers of this or that language, or the followers of this or that religion, or the inhabitants of this or that region. Also, the term *praja* helps to bring out the notion that Indians taken as a whole constitute one democratic entity.

An analysis of the idea of nation in *Hind Swaraj* raises four major issues. First, against those who assert that India is not a nation, the book argues that India is indeed a nation. Secondly, there is the issue of the relationship of religion and language to the concept of nation. Thirdly, the book assesses the contributions that the Indian National Congress made to the evolution of Indian nationalism up to 1909 and evaluates the merits and demerits of its Extremist and Moderate factions. Finally, the book focuses its special attention on the national elite—the lawyers, the doctors, and the rest of the newly educated Indian intelligentsia. It exposes their deficiencies as a national elite and suggests ways and means of correcting them. I shall take up these points by turn.

India is a Nation

Gandhi meets head-on the opinion that India is not a nation, that there is nothing in India's history or traditions that presages nationalism, and that India is an artificial country put together by the British for administrative convenience. And if Indians now talk of India as being a nation, it is due to the introduction of Western ideas and to the changes brought about by modern means of communication such as the railways and the telegraph. He recognizes that such ideas are widespread and that they are sometimes held by even some Indians. The source of such opinions, however, in his view, is the British interpretation of Indian history. "They [the British] have a habit of writing history. They pretend to study the manners and customs of all peoples. God has given us a limited mental capacity, but they usurp the function of the Godhead and indulge in novel experiments. They write about their own researches in most laudatory terms and hypnotize us into believing them. We, in our ignorance, then fall at their feet."[6] The concept of orientalism had not yet been invented. But Gandhi here seems to anticipate the essence of that later theory.[7] The discussion of whether or not India is a nation is introduced by the Reader as a casual aside to the discussion of the railways. One of the hidden benefits of the introduction of railways into India, the Reader claims, is that "we see in India the new spirit of nationalism." The Editor's response is quick and sharp: "I hold this to be a mistake. The English have taught us that we were not one nation before and that it will require centuries before we became one nation. This is without foundations. We were one nation before they came to India."[8]

Gandhi's argument in support of the proposition that India is a nation rests on two bold assumptions. The first is that ancient Indian civilization had an accommodating capacity and the second is that in ancient India the acharyas, in founding certain places of pilgrimage, laid the basis for the evolution of an all-India consciousness.

Though the ancient civilization of India was basically Hindu in character, it was nevertheless a civilization that was potentially open to non-Hindu ideas and values. The Gujarati word that Gandhi uses to express his idea of accommodation is *samas*. According to the grammar of most Indian languages, this term refers to the capacity of these languages to coin new complex words out of existing simple words. To take an example: the word *mahatma* is a new word composed of two already existing words—*maha* and *atma*—, words which have originally their own identity. Yet when they combine, they produce a new but more complex word which then acquires its own unique identity. Similarly, though orginally the Indian word *praja* was composed of simpler identities, in course of time, under certain historical conditions, it became capable of forming a more complex but unified *praja*. Indeed, it may be said that Gandhi's concept of *samas as* applied to Indian sub-national communities is not far removed from Renan's notion of "fusion." It may be remembered that Ernest Renan, in his well-known essay, *Qu'est-c' qu'une Nation?,* spoke of the "fusion of the populations" as being one of the conditions for the formation of the various nations of Europe.[9] Gandhi is in effect saying that India also is the result of a process of *samas* taking place for over several centuries.

There is a corollary implicit in the idea of *samas*. It is that each of the uniting elements should be actually capable and willing to unite and form a more complex population unit. Where many sub-nationalities are involved, national unification cannot be a one-way process. This means that in India the late-comers, whoever they might be—whether Muslims, or Christians, or Parsis, or Sikhs—, should each in their own way be able to adopt the accommodating spirit of Indian civilization. Of course they can and must retain their own individual identity. But, in so far as they are Indians, they must do so within the framework of an all-embracing Indian civilization. "A country is one nation only when such a condition (which enables new-comers to merge with the original group) obtains in it. That country must have a faculty for assimilation. India has ever been such a country."[10] Gandhi's point is that whatever else one may identify as characteristic of ancient Indian civilization, none can be considered as crucial to India's future as its accommodating, open characteristic. And whatever may be the specific identity of the late-comers, nothing should be allowed to stand in their way of accommodating themselves to the temper of Indian civilization.

Gandhi's second assumption concerns the activities of those whom he calls "our leading men" or "the foreseeing ancestors of ours." He is no doubt referring to the acharyas of ancient Indian civilization. These individuals, he points out, travelled the length and breadth of India "either on foot or on bullock-carts," and their activities had the effect of creating a common consciousness. The slowness of their locomotion was the very source of their strength. It enabled them to come to know the people among whom they moved and to establish among them a sense of community. According to Gandhi, their greatest achievement, as far as future national identity was concerned, was the establishment of centers of pilgrimage in key places in India. He mentions, for example, Hardwar in the North, Rameshwaram in the South, and Jagannath in the East. "What do you think could have been the intention of those far-seeing ancestors of ours?" the Editor asks. "You will admit they were no fools." They did not establish these places of pilgrimage merely for religious benefits. Religious benefits, he points out, could have been procured in ways other than by pilgrimage to faraway places. "They knew that worship of God could have been performed just as well at home. They taught us that those whose hearts were aglow with righteousness had the Ganges in their own homes." Yet they instituted these holy places and they had an ulterior motive in doing so. If spiritual benefits were the only or even the chief purpose, travel to North and South, East and West would not have been necessary. No, the reason why the ancient acharyas established these places of pilgrimage had a deeper significance; it was to create and sustain a sense of common identity among Indians scattered over an immense territory. For, "they saw that India was one undivided land so made by nature. They, therefore, argued that it must be one nation. Arguing thus, they established holy places in various parts of India, and fired the people with an idea of nationality in a manner unknown in other parts of the world."[11]

Recent scholars have noted that in ancient India, pilgrimages were powerful means of reinforcing a sense of common identity. Thus David G. Mandelbaum remarks that pilgrimage "helps to continually confirm a sense of identification of people with entire India," and M.N. Srinivas opines that "the concept of the unity of India is essentially a-religious one."[12] But Gandhi anticipated these scholarly discoveries by at least half a century. He is the first major figure in modern India to recognize the significance of the places of pilgrimage for the evolution of a national identity. And it is a sign of his genius that he should single out the ancient acharyas rather than the Maharajas or emperors of the past as the creators of a sense of common identity. It is as if by reading the lives of a Sankara or a Ramanuja, one can learn as much about what India means as by reading the exploits of this king or that or of this dynasty or that.

Also, there is subtle irony in the contrast he draws between railways and bullock-carts. To the Reader who thinks that the sense of nationality came only with the railways, he points out that the bullock-carts do better in this regard. There is no doubt in Gandhi's mind that slow travel is still a very powerful way of reinforcing national sentiment. Throughout his life he maintained that *pada-yatra* or slow motion by foot was an effective means of nation- building and consciousness-raising. One need only think of the Salt March or of his walks through the riot-ridden Noakhali region. But it is clear from '*Hind Swaraj* that, as early as 1909, he had become keenly aware of the communicative value of travel on foot. To get the best out of pilgrimages one had to do them on foot. The use of high-speed travel for the purpose of pilgrimage, he felt, tended to turn holy places in to mere tourist centers, unholy and abominable." Writing to Henry Polak a month before *Hind Swaraj* was completed, he observed: "When there was no rapid locomotion, traders and preachers went on foot, from one end of the country to the other, braving all the dangers, not for pleasure, nor for recreating their health (though all that followed from their tramp), but for the sake of humanity. Then Benares and other places of pilgrimage were holy cities, where as today they are an abomination."[13]

The argument that the slow mode of travel of the ancient acharyas contributed much to the development of a common consciousness in India did not remain a mere *academic* tool for him. Throughout his life, whenever possible, he tried to implement the insight contained in it. He often referred to his political tours as "pilgrimages", fully realizing that the *padayatra* solidified the sense of awakening and enriched his own experience of community. He claimed that his "best work" was done in places which he could reach by foot. As he wrote in the *Harijan:* "It is never a pleasure to me to travel by motor or rail or even a cart. It is always a pleasure to walk. Nor would I mind in the least if every rail was removed and men, except the sick and the maimed, had to walk to their businesses. I can only imagine, but I am working for a civilization in which possession of a car will be considered no merit and railways will find no place."[14] No doubt, for practical reasons, Gandhi made full use of travel by train or car: "Being a highly practical man," he said, "I do not avoid railway travelling or motoring for the mere sake of looking foolishly consistent."[15] But his personal predilection was for the traditional mode of travel. He once recounted an incident in which he had to prevail upon Thakkar Bappa, the "manager" of the tour, to let him travel by foot. "So I put my foot down and insisted on performing the remaining pilgrimage on foot." The "pilgrimage" in question was one of the Harijan tours of the 1930s. He could cover only eight or ten miles per day. But he considered the section he covered on foot as "the most effective part of our tour. The awakening was solid. Our experiences were rich."[16] Travel by foot was an important part of Gandhi's way of nation building: he was doing nothing extraordinary, he would have claimed; he would have protested that he was doing in the present only what the acharyas were doing in the past.

Religion and Language

The argument that Indian civilization supplies the basis for nationhood runs into a major difficulty. The Reader poses it bluntly: "Has the introduction of Mahomedanism not unmade the nation?"[17] Indian civilization may have supplied a basis for a common identity in the pre-Islamic period; "but now we have Mahomedans, Parsis, and Christians. Our very proverbs prove it." The Muslims turn to the West for worship, and the Hindus to the East; the Muslims kill cows, the Hindus worship them. The Muslims do not believe in ahimsa, while the Hindus adhere to it. "We thus meet with differences at every stop. How can India be one nation?"[18]

In approaching Gandhi's position on the relationship between nationalism, religion, and language, it is important to bear in mind that his approach is normative, not positivistic. Certainly, he takes into account historical facts. At the same time he realizes that norms have shaped and will always shape historical facts and that in moral and political sciences there are no such things as pure facts. What are sometimes referred to as pure historical facts have themselves been moulded by their component norms. And if certain facts of Indian history show the existence of animosities between Hindus and Muslims, as undoubtedly they do, it is no reason to conclude that such animosities are inevitable and that they should continue for ever. New norms can and should be developed which in turn can create new historical facts conducive to the growth of India as a *praja*. Thus, though Gandhi recognizes the factual differences between Hindus and Muslims, his normative approach to them disposes him to consider them to be not serious enough to prevent the growth of a composite nationalism. For him the presence of Muslims, and for that matter that of Christians, Sikhs, and Parsis, constitutes not so much a challenge to Indian civilization as an opportunity to manifest its accommodating potential. Furthermore, he takes as norm that religion as sect ought not to be the basis of nationality. That being the case, he reasons: "India cannot cease to be one nation because people belonging to different religions live in it. The introduction of foreigners does not necessarily destroy the nation."[19]

Gandhi's conception of the relationship between nationality and religion deserves close attention. We have to understand first his meaning of religion itself. In religion, according to him, one has to distinguish between the core and the periphery, the ultimate goal and the different paths leading to it. The core and the ultimate goal of religions are compatible with multireligious nationalism. Put differently, one has to distinguish between (i) religion as social organization, as sect, and (ii) religion as the source of ethical beliefs. Religion in the first sense is a social phenomenon, while in the second sense, it is a personal matter. And Gandhi's norm is that the claims of religion in the first sense should be subordinated to the demands of Indian nationalism. If this can be brought about, there would be no unmanageable difficulties between Indian nationalism and religion in the second sense. Gandhi's nationalism, accordingly, is neither fundamentalist nor secular. It is not fundamentalist because it does not identify the nation with the sociological formation that religion as sect creates. It is not secular because it recognizes the autonomy of religion as ethics and the harmony between such ethics and Indian Nationalism. He writes: "In reality there are as many religions as there are individuals; but those who are conscious of the spirit of nationality do not interfere with one another's religion. If they do they are not fit to be considered a nation."[20] "If everyone will try to understand the core of his own religion and adhere to it, and will not allow false teachers to dictate to them, there will be no room left for quarrelling."[21]

Gandhi is quite aware that the fundamentalists think of religion and nationality as identical. The above reference to "false teachers" implies such awareness on his part. We need not take too much space here to determine who these "false teachers" might have been. It is enough to recall that certain schools of *ulemas* and *swamies* were preaching the uncompromising fundamentalist stand of "one religion, one nation." Gandhi totally rejects such theories. "If the Hindus believe that India should be peopled only by Hindus, they are living in dreamland. *If Muslim, believe that only Muslims live here, they are living in dreamland too.* The Hindus, the Mahomedans, the Parsis, and the Christians who have made India their country, are fellow countrymen and they will have to live in unity, if only for their own self-interest. In no part of the world are one nationality and one religion synonymous terms, nor has it ever been so in India."[22]

Given Gandhi's normative position on religion and nationalism, it is not difficult for him to suggest ways and means of reducing the animosities between Hindus and Muslims. If there have been "deadly" proverbs applicable to *mahadevs* and *mians,* so there have been equally vicious proverbs applicable to Vishnavites and Sivites: "Yet nobody suggests that those (last two) do not belong to the same nation."[23] Similarly sectarian differences need not necessarily spell national differences. Thus the Jains and Vedic Hindus differ as sects, yet "the followers of the respective faiths are not different nations."[24] What the Hindus and Muslims therefore ought to seek now is "true knowledge" regarding religion and nationalism. "The more we advance in true knowledge, the better we shall understand that we need not be at war with those whose religion we may not follow."[25]

The argument now shifts to the question of race. There are no racial differences, Gandhi points out, between Indian Hindus and Indian Muslims: "many Hindus and Mahomedans own the same ancestors and the same blood runs through their veins.... Do people become enemies because they change their religion? Is the God of the Mahomedans different from the God of the Hindus?"[26] To fight for separate nations, therefore, has no religious justification. Using the metaphor that should be very familiar to students of Gandhi, *Hind Swaraj* suggests that religions, understood as social formations, are different roads converging to the same point, and it did not matter what road one takes, "so long as we reach the same goal."[27] That is to say, Indian nationalism may legitimately demand that religion as sect accommodate its demands to the needs of the Indian *praja.*

The sincerity of Gandhi's position on religion and nationalism cannot be better expressed than by the stand he takes on the vexed issues of cow protection and cow sacrifice. For his part, in the final analysis, he is willing to accommodate cow protection to the demands of a composite Indian nationalism. Assuming cow protection belongs to the periphery, not the core of Hindu religion, one should be able to treat it within the dictates of a composite nationalism. If the choice was between a unified nation and cow protection, he was prepared to opt for the former. He would no doubt attempt to persuade the Muslims to respect Hindu feelings in the matter. But he was not prepared to go beyond persuasion. "I myself respect the cow, that is, I look upon her with affectionate reverence... But just as I respect the cow, so do I respect my fellowmen."[28] Moreover, the Muslim is the "blood-brother" of the Hindu. That being the case, "the only method I know of protecting the cow is that I approach my Mahomedan brother and urge him *for the sake of the country* to join me in protecting her. If he would not listen to me, *I should let the cow go* for the simple reason that the matter is beyond my ability. If I were over full of pity for the cow, I should sacrifice my life to save her, but not take my brother's. This, I hold, is the law of our religion."[29]

At this point, the Editor reminds the Reader that there have been and there still are meat-eaters among Hindus, and that Hindus mistreat the cow, etc. Yet the cow protection societies do nothing against these Hindus, least of all do they think of them as being anti-Hindu and, anti-national. "Who protects the cow from destruction by Hindus when they cruelly ill-treat her? Who ever reasons with the Hindus when they mercilessly belabour the progeny of the cow with their stick? But this has not prevented us from remaining one nation."[30]

In *Hind Swaraj* Gandhi's attitude towards Muslims is marked by both self-confidence and generosity. He felt that a self-confident majority can afford to be generous towards minorities and that the majority community should take the first initiative to build confidence in their national minorities. "That man who has inspired confidence has never lost anything in this world."[31] The obverse of this principle is that there is nothing more intolerant and more inhumane than a national majority community that feels threatened by its national minorities. One needs only to think of Germans and Jews in Nazi Germany. In the India of 1909 Gandhi felt that the Hindus were "superior in number," "more educated," and therefore "better able to shield themselves from attack on their amicable relations with the Mahomedans."[32] And especially because of this secure position, *Hind Swaraj* is supportive of the separate electorate (what it calls "certain concessions") that the Minto-Morley reforms had made available to the Muslims. He wondered why anyone interested in national unity should oppose them. "There is mutual distrust between the two communities. The Mahomedans, therefore, ask for certain concessions from Lord Morley. Why should the Hindus oppose this?"[33]

Turning now to the language question, Gandhi's approach was guided by three general norms: the need to reject the

Macaulayan concept of the role of the English language in India, the primacy of the mother tongue, (or what *Hind Swaraj* calls "the provincial language"), and the desirability of having an Indian language as the common language of India.

In his letter to Lord Ampthill, referred to above, Gandhi had already declared the following: "I no longer believe as I used to in Lord Macaulay as a benefactor through his Minute on education."[34] *Hind Swaraj* reverts to the same idea: "The foundation that Macaulay laid of education has enslaved us."[35] However, the present problem as he sees it, is not so much with the Minutes of Macaulay, as with the uncritical acceptance of its spirit by some Indians: "by receiving English education, we have enslaved the nation... It is we, the English-knowing Indians, that have enslaved India. The curse of the nation will rest not upon the English but upon us."[36]

What is the "foundation" and what is the "slavery" that Gandhi is alluding to here? He is not alluding to the practical knowledge of the English language as such, which he recognizes as being necessary for improving the quality of the "provincial" languages of India, and for disseminating knowledge of modern science.[37] The "foundation" he objects to is the cultural assumptions underlying Macaulay's thesis, namely that Sanskrit and Persian have no foundational value for the Indian civilization of the future, and that English should replace them as the new foundational language of modern India. To give English language this cultural role, Gandhi recognized, was tantamount to committing national suicide. Those Indians who looked upon English as the foundation of a new Indian culture were enslaving, not liberating, India. Profound as Gandhi's insight here is, it is important nevertheless to understand the distinction that Gandhi makes between English as a means of national slavery and English as a means of national development. His rejection of English is neither total nor mindless. "Do I then understand that you do not consider English education necessary for obtaining Home rule?," the Reader asks. The Editor's response is guarded indeed: "My answer is yes and no."[38] It is "no," as far as the Macaulay thesis is concerned. It is "yes," as far as the practical needs of the nation are concerned. Such needs include, the needs of scientific education, and inter-provincial communication our – dealings with our own people, when we can only correspond with them through that language. Ever the practical man, Gandhi realized in the cultural conditions prevailing in India at the turn of the century, knowledge of the English language was practically necessary. "We are so much beset by the disease of civilization, that we cannot altogether do without English education."[39] It is clear, then, that what Gandhi was objecting to was the wrong kind of use that the new English educated Indian elite was making of their English education. They were looking upon English education as a means of gaining power and prestige and of getting better jobs in relation to their non-English educated fellow nationals. It was setting English-knowing Indians apart from Indians who did not know English. "The object of making money"[40] had become the decisive object of English education in the minds of the vast majority. It had become the means whereby one could become a "doctor" or a "lawyer," or a member of the ruling bureaucracy such as the Indian Civil Service. It was becoming a means of acquiring status in society and control over fellow Indians. It was creating an ambitious, selfish, and unscrupulous Indian elite, with little sense of civic responsibility and national solidarity. "English-knowing Indians have not hesitated to cheat and strike terror into the people."[41] It is this evil tendency among the new Indian elite, and not the knowledge of the English language as such, that *Hind Swaraj* is attacking. On the contrary, it endorses the tactical use of English to bring about national benefits in the areas of communication and scientific progress. But such use of English must be consciously placed within the framework of a robust Indian nationalism.

As for the mother tongue, it had to be the primary basis of the cultural life of each "province." At the same time, Gandhi clearly recognised that English had to be used to bring about the further growth of the mother tongue. *Hind Swaraj* unequivocally states: "We have to improve all our languages. What subjects we should learn through them need not be elaborated here. Those English books which are valuable we should translate into the various Indian languages."[42] Perhaps what is most insightful is his observation that whereas English should be for the time being the language of scientific education, the mother tongue should remain the language of ethical education: "Those who have studied English will have to teach morality to their progeny through their mother tongue."[43] By assigning to the mother tongue the fundamental role in ethical education, Gandhi attempted to show that English education need not have a denationalizing effect on Indians.

As for a common language for India, *Hind Swaraj* reflects Gandhi's thinking in 1909: he opts for Hindi "with the option of writing it in Persian or Nagari characters."[44] No doubt Gandhi is conscious of the fact that his position on the mother tongue is not entirely in sync with his position on the need for a common language. The accent in *Hind Swaraj* is on voluntary, not legal and coercive, methods of bringing about a working harmony between the mother tongue and the common language. It is therefore accommodating to the feelings of linguistic minorities. It proposes a rather elaborate scheme of making the language issue consistent with they demands of Indian nationalism. Thus Gandhi said: "Every cultured Indian will know in addition to his own provincial language if a Hindu, Sanskrit; if a Mahomedan, Arabic; if a Parsee, Persian, all Hindi. Some Hindus should know Arabic and Persian; some Mahomedans and Parsees, Sanskrit. Several Northerners and Westerners should learn Tamil."[45]

Assessment of the Indian National Congress

We have already seen that one of the aims of *Hind Swaraj* was to give an interpretation of the Indian nationalist movement. This meant that Gandhi had to give his own assessment of the achievements of the Indian National Congress up to 1909. Chapters 1-3 and part of chapter 20 address this specific issue. The issue is treated polemically: the Reader taking the offensive and the Editor offering the defence. In the Reader's view, "Young India seems to ignore the Congress. It is considered to be an instrument for perpetuating British rule."[46] The involvement of such Britons as Allan Octavian Hume and Sir William Wedderburn is "beyond my comprehension," says the Reader.[47] The leaders of the Moderate faction—Dadabhai Naoroji, Gopal Krishna Gokhale, and Badrrudin Tyebji—are dismissed unceremoniously for being "subservient" to the British. The Reader wants Indian nationalism to abandon its constitutional approach, the approach of petition and prayer, and to adopt a deliberately violent approach, which would legitimize the use of brute force *(darugolo).* In the Reader's view, split between the Moderates and the Extremists was most salutary, and the latter should be prepared to adopt the methods even of terrorism. Briefly, there was a danger of Indian nationalism becoming by the turn of the century more and more like the violent nationalism of the West. The Reader wanted it to become fully "modern", i.e. "Western" violent, selfish, closed, and exclusive.

Gandhi's response was that the Congress, for all its inadequacies, was the first institution which had "enthused us with the idea of nationality"—it brought together Indians from different parts of India; for that very reason, it was looked upon with suspicion by the colonial government; it had "always insisted that the Nation should control revenue and expenditure;" and it "had always desired self-government after the Canadian model;" and it gave us "a foretaste of Home Rule." To deprive it of "honour" would not only be not proper, it would "retard the fulfilment of the final object" of obtaining true *swaraj.* "To treat the Congress as an instrument inimical to our growth as a nation would disable us from using that instrument."[48]

It is significant that *Hind Swaraj* identifies only three Congress nationalists by name, Naoroji, Gokhale, and Tyebji—a Parsi, a Hindu, and a Muslim, respectively. India's claim to being a *praja* could not have been better substantiated than by such a list. Naoroji is "the Father of the Nation" and "the author of nationalism."[49] He is the model of service to the nation, had he not "prepared the soil," even the Reader could not have spoken of *swaraj,* his drain theory taught us "that the English had sucked our life-blood." In short, "we have learned what we know from him".[50] The case of Gokhale is no less compelling. 'Professor Gokhale, in order to prepare the nation, embraced poverty and gave twenty years of his life. Even now he is living in poverty." He "occupies the place of a parent... His devotion for the Motherland is so great that he would give his life for it". Tyebji is also one of those who "through the Congress, sowed the seed of Home Rule."[51] The conclusion is clear enough: "A nation that is desirous of securing Home Rule cannot afford to despise its ancestors."[52]

Gandhi's unequivocal endorsement of the role that Hume and Wedderburn played in the rise and development of Congress nationalism is equally worthy of attention. It gives evidence not only of his respect for historical facts but also of his normative position on the nature of nationalism as such. He did not see anything inconsistent in the fact that Indians and Britons could work together and nourish Indian nationalism. His nationalism is not ethnocentric, *Hinduttva* as a criterion of Indian nationality is not one of his inventions. He would not support such an invention on philosophical and historical grounds. "Many Englishmen desire Home Rule for India." Some have gone beyond and made India their adopted home. These deserve fair treatment which the Extremists and the terrorists were not willing to accord. "We who seek justice will have to do justice to others." The Editor insists: "How can we forget what Mr Hume has written, how he has lashed us into action, and with what effort he has awakened us, in order to achieve the objects of the Congress?"[53] As for Wedderburn, he has "given us his body, mind and money to the same cause. His writings are worthy of perusal to this day."[54]

Recognition of the historic role that the Moderate wing of the Congress has played does not make Gandhi blind to its defects. He is fully aware that if India is to become free, it would have to go beyond constitutionalism and embrace the principles of *satyagraha*. He found their strategy of petitioning and prayer "derogatory." Neither does he accept their providentialist theory of colonialism which he believes "is almost a denial of the Godhead."[55] He would rather adopt the dictum of an English divine "that anarchy under Home Rule were better than orderly foreign rule."[56]

As for the Extremists, their ideology is more objectionable than that of the Moderates. Their misunderstanding of the true nature of *swaraj* is more profound than that of their adversaries.

They foolishly believe that *swaraj* can be obtained by the use of political violence and the forceful expulsion of the British.[57] They identify *swaraj* with the establishment of the modern, coercive, nation-state or "English rule without the Englishman." They want "the tiger's nature, but not the tiger," they want to make "India English. And when it becomes English, it will be called not Hindustan but Englistan. This is not the *Swaraj* that I want."[58] He is highly critical of their infatuation with the Italian mode of achieving national independence. Chapter 15 of the book is devoted to the analysis of Italian nationalism. If Italy has any valuable lesson for India, it is to show how India ought not to proceed. According to Gandhi, the Extremists were more impressed by Garibaldi and Cavour than they were by Mazzini. Mazzini's vision of freedom has yet to be realized, but Italians think that "the whole of Italian people" have become free simply because Garibaldi and his associates have managed to expel the Austrians by force of arms. "I am sure you do not wish to reproduce such a condition (as that of modern Italy) in India," the Editor observes. "I believe that you want the millions of India to be happy, not that you want the reins of Government in your hands."[59]

The Nation and the National Elite

The contours of Gandhi's conception of nationalism can now be better identified. Indian nationalism should produce a form of self-rule in which (i) the whole community, not just the elite, is free and active; (ii) soul-force, not brute force, should form the basis of public order; and (iii) "the national interest" *(prajana swarth)* is not the ultimate ethical criterion of state action.[60] To state this point differently, he rejects the notion that government by the national elite is beneficial simply because it is government by the national elite. The point is powerfully made by his scathing criticism of tyranny of Indian nawabs and maharajas, which he thinks is worse than the tyranny of the British. "You will admit," he reminds the Reader, "that the people under several Indian princes are being ground down. The latter mercilessly crush them. Their tyranny is greater than that of the English.[61]

It is no wonder that Gandhi is unambiguous in his criticism of Madan Lal Dhingra. "Do you not tremble to think of freeing

India by assassination?... It is a cowardly thought, that of killing others. Whom do you suppose to free by assassination? The millions of India *(praja)* do not desire it. Those who are intoxicated by the wretched modern civilization think these things. Those who will rise to power by murder will certainly not make the nation happy."[62]

Gandhi's interpretation of Indian nationalism reaches its high-water mark in chapter 17, the most important chapter in the whole book. It starts with the question whether there is any historical evidence of "any nation having risen through soul force."[63] Gandhi concedes that historians have paid far too much attention to the violent doings of kings and princes. On the surface, it may appear that brute force is effective and that soul force is ineffective. But Gandhi is not prepared to make his case for nationalism solely on the basis of the behaviour of princes. He would rather base the first premise of his nationalist thought on love and compassion *(daya)* rather than on brute force. Tulsidas, for him is a better guide here than are the Indian princes—the Tulsidas who teaches that *daya* is the true ultimate basis of *dharma* and therefore also of the *dharma* that should govern the *praja*. However widespread the use of brute force may have been in history, it is no reason to doubt the validity of the counterthesis, namely that soul force is the valid basis of the political community. "If the story of the universe had commenced with wars, not a man would have been found alive today... Therefore, the greatest and most unimpeachable evidence of the success of this force is to be found in the fact that, in spite of the wars of the world, it still lives on... Hundreds of nations live in peace... History is really a record of every interruption of the even working of the force of love or of the soul."[64] And it is Gandhi's belief that Indian nationalism has a golden opportunity to give something new to the world, namely the model of a functioning multilingual and multireligious nation. Indian civilization has the potential to bring such a nation into being. But if India is to succeed in producing something new, it should unambiguously reject the political philosophy of both the Extremists and of the terrorists. It should instead adopt something genuinely Indian—for example, the principles of *satyagraha* and *sarvodaya*. The Dhingras and the Savarkars he met in London in 1909 were misled by the nationalist philosophies of the West—of Spencer and Mill. There is delicious irony in Gandhi's use of G.K. Chesterton's analysis of the nationalist ideas propagated by such organs of the Indian terrorist groups as *The Indian Sociologist* published from London. Chesterton readily grants that "Indians have a right to be and to live as Indians." But he is wondering what the philosophies of Spencer and others like him have to do with it. "What is the good of the Indian national spirit if they [Indians] cannot protect themselves from Herbert Spencer?... Do the Indian youths want to pollute their ancient villages and poison their kindly homes by introducing Spencer's philosophy into them?"[65] "But Herbert Spencer is not Indian; his philosophy is not Indian philosophy; all this clatter about the science of education and other things is not Indian. I often wish it were not English either. But this is our first difficulty, that the Indian nationalist is not national."[66] Gandhi thoroughly enjoyed Chesterton's wit. "Indians must reflect over these views of Mr Chesterton," he concluded. The misguided terrorist groups in his view were "endeavouring to destroy what the Indian people have carefully nurtured through thousands of years."[67]

Hind Swaraj does not suggest that state violence can be entirely eliminated. What it suggests is that whatever violence the state may have to exercise must be exercised in the interest of the people as a whole, not just in that of the national elite, and that too, strictly within the bounds of the principle of compassion *(daya)*. The metaphor that Gandhi uses here is that of a child rushing into fire. Is the onlooker justified in using force to restrain the child? Gandhi's opinion is that he/she is justified in doing so, provided it is done from pure motives, namely, the motive of securing the child's welfare. Not otherwise.[68]

What emerges from Gandhi's analysis of nationalism is the stress he places on the need to develop the right relationship between the principle of *daya* and national interest. The error of modern nationalism has been to take for granted that national interest divorced from *daya* is the ultimate principle of national conduct. There is the insidious tendency in modern nationalism to urge the national elite to invoke national interest without any reference to *daya* and to use it (national interest) for its own narrow gains. Gandhi is certain that the interests of the national elite do not necessarily coincide with those of the *praja*. He sees the distinct possibility of the national elite—the "doctors," the "lawyers," and the modern professional class taken as a whole—acting in their own interest, and exploiting, deceiving, and oppressing the people at large in the name of the nation. The national elite is certain to act in this way so long as they remain under the influence of modern nationalism. On the other hand, they would be able to act in the interest of the *praja* only if their nationalism is founded on the principle of *daya*. But to be able to found in this way, they have to undergo a process of inner liberation *(chhutkaro)*. How the emerging Indian elite may achieve this inner liberation is the burden of the final argument of *Hind Swaraj*.

The argument is introduced with great artistic finesse. "What will you say to the nation?," the Reader asks. The Editor responds with a question of his own: "Who is the nation?" It is as if Gandhi wants to emphasize the point that the elite is the nation in a special sense. If up to now Gandhi had been talking of nation in a general sense, as *praja* now, in the concluding chapter, he is talking of it in a narrower sense. Thus through the mouth of the Reader he conveys this narrower meaning: "For our purpose it is the nation that you and I have been thinking of, that is those of us who are affected by (modern) European civilization, and who are eager to have Home Rule." *Hind Swaraj* is addressed to them in a special way.

What Gandhi says in this connection deserves close scrutiny as it outlines the national task lying before the national elite. It anticipates what later would come to be known as "constructive programme." First of all, the elite have to undergo a genuine moral transformation. The transformation in question has to do with their adoption of modern nationalism. They have to free themselves from it and adopt instead a different nationalism, one that is in tune with the spirit of Indian traditions as Gandhi interprets them. That is to say, they have to be "imbued with real love," and must have "experienced the force of the soul within themselves." Only those who are so imbued and who have undergone such an experience can "speak to the English" without fear or hatred. Only such transformed Indian nationals can really understand the threat posed by modern civilization and the promise held by Indian civilization. They would have to grasp the true meanings of *swaraj.* In the first place, *swaraj* is a mental condition (i) of inner liberation from the temptations of greed and power offered by modern civilization, (ii) freedom from hatred towards the national "enemy," the British, and (iii) of active love for the Indian *praja,* a love that can conquer the temptations of greed and power. Secondly, *swaraj* is an external condition (i) of political independence from alien domination and (ii) of life-long dedication to the task of improving the material conditions of poverty and caste oppression of the Indian *praja.* In concrete terms, *swaraj* requires one to take a stand on brute force and soul force. "If there be only one such Indian," the Editor affirms, "the English will have to listen to him."[69] Between such transformed Indians and the morally sensitive Britons there can ensue a genuine dialogue. There would then be no need to resort to the arts of violence and terror as means of achieving national liberation.

It should be clear by now that the task of attaining national liberation is not so much one of getting rid of the British as getting rid of the fascination for modern civilization which teaches the Indian elite to oppress the Indian *praja.* Once Indians liberate themselves from the evils of modern civilization, they would have become morally fit to deal both with the British and with the Indian people. Gandhi's real purpose is as much to find fault with the behaviour of "modern" Britons as it is to cure "modern" Indians from the disease of modern civilization. If Indians must find fault with the British, they themselves should not be guilty of the fault which they find in the British. Moral integrity requires at least that much.

It is to bring about the above-mentioned mental transformation of the Indian elite that the last chapter of *Hind*

Swaraj proposes its nineteen points. They are addressed to the national elite on whom the fate of the nation depends. Gandhi thinks that only such moral transformation can give them "the requisite strength" to make the national effort. There is nothing sacrosanct about number nineteen. Their specific injuctions will have to be understood in the context of the needs and; conditions of the year 1909. But their spirit has to be adapted to the changing needs of the nation.

Of the 19 points, three are addressed to doctors, four to lawyers, and the rest to what Gandhi calls the "wealthy." That is to say, Gandhi's target is the modern professional classes of the nation, whether they be doctors or lawyers, scientists or administrators, politicians or business executives. Modern professions must become means of service to the nation first and means of making money or attaining status only second. That is to say, the pursuit of *artha* must be conducted within the framework of *dharma*. And *dharma* under modern conditions would require that the "machinery" that is adopted for national development be conducive to the health of body and soul, and the well-being of weak and the poor not just the powerful and the wealthy. Gandhi's recommendation of the "handloom" and "hand-made goods" is symbolic of the requirement. Likewise, the mention of "repentance, expiation, and mourning," "gaol," "banishment," and "deportation for life to the Andamans" makes sense only in the context of the particular strategy adopted by the terrorists in 1909. In short, the task before the national elite has to do with love, soul force, and the use of appropriate technology. In other words, self-reform, constitutional reforms, and economic reforms are all activities linked to the pursuit of *swaraj*. That is the national message of *Hind Swaraj*.

Conclusion

If the preceding analysis is correct, it follows that *Hind Swaraj* propounds the thesis that India is a nation, a *praja*, and that everything that one wishes to do for the well-being of India must proceed from this fact. But it does not propound the *modern* concept of nation in so far as the latter is based on the notions of brute force, the priority of national interest, and a principle of exclusiveness based either on religion, or language, or race.

India is a *swadesh* for Indians and for foreigners who wish to adopt India as their adopted *swadesh*. For Gandhi, the idea of *swadesh* is consistent with the idea of an open society, shaped as it is by the legacy of Indian civilization, with its stress on soul force, and its capacity to make *samas* out of diverse ethnic, linguistic, and religious elements.

It follows that Gandhi's concept of the nation imposed certain obligations on the majority community as well as on the minority communities. On the majority community—whether the majority is based on religion or language or race, it imposes the norms of openness, accommodation, and tolerance. On the minorities– whether the minority status is based on religion or language or race– it imposes the norm of adaptation to the ethos of Indian civilization.

The Gandhian concept of national *samas* had, and still has, I think, a special reference to Indian Muslims. Accepting the Gandhian concept of *praja* would mean making a creative adaptation of Islam to the ethos of Indian civilization. Above all, it would mean the legitimization of the principle that Muslims could become the members of the Indian *praja* legally as well as emotionally. For, in the final analysis, the question that faced and still faces Indian Muslims is whether a good Muslim can be an Indian citizen, legally as well as emotionally, but especially emotionally, of a non-Muslim country. Would the Islamic principle of legitimacy legitimize Gandhi's concept of *praja*? The fact that the course of Indian nationalism did not follow the path marked out by Gandhi does not prove that Gandhi's concept was invalid nor that his analysis of Indian civilization was flawed. Partition meant that India was not ready to meet the challenge posed by Gandhi to both tne majority and the minority communities.

Perhaps the most important corollary to the Gandhian theorem is that the fate of India as a *praja* depends on the moral character of the Indian professional classes—the character of its "lawyers," "doctors," and the "wealthy,"—to use the language of *Hind Swaraj.* Gandhi realized with great acuity that India's problems lay not so much with its colonial experience as with her professional classes who have been transfixed by greed, reinforced by caste. He realized that unless these professional classes could be converted to the ideal of nationalism that *Hind Swaraj* proposes, India would not have a bright future. Gandhi's thought here is not dissimilar to that of Plato. There is a link between the health of the soul and the health of the city, and the maintenance of the health of the city depends in practical terms on the moral character of the "guardian class." It is the "guardians" who had to undergo a moral transformation first. Gandhi was equally conscious of the fact that the "guardians" could hijack nationalism and use it for satisfying their own greed and power. Briefly, Gandhi's concept of *swaraj* links the nation *(praja),* the self, the professional classes, soul force, and public service. And the final test of India's nationalism is whether the Indian professional classes will actually dedicate their lives to the attainment of *swaraj* in the dual sense—as personal self-improvement and as the material improvement of the least member of the nation.

Notes and References

1. *The Collected Works of Mahatma Gandhi* (hereafter referred to as CWMG) (New Delhi: The Publications Division, Ministry of Information and Broadcasting, Government of India, 1958-1984), Vol. 9, pp. 508-509.
2. *Ibid.,* p. 509.
3. *Ibid.,* Vol. 10, p. 7.
4. *Ibid.,* p. 190.
5. Sri Aurobindo, *Bande Mataram: Early Political Works I,* (Pondicherry: Centenary Edition, 1972), pp. 571, 585.
6. *Hind Swaraj,* (hereafter referred to as HS) Ch. X, pp. 47-8. The references to HS throughout this article is to the 1989 reprint of second edition published by Navajivan Publishing House, Ahmedabad.

7. Perhaps the following citation might serve as an example of the sort of orientalist British scholarship of the day: "This is the first and most essential thing to learn about India — that there is not, and never was an Indian, or even any country of India, possessing, according to European ideas, any sort of unity, physical, political, social, or religious... That men of the Punjab, Bengal, the North-Western Provinces, and Madras should ever feel they belong to one great nation is impossible." John Strachey, writing in 1888; cited by Ainslie Embree, *India's Search far National Identity.* (Revised Edition), (Delhi: Chanakya Publications, 1988), p. 1.
8. *HS*, ch. IX, p. 42.
9. For the text of Ranan, see Hans Kohn, *Nationalism: Its Meaning and History* (Princetone, NJ: Van Nostrand, 1955), p. 136.
10. *HS*, ch. X, p. 45.
11. *Ibid.*, p. 48.
12. See Surinder Mohan Bharadwaj, *Hindu Places of Pilgrimage in India: A Study of Cultural Geography* (Berkeley and Los Angeles: University of California Press, 1973), p. 217.
13. Letter of 14 Octotober 1909, *CWMG*, Vol. 9, p. 481.
14. *Harijan,* 14 October 1939, p. 303.
15. *Ibid.*
16. *Ibid.*
17. *HS*, ch. X, p. 44.
18. *Ibid.*, ch. IX, p. 43.
19. *HS*, ch. X, p. 45.
20. *Ibid.*, ch. X, p. 45.
21. *Ibid.*, p. 48.
22. *Ibid.*, p. 45. The underlined portion is in the Gujarati version, but not in the English version of *Hind Swaraj.*

23. *Ibid.*, p. 46.
24. *Ibid.*
25. *Ibid.*, p. 46.
26. *Ibid.*, p. 45.
27. *Ibid.*, pp. 45-46.
28. *Ibid.*, p. 46.
29. *Ibid.*, p. 46; emphasis mine.
30. *Ibid.*, p. 47.
31. *Ibid.*, p. 49.
32. *Ibid.*, p. 48.
33. *Ibid.*, p. 48.
34. *CWMG*, Vol. 9, p. 509.
35. *HS,* ch. 19, p. 79.
36. *Ibid.*, p. 80.
37. *Ibid.*, p. 81.
38. *Ibid.*, p. 79.
39. *Ibid.*, pp. 80-81.
40. *Ibid.*, p. 81.
41. *Ibid.*, p. 80.
42. *Ibid.*, p. 81.
43. *Ibid.*, p. 81.
44. *Ibid.*, p. 81.
45. *Ibid.*, p, 81.
46. *HS*, ch. l, p. 18.
47. *Ibid.*, p. 21.
48. *Ibid.*, p. 22.
49. *Ibid.*, pp. 19-20.
50. *Ibid.*, p. 19.
51. *Ibid.*, p. 19.

52. *Ibid.*, p. *20.*
53. *Ibid.*, p. 21.
54. *Ibid.*, p. 18.
55. *HS,* ch. 20, p. 86.
56. *Ibid.*, p. 87.
57. *Ibid.*, p. 86.
58. *HS*, ch. 4, p. 27.
59. *Ibid.*, ch. 15, p. 61.
60. *Ibid.*, ch. 16, p. 68.
61. *Ibid.*, ch. 15, p. 61.
62. *HS*, ch. 15, p. 62. Dhingra, a Punjabi student studying in London, committed a notable assassination, that of Sir William H. Curzon-Wyllie, the Aide-de-Camp to the Secretary of State for India, on 1 July 1909, a few days before Gandhi's arrival in London from South Africa.
63. *HS*, ch . 17, p. 69.
64. *Ibid.*, pp. 69-70.
65. *CWWG*, Vol. 9, p. 425.
66. *Ibid.*, p. 427.
67. *Ibid.*, p. 427.
68. *HS*, ch. 16, p. 68.
69. *Ibid.*, p. 89.

7
Sources and Implications of Sarvodaya in Gandhi's Philosophy

Anil Dutta Mishra

Introduction

Sarvodaya today does not represent a mere vision or utopian notion but makes an attempt at reorienting human mind to reconstruct human society. It has assumed the dimensions of a movement and a socio-economic force of great potentialities. It is a dynamic philosophy, which can make possible the advent of a radically transformed humanity. Sarvodaya seeks to build a new society on the foundations of old spiritual and moral values of India and attempts to meet the challenge of the contemporary problems.[1] The world has witnessed the propagation, experimentation, and implementation of various socio-economic ideologies—capitalist, socialist, and communist, from time to time. But, in overall consideration, Sarvodaya is undoubtedly far more superior to other attributive models. It envisages a well-balanced and integrated development of the nation with no distinction, among haves and have-nots, privileged and underprivileged, ruler and the ruled. The essence of Sarvodaya thought lies in socializing matter through the strength of the spirit. Dogmas have no place in Sarvodaya. "The philosophy of Sarvodaya is not a set of dogmas, in its essence, it is compatible with an attempt of the spirit to prevail over matter and to socialise itself."[2] Sarvodaya is a redeemer's philosophy of social and political orientation; where suffering is, Sarvodaya goes to

* Reprinted with the permission of Gandhi Peace Foundation and *Gandhi Marg* from *Gandhi Marg* (July-September, 2004), pp. 167-186.

mitigate it. It is the culmination of human emotional integration and the highest intellectual aspiration. It is a symbol of platonic detachment and Gita's Anasakti.[3] It is the highest manifestation of love and it aims at a mental transformation of the people. Gandhi denounced the utilitarian principle of the greatest good of the greatest number, and advocated the Sarvodaya philosophy.

Gandhi did not originally coin the word "Sarvodaya." Even before him, the idea of Sarvodaya was found in religious books: Vedas, Upanishads, The Ramayana, The Gita, The Quran, and many others. It was also preached by Indian and Western saints as well as philosophers. But Gandhi gave to these age-old principles and ideals an extended meaning and application. In fact, after the death of Gandhi, the word "Sarvodaya" came into greater prominence, when his fellow-workers assembled at Sevagram (Wardha), in March 1948, and decided to form an organization named Sarvodaya Samaj. This name was chosen in preference to that of Satyagraha Mandal (Satyagraha Circle) because the word "Satyagraha" had come to acquire a restricted meaning which did not include constructive work. Since then the school of thought, which accepts Gandhi's philosophy in all its aspects and of which the central figure is Vinoba Bhave, has come to be known as the Sarvodaya School and its philosophy as Sarvodaya Philosophy.[4] The prominent thinkers of this school were Acharya Vinoba Bhave, Kishorilal Ghanshyam Mashruwala, J.C. Kumarappa, Kaka Kalelkar, Shinkerrao Deo, Dhirendra Mazumdar, Loknayak Jayaprakash Narayan, and Acharya J.B. Kripalani. Except Jayaprakash Narayan, all of them had been associated with Gandhi in his constructive work.

Sarvodaya: Meaning and Genesis

"Sarvodaya" is Sanskrit in origin which is comprised of "Sarva" meaning all and "Udava" meaning rising. The etymological meaning of Sarvodaya is the rising of all. This includes all living beings.[5] In other words, Sarvodaya as the word means welfare of all. The word first appeared in the form of the title for the Gujarati translation of John Ruskin's book entitled "Unto this Last."[6] Sarvodaya was the title of a series of nine articles, which Gandhi wrote and got published in Gujarati in the *Indian Opinion* weekly in South Africa in 1908.[7]

Sarvodaya is essentially a spiritual activity which has two meanings, viz negative and positive. As a negative concept, Sarvodaya is not limited to one person or to one group of persons. Nobody is excluded from enjoying anything from others.[8] It is not something which one man or a set of men can gain or enjoy to the exclusion of others.[9] As a positive concept, Sarvodaya implies the participation of all kinds of people irrespective of class, caste, creed, and religion. It also stands for the total blossoming of all the faculties—physical, mental, and spiritual – of the human being. It is an activity in which all may partake and it is tantamount to a full realization of the human faculties of the human soul.[10]

According to Acharya Vinoba Bhave, the term "Sarvodaya" commands a twofold meaning. Firstly, Sarvodaya means making all happy by removing suffering and poverty with the help of scientific knowledge. Secondly, establishing a world state full with divinity, kindness, and equality is called Sarvodaya.[11] Sarvodaya aims not at the rise of the few or the many, or for that matter the rise of the greatest number. It is not utilitarianism which stands for the greatest good of the greatest number. It contains the germ of minority and majority. Contrary to utilitarianism, it stands for the good of one and all, of the high and the low, of the strong and the weak, the intelligent as well as the dull. As against the laissez faire theory, that is the survival of the fittest, Sarvodaya believes in the survival and development of all. To Vinoba, "the idea of Sarvodaya, as preached by the Gita, is to merge oneself in the good of all."[12]

Apart from connoting the welfare of all, Sarvodaya commands two more meanings: firstly, the universal welfare and, secondly the integrated development of all. The laissez faire philosophy stands for the exploitation of many by a few. The utilitarian school supports the majority, totally neglecting the minority. Sarvodaya rejects these theories which stand for the joy of a few, advocates the welfare of all, irrespective of class, castes, creed, colour, race, region, or religion. The philosophy of Sarvodaya makes the attempt of reorienting human mind, of reconstructing human society. It means welfare and prosperity of all. All must progress together without any collision of interests.[13]

Interpreting the purport of Sarvodaya, Dada Dharmadhikari said: "Sarvodaya is a term with a wider connotation since it conceives of assimilation of all and not only of many or most."[14] Sarvodaya is a philosophy which provides checks against the imperfections of human mind and soul.

As regards the meaning of the word "Sarvodaya", there are broadly two views: the first, in its micro-form, means simply the rise of one and all; secondly, the macro-form connotes the rise of all, the universal welfare and the all-round development of all.[15] But it connotes several other meanings. In its negative sense, it never omits even a single person from enjoying anything from the rest of mankind. As a positive concept it promotes the development of all the faculties of man. According to Vinoba Bhave, it stands for not only making all happy by eliminating suffering from all but also for bringing a world state based on equality. For Gandhi, Sarvodaya as a broader concept stands for the merger of one in all with self-sacrifice and a selfless service. It aims at not only fulfilling the minimum material needs but also at developing the ethico- spiritual aspects of all people. The following sources helped Gandhi to develop his concept of Sarvodaya. These were Ruskin's book *Unto This Last,* Tolstoy's The King*dom of God is Within You, Thoreau's Civil Disobedience,* The Bhagvad Gita, Isavayopanisad, Buddhism Jainism, and Islam.

Ruskin's *Unto This Last*

The Gandhian philosophy of Sarvodaya can be traced to the central teachings of India's spiritual and religious heritage, although Gandhi admits the fact that he had immediate inspiration from Ruskin's *Unto This Last* for which the term "Sarvodaya" is his rendering.[16] The welfare of all became the basic idea of Gandhi's philosophy right from the days when he wrote in Gujarati his most world famous thirty thousand-word book *Hind Swaraj or Indian Home Rule* in 1909.

Gandhi titles one of the chapters of his autobiography as "The Magic Spell of a Book" wherein he describes the effects of

Ruskin's *Unto This Last* (meaning uplift of the last). It is a book from which Gandhi drew great inspiration and he at once determined himself to change his view of life in line with the ideals embodied in Ruskin's book *Unto This Last.*[17]

The central teachings of *Unto This Last*, according to Gandhi, are:

(i) That the good of the individual is contained in the good of all.

(ii) That a lawyer's work has the same value as the barber's inasmuch as all have the same right of earning their livelihood from their work.

(iii) That a life of labour, i.e., the life of the tiller of the soil and the handicraftsman, is the life worth living.

There is a controversy with regard to the meanings of the terms "Unto This Last" and "Sarvodaya." Gandhi himself acknowledged that he translated it later into Gujarati, entitling it Sarvodaya. On the one hand, Benudhar Pradhan opines that the idea of welfare of all formed a part of his mental make-up even before he read this book.[18] This view is further strengthened from what Gandhi has expressed in his own words — "The first of those I knew."[19] On the other hand, Geoffrey Ashe has doubted whether the idea of Sarvodaya is contained at all in Ruskin's *Unto This Last.* Persons like Benudhar Pradhan affirm that "it will be a travesty of truth to say that the objective of "welfare of all" does not remain couched in the pages of *Unto This Last* of Ruskin."[20]

Ruskin and Gandhi both were earnestly concerned with social welfare. While Ruskin aimed at the social welfare of "the greatest number," Gandhi aimed at the welfare of all. Therefore Vinobha Bhave feels that Gandhi is the real author of the term "Sarvodaya," since the term "Unto this last would mean only the uplift of the last (Antyodaya). In fact, one has to accept that Ruskin's *Unto This Last* had directly or indirectly had a profound influence on Gandhi in fulfilling the ideal of Sarvodaya, which he had already cherished as his life's mission.

Leo Tolstoy's *The Kingdom of God is Within You*

Gandhi was greatly influenced by Leo Tolstoy through his book *The Kingdom of God is Within You* and his essay on "Christianity and Patriotism." Tolstoy's simplicity of life and purity of purpose influenced Gandhi deeply. His views on Christianity, its church, its teachings roused Gandhi's feelings. Tolstoy accepted love to be the law of life. The principle of nonviolence is based on love for the entire mankind. Tolstoy and Gandhi both adopted the instrument of love to solve all problems in their lives. In his celebrated book *The Kingdom of God is Within You,* we find a political force creating an indelible mark on Gandhi. Gandhi confessed that its reading cured him of the skepticism and made him a firm believer of Ahimsa. Both Tolstoy and Gandhi firmly believed that nonviolence could cure all social maladies, remove political ills, and establish peace on the earth and goodwill among mankind. In fact, both Tolstoy and Gandhi believed in the efficacy of love for the cure of evil and suffering in this world. Tolstoy perceived the truth, love, and nonviolence and Gandhi grasped the essence of these virtues and led his life directed towards these paths.[21]

Tolstoy also impressed upon Gandhi's mind the importance of bread labour. For Tolstoy, the man who abstains from manual labour is a thief of the society. Gandhi acknowledged his debt to Tolstoy. He says: "The law that to live man must work, first came home to me upon reading Tolstoy's writing, 'On Bread Labour'—only those men deserve to eat bread who actually till the ground, spin cloth and produce things" Tolstoy says: "Let us get off the shoulder of our neighbours" and Gandhi adds that if everyone performed that simple operation, he would have rendered all service God requires of him. Since every man has an obligation to himself as well as to the society, bread labour becomes an imperative duty, which must be performed by each and every man.[22]

The Gandhian philosophy of Sarvodaya comes very close to Tolstoyan philosophy of anarchism. The pure ideal of Gandhi's conception of Sarvodaya is an ideal of philosophical anarchism, a stateless society marked by voluntary cooperation. Profound faith in God, commiseration from the exploited, inherent aversion to violence, deep-rooted belief in the dignity of man led the two philosophers to the same goal and objective. But Gandhi was not a thoroughgoing Tolstoyan. The difference between the two philosophers arises out of fact the that Gandhi is far more practical than Tolstoy. Tolstoy recoils from all expressions of violence. Gandhi permits violence, provided of course, that the motive for violence is not anger but true love. Thus the moral content of Gandhi's doctrine of Ahimsa, which forms the fulcrum around which the entire doctrine of Sarvodaya ideology is based, has a higher significance than that of Tolstoy. This is due to the fact that Gandhi was greatly influenced by the Gita ideal of niskamakarma, *i.e.,* action without attachment.[23]

Thoreau's *Civil Disobedience*

The American pacifist Thoreau was the champion of the free spirit and was repelled by the established political and economic routine of time. In him we discover an element of moral individualism culminating in his concept of "civil disobedience." Thoreau used the term in his speeches in 1849. It is obvious that Gandhi did not derive his idea of civil disobedience from the writings of Thoreau. In fact, the resistance to authority in South Africa preceded before Gandhi got the essay of Thoreau on civil disobedience. This movement was then known as "passive resistance." Gandhi was not satisfied with the term "civil disobedience" because it failed to convey the full meaning of the struggle. Hence he adopted the phrase "civil resistance."[24]

Thoreau did not believe in narrow sectarianism and felt that man is meant to experience God, not to theologise about Him. Man, according to Thoreau, is a social being who is generally disposed to cooperation with fellow-beings for social good. He felt that the moral institutions of the state supported by coercive authority hamper the individual's moral and spiritual freedom. He, therefore, visualized a society in which government will disappear. "That Government is best which governs not at all," or, "which governs least." Like Thoreau, Gandhi also held that the democracy could be realized only in a stable society based on Truth and Nonviolence. And Gandhi described it as Sarvodaya, which promotes not only social welfare but also spiritual upliftment. Thus Gandhi heard an echo of his own thought in Thoreau.[25]

Bhagavad Gita

Gandhi drew his primary strength and inspiration from the Bhagavad Gita. To Gandhi, the Gita is the "Eternal Mother." According to him, the theme of Gita is self-realization and its means is the theme of the Gita.[26] Again he affirms, to one who reads the spirit of the Gita, it teaches the secret of nonviolence, the secret of realizing the self through the physical body."[27]

The sole aim of the Gita is to suppress unrighteousness and to establish Dharma. It wants to bring prosperity and peace to all. It presents in a concise form the Hindu view of life, which in turn stands for the universal brotherhood of all beings. It also highlights the importance of all selfless service for the promotion of the welfare of the whole creation since God and the creation is one. Through Svadharma, the Gita aims at "Sarvabhutahita" or the good of all beings.[28] In this way, Gita preaches the message of the welfare of all or Sarvodaya, which influenced Gandhi's thought and action.

Isavayopanisad

The first verse of Isavayopanisad deals with the ideology of Sarvodaya. The first part of the verse contains the principles of equality and fraternity. And the second part reveals the ideas of renunciation, non-acquisitiveness, non-exploitation and service to the society. According to Gandhi, since the entire universe is pervaded by God, the verse preaches the philosophy of equality and fraternity, which are the fundamental principles of the welfare of all. He confirms: "Universal brotherhood, not only brotherhood of all human beings but of all living beings, I find in this mantra...."[29]

Buddhism

According to Lord Buddha, all life is a suffering. Suffering has to be extirpated in order to enjoy the bliss of nirvana, which is the highest goal in Buddhism. Nirvana is both individualistic and universal or cosmic. It may be realized in this life, here and there. It may also be known as full and perfect enlightenment for the sake of all beings. All can obtain nirvana if they meticulously follow the Noble Eightfold Path of Buddha. Gandhi was highly influenced and deeply impressed by the Buddhist philosophy, which preached universal love, non-injury to living beings, sacrifice, and renunciation for the sake of promoting the welfare of all. The Buddha stressed on purity of means which in turn influenced Gandhi who constantly maintained that there is an indissoluble relationship between pure means and noble end.[30] Buddha preached about the middle path. Similarly, in Sarvodaya, it is understood that no one should take an extreme step.

Jainism

The ideal of the welfare of all forms is the cornerstone of Jainism. Ahimsa forms one of the five vows. The positive aspect of nonviolence is the love for fellow-beings, not only human but also all creatures. A Jain Tirthankara's duty is to devote his whole life for showering happiness on all the beings of the whole universe. About the place of Sarvodaya in Jainism, Benudhar Pradhan states: "The concept of welfare of all was so much an integral part of Jaina philosophy that the term 'Sarvodaya' was used by one Jaina teacher Samantabhadra even before the Christian era."[31] Further, Benudhar Pradhan argues that though the word "Sarvodaya" is used by the Jaina saint Samantabhadra for the first time, yet Gandhi's use of the word is completely his own. According to him, the term "Sarvodaya" came to Gandhi "as if in a flash."[32] Therefore he maintains that "the word 'Sarvodaya'.... was purely his own coinage."[33]

Islam

Gandhi had a great respect for Islam. He learnt the message of universal brotherhood from it. As for Islam, Gandhi declared that in his view, "the point of brotherhood is manifested in no other religion as clearly as in Islam." The reading of the holy Koran convinced Gandhi that the basis of Islam is not violence.[34] In fact, Gandhi showed remarkable catholicity and sympathetic and reverential attitude towards all religions of the world.

Apart from *Unto This Last, The Kingdom of God is Within You,* the Upanishads, the Gita, Buddhism, and Jainism, Gandhi's concept of Sarvodaya was also influenced by Vaishnavism, Zoroastrianism, and Christianity. The revival of the ancient teachings by Gandhi and incorporating them in his philosophy of Sarvodaya is perhaps his greatest contribution to the world of thought. Gandhi attempted the synthesis of the ideas of Vedanta, Buddhism, Jainism, Christianity, and the teachings of prophets like Tulsidas, Tolstoy, Thoreau, Ruskin, and national leaders of the Indian Renaissance movement. The philosophy of Sarvodaya takes up the Gandhian synthesis and tries to work out the implication of their ideas at more critical and analytical levels.[35]

End and Means in Sarvodaya

Morality is the essential means to achieve spirituality and good society or good ends. But people like Machiavelli maintain that end justifies the means. This reveals that through any impure means like cunning, hypocrisy, hatred or violence one can get one's own desired end. To them, ends and means are water-tight compartments. End is everything, no matter what or how the means are. Means become good if they serve the end. Jayaprakash Narayan observed impartially: "In Marxism any means are good means provided they serve the ends of the social revolution."[36]

For Gandhi means determine the end. He says: "As the means so the end."[37] Means are as important as the end. In a way, his unique contribution to the world lies in his maintaining that the means are more important than the end.[38] His emphasis on means rather than on the end is the doctrine of niskamakarma which holds that a person can have control over actions and not on their fruit. Gandhi is fully convinced that man can only strive but cannot command results. He maintains that "means are after all everything. There is no wall of separation between means and end. Indeed the creator gives us control over means, none over the end. Realization of the goal is in exact proportion to that of the means. This is a proportion that admits of no exception."[39] Gandhi's stress on the strength of the means is based on the following reasons: (i) He believes in the progressive evolution of man; (ii) He fixes the end of man as self-perfection; (iii) He feels that the end is always out of man's grip till it is attained; and (iv) He is convinced that if means are subordinated to ends, the ends to which means are subordinated are likely to be less effective. All the above convictions made Gandhi hold the view that man must have complete control over means, despite both means and ends being varied and contradictory.[40]

According to Gandhi, the principle of end justifying the means is dangerous in practice and unsound ethically. If it is accepted, it permits recource to violence, fraud, untruth, opportunism, etc. Gandhi viewed human beings as supreme. They are ends in themselves. If the means are pure, the end also becomes pure. When we take care of the means, the end will take care of itself.[41] By emphasising only the means, Gandhi does not intend to give a secondary place to the ends. To him, means and ends are inseparably connected just like seeds and trees are connected.[42]

By considering means and ends as a continuous process, Gandhi dissolved the age-old opinion of viewing both as water-tight compartments. The difference between them is imaginary.[43] Therefore he takes them as an organic whole. In a way, he proposes that both means and end must be homogeneous. He also holds that the extreme of means is itself the end. That is, the end progressively realizes itself through the means. The end can never result all of a sudden out of the means. In fact, when means slowly progresses, it turns itself into the end. The means, apart from leading to an end, shapes the end. In Gandhian philosophy, self-realization or spiritual freedom is the end of all human actions. Gandhi throughout his life tirelessly tried to use Sarvodaya social order as the means to achieve spiritual-freedom. Sarvodaya society guarantees moral freedom to every individual. This moral freedom, in turn, progresses itself into spiritual freedom, when it is followed meticulously placing faith in the supremacy of God. Moral freedom as means and spiritual freedom as end form a continuous process or organic whole. They cannot be divided into water-tight compartments. Their difference is only imaginary. Both are convertible terms. That is what Gandhi too reveals. What is needed is understanding and practising ethics as God has given. Sarvodaya, as it enjoys ethico-spiritual basis, can also be equitable to both moral freedom and spiritual freedom. Thus, the problem of ends and means, as an organic whole, occupies a unique place in Gandhian thought, contributing to Sarvodaya, moral freedom, spiritual freedom, political freedom, and spiritual economic freedom.

Sarvodaya Social Order

Gandhi with his many-sided personality had a clear vision and definite approach to the problems which faced India of his time. Indian society was full with deep-rooted evils. It had totally degenerated itself socially, politically, economically, and educationally. Penury had further ruined Indian social condition which were already corroded with caste conflicts, child marriages, untouchability, Sati, Pardah, negation of education to women, dowry, polygamy, corruption, exploitation, etc. Gandhi tried to find immediate solutions to all these problems.[44]

In a Sarvodaya society, there is no scope for exploitation, discrimination, inequality, and violence. Gandhi[45] envisaged that Sarvodaya society should also be free from evils like politics without principle, wealth without work, knowledge without character, commerce without morals, science without mankind, and service without sacrifice. It should not be divided into water-tight compartments called social, political, and religious, where all these act and react upon one another. His aim of Sarvodaya made him to establish a close correlation among, these problems. The Sarvodaya society is an indivisible whole. In order to establish a democratic and free society Gandhi suggested that every individual should imbibe the spirit of love, tolerance, kindness, fearlessness nonviolence, etc. A nonviolent society, however small it is, is the strongest one. Non-violence as the law of life includes individuals, societies, and nations. To him, nonviolence is both a personal and social virtue. A society built on the basis of complete Ahimsa is the purest anarchy.[46]

For Sarvodaya a certain mentality, and certain attributes are essential. Gandhi has offered the "eleven vows" to discipline oneself, so that a disciplined society could emerge. Self sacrifice is the essence of Sarvodaya social order. Every individual is to be ready and willing to sacrifice his happiness for the sake of others. Everyone is to follow the policy of giving and not taking. He is to work for others and not expect anything in return for the same. Through Sarvodaya he wanted to rebuild the nation "from the bottom upwards" and establish a new social order based on freedom, justice, equality, and fraternity. Gandhi's ideal (Sarvodaya) society will be marked by the following characteristics :[47]

- There should be no coercive state power in it and social cohesion should be maintained through the citizens' sense of social obligation like the obligations of Varnashram dharma in ancient India.
- It should consist of villages or rural agricultural settlements in which wants are few and cooperation, conservation, and decentralization are the governing norms of social, civil, and economic activity.
- Besides agriculture, other production should be based on cottage industries and handicraft. Even education should be handicraft-centred .
- Besides the ruling principles of decentralized and handicraft-centred production, three other economic norms should be maintained or practised, namely village self-sufficiency, bread labour *(i.e.,* winning one's bread through work done by one's own body labour), and non-possession (acquiring or using the minimum possible articles of consumption). Heavy machines and heavy transport will have no place in this society.
- In such a society, disputes or conflict (generally arising out of the craze for power, property or possession) will be few and far between. But in order to deal with such disputes, as may possibly or occasionally arise, village panchayats should be organized. In the unlikely event of the failure of panchayats, recourse may be had to Satyagraha.

Gandhi had set up his first Sarvodaya community on a farm near Durban and called it Phoenix (c. 1904), followed by another one (*c*. 1910) over Johannesburg named after Leo Tolstoy. The idea behind these two settlements was that the inmates had to perform all chores of running the farms, whatever be their vocation, on living wages, so that they become self-reliant and self-sufficient. In fact, through the pursuit of Sarvodaya ideals, Gandhi wanted to chart out an alternative course. The ideas on Sarvodaya social order found their fullest expression in his constructive work programme that began to unfold itself on his arrival in India from South Africa. Khadi, communal amity, removal of untouchability, promotion of village industries, village sanitation, basic education, etc. came one after another and so did the supporting organizations. Some of these organizations were: All India Spinners Association, All India Harijan Sewak Sangh, Hindustani Prachar Sabha, Hindustan Talimi Sangh, and Akhil Bharat Sewa Sangh. The Sarvodaya society is an ideal society and an ideal cannot be fully realized. Gandhi also believed that "an ideal is never fully realized in life."[48]

Sarvodaya Political Order

Sarvodaya as a political doctrine is mildly anarchist. In fact, the political ideal of Sarvodaya is an anarchism of its own variety. It concedes that a fully stateless society is beyond the reach of man, and the goal of human endeavour can only be to reduce the power and sphere of the state to the minimum. The politics of Sarvodaya is politics of *lokniti* instead of *rajniti*. *Lokniti* is a comprehensive term, which denotes simultaneously a way of life, a form of social order, and a method. As a way of life, it stands for the self-regulation of individual conduct and for a habit to act on one's own initiatives. As a form of social order, it envisages a society in which police and military will have little to do and the law will interfere least with life. A man will have the utmost freedom of action. As a method, it stands for social change in a manner that would maintain man's freedom of action.[49] The Sarvodaya political order is based on certain fundamental political assumptions :

(i) All individuals are equally born.

(ii) People are the custodians of the supreme power in the State.

(iii) Political power should be decentralized both at the individual and at the village level.

(iv) All must train themselves for self-rule.

(v) All should believe in the divinity of every individual and strive for the welfare of all people.[50]

The ultimate goal for Gandhi is the greatest good of all people. Good, to him, means only the self-realization but not the material well-being of the individuals or the society. A study on the nature of Sarvodaya political order demands a brief survey of his view on State, Swaraj, Satyagraha, Democracy, Nationalism, Internationalism, and Ram Rajya.[51]

According to Vinoba Bhave,[52] there are ten criteria of an ideal polity :

(i) International fraternity.

(ii) The conscious, spontaneous (as far as possible) and hearty co-operation of all the inhabitants of the country.

(iii) The identity of the good of the capable minority and the general majority.

(iv) The orientation towards the universal and equal development of all.

(v) The widest dispersion of political sovereignty.

(vi) The least amount of government.

(vii) The easiest availability of tantra or justice (?)-(Sulabhatama tantra).

(viii) The least possible expenditure.

(ix) The lowest degree of external protection.

(x) One universal, uninterrupted, and neutral or objective spread of knowledge.

Sarvodaya Economic Order

Gandhi adopted an integral approach to human problems. His basic aim was to reduce economics to terms of religion and spirituality. For him, ethics and economics are not two different entities. Economics that hurt the moral well-being of an individual or a nation are immoral and therefore sinful.[53] True economics according to Gandhi, "stands for social justice, it promotes the good of all equally including the weakest and is indispensable for decent life."[54] He mainly wants to formulate such an economic constitution for both India and the world that no one suffers from want of food, clothing, and shelter. All necessities of life "should be freely available to all as God's air and water are or ought to be..."[55] Such an economic constitution he aims at building not on material wealth but on spirituality. This is only possible when everyone shows more truth than gold, greater fearlessness than pomp of power and wealth, greater charity than love of self.

The Gandhian Sarvodaya economic order is based on simplicity, decentralization, self-sufficiency, cooperation, equality, non-violence, sanctity of labour, human values, self-sufficient village units, nationalization of basic industries, Swadeshi, and the theory of trusteeship. These, in turn, will solve the problems pertaining to labour, capital, production, distribution, profit, etc.

In the Gandhian economic order, dependence on others is slavery and self-sufficiency is freedom. Regional self-sufficiency is a must in the Sarvodaya economic order. People should produce their own needs of life. Production must be in accordance with the need.

In the Sarvodaya economic order, man is totally free from material bondage. He never becomes a slave to material wants. He lives above his greed and amassing of riches. He views work as service. It is divine for him. He cherishes the principles of self-suffering, sacrifice, dedication, and renunciation. His eating, clothing, or dwelling show no superiority or inferiority. He finds no difference between the rich and the poor. Thus the Sarvodaya economic system is practical, realistic and humane.

Socialism, Communism, and Sarvodaya

Gandhi called himself a socialist and even a communist but for him socialism and communism were transcendental forms of egalitarian social philosophy that find their fulfillment and culmination in Sarvodaya.[56] Although the situational backgrounds from which socialism and Sarvodaya have emerged are different, their humanist idealism is almost similar.[57] According to Jayaprakash Narayan, Sarvodaya represents the highest socialist values. Socialism arose in the West as a philosophy of the industrial proletariat and challenged the pretensions of the contemporary state, which bolstered the interests of the capitalists.[58]

Socialism and communism are basically idealistic, ethical, and humanitarian in nature. They are concerned with the elimination of the misery of the millions, elevation of the status of poor, unfortunate and downtrodden and founding a society based on the principle of economic equality and social justice. Sarvodaya stands for a just society free from all types of exploitation and human miseries. According to Rajendra Prasad,[59] Sarvodaya represents an aspiration "towards a society based on truth and nonviolence in which there will be no distinction of caste or creed, no opportunity for exploitation and full scope for development both for individuals as well as groups." Jayaprakash Narayan[60] writes thus about Sarvodaya. "What we desire is the establishment of a society in which there will be no exploitation, there will be perfect equality and each individual will have equal opportunities for development." Sarvodaya aims at a "classless, casteless, and non-exploitative society."[61] Vinoba[62] said: "There is no permanent conflict between the two ideologies—Marxism and Sarvodaya. Whatever differences there might be between Gandhism and Communism, there are also points of similarity between these and these too are important. The cause of the have-nots is the basic sentiment running through both. Both Gandhism and Communism regard the well-being of the poor and the oppressed with the intensely loving regard of the Mother." K.G. Mashruwala,[63] a prominent Gandhian, observes: "The common point between Gandhi and Marx is the extreme concern of both for the suppressed and the oppressed, the resourceless and the ignorant, the dumb and starving section of humanity." Similarly, Jayaprakash Narayan[64] said: "If we are true socialists, we would be the followers of Sarvodaya as well."

In spite of some fundamental similarities between socialism and Sarvodaya, there are great differences between them on the question of means and methods. From the Sarvodaya standpoint; there are two shortcomings in the socialist philosophy. First, in the socialist philosophy, the basic technique for effectuating socialism is supposed to be nationalization. But nationalization may entrench the control of the bureaucrats and may be another name for state capitalism. According to Sarvodaya the socialist belief in positive state action as the sovereign remedy for human ills is unfounded. Sarvodaya pleads for villagization, while socialism believes in nationalization, Sarvodaya accepts village ownership. Secondly, socialism adheres, at least in some cases, to the concept of violent revolution. But sarvodaya has no place for violence in its philosophy and technique.[65]

The differences between Sarvodaya and communism are far more basic and fundamental. Communism advocates a violent technique for a change-over in favour of egalitarian society, a society free from exploitation and privilege. Sarvodaya, to the contrary, believes in persuasion and change of heart. Both Marx and Engels expressed their conviction that "violent overthrow of the bourgeoisie lays the foundation for the sway of the proletariat." Lenin and Mao used the technique of violence to bring about a change in the Soviet Union and China respectively. While Gandhi has taught the ethics of self-suffering to convert the opponent because violence can never be the foundation of a just and equal society.[66] Violence breeds counter-violence. And on the basis of violence it is not possible to establish a just social order. In fact a new form of exploitation of man has come into existence and that, is exploitation by the party bosses, bureaucrats and the state machine.

Sarvodaya avoids the evils of legislative or legal coercion in democratic socialism and violence and physical coercion involved in communism. It relies on the technique of conversion for bringing about social transformation in the direction of a non-exploitative and egalitarian society. Gandhi was concerned with the welfare of all and hence rejected the view that the welfare of all can ever be attained by physical, intellectual, and moral coercion perpetrated by a section of the people against the rest of the community. Gandhi believed that Sarvodaya could be realized only by the application of a moral and ethical method. Gandhi believed that through the application of the technique of persuasion and appeal to the innate good sense of the rich and the privileged, they might be made to renounce their privileges and apply their superfluous wealth for the welfare of the community. Such renunciation of wealth and privilege was to be for the good of the poor and the rich. "The essence of the revolution contemplated by Sarvodaya is that it plans its faith on human approach, at the root of which stands the concept of revolution by human beings for the proliferation of human values and human virtues, and through a method that is strictly humane."[67]

The advocates of Sarvodaya also differ from the Communists and socialists in respect of the role of the state. Both the communists and the socialists have their faith in the potency of the state to bring about equality in society. In the economic sphere, the communists and socialists advocate centralization and concentration of economic powers in the hands of the state and the proliferation of the economic activities of the state. To quote Jayaprakash Narayan:[68] "Democratic socialists, communists as well as welfarists are all statists." The concentration of both political and economic power in the hands of the state leads to too much of bureaucratization, dehumanization, and loss of individual freedom. To quote Jayaprakash Narayan:[69] "The democratic state remains a Leviathan that will sit heavily on the freedoms of the people." The state is still worse under communism. It is true that the communists talk about the withering away of the state in the long run, but during the transitional period, the state is not only tolerated but also becomes more and more powerful. It devours the lofty ideals of classless society—liberty, equality, fraternity, and fellowship. Jayaprakash Narayan writes: "The remedy is to create and develop forms of socialist living through the voluntary endeavour of the people rather than seek to establish socialism by the use of the power of the state. In other words, the remedy is to establish people's socialism, rather than state socialism."[70]

Considering from all angles, Sarvodaya is a far nobler, subtler, loftier, broader, deeper and transcendental concept than socialism or communism. According to Vinoba, "Sarvodaya" is a better word than "socialist"; it is also our own native word, born from our own soil and carrying a noble meaning. We do not use the word because we are a little doubtful if we can live up to it. So we prefer the word 'socialist.' But our goal is in fact Sarvodaya and our people are being prepared for absorption into the sea of Sarvodaya." It is true that socialism and communism can realize their true meaning and fulfill their objective by merging their identity with Sarvodaya. Jayaprakash Narayan[71] writes: "Socialism, as we understand it today, cannot take mankind to the sublime goals of freedom, equality, brotherhood, and peace. Socialism no doubt gives promise to bring mankind closer to those goals than any other competing social philosophy. But I am persuaded that unless socialism is transformed into Sarvodaya, those goals would remain beyond its reach." Vinoba writes: "There is no permanent conflict between the two ideologies—Marxism and Sarvodaya. As the Ganges becomes wider and wider and moves on and finally merges in the ocean, I hope Marxism will merge in Sarvodaya one day."[72]

Sarvodaya and the Contemporary Crisis

The Sarvodaya principles are capable of meeting the greatest challenge of the age. The most urgent need of today is the abolition of human suffering as well as of war. Sarvodaya will be very important even in the twenty first century due to the complexity of human behavior. Sarvodaya, by laying stress on the goodness of human nature, unity of mankind, service of man, application of moral principle; considered valid for individuals to group life and interstate relations, the nonviolent process of change, social and economic equality, and by economic and political decentralization tries to resolve the various kinds of tensions that disturb domestic and international harmony. Sarvodaya is capable of strengthening the forces of love, creativeness, and joy of life. Sarvodaya takes a holistic view of man and emphasizes his spiritual nature. In the modern context, the concept of Sarvodaya can be interpreted as the "awakening of one and all." Thus, in addition to the awakening of everyone, it refers to the awakening of the total human spirit and personality. Sarvodaya is also related to achieving the highest level of self-realization in which one sees one's manifestation in all others.

Our political, social, and economic life has been seized with a malady. The malady of our times, perhaps of all times, is mad quest for power, whether it is political, social, or economic. Service is being given up in the quest of personal aggrandizement. Humanity is undergoing almost a phase of moral collapse and ethical nihilism. In the era of the mad rush for power, the significance of Sarvodaya lies in its stress on the permanent value of self-abnegation. Sarvodaya is giving expression to a moral principle of cardinal importance because it wants to enshrine the primacy of goodness and character in place of the skill of manipulation and self-assertion. Sarvodaya appeals to the mind and heart in terms of values and goals. The decadence and corruption, which in fact are organized institutional mechanisms, can be removed only by the reassertion of moral and spiritual values and their ever-growing incorporation in social, political, and economic life. Sarvodaya is the only way to solve the problems of unemployment, unequal distribution of wealth, growing corruption in public life, etc. The moral collapse and prostration of our world needs the revitalizing notion of ethical idealism and stress on the moral approach to social and economic problems, which Sarvodaya envisages.

Summing Up

Sarvodaya philosophy, based on the insights and experiences of Gandhi, is a reassertion of the values and moral approach to the problems of mankind, which has been a part of ancient Indian culture for ages. Vinoba Bhave rightly said: "Sarvodaya stands for not only making all happy by eliminating suffering from all but also for bringing a world state based on equality."[73] For Gandhi, Sarvodaya stands for the merger of one in all with self-sacrifice and selfless service. His Sarvodaya ideal, apart from standing for the meaning of the welfare of all, implies the meaning of the universal welfare and integrated development of all. As a universal ideal, it aims at not only fulfilling the minimum material needs but also at developing the ethico-spiritual aspects of all people. The great contribution of Sarvodaya in the present century lies in the reassertion of the Gandhian moral approach to the problems of mankind and a vision that looks forward to the creation of a welfare state and society.

Notes and References

1. V.P. Verma, *The Political Philosophy of Mahatma Gandhi and Sarvodaya* (Agra, Lakshmi Narayan Agarwal, 1980), p. 279.
2. J.N. Mahanty, "Sarvodaya and Aurobindo: A Rapprochment", *Gandhi Marg,* No. 30, July 1960, p. 211.
3. B.P. Pandey, *Gandhi Sarvodaya and Organization* (Allahabad: Chugh Publications, 1988), pp. 20-21.
4. Vishwanath Tandon, *The Social and Political Philosophy of Sarvodaya of Gandhi* (Varanasi: Sarva Seva Sangh Prakashan, 1965), p. 2.
5. Anil Dutta Mishra, *Fundamentals of Gandhian*, (New Delhi; Mittal Publications, 1995), p. 5.
6. Mahajan P. Mani and K.S. Bharati, *Foundations of Gandhian Thought* (Nagpur Dattsons, 1987), p. 68.
7. The Collected Works of Mahatma Gandhi (New Delhi: Publications Division, 1962), Vol. 8, pp. 239-241.
8. K.M. Rathnam Chetty, *Sarvodaya and Freedom. A Gandhian Appraisal* (New Delhi; Discovery Publishing House, 1991), p. 46.
9. B.S. Sharma, "The Philosophical Basis of Sarvodaya", *Gandhi Marg,* Vol. 4, No.3, July 1960, p. 259.
10. *Ibid.*
11. K.M. Ramnan Chetty, *Sarvodaya and Freedom*, p. 47.
12. *Harijan*, 13 February, 1949.
13. B.P. Pandey, *Gandhi Sarvodaya and Organization,* p. 14.
14. Dada Dharmadhikari, *Sarvodaya Darshan* (Varanasi: Sarva Seva Sangh Prakashan, 1957), p. 18.

15. K.M. Rathnam Chetty, *Sarvodaya and Freedom: A Gandhian Appraisal* p. 48.
16. *Ibid.*, p. 38.
17. *Ibid.*
18. Benudhar Pradhan, *The Socialist Thought of Mahatma Gandhi* (Delhi: G.D.K. Publications, 1980), Vol. 1, p. 284.
19. M.K. Gandhi, *An Autobiography: The Story of my Experiments with Truth* (Ahmedabad: Navajivan Publishing House, 1948), p. 365.
20. Benudhar Pradhan, *The Socialist Thought of Mahatma Gandhi*, p. 285.
21. K.M. Rathnam Chetty, *Sarvodaya and Freedom: A Gandhian Appraisal,* pp. 39-40.
22. *Ibid.*, p. 40.
23. *Ibid.*, pp. 40-41.
24. *Ibid.*, p. 41.
25. *Ibid.*
26. *Young India,* 12 November, 1925.
27. *Ibid.*
28. K.M. Rathnam Chetty, *Sarvodaya and Freedom: A Gandhian Appraisal,* pp. 42-43.
29. Anil Dutta Mishra, *Fundamentals of Gandhism*, p. 11.
30. *Ibid.*, p. 11.
31. Banudhar Pradhan, *The Socialist Thought of Mahatma Gandhi*, p. 294.
32. *Ibid.*, p. 301.
33. *Ibid.*, p. 302.
34. K.M. Rathnam Chetty, *Sarvodaya and Freedom: A Gandhian Appraisal,* p. 45.

45\. *Ibid.*

36. Jayaprakash Narayan, *Socialism, Sarvodaya and Communism* (Bombay: A.P.H., 1964), p. 149.
37. *Young India,* 12 November, 1925.

38. S. Gopalan, *Means and Ends: The Gandhian View* (New Delhi, 1959), p. 70.
39. *Young India,* 17 July, 1924.
40. D.G. Tendulkar, *Mahatma* (New Delhi: Publications Division, 1951), Vol. 2, p. 299.
41. *Harijan*, 11 February 1939.
42. M.H. Gandhi, *Hind Swaraj or Indian Home Rule* (Ahmedabad: Navajivan Publishing House, 1946), p. 60.
43. *Harijan*, 27 February 1949.
44. Anil Dutta Mishra, *Fundamentals of Gandhism,* p. 14.
45. *Ibid.*
46. *Ibid.*, p. 15.
47. S.C. Gangal, *Gandhian Thought and Techniques in the Modern World* (New Delhi: Criterion Publications, 1988), pp. 158-159.
48. *Ibid.*, p. 159.
49. Vishwanath Tandon, *The Social and Political Philosophy of Sarvodaya After Gandhi*, pp. 124-125.
50. K.M. Rathnam Chetty, *Sarvodaya and Freedom: A Gandhian Appraisal,* p. 66.
51. Anil Dutta Mishra, *Fundamentals of Gandhism*, pp. 16-17.
52. V.P. Verma, *The Political Philosophy of Mahatma Gandhi and Sarvodaya,* p. 295.
53. Nirmal Kumar Bose, *Selections from Gandhi* (Ahmedabad Navajivan Publishing House, 1994), p. 40.
54. *Harijan,* 9 October 1937.
55. *Young India,* 15 July 1928.
56. V.D. Mahajan, *Modern Indian Political Thought*, p. 569.
57. Jayaprakash Narayan, *Socialism to Sarvodaya* (Madras : Socialist Book Centre, 1956), p. 96.
58. V.P. Verma, *The Political Philosophy of Mahatma Gandhi and Sarvodaya*, p. 283.

59. V.D. Mahajan, *Modern Political Thought*, p. 569.
60. *Ibid.*
61. *Ibid.*, pp. 569-70.
62. *Ibid.*, p. 570.
63. *Ibid.*
64. *Ibid.*
65. V.P. Verma, *The Political Philosophy of Mahatma Gandhi and Sarvodaya*, p. 285.
66. Vinoba Bhave, *Swarajya Shastra* (New Delhi: Sasta Sahitya Mandal, 1953), pp. 58-68.
67. V.D. Mahajan, *Modern Indian Political Thought*, pp. 573-74.
68. Jayaprakash Narayan, *From Socialism to Sarvodaya*, p. 33.
69. *Ibid.*, p. 33.
70. *Ibid.*, p. 34.
71. *Ibid.*, p. 21.
72. V.D. Mahajan, *Modern Indian Political Thought*, p. 574.
73. Anil Dutta Mishra, *Fundamentals of Gandhism*, p. 17.

8
Gandhi and the Politics of Decentralization*

Jayaprakash Narayan

Gandhi's Political, Economic and other ideas are parts of a whole, integrated philosophy of life. Yet Gandhi was not a philosopher in the accepted sense of the word, nor has he left behind him a systematic statement of his thought. He was essentially a man of action, and it was through the adventure of living, his 'experiments with truth, that he came to formulate ideas that are strewn over thousands of pages of writings, speeches and correspondence. That meant, among other things, that he was learning and evolving, and, in the process, ever refining and restating his thoughts. Moreover, his greater experiments were yet to be made - in independent India, when he was to have the opportunity to translate his ideas into practice. But it was just at that moment, when he was perhaps at the threshold of his most creative period, that his life was abruptly cut short by an assassin's bullets. No one who knew him can doubt that in attempting, after independence, to give practical shape to his ideas, he would have modified, innovated and further developed them - keeping perhaps the essentials of his philosophy intact. All of which rather makes it difficult to discuss Gandhi's ideas, particularly those pertaining to politics and economics, because it was precisely in those spheres that his most creative 'experiments' were doubtless going to be made. The essentials

---

* Reprinted with the permission of Professor Sibnarayan Ray from *Gandhi, India and the World*, edited by Sibnarayan Ray (Bombay: Nachiketa Publications Limited, 1970), pp. 226-241, 372-373.

of his philosophy, however, do offer a basis for discussion; and dynamic understanding of them might even help one to relate them to contemporary society.

The essentials of Gandhi's philosophy as related to society and its institutions seem to be centred around his concept of (a) human happiness and development, and (b) the place of man in society and the relationship between the two. Though his *vaishnava* upbringing, reinforced by Jain associations, had inclined him as a boy to belief in non-killing, truthfulness and God, the two great foundations of his mature thought - Truth (or God) and Non-violence (or Love) - came to be developed slowly in the course of the pursuit of his human and social ends. It is all too commonly believed that Truth and Non-violence were Gandhi's *a priori* assumptions - arrived at through a sort of Kantian *a priori* cognition - on which he had built his entire edifice of thought and action. A close study of Gandhi's evolution would hardly support such a view. He had a keenly questioning mind, and hardly ever accepted anything without reason and experience (practice and experimentation). Even the beliefs that he had started with in early life he constantly put to the test of reason and experience and kept on refining and developing them. It was thus that in the course of his inner evolution beginning with a popular faith in God he came to a higher understanding of God being Truth, and finally, of Truth being God. This spiritual journey has led some scholars like D.P. Chattopadhyaya to go so far as to state 'that the ethical contents of Gandhi's thought could be defended without any theistic postulate.'[1]

It was the same with non-violence. It is well-known that in South Africa while he was engaged in his seminal experiments in non-violence, he organized and led a voluntary corps of stretcher-bearers to serve the British side in the Boer War; and on his final return to India he recruited soldiers for the British Indian Army during the last phases of World War I. Even when he had fully developed his philosophy of non-violence, he did not hesitate to emphasize that violence was preferable to cowardice.

Obviously, non-violence was a means and not an end. Man was the end - his material, mental and moral well-being and growth. 'The supreme consideration is man,'[2] he wrote, 'the end to be sought is human happiness combined with full mental and moral growth.'[3] The pursuit of Truth and steadfast adherence to it were not *a priori* values but were conceived as being essential for the fulfillment of 'the end' as defined above. Happiness and moral growth of the individual were not possible without freedom and equal opportunity for all. This was ideally possible only if both man and society were non-violent. Ideal non-violence may not be possible to reach, but to the extent man and society approach the ideal, there will be human happiness and mental and moral development of men.

Having placed man at the center of society, how did Gandhi conceive of their inter-relationship? This is a problem that neither the individualism of the West nor the collectivism of the East has yet been able to resolve. Gandhi tried to resolve it by introducing a moral solvent, that is to say, by assigning mutual moral responsibilities to both. While the well-being of the individual was a social aim, the well-being of society too was to be assured. In Gandhi's concept of society, both were inter-dependent. Neither society was to grow at the cost of the individual nor the individual at the cost of other members of society. 'Unrestricted individualism' he condemned as 'the law of the beast of the jungle.'[4] While the individual was entitled to complete freedom, he must learn to discipline himself so as not only not to infringe the freedom of others, but also to be of service and benefit to his fellowmen and the community at large. 'Willing submission to social restraint for the sake of the well-being of the whole society enriches both the individual and the society of which one is a member.'[5] Society, on the other hand, must work ceaselessly for the well-being of the individual, fully respecting his human rights and treating him as a human person. According to the collectivist philosophy, organized society has the right, in the professed interest of man, to treat the individual as it likes - murder him, suppress his freedoms, use him as a pawn or a mere animal. To Gandhi, that was an obnoxious and immoral doctrine. In a famous passage envisioning his picture of the future world society as made up of 'ever-widening, never-ascending circles' of communities, he wrote: 'it [the world society of men] will be an oceanic circle whose center will be the individual, always ready to perish for the village, the latter ready to perish for the circle of villages, till at last the whole becomes one life composed of individuals never aggressive in their arrogance, but ever humble, sharing the majesty of the oceanic circle of which they are integral units.'[6] Aware that this concept might be brushed aside as utopian, he added: 'I may be taunted that... this is all utopian and therefore not worth a single thought. If Euclid's point, though incapable of being drawn by any human agency, has an imperishable value, my picture has its own for mankind...'[7]

If Gandhi's moral solution of the problem of individual versus society is rejected as impractical, one wonders if there can be any other solution possible. Perhaps a complete solution will never be possible, but to the extent man and society develop morally, individual and social interest and well-being will coincide. The key to such coincidence lies in Gandhi's method of social change and reconstruction through truth and non-violence.

Here then is the rationale of Gandhi's non-violence, of his political, economic and social ideas, the key to his attitude towards the question of power, the question of organization of work, and the question of community. He believed that the human and social ends that he had set before himself could best be achieved in a non-violent society in which there is a thoroughgoing decentralization of power and of production and control of wealth and which is composed of comparatively small autonomous communities, willingly federated and co-operating together. He said, 'Centralization as a system is inconsistent with the non-violent structure of society',[8] because 'centralization cannot be sustained and defended without adequate force.'[9] It is reasonable to suppose that had it been demonstrated to Gandhi that centralization also, under a different system, could lead to the fulfillment of his objectives, he would have withdrawn his objection to it. Hitherto, no kind of centralized system can be found to have done that.

Gandhi was deeply suspicious of the State. 'The State represents violence in a concentrated and organized form. The individual has a soul but the State is a soulless machine, it can never be weaned away from violence to which it owes its very existence.'[10] Discussing his theory of trusteeship in relation to private property he remarked: 'I look upon an increase in the power of the State with the greatest fear, because while apparently doing good by minimizing exploitation, it does the greatest harm to mankind by destroying individuality, which lies at the root of all progress. We know of so many cases when men have adopted trusteeship, but none where the State has really lived for the poor.'[11]

Naturally, the ideal society according to Gandhi is a stateless democracy where social life is so developed as to have become self-regulated. He wrote: 'Political power means capacity to regulate national life through national representative. If national life becomes so perfect as to become self-regulated, no representation is necessary.'[12] In such a society of what he called enlightened anarchy, 'everyone is his own ruler. *He rules himself* [emphasis added] in such a manner that he is never a hindrance to his neighbour. In the ideal state, therefore, there is no political power because there is no state.'[13] Elsewhere he expresses the same thought thus: 'Swaraj [self-government] of a people means the sum total of the swaraj of individuals.'[14]

Believing that means are ends, that every present step taken rightly will automatically lead to the distant goal, Gandhi refused to draw any blueprint of the future. He wrote in 1929: '...we do not know our distant goal. It will be determined not by our definitions but by our acts, voluntary and involuntary. If we are wise, we will take care of the present and the future will take care of itself.'[15] Again, 'I cannot say in advance what the Government based wholly on non-violence will be like.'[16]

However, Gandhi was realist enough to admit that the completely non-violent and stateless society might never be established because everyone in society might not reach the requisite level of moral development. Therefore he conceded that 'A government cannot succeed in becoming entirely non-violent because it represents all the people. I do not today conceive of such a golden age. But I do believe in the possibility of a predominantly non-violent society.'[17] While he thought it possible for non-violence to be so widely accepted and practiced in a society that it can dispense with its army, it may not be able to do the same with its police. But he thought that in such a society the police would be of a 'wholly different pattern from the present-day police force. Its ranks will be composed of believers in non-violence... The police force will have some kind of arms, but they will be rarely used if at all,' because there will be 'ever-decreasing disturbances' and policemen will be 'reformers' and 'servants' of the people who will give them 'instinctive' co-operation.[18]

Even this realism of Gandhi appears to be too idealistic. It would be rash, however, to dismiss him as a dreamer. Gandhi was nothing if not practical, and throughout his life he put into practice what he preached, and with as reasonable a success as perhaps was possible in an imperfect world. For more than a quarter of a century he dominated the Indian scene, drew the attention and respect of the world, converted many of his critics and detractors and silenced many others, not by virtue of his queer ideas, howsoever persistently put forth, but because he succeeded in putting those ideas into practice on a most impressive and effective scale. After independence, though most of his time and energy was taken up with healing the wounds of the partition of India, he wrote and said enough to indicate that the broad outlines of his future plan of action were fairly clear in his mind.

* * *

Gandhi's ideas of decentralization are usually brushed aside as being irrelevant to the modern technological society. Whether one considers Gandhi relevant or not depends very much on what one wants, what values one holds dear. If one has the same human concerns as Gandhi had, then instead of dismissing him one should seriously set about to enquire how in the context of modern technology and centralization those concerns could be fulfilled. Technology is not a force of nature that man cannot control. Man can surely bend technology to his purpose. That is what Gandhi had meant when he said that he was not against the machine, but he did not want it to become the master of man (as, in fact, it has become in modern society). Surely, the advancement of the social and physical sciences has at last made it possible now for society to determine its destiny. Today most of mankind, particularly in the most developed countries, is at the mercy of a few feverishly competing national and international giant business concerns. Even the 'socialist' countries are not immune to this self-driven competition.

While the motivations behind the recent abortive uprising of students and workers in France were rather complex, there is no doubt that a prominent one among them was a profound dissatisfaction with this process. One of the revolutionary leaders, Alain Geismar, a university teacher, when asked to define the aim of the revolution, described it as being 'workers' control and decentralization...'[19] Technologically, France is one of the most modern countries of the West, and if French intellectuals, without any Gandhian inspiration, consider decentralization not only desirable but also practicable, these ideas cannot be brushed aside as the product of a backward society.

In a most valuable study of a pioneering effort towards a new industrial order, The Scott Bader Commonwealth of England, Dr. Fred Blum, while pointing out that meaningful participation and human relations in industry were possible only in comparatively small units of production, says: 'At present size is not primarily the result of the desire to use the "best" methods of production. Most of the giants of industry consist of smaller production units which are combined for financial-power reasons. Technology, furthermore, can be used to make smaller production units viable and not only to make bigger production units bigger.... Once we have understood that technology is not the basic factor determining size we get a new basis for examining the relationships between meaningful participation and the size of an organization... The truth is that the forces now determining our economy - including the forces making for increased concentration - are the reflection of a power and value structure which is incompatible with the true nature and destiny of man.'[20]

One of the most interesting pieces of Gandhian literature is Louis Fischer's *A Week With Gandhi*. That was just two months prior to what came to be known as the 'Quit India' movement, Gandhi's last peaceful campaign against British rule. Fischer was trying to get Gandhi to elucidate his picture of the new order. Fischer asked: '...will you help me to see the new order you speak of?' Gandhi replied: 'You see the center of power now is in New Delhi, or in Calcutta and Bombay, in the big cities. I would have it distributed among the seven hundred thousand villages of India.'[21] But it is remarkable that when India became independent, largely due to his leadership, and a Constituent Assembly was convened to frame its Constitution, Gandhi hardly evinced any interest in its proceedings. When a correspondent drew his attention to the fact that his basic idea of village government had not been even mentioned in the Assembly, he wrote in his weekly journal just forty days before his death: 'I must confess that I have not been able to follow the proceedings of the Constituent Assembly ..... [the correspondent] says that there is no mention or direction about village panchayats and decentralization in the foreshadowed Constitution. It is certainly an omission calling for immediate attention if our independence is to reflect the people's views. The greater the powers of the panchayats, the better for the people.'[22] After Gandhi's death, though there was a clause added to the 'Directive Principles' to the effect that the State should take steps to establish village *panchayats as* 'units of self-government', the Constitution of India cannot be called Gandhian in any respect. Nor are the village *panchayats*, established later, even a pale reflection of Gandhi's *gram-raj* (village government). Gandhi's indifference to the Constituent Assembly might have been due to his feeling that the constitutional framework of a polity that was to be built up from below could more realistically be written by the people's deeds than in the words of constitutional lawyers.

As the village is so basic to Gandhi's polity, it is necessary to understand his meaning of it. The village to him was a 'manageable small group of people', constituting a 'unit of society'. Elsewhere he wrote, 'My imaginary village consists of 1000 souls.'[23] Vinoba Bhave, founder of the *bhoodan-gramdan* movement, speaks of human society being 'organised on the basis of small village communities of, say, 2 to 3 thousand souls'.[24]

Conceivably they could be much larger in a society of a higher technological level, providing better communication facilities. Characteristically, the Gandhian village is a primary community, large enough to offer a diversified life and small enough to generate and sustain a sense of community.

Two further points of clarification. As Gandhi's village was to be a self-governing autonomous community, he considered it necessary that it should be self-sufficient in the matter of its 'vital necessities' - food, clothing, shelter. (Self-sufficiency in these matters was necessary for another important reason too: economic decentralization, conceived as a measure to prevent concentration of wealth and economic power.) Secondly, Gandhi's village was not an exclusively agricultural community; there had to be a balance between agriculture and village industries. Had he been alive now, he might have called it an agro-industrial community. In an unrecorded conversation with one of his co-workers (now Governor of Andhra Pradesh), he spoke of 'urbanizing' the villages and 'ruralizing' the towns and cities.

With this concept of the village before us, we are ready to look at one of Gandhi's rare descriptions of village self-government :

> My idea of village swaraj (self-government) is that it is a complete republic, independent of its neighbours for its vital wants, and yet interdependent for many others in which dependence is a necessity. Thus every village's first concern will be to grow its own food crops and cotton for its cloth. It should have a reserve for its cattle, recreation and playground for adults and children. Then if there is more land available, it will grow useful money crops.... It will have its own water-works ensuring clean water supply.... As far as possible every activity will be conducted on a co-operative basis. There will be no castes such as we have today with their graded untouchability. Non-violence with its technique of Satygraha (non-violent resistance) and non-cooperation will be the sanction of the village community. There will be a compulsory service of village guards, who will be selected by rotation from the register maintained

> by the village. The government of the village will be conducted by the *Panchayat* of five persons annually elected by the adult villagers, male and female, possessing minimum prescribed qualifications. These will have all the authority and jurisdiction required. Since there will be no system of punishments in the accepted sense, this *Panchayat* will be the legislature, judiciary and executive combined to operate for its year of office.[25]

There are a few things about this vision that strike one immediately. Those acquainted with the Indian scene will see at once what a far cry Gandhi's picture is from present realities even after 22 years of freedom and 17 years of official community development programmes. But the most extraordinary thing about it is the large measure of political power, reinforced with the sanction of non-violent opposition, that Gandhi visualized for the village community. Even more interesting than the large measure of power is the fact that it was not conceived as something handed down from above. Gandhi believed that the people, who in *theory* are supposed to be sovereign, shall acquire power in *reality* by just being able to manage their affairs themselves - of course, within the limitation of their resources.

A remarkable fact of Indian socio-political history is that throughout the historical period the Indian village was able, in some measure or the other, to manage its affairs independently of the central authority. In fact, during certain periods, when the central authority over large areas had practically ceased on account of invasion or internal war, the only thing stable in Indian society was village self-government. This condition was drastically altered, by deliberate design of the British, so that by the time India won freedom, the villagers had lost all traditions of corporate life and independence, and had become abjectly dependent upon the Government above.

Gandhi was alone among the national leaders of India at independence to realize this; and believing as he did in power at the ground-level, he not only showed almost complete indifference to power at the top, except perhaps to see that it was held by friendly hands, but also set about - despite his intense pre-occupation with post-partition problems - the task of building India's polity from below. This is evident, first, from the manner in which he formulated his post-independent objectives. In his last piece of writing, described in his *Last Will and Testament* (drafted on the very eve of his martyrdom), he said that while India had won political independence, it still had to achieve 'social, moral and economic independence in terms of its seven hundred thousand villages.'[26] Another rather conclusive piece of evidence is the organizational proposal that he had set forth in that very document, namely, the transformation of the Indian National Congress from a political organization into one devoted to the service of the people. The significance of this proposal can be properly understood only in the light of Gandhi's method of non-violent social revolution and reconstruction.

* * *

Until the success of Gandhi's non-violent national revolution in India all revolutions in history had been brought about by violence. The methods of violent revolution are fairly well understood, but not so the non-violent method. The most important characteristic of this method is that its means must be in harmony with its ends. If the end is a non-violent society, the means also must be non-violent; if human freedom is the end, coercive means (except moral coercion) are ruled out; if man is an end in himself, he cannot be used as a means; if truth is to be the basis of the new life, untruthful means are inadmissible; if the end is dispersal of power, the means cannot be centralized power, etc.

Among other elements of the method are: (a) conversion by persuasion of individuals and groups to new ways of thought and action; (b) a programme of 'constructive work' designed to serve and help the people and to act as a medium through which to touch their hearts and minds; (c) non-violent non-cooperation and resistance when necessary; (d) raising a band of properly trained volunteers committed to non-violence and selfless service to the people, to act as the conscious cadres of the revolution. Just as a violent revolution changes society through the direct action of the people, so too the non-violent revolution.

Regularization by law, in both cases, follows after. The difference is that while in a violent revolution the old society is destroyed in one sweep and the new built slowly brick by brick, in a non-violent revolution change of the old and construction of the new both proceed side by side and step by step.

Gandhi did not live to launch his process of social revolution. After Gandhi his political followers, almost to a man, turned their backs upon his ideas and his vision of a new India. The reason seems to have been that they had accepted non-violence only as a political expedient, rather than as a philosophy of life. The result is that India, instead of contributing something fresh to modern civilization, is floundering in a welter of pale imitations of western capitalism, socialism and communism. The only mitigating factor is Vinoba Bhave's *bhoodan-gramdan* movement, about which space does not permit one to say much here. *Bhoodan* was not just redistribution of land but also introduction of some new values into society. *Gramdan* is carrying the process forward. It is trying to establish the principle of community ownership of land, of regular sharing of labour and income in the community, and of decision-making by general consensus. Fulfilment of the *gramdan* programme will lead, on the moral plane, to ever-growing coincidence between individual and social interests, on the political plane, to direct democracy in a self-governing community; on the economic plane, to community planning and endeavour.

Over a hundred thousand villages out of a total 556,000 in the country have already accepted *gramdan*. Their acceptance, however, is only a declaration of intent; implementation is to follow. Such are the beginnings of a non-violent social revolution in India, including those of a new polity – the polity of dispersal of power, of power to the people. The strength of this polity is proportionate to the strength of non-violence in society.

The relevance of non-violence to what one may call the polity of the people becomes obvious when we take a look at the experience of violent revolutions. 'Power to the people' has been the slogan of so many of the modern revolutions of history. Yet, because they were all born in violence, it happened invariably that those who succeeded in taking hold of the means of organized violence usurped power for themselves, protesting no doubt that they were doing so in the name of the people and for the good of the people. Not that these revolutionary leaders were frauds and charlatans. They were only working out the logic of violence. It is nearly two centuries since the Great French Revolution. Yet the French revolutionaries of the present day are still crying for 'power at the level of the work-place... whether these workers be students, academics, industrial labourers or even peasant.'[27] Lenin marched to power on the crest of the slogan 'all power to the Soviets'. Soviet Russia is a super-power today, but the Soviets of workers, peasants' and soldiers' deputies have no power, if they exist at all. In China the high-priest of ideology has himself ordained that power shall reside in the barrel of a gun; and it is not the people who hold the guns. 'Power to the People' is an empty and mocking slogan without non-violence and thoroughgoing decentralization.

* * *

India's parliamentary democracy, despite its many faults, has proved to be a much greater success than was expected. It has shown far greater strength than the many democracies in the newly freed countries of Asia and Africa. This success becomes the more striking when one takes into account the vast population of the country, its mass illiteracy, its bewildering diversities of language, religion, caste and regional histories. Consider also the fact that it has been able to withstand the shock of Nehru's death and that of Shastri's soon after, as well as the shocks of two wars – withal shortlived – with China and Pakistan, and two severe droughts on top of rising prices, mass poverty and unemployment, and unconscionable economic disparities and social disability (as for the scheduled castes).

It may not be irrelevant to probe into the sources of the strength and stability of India's democracy. The major contributing factor, to my mind, was certainly the peaceful character of the mass movements for freedom led by Gandhi. There is no doubt that had there been a violent revolution, power would have passed into the hands of the army (the new revolutionary or people's army) or of those who had the army behind them. A sort of other side of the coin' of the peaceful campaigns was the emergence, again under Gandhi's active leadership, of a mass political organization, with its roots running deep into the Indian soil, that was able to provide stability to the political system during the initial uncertain years. Another significant source of the strength of Indian democracy and its stability lies in the very nature of that democracy. Experience has shown that in spite of all drawbacks the Indian political system does provide a genuine and credible outlet for mass disaffection and desire for change. The reality and extent of the political and civic freedoms allowed by the Indian Constitution can be judged from the fact that a recently formed party of Indian Maoists, the Communist Party of India (Marxist-Leninist), is able openly to denounce parliamentary methods and preach armed insurrection! The demand for banning this party has been successfully resisted so far by the left parties (including the socialists and communists) on the ground that political opposition and vanquishment was a far better remedy than legal suppression.

Since the break-up of the Congress party's monopoly in the 1967 general election anxiety has been expressed about the future of the Indian system. The cause for anxiety is certainly real, but there is enough flexibility in the system and good sense in the country so that a political collapse is not likely to happen. The factors of regionalism, 'linguism', caste, etc., are prone to be exaggerated. They are certainly there, but mutual adjustments and reconciliation are taking place all the time. There also seems to be a reasonable possibility now of steady economic growth.

While in the respects discussed above Indian democracy is fairly satisfactory, examined from the Gandhian standpoint of power to the people, dispersal of power, participation, direct democracy, communitarian representation, etc., it is highly unsatisfactory. Moreover, the political climate today is far more unfavourable than, let us say, in Nehru's days. During that time a certain scheme of 'democratic decentralization', known as *Panchayati Raj*, had been initiated, handing down certain developmental functions and privileges to elected bodies at the district, (community development) block and village panchayat levels. But partly due to the highly centralized administrative system inherited from the British and still preserved, and partly due to the reluctance of political bosses (no matter of what party) at the State levels, the scheme, though established in form, has hardly got off the ground. Urban local government too, even in the great cities of Calcutta and Bombay, has only minimal powers, as compared to the municipalities of the West. Power still remains confined to New Delhi and the State capitals.

Except for the Gandhians, led by Vinoba Bhave, and a rather small but intellectually able and active group, known as 'radical humanists' (associates and followers of the late M. N. Roy – the famous international revolutionary and thinker and one-time collaborator of Lenin), hardly anyone in India is raising the fundamental questions about power and democracy that had been posed by Gandhi and by Roy.

Had not the hoary institution of village government that had survived until the beginning of British rule been destroyed in order to strengthen the roots of imperialism, the situation might have been very different today. But the situation being what it is, Gandhiji's policy, which Vinoba has called the 'polity of the people' or *Lokniti*, will receive no more than polite mention. Nor would it be possible, in the absence of the foundation, to draw a realistic and convincing picture of the superstructure of this polity. Gandhi himself did not venture to do so. In fact, that would have been contrary to his whole way of thinking. Having a dynamic view of society, and believing that means determined ends, he was averse to drawing any blueprints of the future.

Accordingly, there is little to go by as regards Gandhi's picture of Indian polity beyond village government. There is his picture of ever-widening, never-ascending circles of communities; his statement that there will be 'voluntary co-operation' between the thousands of self-governing village units; there is a brief reference in his speech at the Round Table Conference to an indirectly elected structure. According to Gandhi, 'seven hundred thousand villages of India will be organized according to the will of their citizens, all of them voting. These villages, each having one vote, will elect their district administrations. The district administrations will elect provincial administrations, which in turn will elect a president who will be the national chief executive.[28] "It also appears that Gandhi wanted the representatives of the people to be removable at the will of the people; he was opposed to special representation of interests; he did not consider a majority decision to be sacrosanct and upheld the right of the minority – even the individual – to dissent; he thought a consensus of opinion in certain matters to be advisable.

That is about all that we have. It is reasonable to assume that he would have made many changes in this very sketchy and tentative system. One thing, however, seems to be certain: his political structure would have been based on organized communities rather than the amorphous mass of disparate individual voters. It also seems to be certain that in his decentralized and self-regulated order, there would have been no place for power-seeking political parties, though enough place for different schools of political thought. To Gandhi, party power and people's power could not but have appeared to be mutually contradictory.

Lest it should be overlooked, it is necessary once again to point out that Gandhi's political system is only a part of a whole, and cannot come into existence or survive without the rest. It requires the development of non-violence among the people; an economic order that is just and human and, therefore, decentralized; society that is made up largely of small communities. Without concurrent development along all these lines, Gandhi's polity would be an impossibility.

Reference has been made in a previous section to the *gramdan* movement. So far, as was mentioned there, there are only declarations of intent. When, in the next stage of the movement, the intent begins to be carried out, the foundations of Gandhi's polity will begin to be laid down. Wherever the movement is reasonably well advanced, the contours of a new political system are already taking shape. There is talk, for instance, and some planning about *gram sabhas* (village assemblies) electing their delegates to constituency-wise councils, which shall set up candidates, conduct elections and act as links between the elected representative on the one hand and the village assemblies on the other. It will be these councils of village delegates who will hear reports from the elected representatives and give them guidance and keep them in touch with the opinions of the villages and their needs and problems. Taking the matter a step forward, there is already some discussion as to the functioning of the legislature and the government at the State level. It is too early yet to think of the Parliament and the Central government. Thus it is possible to hope that Gandhi's vision of democracy might yet rise from the soil.

References

1. From an unpublished seminar paper.
2. *Young India*, 13 November 1924, p. 378.
3. *Harijan*, 18 January 1942, p. 5. Happiness certainly included material well-being. Gandhi, though himself a 'half-naked fakir', did not idealize poverty, though he considered self-control and voluntary limitation of wants to be essential for human happiness and social justice. He said, 'Everyone must have a balanced diet, a decent house to live in, facilities for education for one's children and adequate medical relief'. (*Harijan*, 31 March 1945). These are objectives which have yet to be achieved - for everyone - even in the most prosperous societies.
4. *Harijan*, 27 May 1939, p.144.
5. *Ibid.*
6. *Harijan*, 28 July 1946, p. 236.
7. *Ibid.*
8. *Harijan*, 18 January 1942, p. 5.
9. *Harijan*, 30 December 1939, p. 391.
10. N.K. Bose, *Studies in Gandhism* (Calcutta, 1962), pp. 202-04.
11. *Ibid.*, p. 204.

12. *Young India*, 2 July 1931, p. 162.
13. *Ibid.*
14. *Harijan*, 25 March 1939.
15. *Young India*, Vol. 3, p. 547. 'They say means are after all means. I would say means are after all everything. As the means, so the end. There is no wall of separation between means and end. Indeed, the Creator has given us control (and that too very limited) over means, none over the end. Centralization of the goal is in exact proportion to that of the means. This is a proposition that admits of no exception.' N. K. Bose, *Selections from Gandhi, Ahmedabad*, 1957), p. 37.
16. *Harijan*, 11 February 1939, p. 8.
17. *Harijan*, 9 March 1949, p. 31.
18. Mahadev Desai, *The Diaries* (Ahmedabad, 1953), Vol. 1, p. 276.
19. Alain Geismar of the National Union of Higher Education (*SNESup*) in Herne Bourges and B. R. Brester (eds.), *Student Revolt* (London, 1968).
20. Fred H. Blum, *Work and Community* (London, 1968), p. 360.
21. Louis Fischer, *A Week with Gandhi* (New York, 1942).
22. *Harijan*, 21 December 1947.
23. *Harijan*, 4 August 1946.
24. *Bhoodan*, 8 September 1962.
25. *Harijan*, 26 July 1942, p. 238.
26. Pyarelal, *Mahatma Gandhi: the Last Phase* (New Delhi, 1966), Vol. 2, Appendix B, p. 819.
27. Bourges and Brester, *Student Revolt, op. cit.*, pp. 54-55.
28. G. N. Dhawan, *The Political Philosophy of Mahatma Gandhi* (Ahmedabad, 1967), p. 298.

9
Beyond Liberal Democracy: Thinking with Mahatma Gandhi*

Thomas Pantham

Gandhi's case against the West looks ... infinitely stronger than it looked, to us Westerners, thirty years ago.

– *G.D.H. Cole*[1]

Purna Swaraj or Integral Democracy

There is an increasing recognition by political theorists that contemporary liberal democracy is in a crisis that is not confined to the politico-economic sphere, but which has permeated the socio-cultural sphere.[2] The remedy, according to Jurgen Habermas, lies not so much in the critique of political economy as in the critique and supersession of the scientization of politics. In Sheldon Wolin's view, what is needed is nothing short of a long revolution, aimed at deconstituting the present structure of power.[3] In the present article, I shall try to show that such a project of deconstitution is contained in Gandhi's social theory and praxis. I shall try to demonstrate that Gandhi's theory - far from being 'all fine Ruskin-Tolstoyan rodomontade by a lawyer with a printing press'[4] or the primitivist yearnings of a withdrawn mystic - offers guidance in transforming what he called the 'nominal' democracy of the modern Western type into a truer or fuller democracy, which he referred to as *purna swaraj* (complete

* Reprinted with the permission of Sage Publications India Private Limited from Thomas Pantham and Kenneth L. Deutsch (eds.), *Political Thought in Modern India* (Delhi: Sage Publications, 1986), pp. 325-346.

or integral democracy), *ramarajya* ('sovereighty of the people based on pure moral authority'), or *sarvodaya* (a social order promoting the good of all).[5] I shall argue, moreover, that the Gandhian project is aimed at resolving a fundamental contradiction in the theory and practice of liberal democracy, namely, the contradiction between the affirmation of the freedom of the individual in the so-called private sphere of morality and its curtailment in the allegedly amoral or purely technical public/political sphere. I shall try to show that Gandhi repairs this contradiction by de-reifying the objectified state through *swaraj* (participatory democracy combining 'self-rule and self-restraint') and by integrating politics and morality through the *satyagraha* process of socio-political action.

Beyond Utilitarian Ethics

For a proper understanding of 'Gandhi's case against the West,' it is useful to note some of its parallels with Habermas' contemporary critique of the late capitalist state.[6] Both Gandhi and Habermas were reacting to the untruth of the legitimacy claims of the late capitalist state, whose imperialist and fascist manifestations revealed to them the false foundations of Western liberal democarcy. Looked at from the bottom up the contradictions of the late capitalist state were seen earlier in the periphery than at the centre of the world capitalist system.[7] In other words, the untruth of the state's claims to democratic legitimacy, which Habermas sees today in the advanced capitalist countries, was seen earlier by Gandhi in the peripheral states of South Africa and India, which were the arena of his 'experiments' with truthful or authentic politics.

State intervention in the economic, social, and cultural spheres in support of the private appropriation of public wealth is the common feature of the colonial societies and the present-day advanced capitalist countries. Such an interventionist state needs cultural legitimation because it is not engaged in maintaining the natural or inherent 'justice' of the exchange of equivalents as was believed to have been done by the invisible hand of the market in the early, liberal phase of capitalism. But, as Habermas has shown, what it actually experiences is a legitimation deficit; such culturally sanctioned norms of legitimation as possessive individualism, achievement ideology, and utilitarian ethics are offset by the political and administrative considerations, which, under state-managed capitalism, determine the social production and private appropriation of surplus value. Moreover, since such a state is not engaged in promoting 'the greatest good of all' (Gandhi) or 'the generalizable interests' of the people (Habermas), it lacks any basis for a truly democratic legitimation of its actions. To quote Habermas: 'Genuine participation of citizens in processes of political will-formation, that is, substantive democracy, would bring to consciousness the contradiction between administratively socialized production and the continued private appropriation and use of surplus value.'[8]

Gandhi too believed that the capitalist ethos and utilitarian principles militate against participatory or substantive democracy. He realized that 'this age of awakening of the poorest of the poor' is the 'age of democracy' and that the states that are today nominally democratic have either to become frankly totalitarian or, if they are to become truly democratic, they must become courageously non-violent.'[9] According to him, violence is antithetical to democracy because a social system based on the former 'cannot provide for or protect the weak,' while democracy requires that under it the weakest should have the same opportunity as the strongest.'[10] He therefore maintained that a truly democratic or non-violent social order 'is clearly an impossibility so long as the wide gulf between the rich and the hungry millions persists.'[11]

Early in his public life, Gandhi realized that he was a 'pariah untouchable' of the imperialist system, whose claims to be bearing the burden of 'civilizing' and 'democratizing' the colonies he found to be untrue or 'hypocritical'. For instance, taking the meaning of the Gujarati equivalent of 'civilization' as 'good conduct,' he found that what British imperialism did in the colonies was the opposite of it.[12] Similarly, he argued that the electoral democracies of Europe and America are only 'nominal democracies,' belonging to 'the same species' as fascism; both are exploitative systems and 'resort to ruthlessness to the extent required to compass their end.'[13] The only differences he saw between liberal democratic and fascist systems were that the violence of the latter was much better organized than that of the former, and that these 'have the backing of their peoples who imagine that they have a voice in their own government.'[14]

In an article in *Young India* in 1925, he clarified the deceptive, 'hypo critical,' one-dimensional nature of liberal democracy :

> The people of Europe have no doubt political power but no *Swaraj*. Asian and African races are exploited for their partial benefit, and they, on their part, are being exploited by the ruling class or caste *under the sacred name of democracy*. At the root, therefore, the disease appears to be the same as in India. The same remedy is, therefore, likely to be applicable. Shorn of all the camouflage, the exploitation of the masses of Europe is sustained by violence.[15]

As exploitative aspects of Western democracy, Gandhi referred to the British conquest of India 'not through democratic methods,' the white race's domination over the native and coloured people of South Africa, and the oppression of the Blacks in the United States. In an interview with an American journalist at Sevagram in April 1940, Gandhi said :

> My notion of democracy is that under it the weakest should have the same opportunity as the strongest. That can never happen except through non-violence. No country in the world today shows any but patronizing regard for the weak. The weakest, you say, go to the wall. Take your own case. Your land is owned by a few capitalist owners. The same is true of South Africa. These large holdings cannot be sustained except by violence, veiled if not open. Western democracy as it functions today is diluted Nazism or Fascism. At best it is merely a *cloak to hide the Nazi and the Fascist tendencies of imperialism*.[16]

At the outbreak of World War II, Gandhi reiterated his contention that fascism and nazism belonged to the same species as the so-called democracies' and that the end of the war 'will mean also the end of the rule of capital.'[17] He declared that the 'great powers will have to give up the imperialistic ambitions and exploitation of the so-called uncivilized or semicivilized nations of the earth and *revise their mode of life*.'[18] By this 'revision,' he meant the revision of the capitalist ethos. In an article published in 1925 under the title 'What of the West?' he clarified the nature of the needed revision as follows :

> From what will the masses be delivered? It will not do to have a vague generalization and to answer from 'exploitation and degradation'. Is not the answer this, that they want to occupy the status that capital does today? If so it can be attained only by violence. But *if they want to shun the evils of capital*, in other words, *if they would revise the view point of capital*, they would strive to attain a juster distribution of the products of labour. This immediately takes us to contentment and simplicity voluntarily adopted. *Under the new outlook, multiplicity of material wants will not be the aim of life*, the aim will be rather their restriction consistently with comfort. We shall cease to think of getting what we can, but we *shall decline to receive what all cannot get*.[19]

On another occasion, Gandhi defined his conception of true democracy as a post-capitalist social order in which 'inequalities based on possession and nonpossession, colour, race, creed or sex vanish' and 'land and state belong to the people'.[20]

In Gandhi's scheme of transcending the capitalist system, trusteeship is of central importance. That Gandhi envisaged trusteeship as a post-capitalist arrangement may be gathered from the following 'formula,' which he approved :

> Trusteeship provides a means of transforming the present capitalist order of society into an egalitarian one. It gives no quarter to capitalism, but gives the present owning class a chance of reforming itself. It is based on the faith that

> human nature is never beyond redemption. It does not recognize any right of private ownership of property, except inasmuch as it may be permitted by society for its own welfare.[21]

This new outlook of 'declining to receive what all cannot get' was Gandhi's alternative to the utilitarian norms of social organization. He said that the utilitarian, unlike the votary of sarvodaya, takes happiness 'to mean only physical happiness and economic prosperity' and is never willing to sacrifice himself.[22] Gandhi wrote :

> I do not believe in the doctrine of the greatest good of the greatest number. It means in its nakedness that in order to achieve the supposed good of 51 per cent the interest of 49 per cent may be, or rather, should be sacrificed. It is a heartless doctrine and has done harm to humanity. The only real, dignified, human doctrine is the greatest good of all, and this can be achieved by uttermost self-sacrifice.[23]

The Objectification of the State and the Curtailment of Freedom

The 'post-liberal' or post-capitalist thrust of Gandhi's theory of democracy, which I have highlighted above, has not been given sufficient emphasis by Gandhian scholars.[24] This is not without any justification. For, in Gandhi's writings, the main target of attack is the amoral, coercive state, and not any particular class. Not that Gandhi was oblivious of, or tolerant toward, the class conflicts of modern times. He did recognize the reality of class conflicts between capital and labour, and between landlords and landless labourers.[25] He also maintained that capitalism and zamindari should be 'sterilized and that in a truly democratic society, class conflicts would be transcended.[26] He, however, not only opposed the class war approach to social transformation but also regarded the domination by any particular class to be a lesser evil than the violence and oppression of the state. He believed, in other words, that human liberation from 'the evils of capital' is hampered by the fact that the class conflicts of the capitalist imperialist system have become enmeshed with and transformed by a basic conflict between the individual and the state, which, he said, 'represents violence in a concentrated and organized form.'[27] As if in anticipation of the Habermasian diagnosis of the crucial role of state intervention in the maintenance of the late capitalist system, Gandhi wrote that 'the violence of private ownership is less injurious than the violence of the State.'[28] While he recognized the need for mankind to move beyond the capitalist utilitarian system of social organization, he was convinced that 'if the State suppressed capitalism by violence, it will be caught in the coils of violence itself and fail to develop non-violence at any time.'[29] True to his belief in the integral nature of the means-ends continuum, he maintained that through violent means we cannot break out of 'the vicious circle of violence and exploitation'. He wrote :

> The whole reason why labour so often fails is that instead of sterilizing capital, as I have suggested, labour ... wants to seize that capital and become capitalist itself in the worse sense of the term. And the capitalist, therefore, who is properly entrenched and organized, finding among labourers also candidates for the same office, makes use of a portion of these to suppress labour.[30]

Gandhi's objection to the organized and concentrated violence of the state had to do with his commitment to individual freedom. 'The individual,' he said, 'is the one supreme consideration.'[31] 'If the individual ceases to count,' he asked, 'what is left of society?'[32] If fact, Gandhi's entire social theory and praxis were aimed at using and extending civil liberties for the democratization of 'the whole social structure'.[33] He shared the liberal concern for individual freedom. But he found the liberal and liberal-democratic method of securing social order through the supposedly amoral, objectified state to be at the expense of the political dimension of the freedom of the individual. He, therefore, sought to redeem individual freedom even in the political sphere without endangering social harmony. He, in other words, attempted to resolve the contradiction in the theory and practice of liberal democrcay between the *affirmation* of individual freedom in the so-called private sphere of morality and its *curtailment* in the allegedly amoral or purely technical public/political sphere. Let me explain this.

Unlike the pre-liberal world-views, the modern, liberal ideology recognizes the individual's freedom of judgement, choice, contrast, and possessions. This has historically been 'a vast emancipatory achievement for mankind.'[34] But the ensuing inequalities in property and the clash of individual, private interests and judgements, which were unleashed by the liberal revolution, endangered social order. The liberal and liberal-democratic answer to this problem of social order was the invention of a *political* form of government, which excluded individual *private* judgements.[35] That is, the 'rule of one man' (i.e., rule through an individual's private judgement) was replaced by the republican form of government, which, with the eventual democratization of the franchise, became the liberal-democratic state. This state of the 'political' is supposed to be autonomous form or external to, the rest of social life; the standards of expediency or effectiveness of the former are assumed to be divorced from private, moral standards. That the constitution of the liberal-democratic state is based on this artificial dichotomization of social life into the public (i.e., the political) and the private, the amoral and the moral, is argued by Carole Pateman :

> The liberal answer to the problem of social order inherent in such a society was to divide social life into two spheres and to substitute for shared principles a 'political method' or procedure for arbitrating between the conflicting individual interests and deciding on the 'public interest'. In the private sphere of social life, individuals' non-political natural rights are given actual expression; this is the proper sphere for individuals to exercise their private judgement and pursue their interests. In the political sphere individual private judgement is excluded, the natural political right is given up and decisions are made on behalf of individuals by specially chosen representatives.[36]

These representatives, as Pateman goes on to point out are supposedly engaged in representing 'the political or public interest, not the separate, conflicting interests of individuals.'[37] Political decisions are thus assumed to be value-neutral, procedural, or, technical decisions. Similarly, democracy is reduced to an allegedly amoral 'political method,' which, unlike integral or participatory democracy, only gives the people 'the opportunity of accepting or refusing the men who are to rule them.'[38] These rulers or representatives are supposed to embody 'the political selves, the citizen selves, of the members of the community.'[39]

Thus, in liberal democratic theory and practice, the political is reified and objectified into the representative state, which becomes the bearer of the alienated political rights of the citizens. This is what I meant when I said above that there is a fundamental contradiction in liberal democratic theory and practice between the affirmation of individual freedom in the private sphere and its curtailment in the public/political sphere.

Actually, the objectification of the political into the state and its privatization and hierarchization by the technocrats of power, which militate against the requirements of participatory or substantive democracy, serve the requirements of the capitalist-industrial system for state intervention in the process of capital accumulation.[40]

It needs to be emphasized that this technocratization of politics has been going on even in the liberal democracies. Under favourable socio-historical conditions, liberal democracy has indeed served as a peaceful mechanism of securing formal democratic legitimacy for the state. But when the masses have used or threatened to use their civil liberties for pushing the electoral or formal democracies in the direction of a substantive or participatory democracy, which would have offset the state-managed private accumulation of socially produced surplus value, the technocrats of power have raised the cry of 'governability crisis' and have used coercive methods to depoliticize the mass public, thereby further objectifying the state and privatizing it as a purely technocratic enterprise.[41]

Gandhi, as we saw in the foregoing, attacked the late-modern capitalist state for its fascist proclivities. He believed that the de-reification of the objectified state was necessary for redeeming the political dimension of individual freedom: 'I look upon an increase in the power of the State with the greatest fear, because, although while apparently doing good by minimizing exploitation, it does the greatest harm to mankind by destroying *individuality which lies at the root of all progress*.[42]

He maintained that the state is a 'soulless machine' and that amoral politics 'encircle us like the coils of snake.' He therefore sought to repair the liberal democratic one-dimensionalization of freedom and democracy without endangering social harmony by combining *swaraj* (participatory democracy) with the satyagraha mode of integrating politics and morality. He professed his aims in the following words, in which, as he himself clarified elsewhere, 'religious' is used interchangeably with 'moral' or 'spiritual' 'I could not be leading a religious life unless I identified myself with the whole of mankind and that I could not do unless I took part in politics. The whole gamut of a man's activities today constitutes an indivisible whole.'[43] As we see in this quote, the two parts of Gandhi's redemptive project are participatory democracy and the spiritualization of politics.

Swaraj or Participatory Democracy

On several occasions, Gandhi criticized the liberal-democratic reification, objectification, and technocratization of the political and the alienation of the people's political rights. He also put forward the alternative of participatory democracy, which ruptures the positivist disjunction between subject and object, means and ends. To quote him :

> A superficial study of British history has made us think that all power percolates to the people from parliaments. The truth is that power resides in the people and it is entrusted for the time being to those whom they may choose as their representatives.[44]

> Let us not push the mandate theory to ridiculous extremes and become slaves to resolutions of majorities .... Swaraj

> will be an absurdity if individuals have to surrender their judgement to majority.[45]

> The very essence of democracy is that every person represents all the varied interests which compose the nation. It is true that it does not exclude, and should not exclude, special representation of special interests, but such representation is not its test. It is a sign of its imperfection.[46]

> True democracy cannot be worked by twenty men sitting at the Centre. It has to be worked from below by the people of every village.[47]

While admitting that the necessity of a 'central government administration' cannot be ruled out, Gandhi maintained that it need not and ought not be patterned after 'the accepted Western form of democracy'.[48] His objection was to the central government administration becoming the bearer of the alienated political rights of the citizens. 'Under my plan', he said, 'the State will be there to carry out the will of the people, not to dictate to them or force them to do its will.'[49] While he did caution us against converting democracy into mobocracy, he insisted that 'democracy is an impossible thing until the power is shared by all.' He said, 'Most people do not understand the complicated machinery of the government. They do not realize that every citizen silently but nonetheless certainly sustains the government of the day in ways of which he has no knowledge.'[50] Elsewhere he added :

> real swaraj will come not by the acquisition of authority by a few but by the acquisition of the capacity by all to resist authority when it is abused. In other words, swaraj is to be attained by educating the masses to a sense of their capacity to regulate and control authority.[51]

As I said earlier, Gandhi recognised the need for a 'central government administration'. But he said it should be structured not as a pyramid but as an oceanic circle :

> In this structure composed of innumerable villages, there will be ever-widening, never-ascending circles. Life will not be a pyramid with the apex sustained by the bottom. But it

will be an oceanic circle whose centre will be the individual always ready to perish for the village, the latter ready to perish for the circle of villages, till at last the whole becomes one life composed of individuals, never aggressive in their arrogance but ever humble, sharing the majesty of the oceanic circle of which they are integral units.[52]

Politics and Ethics

Gandhi's project of the redemption of political freedom by the individual from the objectified state through participatory democracy is not to be taken to mean that he was unconcerned with the problem of social order. Paradoxic though it may seem, Gandhi, who, compared to the liberal democratic theories, had a greater concern for individual freedom, also had a greater concern for social harmony. He felt that the liberal democratic scheme of securing social order through the supposedly amoral machinery of government not only curtailed individual freedom, but also failed to bring about any lasting or authentic social harmony. He believed that the observance of social norms 'consciously and as a matter of duty' not only was a more secure foundation for social order than their observance for reasons of legality or out of fear of external sanctions but was also conducive to individual freedom. According to him, therefore, both individual freedom and social harmony could be ensured if the participatory process of reclaiming political freedom from the objectified state was *eo ipso* a process of the spiritualization of politics or the reintegration of politics with morality. Anticipating Habermas' contention that the technocratic model of politics is at the expense of democracy and that a society can be ordered democratically 'only as a self-controlled learning process' of communicative ethics,[53] Gandhi said his conception of true democracy was one of 'the reign of the self-imposed law of moral restraint.'[54] He held that 'by learning to adjust his individualism to the requirements of social progress' man could move in the direction of a truly democratic order.[55]

In fact, it was the divorce of politics from morality that Gandhi found most objectionable in the 'modern civilization,' which arose in, and spread out from, the West. In his famous book, *Hind Swaraj*, which he wrote on board the *S.S. Kildonan* during his return voyage to South Africa from England in 1908, he declared. 'This civilization takes note neither of morality nor of religion.'[56] In a lecture he gave at the Muir Central College, Allahabad, in December 1916, he said that it was his 'firm belief that there is little to gain from Britain in intrinsic morality' and that 'if we copy her because she provides us with rulers, both they and we shall suffer degradation.'[57] He therefore proposed and experimented with an action project, namely, satyagraha, for superseding the modernist, amoral, elitist paradigm of government. That action project, it may be noted in passing, ruptures the modern, positivist dichotomies between subject and object, means and ends, politics and morality. Regarding the last mentioned dichotomies, Gandhi wrote that social life 'is not divided into water-tight compartments, called social, political and religious' and that 'every act...has its...spiritual, economic and social implications.'[58] He referred to his ideal of true democracy as 'the square of *swaraj*,' whose four sides are the political, the economic, the social, and *dharma* (i.e., universal morality).[59] The morality or spirituality, which, according to Gandhi, is to be reintegrated with politics, is not any revealed, sectarian religion, but sarvodaya ethics or universal morality. 'The highest moral law,' he said, 'is that we should unremittingly work for the good of mankind.'[60] He singled out truth and non-violence as the most important moral norms, which, he pointed out, 'are no cloistered virtues' but are to be discovered and formed through 'the ordinary activities of life' in the economic, social, and political spheres.[61] Moreover, according to him, an action to be moral has to be done 'consciously and as a matter of duty'; actions that are 'dictated by fear or coercion' or 'promoted by hope of happiness in the next world cease to be moral.'[62] So, instead of withdrawing from politics, he, as I mentioned earlier, introduced and experimented with an emancipatory political project, namely, satyagraha, whose assumptions and action implications are different from those of liberal democracy.

Liberal political thought is based on a pessimistic, one-dimensional conception of man as a brutish and selfish being. It is this conception of man that lies behind the pre-occupation of the pre-democratic and democratic liberal thinkers with political devices or machinery rather than with action techniques for the resolution of social conflicts. The reified and objectified state is their answer to man's brutishness and selfishness. Their reasoning is that because men are brutish and selfish, social order can be secured, not through an action by the individuals, but through the structure of political machinery. This structure is meant to facilitate the process of bargaining and compromise in situations of conflict over relatively minor issues and to impose order through violent force when the conflict is of a fundamental nature. Thus, liberal democratic theory provides no technique of action for avoiding violent revolution in the face of fundamental social conflicts, for example, conflict over the legitimacy claims of the state.

Gandhi argued that if we adopt the pessimistic, one-dimensional conception of man and rely only on the structure of political machinery for securing social harmony, the stronger among the selfish will use that machinery as an additional means of domination or oppression. It is to avoid this vicious circle of violence and exploitation that Gandhi made an inversion of the Hobbes-to-Lenin approach to political theorizing. He based his theory and practice of democracy on a realistic, integral conception of human nature, which, while not denying man's selfishness, acknowledges his potential for rationality and goodness. Accordingly, Gandhi's action project of satyagraha has the twin objectives of enabling humanity to realize its potential for rationality and goodness, and thereby securing a moral or democratically legitimate social order. He wrote that 'the desire to improve ourselves for the sake of doing good to others is truly moral.[63] He discussed the distinctiveness of his assumptions in the following words :

> Socialism and communism of the West are based on certain conceptions which are fundamentally different from ours. One such conception is their belief in the essential selfishness of human nature. I do not subscribe to it for I know that the essential difference between man and the brute is that the former can respond to the call of the spirit

> in him, can rise superior to the passions that he owns in common with the brute, and, therefore, superior to selfishness and violence, which belong to the brute nature and not the immortal spirit of man. That is the fundamental conception of Hinduism.[64]

> In the application of the method of non-violence, one must believe in the possibility of every person, however depraved, being reformed under human and skilled treatment. We must appeal to the good in human beings and expect response.[65]

While the pre-democratic liberal theorists assumed the brutishness of man and justified the role of the Leviathan in maintaining social order, the liberal-democratic theorists assume that men are atomistic beings and that their interests are to be regarded by the political sphere as being morally neutral. For the liberal democrate all the interests of all the people are of equal worth; he does not discriminate between morally justifiable and immoral interests. For him, the task or 'business' of the 'democratic method' is to accommodate or adjust the supposedly amoral interests of the people or, at least, of those who take part in politics.[66] Accordingly, as Immanuel Kant wrote, the problem of securing social order is a problem of arranging :

> the powers of each selfish inclination in opposition... so that one moderates or destroys the ruinous effect of the other. The consequence for reason is the same as if none of them existed, and *man is forced to be a good citizen even if not a morally good person*. The problem of organizing a state, however hard it may seem, can be solved even for a race of devils if only they are intelligent. The problem is: 'Given a multitude of a rational beings requiring universal laws for their preservation, but each of whom is secretly inclined to exempt himself from them, to establish a constitution in such a way that, although their private intentions conflict, they check each other, with the result that their public conduct is the same as if they had no such intentions.'[67]

Gandhi, as I pointed out earlier, repaired this modern scientistic/positivist divorce of morality from politics. He argued that if the stuff of politics is taken to be the atomistic, amoral conception of human interests, there would necessarily ensue the vicious circle of mindless competition, hierarchy, overcentralization and violent coercion. In his view, therefore, we cannot escape the inherent contradictions of liberal democracy without abandoning the liberal-individualistic conception of humanity and the atomistic, amoral conception of its interests. He argued that the promotion of human freedom and fulfilment and the building of human community depend on our ability and willingness to adopt a new conception of humanity and act on the basis of that new conception. That new conception is that humans are essentially social beings, that not all their interests or wants are of equal moral worth, and that they can be educated to discover and pursue their morally justifiable interests.

Satyagraha or Communitarian Ethics

Gandhi argued that we, as *isolated individuals*, are not the sufficient judges of the truth or moral worth of our interests, if they are to be embodied in socially binding norms, claiming democratic legitimacy. In his weekly, *Harijan*, of 31 March 1946, he wrote: 'Individual liberty and interdependence are both essential for life in society.' Again :

> I value individual freedom, but you must not forget that man is essentially a social being. He has risen to the present status by learning to adjust his individualism to the requirements of social progress. Unrestricted individualism is the law of the beast of the jungle. We have learnt to strike the mean between individual freedom and social restraint. Willing submission to social retraint for the sake of the well-being of the whole society enriches both the individual and the society of which one is a member.[68]

According to Gandhi, therefore, only if our interest positions are capable of receiving the uncoerced acceptance of all those who are affected by them, can we advance any truthful or moral claim for their inclusion in socially binding norms. In other words, for Gandhi, as for Habermas, the critical principle of democracy is the principle of uncoerced, consensual or communitarian truth. Gandhi believed that even in situations of fundamental social conflict there is a potential harmony of the essentially human interests of the parties to the conflict.[69] It is for the discovery and formation of such communitarian truth that he developed his satyagraha mode of action.

In a satyagraha movement, the contested truth of social 'system' or norm is sought to be validated through three steps : (i) persuading the opponents through reasoning and being open to, and inviting, the counter-persuasive efforts of the opponets; (ii) appealing to the opponents through the self-suffering of the satyagrahis; and (iii) non-cooperation and civil disobedience.

The various methods of satyagraha are : (a) purifactory or penitential actions by the satyagrahis, such as pledges, prayers, and fasts; (b) acts of non-cooperation, such as boycott, strikes, *hartal*, and the like; (c) acts of civil disobedience such as picketing, non-payment of taxes, and defiance of specific laws; and (d) works of constructive programmes, such as the promotion of intercommunal unity, the removal of untouchability, adult education, and the removal of economic and social inequalities. At each stage of the programme, the satyagrahis, while holding on to the truth as they see it, assume their own fallibility and give the opponents every chance to prove that the satyagrahis' position is erroneous. Satyagraha 'excludes the use of violence because man is not capable of knowing the absolute truth and therefore not competent to punish. The ideal to be kept in mind is that of a self-regulated society of communitarian truth, in which every one rules himself in such a manner that he is never a hindrance to his neighbour.[70] 'The claim for satyagraha,' writes Joan Bondurant, 'is that through the operation of non-violent action the truth as judged by the fulfilment of human needs will emerge in the form of a mutually satisfactory and agreed-upon solution.'[71] Hence the important operative principles to be observed by the satyagrahis are the admission of truths as relative, non-violence and toleration, and the self-suffering of the satyagrahis. Gandhi justified these operative principles in the following passages :

> In the application of satyagraha, I discovered in the earliest stages that pursuit of Truth did not admit of violence being inflicted on one's opponent, but that he must be weaned from error by patience and sympathy. For what appears to be Truth to the one may appear false to the other.[72]
>
> The golden rule of conduct, therefore, is mutual toleration, seeing that we will never all think alike and we see truth in fragment and from different angles of vision. Conscience is not the same thing for all. Whilst, therefore, it is a good guide for individual conduct, imposition of that conduct upon all will be an insufferable interference with everybody's freedom of conscience.[73]
>
> People's conceptions of true interests and just laws differ. That is the main reason why violence is eliminated and a satyagrahi gives his opponent the same right of independence and feelings of liberty that he reserves to himself and he will fight by inflicting injuries on his person.[74]
>
> Evolution of democracy is not possible if we are not prepared to hear the other side. We shut the doors of reason when we refuse to listen to our opponents, or having listened, make fun of them. *If intolerance becomes a habit, we run the risk of missing the truth*. Whilst, with the limits that Nature has put on our understanding, we must act fearlessly according to the light vouchsafed to us, we must always keep an open mind and be ever ready to find that what we believed to be truth was, after all, untruth. This openness of mind strengthens the truth in us.[75]

Regarding the third operative principle of satyagraha, namely, self-suffering, Gandhi believed that it was an extension of the non-violent method or, in other words, 'the chosen substitute for violence to others'.[76] He believed that through self-suffering, the satyagrahis could make extra-rational appeals to their opponents, who may thereby be moved to make the big change expected of them. 'I have found,' he wrote, 'that mere appeal to reason does not answer where prejudices are age-long and based on supposed religious authority. Reason has to be strengthened by suffering.'[77] Further,

> Suffering is the law of human beings; war is the law of the jungle. But suffering is infinitely more powerful than the law of the jungle for converting the opponent and opening his ears, which are otherwise shut, to the voice of reason. Nobody has probably drawn up more petitions or espoused more forlorn causes than I, and I have come to this fundamental conclusion that if you want something really important to be done, you must not merely satisfy the reason, you must move the heart also. The appeal of reason is more to the head, but the penetration of the heart comes from suffering. It opens up the inner understanding of men. Suffering is the badge of the human race, not the sword.[78]

Another reason given for the principle of self-suffering was that it served as the proof of the truthfulness and courage of the satyagrahis.

> Just as one must learn the art of killing in the training for violence, so one must learn the art of dying in the training for non-violence... The votary of non-violence has to cultivate the capacity for sacrifice of the highest type in order to be free from fear... He who has not overcome all fear cannot practise *ahimsa* to perfection.[79]

The Effectiveness of Satyagraha

Several critics of satyagraha have maintained that non-violence and self-suffering and impractical methods against violent oppression, and that self-suffering is too high a price demanded of the democratic emancipators. The Gandhian ideal, they argue, is 'other-worldly, anti-humanist'. For instance, George Orwell has argued that we 'must choose between God and Man,' and that 'Gandhi's teachings cannot be squared with the belief that man is the measure of all things and that our job is to make life worth living on this earth.'[80] Gandhi's great compatriot Lokmanya Tilak, too believed that the Gandhian project of integrating politics and morality was unsuited to this-worldly concerns. In his famous letter to Gandhi, he wrote that politics 'is a game of worldly people and not of *sadhus*,' and that the approach of Sri Krishna is more suited to this world than the Buddhist approach.[81]

In his reply to the Lokmanya (Tilak), Gandhi averred that non-violence and self-suffering were 'not for the unworldly but essentially for the worldly'. He did admit that those principles were very difficult to practise but insisted that we need to, and can, keep on moving along those lines. 'Perfect non-violence whilst you are inhabiting the body,' he wrote, 'is only a theory like Euclid's point or straight line, but we have to endeavour every moment of our lives.'[82] He elaborated this analogy in the following manner: 'Euclid's line is one without breadth but no one has so far been able to draw it and never will. All the same it is only by keeping the ideal line in mind that we have made progress in geometry.'[83] Similarily, 'A government cannot succeed in becoming entirely non-violent, because it represents all the people... But I do believe in the possibility of a predominantly non-violent society. And I am working for it.'[84]

Gandhi maintained that both in the liberal democracies and in dicatorships, satyagraha is an effective way of bringing about a truly democratic transformation of the society. He realized that both violent and non-violent resistance by the oppressed and the exploited become the objects of state surveillance and repression. But he believed that satyagraha has distinctive claim to ennobling consequences and to emancipatory effectiveness as it releases the forces of freedom and love for undermining the paradigm of violence. He pointed out that satyagraha, unlike violent resistance, is 'three-fourths invisible and only one-fourth visible,' and that even though it may appear to be ineffective in its visibility, it is 'really intensely active and most effective in ultimate result.' He illustrated and elaborated this argument as follows :

> A violent man's activity is most visible, while it lasts. But it is always transitory. What can be more visible than the Abyssinians done to death by Italians? There it was lesser violence pitted against much greater. But if the Abyssinians had retired from the field and allowed themselves to be slaughtered, their seeming inactivity would have been much more effective though not for the moment visible. Hitler and Mussolini on the one hand and Stalin on the other are

able to show the immediate effectiveness of violence. But it will be as transitory as that of Chenghis' slaughter. But the effects of Buddha's non-violent action persist and are likely to grow with age. And the more it is practised, the more effective and inexhaustible it becomes.[85]

Regarding the effectiveness of satyagraha against dictatorships, Gandhi wrote :

> Even a Nero is not devoid of a heart. The unexpected spectacle of endless rows upon rows of men and women simply dying rather than surrender to the will of an aggressor must ultimately melt him and his soldiery. Practically speaking, there will be probably no greater loss in men than if forcible resistance was offered; there will be no expenditure in armaments and fortifications. The non-violent training received by the people will add inconceivably to their moral height.[86]

Aldous Huxlcy too believed in the effectiveness and practicality of the Gandhian approach. He wrote :

> In the years ahead it seems possible that satyagraha may take root in the West, *not primarily as the result of any 'change of heart,' but simply because it provides the masses, especially in the conquered countries, with their only practicable form of political action*. The Germans of the Ruhr and Palatinate resorted to *satyagraha* against the French in 1923. The movement was spontaneous, philosophically, ethically and organizationally, it had not been prepared for. It was for this reason that it finally broke down. But it lasted long enough to prove that a Western people - and a people more thoroughly indoctrinated with militarism than any other - was perfectly capable of non-violent direct action, involving the cheerful acceptance of sacrificial suffering.[87]

The sceptic may still object to Gandhi's project on the ground that the individual freedom which he redeems from the objectified, amoral state is sacrificed on the altar of satyagraha, which demands the satyagrahis' self-suffering even unto death. Actually, this is not so.

An element of sacrifice is indeed involved in satyagraha. So also in the case of violent resistance against oppression. Sacrifice even unto death is thus the common element in both the violent and non-violent resistance against oppression. That is why Gandhi approved of the use of satyagraha only in cases of conflict over fundamental issues and only after all milder methods of non-violence have failed. 'I should be deeply distressed', he wrote in 1921, 'If on every conceivable occasion every one of us were to be a law unto oneself and to scrutinize in golden scales every action of our future National Assembly. I would surrender my judgement in most matters to national representatives taking particular care in making my choice of such representative.'[88] But when a situation of violent oppression persists even after all milder methods of non-violent resistance have been tried, Gandhi maintained that the self-suffering even unto death of the non-violent fighter for communitarian truth is a truer assertion of individual freedom than is the death-in-defeat of the violent resister. Gandhi rejected the charge that the non-violence and self-suffering of the satyagrahis are 'a resignation from all real fighting against wickedness'. 'On the contrary,' he stated :

> The non-violence of my conception is a *more active and more real fighting against wickedness than retaliation whose very nature is to increase wickedness.* I contemplate a mental, and therefore a moral, opposition to immoralities. I seek entirely to blunt the edge of the tyrant's sword, not by putting up against it a sharper-edged weapon, but by disappointing his expectation that I would be offering physical resistance.[89]

Gandhi's Audience

Gandhi did not theorize in any historical vacuum or for any atemporal audience. He and his addresses experienced the initial impact of the modern, technocratic, overorganized paradigm of politics. His audience was not confined to the East; it included the people of the West as well. What was needed for human emancipation, he argued, was not any 'revised edition' of the same technocratic paradigm of government (such as, the fascist and Leninist-Stalinist systems), but an alternative, non-violent, educative, mass-based approach to democratization. 'Satyagraha,' he asserted, is a process of educating public opinion, such that it covers all the elements of society and, in the end, makes itself irresistible. *Violence interrupts the process and prolongs the real revolution of the whole structure.*'[90] The method of violence, he said, not only fails to lead us out of the vicious circle of violence and exploitation' but also contributes to the culture of violence and thereby delays the start of the truly emancipatory process. He said :

> The socialists and communists say they can do nothing to bring about economic equality today... They say, 'when they get control over the State they will enforce equality.' Under my plan, the State will be there to carry out the will of the people, not to dictate to them or force them to do its will. I shall bring about economic equality through non-violence, by converting the people to my point of view by harnessing the forces of love as against hatred. *I will not wait till I have converted the whole society to my view but will straightaway make a beginning with myself.* It goes without saying that I cannot hope to bring about economic equality of my conception, if I am the owner of fifty motor cars or even if ten bighas of land. For that I have to reduce myself to the level of the poorest of the poor.[91]

In the Gandhian approach, the oppressed masses are not to be made the objects of domination by their so-called emancipators. Also, the goal of the emancipatory process is not simply to raise the poor to the position of their oppressors, which Gandhi said would be a within-paradigm move, enhancing the forces of violence. The end pursued rather is removing the ignorance of the poor and teaching them to non-cooperate with their exploiters'[92] and thereby bring about a 'real revolution of the whole structure' so that all the members of the initial conflict situation may find their true or moral human interests in a new, communitarian synthesis. As Ashis Nandy has noted, 'All his life, Gandhi sought to free the British rather than the Indians from the clutches of imperialism and the Brahmins rather than the untouchables from the caste system.[93]

Thus the Gandhian praxis of the quest for communitarian truth through non-violence and self-suffering shakes the foundations of both the pluralist-elitist and vanguardist-bureaucratic variants of the late-modern, amoral, technocratic paradigm of government. Hence, as Brian Fay has noted perceptively, Gandhi's praxis of 'educative transformation' through 'free and uncoerced communication' makes him 'the most significant political theorist... in the context of mass society.'[94] Gandhi himself believed that satyagraha was not only an effective and heroic mode of emancipation of the people of a weak country, but also a beacon light... for Europe with all its *discipline, science and organization*. If Europe but realized that, heroic as it undoubtedly is for a handful of people to offer armed resistance in the face of superior numbers, it is far more heroic to stand up against overwhelming numbers without any arms at all, it would save itself and blaze a trail for the world.[95]

Notes and References

1. G.D.H. Cole, *Reflections on 'Hind Swaraj' by Western Thinkers* (Bombay: Theosophy Company, 1948), p. 17. See also note 5 below.

2. Jurgen Habermas, *Legitimation Crisis,* tr. Thomas McCarthy (Boston: Beacon Press, 1975); William Connolly, *Appearance and Reality in Politics* (Cambridge University Press, 1981); Christian Bay, *Strategies of Political Emancipation* (University of Notre Dame Press, 1981, and Bombay: Somaiya, 1982); Alan Wolfe, *The Limits of Legitimacy: Political Contradictions of Contemporary Capitalism* (New York: Free Press, 1977); Daniel Bell, *The Cultural Contradictions of Capitalism* (New York: Basic Books, 1976); George Kateb, 'On the "Legitimation Crisis", *Social Research* (Winter 1979); and Richard Lowenthal, 'Political Legitimacy and Cultural Change in West and East,' *Social Research* (Automn 1979).

3. Sheldon Wolin, 'The People's Two Bodies,' *Democracy* (January 1981), p. 24. That 'the world needs cultural alternatives to the dominant Western paradigm of development' is argued in Rajni Kothari, 'Symposium

on a New International Development Strategy: A Report.' *Alternatives*, Vol. 5 (1979-80).

4. George Catlin, *In the Path of Mahatma Gandhi* (Macdonald, 1948), p. 245, as cited in Raghavan N. Iyer, *The Moral and Political Thought of Mahatma Gandhi* (Delhi: Oxford University Press, 1973), p. 30.

5. Gandhi's most significant tract on political thought is his *Hind Swaraj* (Ahmedabad: Navajivan, 1938). There anthologies particularly useful for the present article are M.K. Gandhi, *Democracy: Real and Deceptive*, comp. R.K. Prabhu (Ahmedabad: Navajivan, 1942); M.K. Gandhi, *Sarvodaya* (Ahmedabad: Navajivan, 1954). Among the secondary sources, the most comprehensive and penetrating is R.N. Iyer, *Moral and Political Thought*. Special mention may also be made of Joan Bondurant, *Conquest of Violence: The Gandhian Philosophy of Conflict* (Bombay: Oxford University Press, 1959); Buddhadeva Bhattacharya, *Evolution of the Political Philosophy of Gandhi* (Calcutta: Calcutta Book House, 1969); and Arne Naess, *Gandhi and Group Conflict* (Oslo: Universitatforlaget, 1974).

6. Habermas, *Legitimation Crisis*. I have benefited from the treatment of Habermas' theory in Thomas McCarthy, *The Critical Theory of Jurgen Habermas* (Cambridge, MA: MIT Press, 1978).

7. Some of the implications of the world-system perspective for comparative political analysis are spelt out in Immanuel Wallerstein, 'The Rise and Future Demise of the World Capitalist System: Concepts for Comparative Analysis', *Comparative Studies in Society and History* (September 1974), pp. 387-415. See also Thomas Pantham, 'Integral Pluralism – A Political Theory for India?' *Indian Quarterly*, Vol. 36, Nos. 3-4 (July-December 1980).

8. Habermas, *Legitimation Crisis*, p. 36. For a related treatment of the relationship between participation and legitimacy, see Dennis F. Thompson, *The Democratic Citizen* (Cambridge University Press, 1970), pp. 62-64.

9. Gandhi, *Democracy: Real and Deceptive*, p. 68.
10. Gandhi, *Nonviolence in Peace and War*, Vol. 2, p. 269.
11. Gandhi, *Democracy: Real and Deceptive*, p. 68.
12. *The Collected Works of Mahatma Gandhi*, Vol. 10 (Government of India, Ministry of Information and Broadcasting), p. 37.
13. Gandhi, *Democracy: Real and Deceptive*, p. 78.
14. *Ibid.*, p. 9.
15. *Ibid.*, p. 76. Emphasis added.
16. *Ibid.*, p. 11. Emphasis added.
17. Gandhi, *Nonviolence in Peace and War*, Vol. 1, p. 373.
18. *Ibid.*, pp. 158-59. Emphasis added.
19. Gandhi, *Democracy: Real and Deceptive*, pp. 76-77. Emphasis added.
20. M.K. Gandhi, *Towards Lasting Peace*, ed. A.T. Hingorani (Bombay: Bharatiya Vidya Bhavan, 1956), p. 217.
21. This is the final version of a trusteeship formula which was originally drafted by Professor M.L. Dantwala and modified by Gandhi. See Pyarelal, *Mahatma Gandhi: The Last Phase*, Vol. 2 (Ahmedabad: Navajivan, 1958), pp. 633-34.
22. Gandhi, *Sarvodaya*, pp. 4, 7.
23. *The Diary of Mahadev Desai*, Vol. 1, tr. V.G. Desai (Ahmedabad: Navajivan, 1953). p. 149. Emphasis added.
24. Some notable exceptions are Ashis Nandy, 'From Outside the Imperium: Gandhi's Cultural Critique of the "West",' *Alternatives*, Vol. 7 (1981), pp. 171-94; J.D. Sethi, *Gandhi Today* (New Delhi: Vikas, 1978); and V.R. Mehta, *Beyond Marxism* (New Delhi: Manohar, 1978). On the notion of post-liberal democracy, see C.B. Macpherson, *Democratic Theory: Essays in Retrieval* (London: Oxford University Press, 1973), Ch. 9; and Alan Wolfe, *Limits of Legitimacy*.
25. See A.K. Das Gupta, 'Gandhi on Social Conflict,' *Economic and Political Weekly*, Vol. 3, No. 49 (7 December 1968);

Abha Pandya, 'Gandhi and Agrarian Classes,' *Economic and Political Weekly*, Vol. 13, No. 26 (1 July 1978); and V.K.R.V. Rao, 'Gandhi and Social Change,' *Mainstream*, Vol. 18, No. 11 (10 December 1979).

26. Gandhi, *Sarvodaya*, pp. 95-97.
27. *Ibid.*, p. 74.
28. *Ibid.* According to Habermas, 'State-regulated capitalism, which emerged from a reaction against the dangers to the system produced by open class antagonism, suspends class conflict.' Habermas, *Toward a Rational Society* (Boston: Beacon Press, 1970), p. 107. In *Legitimation Crisis* (p. 57), he speaks of 'a partial class compromise' under state-managed capitalism.
29. Gandhi, *Sarvodaya*, p. 74.
30. *Ibid.*, p. 92.
31. Gandhi in *Young India* (13 November 1924), p. 378.
32. Gandhi in *Harijan* (1 February 1942), p. 27.
33. Gandhi, *Nonviolence in Peace and War*, Vol. 1, p. 353, and Vol. 2, p. 61.
34. Christian Bay, *Strategies of Political Emancipation*, p. 21.
35. Carole Pateman, 'Sublimation and Reification: Locke, Wolin and the Liberal Democratic Conception of the Political,' *Politics and Society* (1975), p. 451.
36. *Ibid.*, p. 454.
37. *Ibid.*, p. 456.
38. For a critique of this democratic Methodism, see Thomas Pantham, 'On the Theory of Democracy: A Critique of "the Schumpeter Dahl Axis",' *Journal of the M.S. University of Baroda* (Social Sciences), Vols. 25-26, 1976-1977.
39. Pateman, 'Sublimation and Reification,' p. 456. Similarly, Benjamin R. Barber writes: 'The chief obstacle to political participation is, paradoxically, the chief instrument of political participation in the United States –

representation. Representation, intended by the Founders to mediate the value conflict between active local citizenship and effective central administration, has been far too efficacious; it has made citizens unnecessary,' Barber, *Political Participation and the Creation of Res Publica* (Bloomington, IN: Poynter Center, 1977), p. 10.

40. See Brian Fay, *Social Theory and Political Practice* (London: George Allen & Unwin, 1975), p. 46. Alvin Toffler writes: 'Representative government – what we have been taught to call democracy – was, in short, an industrial technology for assuring inequality.' Toffler, *The Third Wave* (Bantam Books, 1981), p. 77.
41. See Walter Dean Burnham, 'Thoughts on the "Governability Crisis" in the West,' *Washington Review of Strategic and International Studies* (July 1978), pp. 46-57; and Jurgen Habermas, 'The Public Sphere,' *New German Critique*, Vol. 3 (1974), pp. 49-55, as cited in T. McCarthy, *Critical Theory of Jurgen Habermas*, p. 382.
42. Gandhi, *Sarvodaya*, p. 74. Emphasis added.
43. D.G. Tendulkar, *Mahatma: Life of Mohandas Karamchand Gandhi*, Vol. 4 (Bombay: 1951-1954), pp. 387-88.
44. Gandhi, *Constructive Programme* (Ahmedabad: Navajivan, 1945), pp. 8-9.
45. Gandhi, *Democracy: Real and Deceptive*, p. 45.
46. *Ibid.*, p. 7.
47. *Ibid.*, p. 7.
48. As told to Louis Fischer. See Fischer, *A Week With Gandhi* (Bombay: International Book House, 1944), p. 44.
49. Gandhi, *Democracy: Real and Deceptive*, p. 70.
50. *Ibid.*, p. 30.
51. *Ibid.*, pp. 4-5.
52. *Ibid.*, pp. 73-74.

53. Habermas, as cited in T. McCarthy, *Critical Theory of Jurgen Habermas*, p. 331.
54. Gandhi, *Towards Everlasting Peace*, p. 217.
55. Gandhi, *Democracy: Real and Deceptive*, p. 32.
56. Gandhi, *Hind Swaraj*, p. 27.
57. Gandhi, *Economic and Industrial Life and Relations*, Vol. 2 (Ahmedabad: Navajivan, 1957), p. 8.
58. *Young India*, 2 March 1922, p. 131.
59. *Harijan* (2 February 1937), p. 374. Emphasis added.
60. M.K. Gandhi, *Ethical Religion*, tr. A. Ramaiyer (Madras: S. Ganesan, 1922), p. 7. Emphasis added.
61. *Harijan*, 8 May 1937, p. 98.
62. Gandhi, *Ethical Religion*, pp. 8-11.
63. *Ibid.*, p. 7.
64. M.K. Gandhi, *Socialism of My Conception* (Bombay, 1957), p. 270.
65. Gandhi, *Democracy: Real and Deceptive*, p. 64.
66. Alvin Toffler says that the votes are the atoms of the Newtonian mechanism of representive government. Toffler, *The Third Wave*, p. 72.
67. 'Perpetual Peace,' in L.W. Beck, ed., *Kant on History* (New York: 1963), p. 112. Emphasis added.
68. Gandhi, *Democracy: Real and Deceptive*, p. 32.
69. C.B. Macpherson has argued that an optimistic assumption about the potential harmony of the essentially human interests has always been at the root of the democratic vision. Macpherson, *Democratic Theory*, pp. 54-55. See also the discussion of Habermas' theory of communicative ethics in Thomas McCarthy, *Critical Theory of Jurgen Habermas*, and Stephen K. White, 'Reason and Authority in Habermas: A Critique of the Critics.' *American Political Science Review*, Vol. 74 (1980), pp. 1007-17.
70. Gandhi, *Sarvodaya*, p. 73.

71. Bondurant, *Conquest of Violence*, p. 195.
72. Gandhi, *Satyagraha* (Ahmedabad: Navajivan, 1958), p. 6.
73. *Young India*, 23 September 1926, p. 334.
74. *Young India*, 1919-1922, p. 18.
75. Gandhi, *Democracy: Real and Deceptive*, pp. 34-35, Emphasis added.
76. *Young India*, 8 October 1925, p. 345.
77. *Young India*, March 1925.
78. M.K. Gandhi, *India's Case for Swaraj* (Yeshanand, 1932), p. 369.
79. *Harijan*, 1 September 1940. For a discussion of Gandhi's conception of self-suffering as an efficient instrument of social persuasion, see W.H. Morris-Jones, 'Mahatma Gandhi – Political Philosopher?' *Political Studies* (February 1970).
80. George Orwell, 'Reflections on Gandhi,' *Partisan Review*, Vol. 16 (January 1949).
81. For Tilak's letter and Gandhi's reply to it, see *Young India*, January 1920.
82. Gandhi, *Nonviolence in Peace and War*, Vol. 1, p. 292.
83. Gandhi, *My Socialism* (Ahmedabad: Navjivan, 1959), pp. 49-50.
84. *Ibid.*, pp. 50-51.
85. Gandhi, *Nonviolence in Peace and War*, Vol. 1, pp. 128-29.
86. Gandhi, *Democracy: Real and Deceptive*, p. 21. That the 'inner strength' of the satyagrahi and not the civility of the opponent is the crucial requirement of the Gandhian satyagraha is persuasively argued by Indira Rothermund in her paper, 'Gandhi's Satyagraha and Hindu Thought,' in this volume, Unlike Gandhi, John Rawls is reluctant to command civil disobedience against dictatorships because they would use 'more repressive measures if the calculation of advantages points in this direction.'

Rawls, *A Theory of Justice* (Oxford: Clarendon Press, 1972), p. 387. For an excellent comparison of Rawls' and Gandhi's views, see Vinit Haksar, 'Rawls and Gandhi on Civil Disobedience,' *Inquiry*, Vol. 19 (Summer 1976), pp. 51-92.

87. Aldous Huxley, *Science, Liberty and Peace* (New York: Harper Brothers, 1946), pp. 7-8. Emphasis added.
88. Gandhi, *Nonviolence in Peace and War*, Vol. 1, pp. 22-23.
89. *Ibid.*, p. 44. Emphasis added.
90. *Harijan*, March 1946. Emphasis added.
91. Gandhi, *Democracy: Real and Deceptive*, pp. 69-70. Emphasis added.
92. *Ibid.*, p. 67. Gandhi believed that 'the rich cannot accumulate wealth without the cooperation of the poor in society. If this knowledge were to penetrate to and spread among the poor, they would become strong and would learn how to free themselves.' *Ibid.*, p. 66.
93. Ashis Nandy, 'Oppression and Human Liberation: Towards a Third World Utopia,' *Alternatives*, Vol. 4 (October 1978), p. 172.
94. Fay, *Social Theory and Political Practice*, pp. 100-1.
95. Gandhi, *A Pilgrimage for Peace* (Ahmedabad: Navajivan, 1950), p. 56. Emphasis added.

10 Problematizing Modernity: Gandhi's Decentering Impulse

Ronald J. Terchek

Gandhi Provides a powerful voice that challenges some of the central axioms of modernity. In the process, he champions those who have been ignored or dominated in the grand narrative of modernity and denies its claim that it is natural, objective, and neutral. For him, modernity is only one way of thinking, and frequently a flawed one at that. Among his major objections to modernity is its proclivity to deny the validity of other claims to knowledge/truth and to universalize its applications for all conditions.

Today, questioning modernity is widespread, and Gandhi's voice represents an early refusal to accept the story that modernity is telling about itself. In some ways, his critique is as radical as many post-modern efforts to challenge modernity, but in other ways, he departs markedly from most post-modern thinking.[1] He believes, for example, that it is possible to repair our fragmented world with a cosmological outlook and holds that truths exist and parts of them can be found and practised.

In this paper, I enlist Gandhi as a critic of the universalizing impulse and fatalism of late modernity and argue that his primary interest is in preserving the autonomy of individuals. I argue that Gandhi insists on questioning modernity, not to conclude that it has nothing to offer, but to maintain that modernity cannot

* Reprinted with the permission of Gandhi Peace Foundation and *Gandhi Marg* from *Gandhi Marg* (April-June, 2001), pp. 5-20.

set the exclusive standards of what constitutes the good life.[2] One reason he finds alternative logics require a hearing is not that they are invariably correct but that they offer contestation and controversy, that is, they are political.[3] On Gandhi's account, these lost or neglected alternatives usually grasp parts of the truth and often provide fresh ways of seeing the world and the means to challenge late modern versions of orthodoxy.

Gandhi's interrogation of modernity is one of a selective but skeptical borrower. Even though he finds the Enlightenment project encumbered with pretentious claims to know the truth, he sees no need to completely reject modernity out of hand.[4] Hence Gandhi talks about the equality of everyone in his assault on untouchability; he speaks of the rights of women, including their right to govern themselves; and he attacks colonialism as a negation of the modern ideal of equal regard and respect.

Gandhi's Problematizing Impulse

In whatever variant, post-modernism is characterized by its questioning of matters we commonly take as good, natural, or right in the modern era. In its efforts to unsettle and decenter the premises that moderns hold to be beyond the realm of scrutiny, the post-modern temper seeks to show how the constructedness of the modern world favours some over others, leads to practices of domination, and legitimizes disciplinary practices. In many ways, this approach parallels the problematizing proclivities of Gandhi who continually questions much that has been taken for granted in the modern world. He means to show that modernity is not neutral or objective but carries extraordinary costs, even though many of its products provide welcome goods. Gandhi extends his argument to claim that what the modern world has constructed is not the culmination of a universal rationality but a particular rationality that legitimizes disciplinary networks that deprive modern men and women of their autonomy, some more severely than others.

This critique can be seen in his quest for Indian national independence or what he calls *Hind Swaraj*. As an advocate for Indian independence, he claimed that his primary quarrel is not with the British; his fight is with modernity.[5] In its effort to become the dominant way we think and organize the world, modernity makes diversity and plurality remainders of a forgotten past. And Gandhi goes on to argue that Indian independence cannot mean only, or even primarily, Indian national sovereignty.[6] For him, it must mean that every Indian is self-governing. In this context, British imperialism is only a part of the problem.

As Gandhi understands matters, modernity advances the claim that its knowledge supersedes all other claimants to knowledge. On his account, it does this in several ways. For one, it introduces a science and a technology which can discover and produce things that traditional science and technology cannot. In the process, modernity introduces its own way of organizing things, determining what is important and what is not. And it does this, according to Gandhi, not with brute force, although this is sometimes employed, but by disciplining individuals into accepting the many practices of modernity as legitimate. On his account, too many Indians have already acquiesced in accepting claims of the superiority of modernity and have, in the process, been drawn into a web of discipline where they reconstitute themselves and their understanding of the world.[7] This can be seen in his observation that his "resistance to Western civilization is really a resistance to its indiscriminate and thoughtless imitation based on the assumption that Asians are fit only to copy everything that comes from the West".[8]

Gandhi's assaults on modernity emerge clearly in his famous, or infamous, attacks on modern medicine, railroads, and machinery in *Hind Swaraj.*[9] One way of reading Gandhi on these matters, and not an uncommon way in either India or elsewhere, is to find him reactionary. But there is another way of grasping his meaning and that is to notice that he wants to problematize the apparent benefits of science and technology and see it as constructed phenomena that hide their unwelcome consequences and disciplinary character. He believes that if he can demonstrate that modernity is not benign and that it carries its own forms of inequality, domination, and abnormalization, then he can energize Indians to mobilize and resist.[10]

This can be seen in his critique of science where he calls attention to its paradoxes. Science promises both control and the truth, but Gandhi questions these claims. He thinks that in a perverse and unexpected way, we have lost control of the march of science.[11] When he writes about medicine, for example, he fears people have handed over control of their bodies to others.[12] He also argues that modern medicine's focus on the individual body de-emphasizes other reasons for sickness (such as environmental).

Gandhi finds that as modern science reaches to control nature, it is frequently employed to control people. As he understands matters, India would not have been colonized without modern science which enables the British to assert their sovereignty. As he puts, "It is not the British people who are ruling India but it is modern civilization, through its railways, telegraph, telephones, and almost every invention which has been claimed to be a triumph of civilization."[13]

Science is animated by doubt, but no single discovery quiets its uncertainty about the world and conventional reason. Doubt has become, as Hannah Arendt observes, universalized in science which is ever-pressed to investigate new fields and, undermines, revises, and supplants its own current certainties.[14] For this reason, the knowledge provided by science can never be settled, fixed, or stable. Any home it finds on the earth is subject to reconstruction and, in time, to demolition and replacement. But Gandhi holds that ordinary people desire and require some measure of stability to build a self-governing life for themselves. As he understands matters, fluidity, novelty, and incessant change create background conditions that are confusing and fragmented. In such a world, we become both preoccupied with day-to-day problem-solving and less interested, Gandhi fears, in finding stable truths.

For all of his misgivings about modern science, he denies that he is "an opponent, a foe of science." Rather, he claims, he is concerned "about the misuse of science"[15] What this means in practice can only be controversial, but Gandhi insists that too often the subject-matter of modern scientific inquiry and the ways that science is applied are hardly neutral. Unless modern science is problematized, he argues, it will never be resisted. Even though Gandhi is not forthcoming about the appropriate boundaries for modern science and its uses, he insists that scientific knowledge should ultimately contribute to self-knowledge.[16] And he insists that its material benefits must be directed at the most vulnerable. For Gandhi, "the individual," not science or technology, "is the one supreme consideration."[17] With this is mind, he directs his problematizing efforts to a critique of the grand narrative of progress that is at the heart of modernity.[18]

The Grand Narrative

The grand narrative attempts to gather all of the disparate, sometimes messy, pieces of life and society into a coherent whole which explains why things are what they are and what must be done to make them fit better, if not perfectly. In the process, the grand narrative is able to assign labels to people, practices, and all sorts of other things, holding some are positive and some are not. From this perspective, some must be nurtured and some impeded and some must be counted as allies and some as enemies. The successful culmination of the grand narrative comes when we are left with only the positive, mature, and friendly. Such a stance characterizes Marxism, market analysis, and nationalism; but for Gandhi, these are expressions of the core problem, that is to say, modernity.

With the grand narrative, we are asked to surrender what is unique when it fails to conform to the plan and pace of progress. Progress becomes a benevolent but blind process that proclaims we are, on the whole, better off than we had been and promises that the future will be better still. Such promises can be honestly made and even met because of the specific meaning accorded to "better off" and because they receive their validation by looking at the successful members of the modernized sectors of society and ignoring the rest.

Gandhi recoils at this account because it smothers community and the autonomy he believes community promotes.

For him, autonomy is not to be confused with modern conceptions of individualism which, he insists, separates persons from one another. On Gandhi's reading of modern individualism, persons are largely left to their own devices and made respossible for the successes and failures that visit them. Gandhi fears that such a stance ignores how much individuals depend on others.

He cannot imagine human beings alone and isolated from one another. As I shall elaborate later, he places men and women in an interdependent cosmos where he imagines that they not only respect one another but also carry duties to each other. For Gandhi, human beings become autonomous when they are embedded in a vibrant community which provides them with moral standards to judge themselves as well as networks of cooperation which serve as a source of mutual assistance and respect.[19] For this to occur, Gandhi believes that power must be dispersed and inequalities narrowed. Then, he argues, a self can emerge that is confident in its own integrity as well as proud of the contribution it is making to the broader community.

But Gandhi does not believe this happens when modernity appears; initially, its occupation is partial. Some parts of society are modernized but others are not, and society becomes incoherent as the old and new parts move in different, often conflicting, directions. It frequently means that some are much worse off — socially, psychologically, economically, and / or politically — man they were before. From the story told in the grand narrative, however, this is a transition cost which, over time will lead to increasing productivity and growth, eventually reaching those now excluded. Notice this argument holds that modernity can keep its promises and is, therefore, the legitimate way to proceed. This Gandhi rejects. As he sees matters, modernity can never fulfil its promises. One reason is that they are incommensurable: greater growth requires more discipline; more science leads to more fragmentation; more individualism diminishes a sense of community and personal rsponsibility. Taken together, these consequences contradict the humanitarian impulses of modernity. The more modernity honours its economic promises of prosperity, the more it needs to normalize, regularize and supervise. From Gandhi's perspective, it cannot help but discipline deviant identities and diminish alternative ways of thinking and acting.

In accepting the grand narrative, according to Gandhi, individuals usually do not recognize what is happening to them and accept its story as natural and inevitable. As a consequence, they allow themselves to become the playthings of a historic process they cannot fully understand, much less control. The idea of inevitable progress introduces, for someone like Gandhi, not a march to emancipation but a new form of fatalism which disenfranchises individuals who are now assigned places in a process outside of their reach and control.

Modern Fatalism

The grand narrative tells a story about how many of the most important things in the world and the people we have become are matters that cannot be significantly otherwise. If we stop growth, then the economy falls apart. If we do away with centralization and bureaucratic structures, we invite chaos. If we challenge complexity, we give up all kinds of future good things. If we undermine progress, we unglue all that is positive. If, if, if, ... then all kinds of bad things happen. However, Gandhi finds that we do not control growth, progress, centralization, bureaucracies, or complexity. He fears that we have allowed ourselves, in very critical ways, to be controlled by them. Here I have in mind much more than such matters as bureaucratic regulations which tell us to do this but not that or economic imperatives that displace traditional occupations, although each is part of the picture for Gandhi.

Rather, I argue that Gandhi holds that because (and not in spite of) modernity, the transformations that mark the late modern period, human beings are not, in the ordinary course of events, in control. A process (or many processes) beyond their comprehension propel matters along. The best that people can do is to explain matters after the fact and hope for the best in the future. However much we critique the mega institutions that have become a central part of late modern society and the practices associated with the modern metanarrative of progress, matters do not seem to respond appreciably to our best efforts.[21] This fatalism in the late modern era is something that Gandhi finds disturbing and debilitating.

Are we, then, fated to take the current situation as intractable, carried along by an uncontrollable momentum and robbed of the chance to have a say in these matters? To have a say about who we are? Gandhi things not.[22] To have a chance in gaining some of the control we want, he thinks it is necessary to have a clear understanding of the causes that distress us. This leads him to question modernity at its core. He takes up the axioms and assumptions we take for granted and exposes their consequences.

For Gandhi, this can lead to *satyagraha* or civil disobedience which can be seen as not only challenging injustice but also fatalism. In mounting challenges to what appears to be solid and permanent obstacles that are unaffected by human aspirations or actions, Gandhi holds that apparently weak and powerless individuals are now able to take charge of their own lives. On Gandhi's account, this sometimes leads to change, but even when it does not, he believes that the moral assertiveness of individuals put them in charge of what they make important and what they do. In his own life, Gandhi confronts fatalism with his civil disobedience, taking on the British empire and challenging the cultural and religious elite of India.

Gandhi's Archaeology

In order to resist the totalizing claims and fatalism carried by the grand narrative, Gandhi offers his own archaeological approach to digging out truth as a way of empowering those who have been dominated or marginalized by the prevailing order, whether traditional or modern.[23] In proceeding in his nonacademic way, he devotes himself to uncovering actual practices that disable and then challenges them. In his archaeological excavations, he searches for fragments of the truth that he believes have been covered over. For Gandhi, these fragments speak to the autonomy of all persons as well as to the transcendent nature of everyone. What follows in this section focuses on Gandhi's excavations of his own tradition, but he employs an archaeological strategy in his critique of modernity.

As he understands matters, each tradition expresses fragments of the truth in its own vernacular and symbols. But because these are the expressions of human beings they are subject both to the decay that describes the human condition as well as to the possibilities for renewal and revitalization.[24] His archaeological exercises have three dimensions. One is to identify the fragments of the truth he believes lie at the core of traditions, including his own; a second is to uncover the layers of sediment that have hidden the core and seek to stand in its place. Finally, he means to convey the findings of his excavation in the local dialect of the marginalized so they can act.

He employs these strategies in his campaign on behalf of untouchables attempting to open the Vykom Temple Road, in his work with striking textile workers in Ahmedabad, and in his salt *satyagraha*.[25] And they appear in his arguments regarding the equality of women.[26] His archaeological approach does not look at traditional texts or practices as sacrosanct expressions of unchallengeable knowledge. Rather, he wants to move beyond standard readings of traditional texts or practices and expose those that spawn domination. When he turns to gender relations, he finds: "The ancient laws were made by seers who were men. The women's experience, therefore is not represented in them. Strictly speaking, as between man and woman, neither should be regarded as superior or inferior."[27] For equality to emerge, he urges women to deconstruct what has been fabricated for them. To do this, it is essential for women to refuse to be intimidated by traditional practices and to decline to accept an inferior position in the social order that they have been taught is natural.[28] Pursuing his archaeological strategy, Gandhi finds that gender relations have been evolving and that what we have now is not neutral or natural. This can be seen in his commentary regarding polygamy and monogamy.

> Draupadi had five husbands at one time and yet has been called "chaste". This is because in that age, just as a man

could marry several wives, a women (in certain regions) could marry several husbands. The code of marriage changes with time and place.[29]

Just as marriage "codes" change, so do other social "codes", some in ways that are emancipatory and some debilitating to the autonomy of persons. Gandhi, often the traditionalist, turns out to be one of the harshest critics of his own tradition as he digs through what he takes to be its decay and rubble in order to find its core.

We see this again in his critique of untouchability and his excavation of layers of sedimentation to uncover what he takes to be the true Hinduism. His reading of ancient texts reveals to him that although untouchability is sanctioned in contemporary Hindu practice, it "disfigures" the core of Hinduism and "is a morbid growth".[30] Holding that Hindu practice roams from its ideals when it embraces untouchability, he calls for its elimination. Part of his reconstructive archaeology is to deny commonly held interpretations in order to propose an alternative that he thinks embodies the original meaning of his own tradition. So, he argues, "Untouchability is not only not a part and parcel of Hinduism, but a plague, which it is the burden of every Hindu to combat."[31]

For all of the variety in his many archaeological efforts, the underlying purpose of each of them is to offer emancipatory materials to those at the periphery to enable them to voice their own needs and assert their own dignity.[32] He argues that there is an underlying unity in the core of ancient traditions that has been lost over the centuries and needs to be uncovered and practised. He sees the members of different traditions grasping different fragments of the truth, and when they adhere to its core, Gandhi argues, they have materials to judge themselves and others.[33] However, he insists, these fragments, precisely because they are fragments, do not give anyone warrant to impose their truths on others.[34]

At the same time, Gandhi finds these fragments are sufficiently robust to challenge the fatalism he sees embedded in modernity as well as to confront the fatalism that is spawned by an unreflective acceptance of traditional practices that justify domination. Freed from such fatalism, women, untouchables, and others need not accept the way things are.

Old and New Expressions of Power

For some, the modern state serves as the primary vehicle for emancipation; others find the state oppressive and hold that if confined, civil society can become free. What we find in each of these accounts is the prominence given to the state and the need to make it a focal point of our attention. These are logical arguments stemming from conventional ideas of sovereignty. There can only be one sovereign; some power must stand above all other forms of power and, therefore, should have the ability to command. Gandhi is not content to concentrate on the state as the exclusive site of domination. To be sure it is an important locale of power for him, but he finds the state sharing power with myriad other repositories of power.[35]

Gandhi believes the state has been assigned an exaggerated role in contemporary society. It is not merely that the state is pretentious in what it claims for itself but that the attention paid to it deflects us from looking at the many other sites of power. Wanting to move beyond conventional readings of the modern state, he finds that it is part of a much larger phenomenon and cannot be treated as something that stands above modernity.

Gandhi holds that power is embedded in traditional practices such as caste and gender relations as well as in modern economic and social practices and modern claims to knowledge. This theme is prominent in *Hind Swaraj* where Gandhi denies that if only the seat of sovereignty changes from London to New Delhi, then India will be emancipated.[36] What is necessary, on his account, is that the institutions of civil society change and the debilitating consequences of modernity be openly challenged.

Gandhi participates in politics, he tells us, "only because politics encircle us today like the coil of a snake from which one cannot get out, no matter how much one tries. I wish, therefore, to wrestle with the snake."[37] In this way he departs from those who ignore the state or take a fatalistic position that nothing can be done.[38] He finds, for example, that the British colonial state cannot be escaped or ignored. But any effective resistance in the name of autonomy, he argues, must do more than take on the coercive state. As important as the state is as a site of power, Gandhi thinks that is represents only a part of the problem. He finds that in the modern world, disciplinary networks have evolved which direct and manage people and deprive them of their autonomy. For Gandhi, disciplinary power does not rely on the visible coercion of conventional state power. From his perspective, modernity coughs up rules that, to be followed, require people to redefine themselves. For him, this reconstructed self accepts the new rules as necessary and takes their construction as appropriate. Modern disciplinary power is so dangerous, according to Gandhi, because it attempts to disguise itself and pretends it is not power. Hiding behind appearances which mask its real nature, disciplinary power departs from state conceptions of power.

Why should individuals not recognize that they are being redefined and disciplined? Gandhi thinks that much of the answer comes with the way discipline is often tied to necessity, that is, to the economy.[39] Necessity not only has to do with the ways households meet their elementary needs in order to survive biologically, but today it also has been greatly expanded to include all manner of things that are considered needs.[40]

Gandhi thinks that any social system creates its own unique set of systemic needs layered on top of basic ones. These needs address what is takes to get along in that society. To meet these needs, it is necessary to work: how persons work,[41] how they are rewarded, and what goods they consume or want to consume are important to individuals. He holds that with modernity, needs expand all over the place, and it becomes impossible to satisfy all of them. The explosion of needs stems not only from the burgeoning of systemic needs but also from the materialistic character of modernity which ties identity to a consumption that is never satiated.[42]

It is not the case that the privileged classes discipline other classes but are not disciplined themselves. Gandhi's critique of modernity holds that those most likely to be disciplined by modernity are those in the modern sectors, accepting the claims of modernity about its humanitarian impulses, its commitment to rationality, its debts to science, and its promise of progress. Those who have been or seek to be integrated in the modern sector find their success depends on their "self-discipline". The "self-discipline" Gandhi has in mind concerns the ways persons redefine themselves to accommodate to modern norms in order to take advantage of as much of the material as of status, advantages that the modern age offers.[43]

Among the Indians Gandhi targets as falling victim to modern discipline are those who are attempting to insert themselves into the modern sector, such as lawyers in British courts.[44] Ironically, those outside the orbit of modernity often escape many of its pressures of normalization, but they frequently fall under its coercive power.

Surely, the question can be asked whether modern society is more disciplinary than other societies. Probably not, but modern discipine takes place within the context of freedom. The things we want are seen as free expressions on our part. But are they? Gandhi believes that modern freedom often clouds an understanding of how people are being disciplined and shaped. For him, the order imposed in modern society comes not primarily from the state but from the disciplinary practices that are scattered throughout modern society.

Plurality and Universalism

With modernity, several changes occur: the preferred politics that develops is of a certain sort (democracy as centralized, bureaucratic, representative, and interest alternative) the norms of modern culture are secular, consumer-oriented, and pleasure-driven; economics rotates around production, efficiency, growth, and consumption, education becomes the acquisition of skills valued in the economy. These changes signal the invasion of traditional and transcendent modes of understanding and acting in the world. For Gandhi, such developments also crush what was once a robust diversity.

What is important about diversity to someone like Gandhi is that much of it makes room for what modernity ignores, namely transcendent ways of thinking about the self. He sees people with a material, biological nature and a transcendent spiritual nature, and as I have argued elsewhere, Gandhi argues that to be fully human it is necessary to attend to both. For him, transcendence means moving outside oneself, something that requires detachment and results in service to others.[45] Gandhian transcendence is something anyone is said to be able to achieve, independent of income, education, or religious commitment.[46] For him, the universalizing materialism of modernity stands in the way of the many different expressions of transcendence that he believes once flourished and are in danger of being lost. He also fears that detachment becomes difficult when the self-referential self, particularly the materially oriented self-referential self, is the primary way people understand themselves.

Gandhi's celebration of transcendence does not require an external standard that purports to be objective and applicable to all situations. Although he believes that real truth exists, he holds that no single creed, tradition or philosophy grasps the truth in its entirety.[47] On Gandhi's view, most traditions grasp important fragments of the truth which are translated into local idioms. For him, Hinduism, Islam, and Christianity, in their highly distinctive ways, do this in confronting the raw ego and providing individuals with a meaning beyond their biological properties.[48] Believing that every tradition is partial in the sense that it cannot grasp, much less incorporate, the entire truth, Gandhi resists efforts to appropriate dogmatic truth claims by any tradition, including his own, or to use its understanding of the good to claim a privileged status for itself in relation to other traditions.

With modernity, Gandhi fears that many diverse expressions of culture are in danger of disappearing and the rest must explain themselves by reference to modernity. On his account, many different logics carry challenges to modernity and what I have in mind is not the shaman or magician but such logics that emphasize the relationship of human beings to one another and to their environment and the responsibilities the members of a community have to each other. For Gandhi, this requires moral agents to move away from their material attachments and see themselves as part of an interrelated and interdependent cosmos where all of the parts are equal and united.

Gandhi's Cosmos

Throughout this paper I have used some conceptual frameworks that Gandhi shares with post-modernism. But these similarities become exhausted after a while, and one place where this is the case concerns Gandhi's view of the cosmos.[49] Post-modern writers would find that his cosmos looks too much like a *telos*, with its own imperatives, and is unwittingly open to domination. This Gandhi would deny.

For him, the cosmos is ideally characterized by the interdependence and interrelatedness of the parts which simultaneously retain their own integrity and coexist together harmoniously.[50] These two latter characteristics are what I want to pursue in terms of Gandhi's critique of modernity. Gandhian harmony cannot evolve out of a discipline which seeks to universalize rules and conduct; rather he imagines that any real harmony reflects the rhythm of life with all of its diversity. One thing this requires is that the many aspects of a person's life coexist in some reasonable harmony.[51] This internal rhythm is interrupted when one aspect of our life, such as economics, dominates the other aspects. The diversity within our own lives needs to be safeguarded, and part of Gandhi's quarrel with modernity is that he believes it cancels the multiple needs of individuals in favour of making economic ones primary.[52]

Gandhi presents his cosmic harmony as something on the horizon, something to aim for. Standing away from us, it remains elusive and, at the same time, is the embodiment of what Gandhi considers to be the highest human aspirations. From his perspective, if all that we have are practicalities and no ideals, we remain bogged down in the world, its captives, as we find how best to adjust and adapt rather than to aspire to take control of our own lives.

The coherence and intelligibility Gandhi finds in his cosmos are shattered in the modern world which offers a series of discreet rules to apply to the many separate and distinctive roles which individuals carry. He fears that when a person's life is splintered by conflicting standards, eventually one or another dominates, and the weaker ones no longer contribute organizing principles for the person. For him, modernity supplies the dominant standard for individual well-being today. The surviving fragments of a tradition roam only in marginal realms of a person's life or line in the shadows of ritual and nostalgia.

Gandhi offers *swaraj* or self-rule as an alternative to modernity, not as an abstraction but as an affirmation of the dignity of ordinary people in the countless, diverse villages of India.[53] He sees each community as a minicosmos reflecting the rhythm, cooperation, responsibilities, and opportunities resident in his idealized cosmos. Each community is said to have its own particular mixture of tradition, religion, language, economics, and myriad other properties. In emphasizing each distinctive community as integral parts of the foundation of Indian society, Gandhi opposes one of the most characteristic features of the modern age: its tendency to homogenize.

Gandhi's cosmos is not guided by comprehensive standards which replace diversity and plurality with uniformity. For him, ordinary men and women need to work with familiar materials when they construct a moral life for themselves and meet necessity. The intersection between a (local) tradition and an active, sentient person creates Gandhi's autonomous person, situated with others who share a common life built on mutual respect. To eliminate various local traditions because they do not accord with the grand narrative of modernity is to deny people their familiar identities and assume they can readily accept some unfamiliar, universal construction that coherently covers them and everyone else. This, Gandhi holds, is not possible and efforts to make it so are destined to be cruel.

In his unique way, Gandhi offers a response to late modernity, whether modernity is characterized by modern science, economics, or culture. He also takes on traditionalists who want to vitalize hierarchical understandings of citizenship and duty as well as depoliticize much that Gandhi wishes to contest. In proposing everyday autonomy in a plural setting as the standard for judgment, rather than abstract standards such as justice or the modern standard of progress, he seeks a society that is open-ended and fluid and whose practices are under constant scrutiny and potential revision. This is why he wants civil disobedience to remain part of his idealized society. It is to be a place where its primary, self-conscious goals speak to the autonomy and equality of everyone and where efforts to deny these goods can be challenged.

With this vision, Gandhi parts company with a major strand of the Enlightenment which exudes a confidence that the good material life will be the good life and the engine of progress will deliver prosperity and personal fulfilment. For his part, Gandhi disputes these claims and calls attention to the many sites and abuses of power and calls for resistance to domination. In the process, he means to defend the idea that the autonomy of individuals must be the standard with which to judge claims to knowledge and social practices.

Notes and References

1. Both Gandhi and several post-modern writers offer alternative modes of discourse and analysis to the modern paradigm. In this paper I will deploy some conceptual categories used by various post-modern writers to show that the post-modern temper shares much with an unlikely voice, one which talks about love, truth, tradition, and autonomy. In drawing parallels between some post-modern writers and Gandhi, I do not mean to make the two interchangeable or to argue that post-modernism implicitly contains such Gandhian imperatives as love and self-sacrifice any more than I claim that Gandhi can comfortably fit into a thoroughgoing post-modernism.

   Then why use some of the post-modern perspective to think about Gandhi's critique of modernity? There are several reasons for embarking on such a discussion. For one, the exercise shows that neither is a totally distinctive language but shares some reading of the modern world and how that world has exhausted itself. Moreover, the exercise demonstrates that the logic of post-modernism about constructiveness and deconstruction does not necessarily lead to the kind of skepticism that characterizes much post-modernism.

2. One of the primary complaints with modernity is that it judges not only the world but itself by its own internally generated standards. For Gandhi, any practice must do more than show it is good or efficient by its own standards.

3. M.K. Gandhi, *Hind Swaraj*, Chapter 17, p. 92. The edition cited here is *Hind Swaraj* edited by Anthony Parel (Cambridge: Cambridge University Press, 1997).

4. *Ibid.*, Chapter 13, p. 71. For a further discussion of Gandhi's selective reliance on modern concepts, see Ronald Terchek, *Gandhi Struggling for Autonomy* (Lanham: Rowman and Littlefield, 1998), Chapters 2 and 3; Bhikhu Parekh, *Gandhi's Political Philosophy* (Norte Dame, Norte Dame University Press, 1989); Anthony Parel, "Introduction" in his *Hind Swaraj and other Writings* (Cambridge: Cambridge University Press, 1997); Mahendra Kumar, "Gandhi in the Twenty-first Century" in Anthony Copley and George Paxton, eds., *Gandhi and the Contemporary World* (Chennai: Indo-British Historical Society, 1997); and Thomas Pantham, "Gandhi, Nehru, and Modernity" in Upendra Baxi and Bhikhu Parekh eds., *Crisis and Change in Contemporary India* (New Delhi: Sage, 1995).

5. *Hind Swaraj*, Chapter 5, p. 33.

6. *Ibid.*, Chapter 14, p. 73.

7. *Ibid.*, Chapter 8, p. 43.

8. *Young India*, 21 March 1928.

9. *Hind Swaraj*, Chapters 8, 11, 12, and 19 and pages 164-79. But he continually makes it clear that he is not

opposed to everything modern. Regarding machinery, he says that he rejects it when it ceases "to help the individual and encroaches upon his individuality" (*Young India*, 20 November 1924).

10. See *Hind Swaraj*, Chapter 3, p. 24 on the need to be discontented.
11. On Gandhi's views linking science and ethics, see "Ethical Religion", in Raghavan N. Iyer, *The Moral and Political Writings of Mahatma Gandhi* (New York: Oxford University Press, 1973), 2, 51-52.
12. See *Hind Swaraj*, Chapter 5 and Anthony Parel's notes in this chapter.
13. Letter to H.S.L. Polak, 14 October 1909 in Raghavan N.Iyer, ed., *The Moral and Political Writings of Mahatma Gandhi*, Vol. 1, p. 293.
14. Hannah Arendt, *The Human Condition* (Chicago: University of Chicago Press, 1958), p. 275. For extended discussions of Gandhi and Science, see Ashis Nandy, *Traditions, Tyranny, and Utopia* (Delhi Oxford University Press, 1987) and Partha Chatterjee, *Nationalist Thought and the Colonial World: A Derivative Discourse* (Delhi: Oxford University Press, 1986).
15. *The Hindu*, 19 March 1925 in Raghavan N. Iyer, ed., *The Moral and Political Writings of Mahatma Gandhi*, Vol. 1, pp. 310-11. Here and elsewhere, Gandhi shows that he carries his own appreciation of modernity of a certain sort.
16. *The Hindu*, 19 March 1925.
17. *Young India*, 13 November 1924.
18. Gandhi writes that "what may be, therefore, true of Europe is not necessarily true of India... [Each nation has its own characteristics and individuality. India has her own; and if we are to find out a true solution for her many ills, we shall have to take all the idiosyncrasies of her constitution into account." Vide *Young India*, 6, August, 1925.

19. See M.K. Gandhi, *Constructive Programme* (Ahmedabad: Navajivan Publishing House, 1941).

20. For Gandhi's discussion of his idealised village as a minicosmos, see his *India of My Dreams* (Ahmedabad: Navajivan Publishing House, 1959) and *Rebuilding Our Villages* (Ahmedabad: Navajivan Publishing House, 1952).

21. There is a vast literature on this subject, ranging from Marx to Foucault and from Tocqueville to MacIntyre. Rather than picking and choosing which of the various alternatives to follow, I plan simply to build on the overall arguments that this body of critiques offers.

22. See *Young India*, 25 August 1920; and *Harijan*, 21 July 1940 for examples of defying fate.

23. Gandhi's critique of modernity cannot be understood apart from his critique of tradition. He is no nostalgic communitarian who seeks relief from the present by escaping into the past. As he understands matters, domination is no exclusive characteristic of either the past or the present and needs to be exposed and resisted whenever it asserts itself.

24. According to Gandhi, sacred texts "suffer from a process of double distilation. Firstly, they come through a human prophet, and then commentaries of interpreters. Nothing in them comes from God directly." Vide *Harijan*, 5 December, 1936.

25. See Joan Bondurant *Conquest of Violence* (Berkeley: University of California Press, 1967), pp. 46-50, 53-61, and 65-71. Also see Yogesh Chaddha, *Gandhi: A Life* (New York, John Wiley, 1997), pp. 218-25.

26. See Ronald Terchek and Nitis Das Gupta, "Gandhi and the Autonomous Woman," *Journal of Gandhian Studies*, 1998.

27. "Talks to Ashram Women", 1926 in Raghavan N. Iyer, ed., *The Moral and Political Writings of Mahatma Gandhi*, Vol. 3, p. 394.

28. See *Harijan*, 24 February, 1940.

29. "Talks to Ashram Women", 1926, referred to earlier.

30. *Harijan*, 20 April 1934.

31. M.K. Gandhi, *From Yeravda Mandir* (Ahmedabad: Navajivan Publishing House, 1935), p. 47. As Gandhi understands matters, "Caste, if you will, is undoubtedly a drag upon, Hindu progress, and untouchability... is a weedy growth fit only to be weeded out. If I again interpret the Hindu spirit rightly, all life is absolutely equal and one". Vide *Young India*, 20 October 1927.

32. See his advice to women that they must be in charge of their own emancipation in "Talks to Ashram Women".

33. Krishna Kripalani, *All Men are Brothers* (New York Columbia University Press, 1958), pp. 72-73.

34. He reports that "After long study and experience, I have come to the conclusion that all religions are true, (2) all religions have some error in them" (*All Men are Brothers* edited by Krishna Kripalani (New York Colombia University Press, 1958), 60.

35. When some people talk about power and Gandhi, they discuss his theory of the power of love. Here, I want to take up another aspect of power in his writings. I do not mean to discount the importance of love in Gandhi's conceptualization of power. See Bhikhu Parekh, *Gandhi's Political Philosophy*, Ronald Terchek, *Gandhi: Struggling for Automony*; and Joan Bondurant, *Conquest of Violence*.

36. See *Hind Swaraj*, Chapter 19, p. 198.

37. *Young India*, 23 May, 1920.

38. Gandhi regards the rise of the nation-state and its accompanying bureaucracy as a threat to the power of the periphery. For a further discussion of Gandhian politics, see Ronald Terchek, "Gandhi's Democratic Theory", in Thomas Pantham and Kenneth Deutsch, eds., *Political Thought of Modern India* (New Delhi: Sage, 1986).

39. In this way, he departs from most post-modern writers who tend to devalue the economy.

40. Gandhi holds that modernity feeds on the proclivity of the biological nature of human beings always to crave more. On his account. "The mind is a restless bird; the more it gets the more it wants and still remains unsatisfied. The more we indulge our passions the more unbridled they become". Vide *Hind Swaraj*, Chapter 13.

41. Gandhi is as interested in production as distribution. He argues that if production or work is degrading and thwarts autonomy, then it is not good enough to concentrate on distributive policies. See *Young India*, 2 July 1931.

42. He complains: "The distinguishing characteristic of modern civilization is an infinite multiplicity of human wants". Vide *Young India*, 2 June 1927.

43. He complains that the British "spend their days in luxury or in making a bare living and retire at night thoroughly exhausted. In this state of affairs, I cannot understand when they can" transcend their worlds of work and consumption. Vide *Collected Works of Mahatma Gandhi*, Vol. 9, p. 389.

44. See *Hind Swaraj*, Chapter 11.

45. Gandhian detachment is a prelude to action, not an escape from the world. See Ronald Terchek, *Gandhi: Struggling for Autonomy*, pp. 29-32.

46. According to Gandhi, "God is Truth and Love; God is ethics and morality; God is fearlessness ... God is conscience. He is even the atheism of the atheist". Vide *Young India*, 5 March 1925.

47. Gandhi holds that all "religions are more or less true. All proceed from the same God but all are imperfect because they come down to us through imperfect human instrumentality" (*Young India*, 24 May 1924). He returns to this theme in *Harijan*, 7 March 1929. Also see, Ronald Terchek, "Gandhi and Moral Autonomy", *Gandhi Marg*, Vol. 13, March 1992, and Joan Bondurant, *Conquest of Violence*, p. 19.

48. Gandhi announces that he is "a Muslim, a Hindu, a Buddhist, a Christian, a Jew, a Parse". On another occasion, he asks, "why blaspheme God by fighting over different media? Koran, Bible, Talmud, Avesta, or Gita? ... Why make of books and formulas so many fetters to enslave rather than to unify"? See G.N. Dhawan, *The Political Philosophy of Mahatma Gandhi* (Ahmedabad: Navajivan Publishing House, 1951, p. 9). Also see Joan Bondurant, *Conquest of Violence*, p. 152.

49. Gandhi finds that every living being has a role in the continual cycles of life and must be respected. On his reading, human beings have duties and responsibilities in the cosmic cycle. One reason is that every individual is a debtor, not only taking from nature but also in living in a particular community with its own language customs, divisions of labour, and patterns of cooperation and support. As such, individuals are said to owe debts to the many persons who contribute to their well-being.

50. See V.R. Mehta, *Foundations of Indian Political Thought* (New Delhi: Manohar, 1992).

51. *See* Bhikhu Parekh, "Is Gandhi Still Relevant?" in Anthony Copley and George Paxton, *Gandhi and the Contemporary World.*

52. The multiple needs of individuals are not stationary, according to Gandhi, but change as people move into new stages of their lives.

53. See *Harijan*, 20 January 1940.

11
Bringing Gandhi Back into Independent India

T.K. Oommen

Implied in the title of my lecture is an apprehension that Gandhiji has receeded into oblivion in Independent India. Some of you may be hurt by this and others may contest this proposition. The fact is that Mohandas Karamchand Gandhi has been subjected to a cognitive blackout in Independent India and I will attempt to explicate it in the course of my lecture. Although he has been christened as Father of the Nation, his ideas are scarcely practiced in the nation he fathered. He lived barely six months in Independent India and there is a widespread tendency to consign him to Colonial India. While there is Consensus that he was the single most important figure in the realization of Swaraj his ideas are pronounced to be irrelevant, by an influential section in the country, in building the nation. What I propose to do is to dispel this naive notion. As a prelude to this we need to have an orientation towards the prevailing dominant ideas and contestations about them.

Human society has been in existence for three million years but the discourse on development is barely three hundred years old. Initially development was sought to be achieved through industrialization. This in turn meant two things. First, it attempted the replacement of agriculture by industry and the rural population by urban population. Second, it aimed at the

---

* Gandhi Peace Foundation Annual Lecture 2006; published by the Gandhi Peace Foundation (Delhi: 2006), pp. 1-14. Reprinted by kind permission of Professor T.K. Oommen.

progressive displacement of animate energy by inanimate energy. The two elements — industrialization and technologisation — conjointly gave birth to the notion of modernization. Irrespective of ideological variations, that is capitalism and socialism, industrialization was a common refrain. Industrialize or perish became the new populist cry.

While both capitalism and socialism invoked industrialization as the primary tool of development, the former combined it with multi-party democracy and the latter with one-party democracy giving birth to two models of development. Capitalist democracies claimed that their modernity is natural and they combined the process of economic growth with equality of opportunity giving birth to the First World. While state played an important role in development in capitalist welfare states, adequate space was gradually conceded to market and civil society. In contrast, the socialist one-party systems labeled their modernity as enlightened; they rolled up the state, civil society and market into one entity, firmly positioning the state at the commanding height. However, the socialist states pursed economic development with a firm thrust on distributive justice and material equality. The Second World is the product of this process.

If the 'bourgeoisie revolution' produced the First World and the 'socialist revolution' created the Second World, the anti-colonial revolution gave birth to the Third World. Most of the Third World countries opted for one of the two modernities, but India opted for the Third Way, combining planned economic development of the Second World and multi-party democracy of the First World. This was then widely hailed as the hope of the future.

However, all the three worlds had industrialization as their common route to development. In fact development came to be measured in terms of the level of industrialization. But the devastation caused by industrialization on environment produced a new trend in development thinking. Development produced a 'risk society' as the whole world is exposed to ecological problems. Globalization of risk through global ecological hazards, export of polluting industries and waste materials, the risks of biogenetic engineering etc. are fast spreading. Understandably sustainable development became the new refrain.

Capitalist democracy could not satisfactorily address the problem of inequality, indeed it was indifferent to distributive justice, although it did champion the notions of equality of opportunity, liberty and freedom. Communist one-party regimes did attend to the problem of material inequality but failed to tackle the issue of centralization of political authority. Faced by the fierce competition posed by communism, capitalist democracy invented the institution of welfare state and attempted to moderate the deepening inequality. But with the demise of the Second World, capitalist democracy returned to its original mission namely unbridled accumulation of wealth by a few through the instrumentality of market fundamentalism. The fatal flaw of capitalism is excessive concentration of wealth, the basic problem of communism is excessive concentration of authority. It is against this backdrop that we must situate the robust relevance of the Gandhian alternative.

II

Mohandas Karamchand Gandhi used to say: "India lives in her villages". Even to-day, after considerable progress in industrialization, 71 percent of India's population are rural according to the 2001 census. Therefore, rural development is synonymous with development even today in India.

Gandhiji advocated a village-based development process. He wanted to "...make each village self-governing and self-contained as regards essential needs of its inhabitants...". That is, both political decentralization and economic autonomy were envisioned by him. But it has been castigated for several reasons. I shall list just two of these. First, development was, and continues to be, wrongly equated with industrialization as noted above. Second, leaders like Pandit Jawaharlal Nehru and Dr. Baba Saheb Ambedkar viewed the Indian villige as an intellectually and culturally backward entity, indeed a den of ignorance and illiteracy and a habitat which perpetuates both physical and mental ill-health. That is, they were referring to villages as they existed.

The fact is that Gandhiji himself did not endorse Indian villages as they were. He admitted that: "The approach to many villages is not a refreshing experience. Often one would like to shut one's eyes and stuff one's nose; such is the surrounding dim and offending smell". However, he refused to accept this state of affairs as a fait accompli, as an irredeemable situation. Gandhiji wanted to change the village radically and held the view that. "...if the village perishes. India will perish too". And he did not advocate village primitivism. He wrote in 1936: "... there would be no objection to villagers using even the most modern machines and tools they can make and can afford to use". He was only wanting to save rural India being exploited by urban India, the villages "from catching the infection of industrialism". That is, he was speaking about villages as they ought to be.

However, Gandhiji insisted that "... nothing will be allowed to be produced by cities which can equally well be produced by villages": goods produced in villages are not to compromise on quality. And when the villages are developed "... there will be no dearth in them of men with high degree of skill and artistic talent". Therefore what Gandhiji advocated was the co-existence of village and city, agro-industrial communities which are mutually interdependent. Further, he has not even advocated self-sufficiency of single villages. He held the view that, "It will be possible to reconstruct our villages so that villages *collectively*, not-villagers *individually*, will become self-contained". Gandhiji abandoned the rural-urban dichotomy and advocated rural-urban continuum.

I have spent a little time to explicate Gandhiji's position because he was/is widely misunderstood and misrepresented even by his outstanding contemporaries. But there were others who shared his perception. Permit me to cite just one case. William Digby the British scholar-administrator wrote in 1901 i.e. 105 year ago: "There are two Indias: the India of the Presidency and the chief-provincial cities, of the railway systems, of the hill stations... There are two countries: Anglostan, the land especially ruled by the English, in which English investments have been made and Hindustan, practically all India fifty miles from each side of the railway lines". It will be dishonest to insist that there have been no changes in the past one century but it is a truism that the basic wedge between Bharat i.e., rural India and India, that is, urban India persists obstinately. That is why Mohandas Karamchand Gandhi continues to be absolutely relevant for Independent India.

Now the question is who should undertake this stupendous task? I have alluded to Independent India opting for the Third Way to bring about development. Planned economic development launched through Five Year Plans in which the state played a crucial role was and continues to be an important instrument in this context. And people's participation was consciously solicited by the state in the formulation and implementation of Five Year Plans. The modus operandi invoked to elicit participation was indeed unique. Usually draft outlines of Five Year Plans are circulated to ensure the widest possible discussion. The rationale of this procedure was enunciated in the First Plan: "Planning in a democratic state is a social process [in] which in some part, every citizen should have the opportunity to participate. To set the patterns of future development is a task of such magnitude and significance that it should embody the impact of public opinion and the needs of the community.... The draft is intended to be a *document for the widest possible discussion*" (italics mine).

The process of planned development through people's participation was intended to bring about distributive justice as is evident from the following statement from the draft outline of the Second Five Year Plan: "The benefits of economic development must accrue more to the relatively less privileged classes of society and there should be progressive reduction of the concentration of incomes, wealth and economic power."

These laudable objectives notwithstanding and in spite of introducing institutional innovations such as the Community Development Programmes (CDP), Panchayati Raj Institutions (PRI) and Co-operatives it cannot be said that participation by the weak achieved a high pitch in rural India. The basic reason for the alienation of the poor from the development process is the lack of economic content in India's political democracy.

The state in India had recognized the inadequacy of PRIs in promoting participatory development as articulated in the Fifth Plan document. It notes: "In actual practice... the resources envisaged have not had adequate impact on the direction or tempo of development." Therefore, the strategy was radically changed when the Seventh Plan was launched in 1985 which recognized the importance of education. "Education in all its aspects, and people's participation in development programmes through their own organization hold the key to rapid and sustained social and economic advance". Thus a major shift of tool to elicit people's participation has been recognized. The role of civil society in development came to be accepted by the state and the proliferation of NGOs started. The Seventh Five Year Plan (1985-90) document advised NGOs to:

> ...give greater attention to mobilize locally available human and financial resources, identify people in the poorer and vulnerable occupations like farmers, rural artisans, scheduled castes, scheduled tribes, agricultural labourers, girijans, bonded labour upgrade their skills give them the tools to make them economically self-sufficient as well as productive.

This in an acutely Gandhian statement. As usual we are rich in rhetoric but abysmal in performance. Thus the high point of state-civil society partnership was achieved by the Seventh Five Year Plan which ended in 1990. It was precisely at this point of time liberalization of the Indian economy was initiated. The last one and a half decades (1990-2005) was somewhat ambiguous with regard to the roles of the three agencies — state, civil society and market — with regard to development. The state's role in planned development became nebulous, the institutions of market scarcely took on board the developmental agenda and the civil society largely became a mere interrogator of the policies of state and market. Given the above scenario this is the most opportune time to think about the roles and responsibilities of the three pillars of the evolving society — state, market and civil society — and their central actors, namely citizen, consumer and communitarian.

III

Gandhiji's observation that there is enough in the world to meet everybody's need but not enough to meet the greed of even a few, was an astute statement against consumerism. His first priority was to meet the basic needs of all human beings. He went to the extent of suggesting that all men should get equal wages for a day's honest work be they doctors, lawyers, merchants, teachers or scavengers. But this is not to be imposed on people but to be the end-product of moral enrichment manifesting through voluntary restriction of wants. It could be legitimately asked: why should people work hard if they are not rewarded adequately?

The fatal flaw here is to view rewards purely in material terms. For Gandhiji, material reward makes an insignificant aspect of rewards, the more important dimension is symbolic satisfaction one gains through giving. The wealth one accumulates is not to be used for indulging in conspicuous consumption but to be held in trust and to be given to the needy, *antyodaya* being the ultimate aim.

I am afraid the widespread tendency to interpret Gandhiji's advocacy in this context literally robs it off its true spirit. I suggest that the true intent of his advocacy was to reduce the ever widening income disparity as the process of economic development advances. Let me recall some statistics for you. The ratio between the incomes of the richest and the poorest country was 3:1 in 1820. it became 35:1 by 1950 and shot up to 72:1 in 1992. What is true of countries is also true of classes. In 1960 the richest 20% of humankind was earning 30 times of what the poorest 20% earned. By 2000, this disparity doubled, it became 60 times. In 2000 the richest one percent of world's population received as much income as the poorest 57%.

Income disparity is a phenomenon which exists across countries irrespective of their ideological dispositions. In the

Soviet Union, before the break up, the wage disparity between the highest paid and the lowest paid was 40 times. In the United States of America, usually referred to as the most successful democracy in the world, in the last 30 years 40% of all income earners have experienced decline of income but two percent citizens own 90% of the country's wealth. In Gandhi's India which pledged to reduce income disparity to the tune of 1:20 the situation is no better. With the advent of globalization the situation has further deteriorated. It is true that some 100,000 Indians are shining but three hundred million Indians are sinking: they are below the poverty line. *Antyodaya* is more relevant now than ever before. To realize it the abandoning of consumerist craze is an absolute pre-requisite.

Consumerism is condemned by a few, but it is an aspiration for the vast majority and remains unachievable for most. It is the huge gap between the unrealistic aspiration assiduously promoted by commercial advertisements and the sheer impossibility of its realization which is at the root of much of the corruption and crime. As accumulation of wealth has become a culturally valued goal and as culturally prescribed means are inadequate and/or unavailable to achieve this goal, the human tendency is to resort to illegitimate means. This muddled opposition between means and end was well recognized by Gandhiji. His Golden dictum that means and end should be equally pure and they are convertible terms is completely ignored in contemporary India.

Modern development is driven by high technology. Understandably Jawaharlal Nehru's evocative phrase. "the temples of modern India", found instant appeal among those who stood to profit by these huge ventures. But gradually he realized his mistake and in 1958 Nehru deplored a "dangerous outlook developing in India", which he designated as "the disease of giganticism". While such undertakings can demonstrate to the world our capacity to do big things he underlined the importance of "the small irrigation projects, the small industries and the small plants for electric power which will change the face of the country, far more than a dozen big projects in half a dozen places". He also referred to the large scale displacement caused by these big projects. This conversion of Nehru to Gandhism came little too late. The nexus between the vested interest forces consisting of contractors, engineers and bureaucrats became too formidable to desacralise the temples.

One of the pathological manifestations of technology driven huge projects is displacement. The estimates regarding displacement vastly vary. According to one such estimate some 35 to 55 million people have been displaced in Independent India. Of these, displacement due to large projects according to the government, between 1951 and 1985, is sixteen and a half million. But according to another estimate the displaces, between 1951 and 1990, count twenty one million. Even if we go by the most conservative estimate the numbers are huge. It needs to be underlined here that only eight percent of India's population is tribal, numbering eighty million, but sixty percent of the displacees are tribals. Thus the worst affected because of the current model of development are the already marginalized. Disparity and displacement in conjunction impoverish and uproot them. Gandhian approach to development would have completely averted their immiserisation.

Gandhiji condemned untouchability as the greatest blot on Hinduism. Independent India's legislative generosity is loud and clear in this context also. The Untouchability (Offences) Act passed in 1955 gave access to the erstwhile untouchables to all public places, including places of worship and public utilities. To augment the scope of this Act and to plug some of its loopholes the Protection of Civil Rights Act, 1976 was passed. As the socio-economic conditions of the Scheduled Castes improved they started interrogating the traditional intimidations and violence unleashed against them by the land-owning castes. To cope with this new development, the Schedules Castes and Scheduled Tribes (Prevention of Atrocities) Act, 1989 was passed. In spite of all these Acts the practice of untouchability continues. Between 1955, the year in which the first anti-untouchability act was passed, and 1995 some 2,74,438 cases of offences have been registered which works out to be 6,693 cases per year. If the

Indian state were uncompromising in its implementation of the Acts passed, and the Indian society were sensitive in the indignation heaped on fellow human being, the 'blot on Hinduism' about which the Mahatma was agonized would have substantially eroded, if not completely erased.

The worst sufferers of the practice of untouchability in India are the scavengers. The Bhangi Mukti was an important item on the agenda of constructive programme conceived by Gandhiji. Out of the 300 million people who live in Urban India, 76% do not have toilet facility and most of the available ones are dry-latrines manually cleaned by the Bhangis, a caste group with the lowest position in India's social hierarchy. Although the sewerage system was introduced in 1870 in India, it was mainly confined to the civil lines, those days inhabited by whites. Even today only little over 300 out of the 4800 towns and cities in India have sewerage lines. Even in big cities, a substantial proportion of population lives in slums which do not have any sanitation facility. According to one estimate, sanitation facilities are now available only to 48% of urban and three percent of rural population in India. One can very well imagine the stigma associated with those who do scavenging in a caste-ridden society like ours. Small wonder, the Mahatma averred: "Toilet is Temple" and "...sanitation is more important than independence". Alas, his dream of Bhangi Mukti remains unrealized even as India is fast racing to become a super power!

While the advocacy of Hindu Rashtra by Hindu nationalists, crystallized by the 1930s, latterly it has become a major credo. With the political legitimation achieved by them in the1990s India's proverbial cultural pluralism is getting sidelined and cultural monism is gaining centrality. Gandhiji dispelled the pernicious notion of Hindu Rashtra as early as 1938 when he wrote: "If the Hindus believe that only Hindus should people India, they are living in Dreamland. The Hindus, the Mohammedans, the Parsis and the Christians who have made India their country are fellow countrymen". In spite of this, externalization of some of the religious minorities persist in Independent India. Our co-citizens who are legal insiders are defined and treated as aliens and cultural outsiders by a section of Indians.

Inter-religious conflicts, referred to as communal riots in popular parlance, have become a recurring event in India. While the anti-Sikh riot of 1984 in Delhi and the Muslim carnage of 2002 in Gujarat shattered the collective conscience of India, communal riots have become an industry in the country prompted by brain activists and executed by muscle activists. Communal riots have their own infra-structure, production and deployment of weapons, middle men, collective actors and profit makers. From 1954 to 1988 there were more than 10,000 communal riots in India, small and big. This is indeed a persisting blot on democratic and pluralistic India. How one wishes Mohandas Karamchand Gandhi were in our midst now!

IV

I want to conclude my lecture with a short reference to the current credo namely autonomisation of state, market and civil society. It is widely accepted today that state is a coercive agent and motivated by political authority. Rolling back the state is a contemporary refrain. Interestingly enough Gandhiji said: "I look upon an increase in the power of the state with the greatest fear...". But he knew that the state will not wither away and it cannot be wished away. Therefore he advised: "We should strive to create a state which would not need to exercise its coercive authority". That is, the state should govern with the consent of the people which would be a consensual and not a coercive state. Contemporary states, including democratic states, are a far cry from this. The expression, state terrorism, is often invoked to refer to some of the actions of democratic states also.

The present tendency is to let the market occupy the space vacated by the shrinking state so that economic activity which is motivated by material incentives can function without any state regulation. The market mechanism should function in terms of free exchange according to this rendition. But all available empirical evidence suggests that a 'free market' is characterized by rapacity and prompted by greed. If the state is to function without coercive authority and if the market is incapable of self-regulation, the way out is aparigraha or non-possession of material goods and services beyond one's need. Herein lies the seminal importance of Gandhiji's advocacy of voluntary restriction of wants by human beings.

Civil society is the space for free voluntary activity for all citizens, the space between market and state. There is widespread tendency to oppose the authoritarianism of the state and rapacity of the market but to view civil society as positive. But it is important to keep in mind that just as a state could be authoritarian or democratic and the market could be monopolistic or competitive, the civil society too consists of positive and negative elements. Gandhiji recognized this seminal truth. That is why, while firmly holding the view that "No society can possibly be built on a denial of individual freedom", he insisted that "... unrestricted individualism is the law of the beast of jungle". Civil society the space for free voluntary activity, is constituted by individuals who are capable of self restraint as well as those who may behave like beasts. Therefore the current proclivity to declare civil society as an entity without blemish sits uneasily with Gandhian understanding.

Citizen is the creature of state; one cannot meaningfully think of entitlements, duties and rights of citizens without reference to a state. Market produces the consumer; much of her needs and aspirations are created and sustained by the market. Civil society prompts the emergence of communitarians; ideally the communitarian spirit of interrogation is informed of altruism. If the ongoing market fundamentalism gains momentum we will enter a world torn asunder between the citizen, consumer and communitarian. And this should be arrested.

The role and responsibility of citizen will reduce with the shrinkage of state, the dependence of consumer will increase with the expansion of market and the vitality of communitarian will not be very relevant in the changed situation. That is the hegemony of market will adversely affect not only the citizen and the communitarian but the consumer too. The citizen may opt out and become apathetic and alienated. The communitarian may limit her involvement and participation in society, become a retreatist and a recluse, out of sheer disgust. The consumer may tend to catch up, to cope with the intense global competition, becoming an atomized individual indulging in reckless consumption. These are dangerous portents.

Why should this scenario emerge? Because of the contradictory expectations the present regime of globalization have from each of the three societal pillars. It wants that the state should promote and facilitate high quality of life for citizens. The state is expected to be responsible, responsive, transparent and decentering. But at the same time it recommends that the state should roll back and shrink. A shrinking agency cannot be responsible and responsive.

On the other hand, the expanding market is not charged with the responsibility of being a promoter or facilitator of high quality of life. Rarely does one hear in the wake of globalization the need for market institutions to be responsible and responsive. An expanding agency should not be let off without its share of social responsibilities. If taxes collected by the state from citizens are to be invested for their welfare, the profits made through consumers should also be shared with them. It is necessary to postulate a consumer-friendly market ethic.

Institutions of civil society come for frequent approbation in the media. But are they free of the malaise which beset institutions of state and market? The fact is civil society like the curate's egg is partly good and partly rotten. Civil society which produces communitarians who participates in caring and sharing activities also produces criminals, crooks and communalists. The Non-Governmental Organizations and even the media are not necessarily transparent. None is above reproach, beyond blemish. Therefore, we need a New Consensus which is comprehensive enough to encapsulate the roles and responsibilities of state, market and civil society.

Active citizenship is a popular refrain in the contemporary world particularly in liberal democracies. But capitalism and democracy have become ideological Siamese twins and the consumer created by the market has become the slave and not the king as promised. Further, with the onset of globalization the state is rolling back and the creature of the state namely citizen, is losing salience. Even as the consumer is forging ahead and going berserk there are no controlling radars applied to him. The state is rendered weak and hence incapable of performing this task and the market has a vested interest in boosting consumerism. Indeed there is a conspiracy of silence about responsible consumership which was a Gandhian refrain. Finally, the communitarian the creature of civil society need to be disciplined, neither by the state nor by the market, but has to be self-disciplined. The crucial characteristic of the human being of Gandhian conception is self-restraint. To nurture such an entity remains the single most important task of Independent India and hence the eternal relevance of Mohandas Karamchand Gandhi.

12

The Spinning– Wheel and the Seed: Gandhi's Legacy, Humanity's Hope

Vandana Shiva

Gandhi lives as a perennial source of inspiration and political innovation to defend our freedoms. Globalisation as a project is a plan to extinguish all freedoms of people through the total control of trade, technology, and property rights. The freedom of river to flow and organisms to evolve, of farmers to save seeds and grow crops, of consumers to be free to choose what they eat and know how their food is produced constitutes the fundamental freedoms of all species. Ordinary humans are being robbed in the name of "free trade" or globalisation.

Globalisation is often presented as a process of new interconnections between societies. However, if it is geographical, it is about the global reach of giant corporations, not about a global joining of the hearts of people worldwide. But the real project of globalisation is colonisation and commodification of the very resources and processes that give us life-our biodiversity, our food, and our water.

Over the past decades my ideas and actions to defend life's freedom and diversity have come from the inspiration from Gandhi. Without his legacy it would be impossible even to imagine a response to the totalitarianism built into the project of owning life, owning seeds, owning water. Patents on life and the new biotechnologies are today's tools of imperialism, and

* Reprinted with the permission of Gandhi Peace Foundation and *Gandhi Marg* from *Gandhi Marg* (April-June 2004), pp. 19-30.

they are a core part of the global "constitution" called the WTO rules of free trade in the form of Trade Related Intellectual Property Rights (TRIPS). The phrase "trade related" had to be forcefully linked to intellectual property precisely because intellectual property has no place in a trade treaty and patents should not have been extended to cover life forms as they were under Act 273(b) of TRIPS which forces countries to patent life forms, in particular micro-organisms and genetically engineered plants and animals. These rules and laws were made by and for corporations. As a Monsanto spokesperson stated about the drafting of TRIPS, "we were the patient, the diagnostician, the physician".

Patents of life are a total control system. They allow corporations to claim ownership over life forms-micro-organisms, plants, animals. They allow corporations to define the acts of saving and sharing seeds as "intellectual property crimes". And they allow the crime of biopiracy-the theft of traditional knowledge and biopiracy to be treated as a right.

A patent is an exclusive right to own, make, sell, produce, use a patented product. A patent on seed implies that a farmer saving seed is an "intellectual property thief." But it means more. A system in which seed has become a corporate monopoly, a system in which a few companies control the seed supply is in effect a system of slavery for farmers. Where the freedom of seed disappears, the freedom of farmers disappears.

That is why, in 1987, when I first came to know about GATT and TRIPS and Patents on life, I searched for ways to defend the freedom of biodiversity and the freedom of peasants. And Gandhi's spinning wheel inspired my dedicating my life to saving seeds to save small farmers and protect life.

Spinning Freedom

It was to regenerate livelihood in India that Gandhi thought of the spinning-wheel as a symbol of liberation and a tool for development. Power driven mills were the model of development in that period of early industrialisation. However, the hunger of mills for raw materials and markets was the reason for a new poverty, created by the destruction of livelihoods either by diverting land and biomass from local subsistence to the factory, or by displacing local production through the market.

Gandhi had said that "anything that millions can do together, becomes charged with unique power". The spinning wheel had become a symbol of such power. "The wheel as such is lifeless, but when I invest it with symbolism, it becomes a living thing for me'.

When Gandhi described the Charkha in 1908 in his *Hind Swaraj* as a panacea for the growing pauperism of India, he had never seen a spinning-wheel. Even in 1915, when he returned to India from South Africa, he had not actually seen a spinning wheel. But he saw essential element of freedom from colonialism in discarding the use of mill woven cloth. He set up handlooms in the Satyagraha Ashram at Sabarmati, but could not find a spinning wheel or a spinner, who were normally women. In 1917, Gandhi's disciple Ganga Behn Majumdar started a search for the spinning wheel, and found one in Vijapur in the Baroda State. Quite a few people there had spinning wheels in their homes, but had long since consigned them to the lofts as useless lumbers. They now pulled them out, and soon Vijapur Khadi gained a name for itself. And Khadi and the spinning wheel rapidly became the symbol for India's independence movement.

The spinning-wheel symbolised a technology that conserves resources, people's livelihoods, and people's control over their livelihoods. In contrast to the imperialism of the British textile industry, the Charkha was decentred and labour generating, not labour displacing. It needed people's hands and minds, instead of treating them as surplus, or as mere inputs into an industrial process. This critical mixture of decentralisation, livelihood generation, resource conservation and strengthening of self-reliance were essential to undo the waste of centralisation, livelihood destruction, resource depletion and creation of economic and political dependence that had been engendered by the industrialisation associated with colonialism.

Gandhi's spinning-wheel is a challenge to notions of progress and obsolescence that arise from absolutism and false universalism in concepts of science and technology development. Obsolescence and waste are social constructs that have both a political and ecological component. Politically, the notion of obsolescence gets rid of people's control over their lives and livelihoods by defining productive work as unproductive and removing people's control over production in the name of progress. It would rather waste hands than waste time. Ecologically too, obsolescence destroys the regenerative capacity of nature by substituting manufactured uniformity in place of nature's diversity. This induced dispensability of poorer people on the one hand and diversity on the other constitutes of the political ecology of technological development guided by narrow and reductionist notions of productivity. Parochial notions of productivity, perceived as universal, rob people of control over their means of reproducing life and rob nature of her capacity to regenerate diversity.

Ecological erosion and destruction of livelihoods are linked to one another. Displacement of diversity and displacement of people's sources of sustenance both arise from a view of development and growth based on uniformity created through centralised control. In this process of control, reductionist science and technology act as handmaidens for economically powerful interests. The struggle between the factory and spinning-wheel continues as new technologies emerge.

As seeds are genetically engineered and patented, a crisis is being engineered for farmers and farming. And the seed becomes the Charkha of today. That is why I started Navdanya.

Diversity and Freedom

The Green Revolution was an exemplar of the deliberate destruction of diversity. The new biotechnologies are repeating and deepening these tendencies, rather than reversing them.

Further, new technologies in combination with patent monopolies being pushed through intellectual property rights regimes in GATT and other trade platforms as well as the biodiversity convention are threatening to transform the diversity of life forms into mere raw material for industrial production, and limitless profits. They are simultaneously threatening the regenerative freedom of diverse species, and the free and sustainable economy of small peasants and producers which is based on nature's diversity and its utilisation.

The seed, for example, reproduces itself and multiplies. Farmers use seed both as grain as well as for the next year's crop. Seed is free, both in the ecological sense of reproducing itself, as well as in the economic sense of reproducing the farmers' livelihood.

This seed freedom is, however, a major obstacle for seed corporations. If the market for seed has to be created, the seed has to be transformed materially, so that reproducibility is blocked and its status has to be changed legally, so that instead of being the common property of farming communities, it becomes the patented private property of seed corporation.

As my involvement in these issues grew, the seed started to take shape as the site and symbol of freedom in the age of manipulation and monopoly of life in its diversity.

Ethically and ecologically, unrestrained biotechnology development gives new tools for manipulation, patents offer new tools for monopoly ownership of that which is by its very nature free. I thought of Gandhi's spinning wheel which had become such an important symbol of freedom, not because it was big and powerful but because it was small and could become alive as a sign of resistance and creativity in smallest of huts and poorest of families. In small lay its power.

The seed too is small. It embodies diversity. It embodies the freedom to stay alive. And seed is still the common property of small farmers in India. Seed freedom goes far beyond freedom for the farmer from corporations. It indicates freedom of diverse cultures from centralised control. In the seed, ecological issues could combine with social justice. I could see that it was the seed that could play the role of Gandhi's spinning wheel in this period of recolonisation through "free trade".

In spite of many blocks and pressures, I launched a national programme to save seed diversity in farmers' fields in cooperation with the movements I have been working with over many years. We call it "Navdanya", which literally means nine seeds and is a beautiful symbol of the richness of diversity.

Ours was not the first seed conservation programme. Genetic resources have always been collected for breeding. The risks for breeding towards uniformity led to the emergence of government gene banks in the 1970s. However, while gene banks collect biodiversity from farmers' fields, they do not conserve it through and with farmers. Instead, diversity flows from farmers' fields to gene banks and then on to corporate breeders, but is systematically eroded at the source. The farmers then become mere consumers of corporate seed, which in the future will also have IPR protection, thus forcing farmers to buy seed every year. This excludes the farmer from playing the critical role of conserver of genetic diversity and innovator in the utilisation and development of seed. It robs farmers of their rights to their biological and intellectual heritage. It also separates conservation from production, and scientists from farmers. We wanted to build a programme in which farmers and scientists relate horizontally rather than vertically, in which conservation of biodiversity and production of food go hand in hand, and in which farmers' knowledge is strengthened, not robbed.

While the fundamental changes we are working toward can only be achieved in the long-term, at the small-scale level, Navdanya has already had major impact in the villages in which we work. Realising that our small efforts in the conservation of indigenous seed diversity are not enough, we have also joined hands with the farmers' movement to urgently mobilise public opinion against the emerging threat of multinational corporations gaining monopoly control on all life through the new biotechnologies and intellectual property rights.

In 1991, I started to contact the farmers organisations to alert them on the new trends, to work with them on protecting farmers' rights to freely conserve, use, exchange and modify the seeds. In February 1992, we organised a national conference on

GATT and Agriculture with the Karnataka Rajya Ryota Sangha (KRRS). In October 1992, at a massive farmers rally in Hospet organised by the KRRS, the Seed Satyagraha was launched following Gandhi's politics of Satyagraha as a fight for truth based on non-cooperation with unjust regimes. In March 1993, we held a national rally in Delhi at the historic Red Fort under the leadership of the national farmers organisations, the Bharatiya Kisan Union. Independence Day (15 August 1993) was celebrated with farmers asserting their "collective intellectual property rights" (Samuhik Gyan Sanad). On 2 October 1993, one year of the seed satyagraha was celebrated in Bangalore with a gathering of 5,00,000 farmers. We also had farmers from some other Third-World countries as well as from amongst scientists who work on farmers' rights and sustainable agriculture in an expression of solidarity. The internationalisation of the Seed Satyagraha within one year has given the word globalisation a new meaning. From representing global markets as in the parlance of free trade proponents, it has come to mean for us the globalisation of people's resistance to centralised control over all aspects of their life.

The native seed has become a system of resistance against monocultures and monopoly rights. The shift from uniformity to diversity respects the rights of all species and is sustainable. Diversity is also a political imperative because uniformity goes hand in hand with centralisation, while diversity demands de-centred control. Diversity as a way of thought and a way of life is what is needed to go beyond the impoverished monocultures of the mind.

For us, protecting native seeds is more than conservation of raw material for the biotechnology industry. The diverse seeds now being pushed to extinction carry within them seeds of other ways of thinking about nature, and other ways of producing for our needs. Uniformity and diversity are not just patterns of land use, they are ways of thinking and ways of living.

Conservation of diversity is, above all, the commitment to let alternatives flourish in society and nature, in economic systems and in knowledge systems. Cultivating and conserving diversity is no luxury in our times. It is a survival imperative, and the precondition for the freedom of all, the big and the small. In diversity, the smallest has a place and significance. Allowing the small to flourish is to me the real test of freedom in the life of an individual, the life of an organisation, the life of a society, and the life of this planet. It is this connection between diversity, decentredness and democracy which has guided my ideas and actions, at the local as well as the global level.

Seed Saving: Our Ethical Duty, Our Human Right

Seed is the first link in the food chain. In Sanskrit, *Bija*, the seed, means the source of life. Saving seed is our duty, sharing seed is our culture.

Patents on seeds and genetic resources rob us of our birthright to derive our livelihoods by transforming seed saving and seed sharing into "intellectual property crimes". This is an assault on our culture, our human rights, our very survival.

Seed patents and seed monopolies are also becoming a major source of seed insecurity and food security. As seed is transformed from the common property of peasant communities into the private property of giant corporations like Monsanto, a number of associated transformations take place.

As seed saving is prevented by patents as well as by the engineering of seed with non-renewable traits, seed has to be bought for every planting season by poor peasants. A free resource available on farm becomes a commodity which farmers are forced to buy every year. This increases poverty and leads to indebtedness. As debts increase and become unpayable, farmers are compelled to sell kidneys or even commit suicide. More than 25,000 peasants in India have taken their lives since 1997 when the practice of seed saving was transformed under globalisation pressures and multinational seed corporations started to take control of the seed supply. Seed saving gives farmers life. Seed monopolies rob farmers of life.

The shift from farm saved seed to corporate monopolies of the seed supply is also a shift from biodiversity to monocultures in agriculture. This District of Warangal in Andhra Pradesh used to grow diverse legumes, millets, oilseeds. Seed monopolies created crop monocultures of cotton, leading to disappearance of millions of nature's evolution and farmers' breeding.

Monocultures and uniformity increase the risks of crop failure as diverse seeds adapted to diverse ecosystems are replaced by rushed introduction of unadapted and often untested seeds into the market. When Monsanto first introduced Bt. Cotton in India in 2002, the farmers lost Rs. 1 billion due to crop failure. Instead of 1,500 kg./acre as promised by the company, the harvest was as low as 200 kg. Instead of increased incomes of Rs. 10,000/acre, farmers ran into losses of Rs. 6,400/acre.

In the state of Bihar, when farm saved corn seed was displaced by Monsanto's hybrid corn, the entire crop failed creating Rs. 4 billion losses and hence increased poverty for desperately poor farmers.

Poor peasants of the South cannot survive seed monopolies. That is why the case of Percy Schmeiser will decide the fate not just of one Canadian farmer but billions of peasants. The unjust and unethical case brought by Monsanto against Percy is a double crime against farmers. Firstly by creating and enforcing illegitimate patent rights to seed, it robs us of our human right and human duty to be seed savers. Secondly, it rewards the polluter with enhanced property rights and profits. The principle of "polluter pays" has been transformed into the "polluter gets paid" principle.

This perverse jurisprudence must be corrected for the sake of all farmers, and all species. Farmers' freedoms must come before corporate monopoly. Farmers survival must come before corporate greed. Percy's future is our future. Percy's seed freedom is our freedom. Percy's rights as a farmer are symbolic of the human rights of all farmers.

The Suicide Economy of Corporate Globalisation

While the government spends millions on advertisements saying "India Shining", a large part of India is dying. The Indian peasantry, the largest body of surviving small farmers in the world, today faces a crisis of extinction.

Two-thirds of India makes its living from the land. The earth is the most generous employer in this country of a billion, that has farmed this land for more than 5,000 years.

However, as farming is delinked from the earth, the soil, the biodiversity, the climate and linked to global corporations and global markets, and the generosity of the earth is replaced by the greed of corporations, the viability of small farmers and small farms is destroyed. Farmers' suicides are the most tragic and dramatic symptom of the crisis of survival faced by Indian peasants.

The year 1997 witnessed the first emergence of farm suicides in India. Rapid increase in indebtedness was at the root of farmers taking their lives. Debt is a reflection of a negative economy, a losing economy. Two factors have transformed the positive economy of agriculture into a negative economy for peasants - the rising costs of production and the falling prices of farm commodities. Both these factors are rooted in the policies of trade liberalisation and corporate globalisation.

In 1998, the World Bank's structural adjustment policies forced India to open up its seed sector to global corporations like Cargill, Monsanto, Syh genta. The global corporations changed the input economy overnight. Farm saved seeds were replaced by corporate seeds, which needed fertilizers and pesticides and could not be saved.

As seed saving is prevented by patents as well as by the engineering of seed with non-renewable traits, seeds have to be bought for every planting season by poor peasants. A free resource available on farm becomes a commodity which farmers are forced to buy every year. This increases poverty and leads to indebtedness. As debts increase and become unpayable, farmers are compelled to sell kidneys or even commit suicide. More than 25,000 peasants in India have taken their lives since 1997 when the practice of seed saving was transformed under globalisation pressures and multinational seed corporations started to take control of the seed supply. Seed saving gives farmers life. Seed monopolies rob farmers of life.

And the crisis of suicides shows how the survival of small farmers is incompatible with the seed monopolies of global corporations.

The second pressure Indian farmers are facing is the dramatic fall in prices of farm produce as a result of free trade policies of the WTO. The WTO rules for trade in agriculture are in essence rules for dumping. They have allowed an increase in agribusiness subsidies while preventing countries from protecting their farmers from the dumping of artificial cheap produce. High subsidies of $ 400 billion combined with forced removal of import restrictions is a ready-made recipe for farmers' suicides. Global prices have dropped from $ 216/ton in 1995 to $ 133/ton in 2001 for wheat, $ 98.2/ton in 1995 to $ 49.1/ton in 2001 for cotton, $ 273/ton in 1995 to $ 178/ton for soyabean. This reduction of half the price is not due to a doubling in productivity but due to an increase in subsidies and an increase in market monopolies controlled by a handful of agribusiness corporations.

Thus the US government pays $193 per ton to US soya farmers, which artificially lowers the price of soya. Due to removal of quantitative restrictions and lowering of tariffs, cheap soya has destroyed the livelihoods of coconut growers, mustard farmers, producers of seasame, groundnut and soya.

Similarly, cotton producers in the US are given a subsidy of $ 4 billion annually to 25,000 cotton producers. This has brought the cotton prices down artificially, allowing the US to capture world markets which were earlier accessible to poor African countries such as Burkina Faso, Benin, Mali. The subsidy of $ 230 per acre in the US is genocidal for the African farmers. African cotton farmers are losing $ 250 million every year. That is why small African countries walked out of the Cancun negotiations, leading to the collapse of the WTO ministerial.

The rigged prices of globally traded agriculture commodities are stealing incomes from poor peasants of the South. Analysis carried out by the Research Foundation for Science, Technology and Ecology shows that due to falling farm prices, Indian peasants are losing $ 26 billion or Rs. 1.2 trillion annually. This is a burden their poverty does not allow them to bear. Hence the epidemic of farmer suicides.

India was among the countries that questioned the unfair rules of WTO in agriculture and led the G-22 alliance along with Brazil and China. India with some other Southern countries addressed the need to safeguard the livelihoods of small farmers from the injustice of free trade based on high subsidies and dumping. Yet at the domestic level, official agencies in India are in deep denial of any links between free trade and farmers' survival.

An example of this denial is a Government of Karnataka report on "Farmers' suicide in Karnataka — A scientific analysis". The report, while claiming to be "scientific", makes unscientific reductionist claims that the farm suicides have only psychological causes, not economic ones, and identifies alcoholism as the root cause of suicides. Therefore, instead of proposing changes in agricultural policy, the report recommends that farmers require to boost up their self-respect (swabhiman) and self-reliance (swavalambam). And ironically, its recommendations for farmers' self-reliance are changes in the Karnataka Land Reforms Act to allow larger land holdings and leasing. These are steps towards the further decimation of small farmers who have been protected by land "ceilings" (an upper limit on land ownership) and policies that only allow peasants and agriculturalists to own agricultural land (part of the land to the tiller policies of the Devraj Urs government).

While the "expert committee" report identified "alcoholism" as the main cause for suicides, the figures of this "scientific" claim are inconsistent and do not reflect the survey. On page 10, the report states in one place that 68 per cent of the suicide victims were alcoholics. Five lines later it states that 17 per cent were "alcohol and illicit drinkers". It also states that the majority of suicide victims were small and marginal farmers and the majority had high levels of indebtedness. Yet debt is not identified as a factor leading to suicide. On page 32 of the report it is stated that of the 105 cases studied among the 3544 suicides which had occured in five districts during 2000-2001, 93 had debts,

54 per cent victims had borrowed from private sources and moneylenders. More than 90% suicide victims were in debt. Yet a table on page 63 has mysteriously reduced debt as a reason for suicide to 2.6% and equally mysteriously, "suicide victims having a bad habit" has emerged as the primary cause of farmers' suicides.

The government is desperate to delink farm suicides from economic processes linked to globalisation such as rise in indebtedness and increased frequency of crop failure due to higher ecologic vulnerability arising from climate change and drought and higher economic risks due to introduction of untested, unadopted seeds. This is evident in recommendation No. 4.3.24.3. "The government should launch prosecution on the responsible persons involved in misleading the public and government by providing false information about farmers' suicides as crop failure or indebtedness" (page 113 of expert committee report).

But farmers' suicides cannot be delinked from indebtedness and the economic distress small farmers are facing. Indebtedness is not new. Farmers have always organised for freedom from debt. In the nineteenth century the so-called "Deccan Riots" were farmers' protests against the debt trap into which they had been pushed to supply cheap cotton to the textile mills in Britain. In the eighties they formed peasant organisations to fight for debt relief from public debt linked to Green Revolution inputs. However, under globalisation, the farmer is losing her/his social, cultural, economic identity as a producer. A farmer is now a "consumer" of costly seeds and costly chemicals sold by powerful global corporations through powerful landlords and moneylenders locally. This combination is leading to corporate feudalism, the most inhumane, brutal and exploitative convergence of global corporate capitalism and local feudalism, in the face of which the farmer as an individual victim feels helpless. The bureaucratic and technocratic systems of the state are coming to the rescue of the dominant economic interests by blaming the victim.

It is necessary to stop this war against small farmers. It is necessary to rewrite the rules of trade in agriculture. It is necessary to change our paradigms of food production. Feeding humanity should not depend on the extinction of farmers and extinction of species. Another agriculture is possible and necessary - an agriculture that protects farmers' livelihoods, the earth and its biodiversity and health.

From the Suicide Economy to Living Economics

Gandhi's creative vision of Swadeshi, Swaraj, Satyagraha, and Sarvodaya inspires us to build living economies and living democracies. In his legacy we find hope, we find freedom, we find our own creativity. Gandhi's philosophy is a living philosophy both because it is not dead and because when it informs our actions, they become charged with life. Only through Gandhi do we begin, with constructive action and turn it into our best resistance. Our seed saving is a resistance to seed monopolies and seed patents. And when our government begins to implement TRIPS as it has done through three amendments of our Patent Act and the creation of a new plant variety legislation, we remember Gandhi's words "As long as the superstition that people should obey unjust laws exists, so long will slavery exist". And we renew our commitment to the Bija Satyagraha. Like Mahatma Gandhi started the Salt Satyagraha to protest against the colonisation of salt by the Salt Laws imposed by the British Empire, people's movement in India are committed to the Bija Satyagraha based on non-cooperation with unjust and immoral IPR laws being imposed on MNC's and the rich countries. These laws are : -

(i) The protection of plant varieties and farmers' rights act which establishes MNC's monopoly over seeds, makes Indian farmers bioserfs and robs them of their age-old freedom to save, exchange and sell seeds.

(ii) The amended patent act which allows seeds, plants, animals, genes and all life forms to be patented and indigenous knowledge to be pirated.

(iii) The biodiversity act which gives free access to our genetic wealth and indigenous knowledge to biopirates within and outside India.

As genetic pollution threatens our biodiversity and globalisation threatens our farmers, we create living economies and living democracies based on swadeshi and swaraj. Just as the seed has the potential to germinate and evolve and renew itself perennially, Gandhi's legacy has the potential to germinate, evolve, and renew our actions and strategies for freedom appropriate to our times and context.

From the seed, our swadeshi efforts have grown to organic farming or *jaiv kheti*, fair and just trade, and swadeshi in the form of biodiversity conservation has evolved organically into the swaraj of Jaiv Panchayat or living democracy, resting on the resistance of satyagraha – non-cooperation with immoral, unjust laws that force patenting of life.

Gandhi's legacy lives and gives us the hope to shape ever new instruments to keep life in its diversity and integrity free. Gandhi's legacy carries the seeds for the freedoms of humans and all species. Gandhi's legacy is humanity's hope.

13 Morality in Political Practice: Marx and Gandhi*

M.N. Roy

The controversy about the philosophical consequences of the New Physics, particularly the Quantum Theory, prepared the intellectual background of the present crisis of culture. A good many philosophizing scientists of the first rank advanced the view that recent discoveries of physics had shaken the foundation of the mode of thought which, heralded by the Renaissance, was cultivated and preached by a long succession of scientists and philosophers during the sixteenth and seventeenth centuries, elaborated in a comprehensive system by the Encyclopedists of the eighteenth century, and thereafter gained ground steadily as the most characteristic feature of modern civilization and culture. Scepticism about the objective validity of scientific knowledge became fashionable; scientific agnostics preached a neomysticism; and the world was flooded with a literature to ridicule the naivety of the nineteenth century scientists, to cast doubt on their Natural Philosophy, to exorcise the evil spirit of Materialism and to call for a religious revival with the sanction of science.

The modern world had just emerged from the twilight of the Middle Ages dominated by transcendentalism and the religious mode of thought. A few centuries are but a moment in

---

* Reprinted with the permission of Indian Renaissance Institute (IRI) from *The Marxian Way*, 3:2 (1948-49); also in R.M. Pal (ed.), *Selections from The Marxian Way and the Humanist Way* (Delhi, Ajanta, 1999), pp. 252-260.

the long history of man. The predisposition to believe, which makes life so much simpler, as against the spirit of enquiry, so very difficult to cultivate, was still lingering in most modern men. The lingering predisposition to atavism was encouraged in the intellectual atmosphere of inverted agnosticism and scientific mystery - mongering. The modern man in search of God was a curiosity of our time. That process culminated in the present widespread tendency of falling back upon religious and transcendental authorities not only for defending morality in public life, but for rehabilitating ethics generally.

This spiritual atavism, amounting to an admission of the defeat of man in his age long quest for freedom and search for knowledge, is the essence of the present crisis, the severest of all ever experienced by mankind. A relapse seems to be unavoidable, unless the possibility of an ethics without any transcendental sanction can be established. And that can be done by a truly philosophical interpretation of the scientific knowledge on the basis of an integration of the achievements made in the different field of scientific enquiry.

While the world appears to be sinking deeper and deeper in the crisis, the way out of it is actually being found by those who are qualified and competent for the great task. During the closing years of his life, Paul Langevin threw the entire weight of the reputation of a great scientist on the side of the rationalist and naturalist tradition of modern culture and civilization. Notwithstanding the fact that, in the light of the present knowledge about the foundation of the physical Universe, the classical concept of matter has lost all meaning, he held that the philosophy traditionally known as Materialism is the only philosophy consistent with rationalism and science, and even used the odious term in the absence of a more appropriate denomination.

But the wisdom of distinguishing dialectical Materialism from the classical Mechanistic naturalism is doubtful. If Materialism by itself cannot stand the test of scientific knowledge and rationalist judgment, a misfitting adjective will not save it. The objective reality of physical processes cannot be qualified by a method of thinking. Dialectical Materialism is a contradiction in terms, because dialectic belongs to the world of ideas.

At the time of Marx, the classical mechanistic view of the Universe stood unchallenged, supported by the great achievements of Newtonian physics. The introduction of the term dialectic was entirely gratuitous. Marx's attack upon mechanical Materialism could have served no other purpose than that of claiming the credit of founding a new philosophy - essentially of the Hegelian tradition. The extravagance of the nineteenth century German materialists like Buechner, Moleschott, Vogt, etc. was a caricature of the philosophy of the Enlightenment physiocrats.

If it is true that classical determinism might have a fatalistic connotation, the tendency is much stronger in the philosophy of history deduced from dialectical Materialism. Economic determinism is the basic principle of Marxist historiology (Historical Materialism). According to it, the evolution of society is predetermined in minutest detail; man is reduced to a marionette; the operation of the forces of production, which becomes almost a metaphysical concept, is as inexorable as the Providential Will. Historical (economic) determinism is a teleological notion. It admits of more absurd fantasies than the Super-Intelligence of Laplace.

The history of the notion of dialectic should expose the meaninglessness of such phrases as "dialectics of nature", "dialectics of history", "dialectics of social evolution", etc. Dialectic is a method of thinking and discussing; neither nature nor history, nor again society, thinks or discusses. These phrases, freely and frequently used in a pseudo-philosophical literature, smack of anthropomorphism, if not of animism of the savage.

Originally a method of disputation used by the Eleatic philosophers, dialectic was developed by Plato as an art of analyzing the "Ideas". Previously, the function of Socratic dialectic was to expose the fallacy of popular belief. With Aristotle, dialectic became the universal law of reasoning-an *a priori* category of thought, an intellectual process, a system of logic. Therefore, it is not historically true that dialectic is essentially different from the "formal" Aristotelian logic. In Hegelian philosophy, the old notion reappears in the Socratic as well as Aristotelian sense. It was entirely arbitrary of Marx to maintain that he had taken over the notion of dialectic without its intrinsic meaning. The notion is intrinsically as well as historically idealistic, and as such, cannot be used as an adjective to the process of nature and history. Such an inappropriate adjective is not necessary for a defense of Materialism, which can today be done epistemologically as well as ontologically.

The error of the venerable dictum, "Natura non facet saltus", has been exposed not by dialectic, but simply by a greater knowledge of nature. On the other hand, gratuitously hitched on to the mysticism of dialectic, Materialism is committed to a series of historically, untrue and logically untenable propositions; unity of thought and action, of theory and practice, is the most vicious of them. Priority might be a conceivable question; unity of the two is a palpably absurd notion. And the problem of priority is no less baffling than in the case of the chicken and the egg. *Homo Faber* and *homo sapiens* may be identical; but anthropology will find it extremely difficult to pronounce a rationalist judgment on the question of priority, if it is raised. And the question must be raised, because thought and action are never simultaneous. What distinguished the progenitor of the human species from lower animals? Was it mere action or primitively intelligent action, as distinct from mechanical adaptation? And is not the very phrase-intelligent action a pointer to the solution of the problem of priority?

There is little room for disagreement about the interdependence of thought and action. It is also true that theory is tested in practice. But it is an unchallengeable empirical proposition that human action presupposes thought; even in lower vertebrates, traces of an incipient intelligence may be noted as impelling certain physical behaviour. The brain is not created by human hands, through the manipulation of tools; on the contrary, fabrication and manipulation of tools presupposes not only the physical existence of the brain, but its functioning as intelligence. Thoughts may be born of action; but thoughtless action is not a desirable human attribute.

It is difficult to accept the view that science evolved in response to the requirements of action, even when it carries the authority of a great scientist. It may be valid in the case of technology, and even then one cannot be dogmatic; many inventions as well as discoveries are accidental. It would be difficult to trace a utilitarian motive, or even any conscious urge for action, in the first inventor of the steam-power, for instance. In the realm of pure science (and it would be incredible if a mathematician denied the possibility of pure science), the view is palpably wrong and utterly unfounded. Take, for instance, Copernican astronomy, or Cartesian cosmology, or Newtonian physics, or non-Euclidean geometry, or Einstein's Theory of Relativity or, finally, the contributions to pure mathematics of Langevin himself. Were they evolved in response to any requirement of action? Knowledge certainly enables man to act more effectively, and the experience of action again makes his quest for knowledge more fruitful. In this sense thought and action are interdependent. But the age long quest for knowledge has no utilitarian motive. The search for truth is an independent human function.

Dialectic can be associated with Materialism as its logic. But Marxian dialectic distinguishes itself from logic by freeing Materialism from the encumbrance of an ethics. The defect of classical mechanistic natural philosophy was that it had no necessary connection with ethical principles. As such it could degenerate into a dehumanized system of thought having no bearing upon the realities of life. Dialectic Materialism is no improvement in that respect. On the contrary, it expressly rejects generally applicable moral principles and abiding ethical values. Having no logical connection with ethics, classical naturalism, nevertheless, did not preclude the possibility of a moral philosophy. The attitude of dialectic Materialism in that respect is clearly negative. Placing human action above all moral considerations, dialectic Materialism has precipitated the present crisis of culture.

If it is true that a "scientific philosophy of revolution and freedom" eliminates moral considerations from political actions and social behaviour, then the very humanness of man-kindness, compassion, loyalty, honesty, indeed ordinary decency – must drive him back to some form of religion and transcendentalism. The vicious circle of the crisis is thus completed by religious predisposition, from the one side, and the moral callousness of dialectical Materialism, from the other. The flaunting attitude of the latter provides the former with greater impetus. While a morally callous determined minority heralds a revolution and a new order, the great bulk of thoughtful, sensitive, cultured men and women, out of sheer fright and frustration, fall back upon a lingering predisposition, which process, if not checked, may mean a relapse into medievalism.

Marxian dialectics is an unmitigated evil. Associated with it, Materialism, on the one hand, degenerates into a neo-mystic teleology and, on the other hand, provides a pseudo-philosophical sanction to the Jesuitic doctrine that the end justifies the means, which is a flat negation of ethical principles and moral values, and thus deprives human life of its humanness and may transform the modern world into a grim habitat of "Twentieth Century Neanderthalers".

Faced with this deadly and dreadful possibility, human genius must rise up to the occasion and show a way out of the dilemma; a choice between civilized barbarism and cultural reaction casting doubt on the spiritually liberating significance of modern scientific knowledge. A legitimate distrust for this latter tendency may only push the modern world of light and learning to the opposite direction, over the precipice. A man like Langevin failing to separate the chaff from the corn symbolises the danger.

Is there not a third alternative? Cannot the rationality of man and the vast store of positive knowledge, acquired during several creative centuries, provide a sanction for morality? Must ethics be either transcendental (intuitive) or utilitarian? Is there no way out of Spratt's "dilemma", except the blind-alley of Gandhism, which really has nothing new to say? Must modern man necessarily be in search of God to evade moral degradation and relapse into bestiality? Can we not be good, just, kind, truthful, simply because it gives us joy to be so, instead of being wicked, cruel and false?

The martyrdom of the Mahatma may elevate him to the high pedestal of the Messiah of morality in politics. Spratt's paper published in this issue was written before the tragedy; it was actually being read in a meeting in Calcutta on the very day of the Mahatma's assassination. The terrible news came just when the reader was on the last page of the paper, where Spratt's appreciation of Gandhism was recorded. While conceding that the doctrine, of non-violence did represent an effort to introduce morality in political practice, one may find it difficult to accept the view that Gandhism allows individual freedom, rational thinking, and cherishes the ideal of cosmopolitanism. Gandhism is not a logically coherent system of thought. Consistent thinking, indeed, was not the *forte* of the Mahatma. Often moved by good sentiments, he preached a heterogeneous conglomeration of dogmas, which frequently contradicted each other. He never concealed his distrust for reason and intelligence. Blind faith in a divine power, and also in his being its vehicle, was the sheet-anchor of the Mahatma's life. That certainly was fanaticism and intellectual narrowness. In philosophy, the unity of theory and practice may be the most poisonous error; but crass inconsistency between theory (profession) and practice in actual life is not an antidote to the poison. Therefore, for the sake of introducing morality in political practice, Gandhism is hardly preferable to Marxism. There is really not much to choose between cant and callousness. In fact, the former may be more dangerous, because of its insidiousness. Callousness repels and therefore may provoke revolt.

If the proof of the pudding is in the eating, then Gandhism should be judged by the present political atmosphere of India, which is its creation. It certainly has not succeeded in the least in introducing morality in political practice. A rigorous system of thought may be appreciated on its abstract merit. Any reference to practice is irrelevant for judging it. But Gandhism is a practical philosophy, if it is to be granted that distinction; it lays down codes of conduct. Therefore, it must be pragmatically judged. If practice warrants a favorable judgment, its logical inconsistencies may be overlooked as irrelevant. Gandhism is not utopian; it does not pursue a distant ideal. It is evangelist, like a revealed religion. The prophet delivers his message not through precepts, but by the example of his life. Gandhi may be remembered in history as one whose life was his message. And on that token, he failed. Christ gathered around himself at least a dozen apostles who not only preached the gospel, but tried to live it. How many are there among the thousands of professed Gandhists who preach the gospel as well as live it? There is certainly none among those who are supposed to have succeeded in politics by following the Messiah of morality in public life. Is there any difference between the political practice of the Gandhists in power and that of others in a similar position, including the Marxists? Only there is more of hypocrisy, cant and demagogy. That is hardly a recommendation. A pragmatic judgment of Gandhism, therefore, must be that it has failed to introduce morality in political practice. In view of that signal failure, Gandhism offers no solution of the crisis of modern culture. The remedy is ineffective, because it is antiquated. It does not take into account the causes of the disease it wants to cure. It is quackery.

Nevertheless, the Gandhi cult is not only sweeping India, but finding an echo in other parts of the world. In India, the phenomenon is understandable: apart from the vulgar desire of making a political capital for the established regime and the party in power, a mediaeval mentality creates a suitable atmosphere for the cult of hero worship. Therefore, Gandhism, whatever might have been the purpose of the prophet, is bound to serve an immoral purpose. Spiritual regimentation of a people as the precondition for the stability of a dictatorial regime, forsooth, with a democratic facade, is the greatest act of immorality in political practice. The spread of the Gandhi cult abroad is yet another manifestation of the crisis of our time. The modern world is in the danger of losing faith in its spiritual heritage– the declaration of the sovereignty of man. Having lost faith in the innate rationality and endless creativeness of man, it is looking out for a Messiah. In this atmosphere of frustration and despair, any charlatan may fill the role. Hitler almost succeeded. Even after his downfall, others are in the run, and they all pretend to be pious men alarmed by the moral malaise of the modern world. Therefore, the disgust and disillusionment caused by the moral callousness of dialectical Materialism should not lead to an uncritical acceptance of Messianic doctrines or counsels of despair calling upon mankind to turn its back upon modern civilization with its scientific mode of thought.

The world is ailing from what the Germans call *Kultur-krankheit* - a malady resulting from new habits cultivated under new social environments - which, therefore, can be cured only by readjustment of behaviour on a higher cultural level. Neither Marxian Materialism, nor the lust for power expressing itself in a mad race for world domination, is a necessary consequence of modern science and civilization. Both are abuses of a precious human heritage - the great achievements of modern science and civilization. The world needs not a revival of God, but a resurrection of man, not Messiahs claiming mystic power to thwart the forces of evil and invoking transcendental sanction for a utopian moral order but moral men and women and possessed of the courage and capacity to build a system of secular ethics on the basis of rationalism, scientific knowledge and aesthetic sense, which distinguish the modern world from barbarism, either of the past or of the future.

14
Mr. Gandhi: An Analysis*

Santi Devi (Evelyn Roy)

And so, Mahatma Gandhi, variously described as "the greatest apostle of non-violence since the days of Buddha and Jesus", "the prophet of spiritualized democracy", and "the greatest man of the world", is in jail, condemned to six years' incarceration by the very judge who in passing sentence paid tribute to him as "a great patriot and a great leader, and even those who differed from you in politics look up to you as a man of high ideals and leading a noble and even saintly life". It is not the purpose of this article to add or detract from the praise that has been heaped upon the head of this unique leader of Indian nationalism.

Rather it is aimed to estimate, as carefully and impartially as may be, the essential qualities of Gandhi the saint, philosopher, politician and patriot, as applied to present-day Indian conditions, and to derive what valuable lessons we may from his failures as well as successes of the past three years.

Gandhi the Saint

No one can know of the life and personality of Mr. Gandhi and fail to render tribute to him as "a saintly man who purifies us at sight". In an age of intense individualism, of uncompromising struggle for existence, in which national, racial

---

* Reprinted with the permission of the Indian Renaissance Institute (IRI) from *Radical Essays on Gandhi and Gandhism*, I.R.I. Essays and Monograph No. 11 (Calcutta: Renaissance Publishers Private Limited, 1986), pp. 14-30.

and class conflicts are hardening for the final battle that will usher a new era of social relationships and civilization, the golden legend of this idealist and ascetic who has carefully given his whole life in service of his fellows, upon whose personal character no faintest blemish rests, whose fearless courage and love of truth stand proven before the whole world, and who combines the naive purity and innocence of a child with the iron will and unbending principles of a man,—such a character will go down in history with the same moral force upon posterity as those saintly prototypes of the past, Thomas Aquinas and St. Francis of Assisi. Gandhi the individual has impressed, individually, thousands of lives who are uplifted and inspired to better things for having known him. His personal example gives force to his moral precepts, for no man can say of him that he does not practice all that he preaches. And it is this moral force of his, dimly radiating beyond the confines of vast India to the indifferent world beyond, which has brought him into prominence as a figure of international interest. Gandhi the philosopher, the politician and patriot is but one of many on this storm-tossed sea of Indian nationalism, unknown and uncared for by the heedless nation which has long since learned not to tread on the tail of British imperialism. But Gandhi the saint—here is a spectacle unique in every age, and as one of the great men cast up by the waters of time, he belongs to every country.

Here is in this half-naked, slender, brown body so completely dominated by the mind within, a strength that dreadnoughts cannot conquer nor machineguns subdue though they shatter it to bits, and out of the respect bred of this certain knowledge, the British empire leaves him unharmed. Six years' simple imprisonment, "with everything possible to make him comfortable", is the utmost they dare attempt, and this merely to remove him from the arena of active politics. When the storm dies down a little, they will let him free. For they will soon learn, if they do not already know, that Gandhi the saint in prison becomes to India's adoring millions Gandhi the martyr, and from the days of the Roman empire onward, the spectacle of martyrdom has exercised a potent and irresistible effect upon the massmind. It is well and truly said that, "Mahatma in jail is more powerful than Mahatma free", not alone for the constant impetus it gives to Indian nationalism by working upon the sympathetic indignation of the masses, but because in jail his qualities of sainthood can radiate at their fullest and best uncongested by the exercise of those more worldly faculties of political leadership in which Mr. Gandhi is not so conspicuously successful.

Gandhi the Philosopher

As a philosopher, Mr. Gandhi is neither original nor unique. He merely reiterates, in an age peculiarly out of tune with his teachings, the ancient doctrine of Hinduism whose ramifications are spread through the world and which are spread at various times to inspire the prophets and saints of other lands. To say that he is a disciple of Buddha and Christ is merely to confirm this statement, for the best teachings of Buddha and Christ were drawn from a common fountainhead which made India and the Orient the mother of all religions. Nor does Mr. Gandhi claim originality in any sense. He frankly professes the teachings of pure Hinduism as interpreted through the Bhagvad Gita and the Bible and seeks to lead not only India, but all humanity back to the golden age of the Vedic cult, when the heresy of materialism and the social conceptions of caste and class did not exist. Like Tolstoy, who was himself fed upon Hindu philosophy and whose place in the revolutionary movement of Russia is peculiarly similar to the role of Mr. Gandhi, non-violence is the first article of faith, "it is my faith". In an article on non-violence published in *Young India,* the tenets of this faith are very clearly outlined and it is necessary to quote the gist of it in order to appreciate its bearing on the political creed which is merely the application of philosophy to contemporary Indian politics.

"Non-violence is complete innocence. Complete nonviolence is complete absence of ill will against all that lives—and in its active form good will towards all life. It is pure love, and, as I read it in the Hindu scriptures, in the Bible, in the Koran, nonviolence is a perfect state. It is the goal towards which mankind moves naturally, though unconsciously. Man does not become divine when he personifies innocence in himself, only then does he become truly man.

"Restraint is the law of our being. Highest perfection is unattainable without highest restraint. Suffering is "thus the badge of the human tribe... Satisfaction lies in the effort, not in the attainment."

Again in *Young India* of February 16, commenting on the remarks of Sir William Vincent in the Bengal Legislative Council, Mr. Gandhi enunciates the purest Hindu gospel of self-renunciation, beloved by Schopenhauer :

"Willing death is deliverance. According to Hindu belief the highest known form of freedom, that is salvation, is possible only when a man voluntarily surrenders his body and becomes totally indifferent to bodily wants. Political freedom of a disciplined character is a prelude to a higher type. It is therefore in the fitness of things that we should voluntarily surrender our possessions, including our bodies for the attainment of national freedom. We must therefore develop an equally infinite capacity for suffering, if we are to replace government by force with government based on popular will".

Thus then, nonviolence is pure love, perfection towards which man is naturally, progressing as a goal, through the highest restraint and suffering. Satisfaction lies not in the attainment of the goal but in the effort. Satisfaction, the beatification of freedom, is attainable through the willing death and surrender of all earthly possessions, and political freedom—the prelude to a higher type—is attainable by developing an infinite capacity for suffering. Nonviolence or love, in its negative state, is complete absence of ill will towards all that lives, and in its positive aspect it is good will towards all life.

What does this doctrine mean applied to the realm of practical politics? It means, to call a spade a spade, that India will be free when two things are accomplished—first, when three hundred millions of Indians living under the most refined and perfected system of imperial exploitation ever devised, starved, maltreated, ignorant and brutalized by armed oppression of a tiny fraction of overlords, reduced to grovelling impotence and hopelessness by constant threat of every engine of destruction which modern civilization has invented, directed against their disarmed helplessness—that these three hundred million slaves will be free when they have learnt to the last man, not only to bear no ill will but practice nonviolence against their oppressors, but to love them completely and perfectly. But not yet free, only half free, for there remains another equally important thing to be accomplished. The realization of such a perfect atmosphere of complete nonviolence of infinite love means that three hundred million Indians will cheerfully endure all kicks and insults, all hunger and nakedness, all poverty and wretchedness until those touched and overcome by such demonstration of man's innate divinity will respond to it by throwing away their machineguns and fleshpots, their treasure hoards and princely power, and will welcome their three hundred million brethren to a new fraternity of man, where liberty and equality will rule the human race under the aegis of perfect love.

Such was the dream of Gautama, of Christ and such is the millennium of Gandhi. Do you doubt it ? Listen to his words of applied philosophy :

"The political nonviolence of the noncooperator does not stand the test in the vast majority of cases. Hence the prolongation of the struggle. Let no one blame the unbending English nature. The hardest fibre must melt in the fire of love. When the British or other nature does not respond the fire is not strong enough.

"If nonviolence is to remain the policy of the nation, we are bound to carry it out to the letter and in the spirit. We must then quickly make up with the English and the cooperators. We must get their certificate that they feel absolutely safe in our midst, that they regard us as friends though we belong to a radically different school of thought and politics. We must welcome them to our political platform as honoured guests; we must meet them on a neutral platform as comrades. Our nonviolence must not breed violence, hatred or ill will.

"If we approach our programme with the mental reservation that, after all, we shall wrest power from the British by force of arms, then we are untrue to our profession of nonviolence—if we believe in our programme, we are bound to believe that the British people are not unamenable to the force of affection as they are undoubtedly amenable to the force of arms.

"Swaraj is a condition of mind and the mental condition of India has been damaged. India will win independence and swaraj only when the people will have acquired the strength to die of their own free will. Then there will be swaraj."

Mr. Gandhi's political philosophy is more difficult to define than his moral one. But Russians who are versed in all shades of political thought would place him in the slender category of "anarchist-mystics". He is an anarchist because he appeals essentially to the individual man and the only possible response to his cult is an individual one; to expect to move masses of men by moral predications that rest ultimately with the individual for fulfilment is utopianism. The gigantic failure of Christianity is the best proof of this. He is a mystic, because he appeals to the intangible something which he turns into "soul force" as the dynamics of his movement towards emancipation. He is above all a subjectivist who looks to psychology to explain that which the objective working of material laws is alone responsible for. "Swaraj is a condition of mind." It is the subjectivism of the man who sees man everywhere controlling the material force of his existence, and who does not stop to reckon that man himself is the product of his material environment, which has predetermined the working of his mentality.

If mere voluntary self-immolation upon the altar of national freedom be the price of swaraj the Indian people ought long ago to have attained the blessing, for nowhere else has the cult or self-annihilation been so practically fulfilled, be it by the philosophers and sannyasis of the past or by the millions of deaths through poverty and plague and famine which the Indian masses have patiently endured, or by the vicarious sacrifice of thousands of lives by the young patriots of India reborn. Mr. Gandhi himself sometimes doubts the possibility of the attainment of perfect nonviolence, that first prerequisite of swaraj, but smothering his doubts he bids the people to struggle towards its realization. "Each time I fail, my effort will be all the more determined for my failure." It is the splendid but impractical idealism conceived in much the same spirit with which Christ bade the rich man give away his all to the poor, and comforted those who had nothing, telling them "Blessed are the humble, for they shall inherit the Kingdom of Heaven." Is it because Mr. Gandhi sees his people disarmed and bleeding, helpless and hopeless before the superior might of the conqueror, that he counsels the philosophy of nonviolence which is after all a philosophy of despair when by analysis it is patent that no one believes in its ultimate fulfilment ? For thousands of years the Indian people have listened to such counsels; for thousands of years they have heeded them, bowing their broken lives before the inscrutable working of providence, accepting their earthly lot without complaint and looking to death willingly for their deliverance. Nonviolence, resignation, perfect love and the release from the pain of living—this is the substance of Indian philosophy handed down through the ages by a powerful caste of kings, priests and philosophers who found it good to keep the people in subjection. Mr. Gandhi is nothing but heir of this long line of ghostly ancestors—he is the perfect product of heredity and environment. His philosophy of satyagraha is the inevitable fruit of the spiritual forebears.

What is unfortunate is that Mr. Gandhi's revived philosophy of other-worldliness coincides with a most unprecedented growth in Indian national life—the growth of a spirit of revolt against material privation on the part of the Indian masses. His time-honoured doctrines of orthodox Hinduism have conflicted with this new spirit of rebellion, have temporarily controlled and arrested its development, thanks to his saintly personality, which has more hold on the imagination of the Indian people than his outworn doctrines of self-annihilation. For this involuntary service, the British government has every reason to be grateful to him, and it was a dim realization of his pacific influence upon the unruly masses as well as a very wholesome fear of rousing the fury of the people to the breaking point, that made the government stay its hand so long before arresting him. It was only when Mr. Gandhi had himself prepared the way to his own arrest by schooling the masses to calmness and had stemmed the flood tide of the spontaneous upheaval of social and economic emancipation by rebuking every outbreak of mass energy, every manifestation of force on the part of the people, and by throwing the entire weight of his loved personality on the side of peace, nonviolence and nonresistance that the bureaucracy dared to arrest him. The story of his political career is best studied in a separate chapter which we will title "Gandhi, the Politician and Patriot". (May 15, 1922).

II

Mr. Gandhi is in jail, but Gandhism as a force in Indian politics lives on, influencing the course of the movement for good or ill. It is the purpose of this article to point out the mistakes of Gandhism in the past, as well as its triumphs, so that those who guide the present struggle for Swaraj may apply these lessons of the past to future action. Until his arrest, Mr. Gandhi was the head and forefront of the Indian Nationalist Movement,—his ideas, his judgment and his final decision on questions of program and tactics were what counted most, influenced though he may have been by other leaders less powerful, because lacking his command of the wide masses of the Indian people. It is, therefore, necessary to study Mr. Gandhi as an individual to fully understand what Gandhism is. In a preceding article, we have already analysed him as Saint and Philosopher; it is essential for our thorough understanding to study him as politician and patriot. A careful survey of his speeches and writings, as well as of his program and tactics, is enough to convince anyone that his personal and political life are merely an application of his philosophical doctrines of Soul-Force, Self-Abnegation and Non-violence, – of the ultimate triumph of Spirit over Matter. The result has been to create as the dominating force in Indian nationalism for the past three years what has cleverly been dubbed "transcendental politics". The effect of this transcendentalism, not only upon British

Imperialism but upon the Indian people, can best be seen in a brief review of Mr. Gandhi's leadership of the Nationalist Movement.

Gandhi the Politician

"Swaraj by nonviolent means can, therefore, never mean an interval of chaos and anarchy. Swaraj by nonviolence must be a progressively peaceful revolution such that the transference of power from a closed corporation to the peoples' representatives will be as natural as the dropping of a fully-ripe fruit from a well nurtured tree. I say again, that such a thing will be quite impossible of attainment, but I know that nothing less is the implication of Nonviolence" (M.K. Gandhi).

Here is Mr. Gandhi's political philosophy in a nut-shell. On reading it one is tempted to enquire, in what way does this differ from the conception of the sincere British Imperialist, who openly declares his civilizing mission to be to fit the Indian people for self-government by an evolutionary process of gradual, progressive stages. He too desires peace, nonviolence and "law and order", if not perfect love. There is no contrast between his and Mr. Gandhi's professed goal and the means to attain it. To find a contrast, one must turn to the histories of past revolutions, which were made, not by love and peace, but by blood and iron. The English Revolution of 1640; the French Revolutions of 1789, 1848 and 1870; the German, Italian and Hungarian Revolutions of '48; the Russian Revolutions of 1905 and '17, to cite only a few of the great liberation movements of modern times. Was there ever a revolution in the history of the world which was not ushered in by force ? Gandhism could learn something by a study of the past. But no, it declares, "India is a special creation of Providence, she has a spiritual heritage to transmit to the world ; she has evolved a spiritual civilization like to none ever witnessed before in the evolution of the human race, and India can do that which no race, no nation in bondage has heretofore been able to accomplish. She can melt the stony heart of her conqueror and win freedom by Nonviolence".

On the subject of India's "spiritual civilization", ...suffice it to say that while India's starving millions are rioting, striking, looting and killing—in a word, behaving exactly like every other normal people under the stress of hunger, overwork and privation,—the burden of proof as to India's spiritual heritage rests upon Indians themselves. A few ascetics practicing Ahimsa, an abnormally large number of monks and begging friars infested Europe in the Middle Ages as well as India today; but Europe nevertheless, despite the Christian Church and the Holy Roman Empire, underwent her bloody baptism of countless wars and revolutions before emerging into the nations of modern times. We venture to suggest that India's spirituality is merely the remnant of medievalism clinging to the new organism about to be ushered into Nationhood. And in this connection we can but quote the profound saying of Marx— "Force is the midwife of Revolution".

So much for the philosophy,—now for the program and tactics of Gandhism. The program can be dismissed in one short word— "swaraj", with the accompanying addenda, "righting the Punjab wrongs" and "restoring the Kalifat." What Swaraj is, what kind of Government it implies, what definite benefit it will confer upon the various classes of the Indian people, remains a vague and undefined uncertainty. We know what Swaraj is not, only since the Ahmedabad Congress of December, 1921, full three years after the movement was under way. Swaraj is not "outside the British Empire", as the rejection of Hazrat Mohani's resolution definitely shows. Swaraj, therefore, is some form of Dominion Home Rule, as Mr. Gandhi himself reluctantly defined it, based upon the "four anna franchise", that is, the right to vote being limited to those who had attained the membership in the Congress Party by paying the regular dues. The Moderates themselves are aiming at Home Rule. Wherein then, lies the difference between them and Gandhism?

The difference, and there is a real even though imperfectly defined one, lies in orientation and tactics. The Moderates look to the attainment of Swaraj through "constitutional" means; their hope is in voluntary concessions from the British Government. The Extremists base their Swaraj upon the dynamic action of the masses, which will force concessions from the foreign ruler by "legitimate and peaceful" means. These means, under the inspiration and leadership of Mr. Gandhi, took the form of Non-cooperation with the present government; Boycott of schools, law courts, liquor and foreign cloth; the manufacture and use of Khaddar or homespun, by the Charka (spinning wheel); and Civil Disobedience, chiefly in the form of Non-payment of taxes,—all to be practiced with absolute nonviolence.

Since the tactics of the Non-cooperator are based upon and depend for ultimate success upon mass action and call upon active cooperation of the vast majority of the nation, the Indian workers and peasants, at every step of the way,—it is but logical to assume that this indispensable support of the masses would be won by adopting a program suitable to their immediate needs and desires. The Indian peasantry who awoke from their agelong resignation during and after the war to demand improvement in their earthly lot by remission of taxes, lowering of rents and access to land, began a spectacular career of looting and burning, rioting and killing in various parts of the country, which presaged a peasant revolt of serious dimensions, and which gave the government grave concern. Similarly, the Indian proletariat, that comparatively new creation of Indian industrialism, who had been herded into the great manufacturing centres and mercilessly exploited, began to rebel and to enforce their demands for fewer hours, higher wages and better living conditions by means of strikes which spread with lightning rapidity and threatened to paralyse the industrial life of the country. The awakening of both peasants and proletariat was independent of the nationalist movement for swaraj ; one was economic, the other political. But the nationalist movement, which needed the support of the masses, immediately stepped into the leadership of this economic revolt ; it sought to guide and control the activities of the people to enforce its own demands ; it called hartals or strikes and suspended them at pleasure ; announced boycott of foreign cloth and liquor shops, the universal use of the Charka, and commanded the masses to obey. In return for this usurpation of a popular upheaval for economic betterment, what did the Congress give the masses ? Did it hold out the promise of a swaraj with better wages, lower taxes, enough to eat and to wear and a decent place to live in for the millions of Indian workers on the land and in the factories ? Did it hold up the banner of a material swaraj within the comprehension and necessities of the rebellious Indian people ?

No. On the contrary, it held before the eyes of the famished workers a fabulous, "spiritual" Swaraj, to be attained not by the brief, energetic and wholesome birth-pangs of revolution, but by the old, familiar method of suffering, sacrifice, non-resistance, repentance and prayer. The Indian masses, who had come to the end of their capacity to suffer and endure, must "purify" themselves and become perfectly nonviolent in thought, word and deed before the Swaraj of the Rishis, the Swaraj of a hand-spinning, hand-weaving, beast-of-burden India would descend upon them like a boon from Heaven. Swaraj would come, next week, next month, next year, when the hungry, naked Indian toilers had transcendentalized themselves. Mahatma Gandhi said so ; Mahatma Gandhi was a great saint, a great sage, an incarnation of God Himself, whom the white rulers could not harm, did not dare to touch ; therefore, simple, ignorant men must trust, believe and blindly obey. The mass movement of riotous peasants, of striking city workers, fell into line with the Nationalist movement, danced to the tune of its leaders, obeyed, insofar as lay within his power, the gentle behests of the Mahatma, and waited three years for a Swaraj that like a will-o'-the-wisp, fled further and further away. Tremendous nation-wide Hartals paralyzed for a day, two days, the national life and displayed the majestic strength of the Indian masses; burning of foreign cloth, boycott of cloth and liquor, nonpayment of taxes, drained the national exchequer. The British Government felt, for the first time of its rule in India, a challenge to its authority. Occasional bloody conflicts between the armed legionaries of the State and the rebellious Indian masses testified to the grimness of the struggle. Twenty-five thousand people were led off to jail unresisting. The Indian massess were fighting under discipline for Swaraj.

But Swaraj never came. One by one, then in dozens and hundreds, the national leaders went to jail. Every attempt at self-defense, at aggressive action by the massess, met with sharp reproof from Mr. Gandhi—with worse than reproof,— with public lamentations, fasting and prayer. The golden promise of Swaraj was growing dimmer; the daily misery of the people grew ever worse : governmental repression, machine-guns and jails killed all the spontaneity and enthusiasm of the early struggle. Every chance for direct action was curbed by the mandate of the Mabatma; after Bardoli, the very non-payment of taxes that had swept the peasants with a thrill of hope, as well as all forms of aggressive mass-action, were called off. The bewildered people were told to spin and pray for Swaraj. Then came the final blow. The Mahatma, divine Incarnation, All-wise, All-powerful, was arrested by the white infidels, tried and sentenced to six years in jail. The heavens did not fall, neither did the earth yawn open at this blasphemy. The doors of the jail remained locked upon the Savior of the Indian people, who remained peaceful, mute and unresisting, as he had bidden them, in expectation that a miracle would justify their obedience. There came no miracle to reward their faith. The British Raj remained securely enthroned. Swaraj was locked in the cell of the Mahatma. The waiting masses were told from behind the bars to "spin and pray".

Mr. Gandhi as political leader cannot escape responsibility for the lamentable state of chaos that besets the Indian movement today. Gandhism must be held accountable for its mistakes as well as honored for its achievements. The constructive contributions of Gandhism to the nationalist movement as a whole are : (1) the use of mass-action for the enforcement of political demands; (2) the building up of a nation-wide organization such as the Congress Party ; (3) the liberation of the national forces from governmental repression by the slogan of Non-violence; (4) the adoption of Non-cooperation and Civil Disobedience, especially Non-payment of taxes as tactics in the struggle against foreign rule. Non-cooperation and Civil Disobedience, if properly wielded, are powerful weapons in the hands of a disarmed people against machine-guns and bombing planes. But Mr. Gandhi has always shrunk from putting his brilliantly conceived tactics to proper use. The Boycott was not an original contribution of Gandhism; it had been used in the

Partition of Bengal crisis in 1906, and Gandhism spoiled the possibility of its successful application by stressing homespun Khaddar at the expense of mill-made Swadeshi, instead of encouraging Indian industrialism by every means.

The shortcomings and failures of Gandhism may be summarized succinctly. The most glaring defect was lack of an economic program to win the interest and allegiance of the masses, and to make Swaraj intelligible to them. Next, and closely related to this omission, was the obstinate and futile desire to unite *all* the Indian people, landlords and peasants, capitalists and proletariat, Moderates and Extremists, in a common struggle for an undefined goal. Oil and water cannot remain mixed; the lion and the lamb do not lie side by side; each man follows his own material interests, even in the fight for a spiritual Swaraj. At the slightest danger to their property and profits the Zemindars and mill-owners rallied to the side of the Government of "law and order". If it was desired to change this Government for the benefit of the majority of the people, it was necessary to sacrifice the interests of the handful of landlords and capitalists to the needs of the hungry stomachs and the naked bodies of the Indian workers and peasants. This the Congress never had the courage to do, and we cannot see that it had even the desire. Resolutions 6 and 7 of the Bardoli Conference ordering the ryots to pay rent to the Zemindars, prove it. The Nationalism of the Moderate does not extend beyond his pocket-book: the nationalism of the masses lies in their stomachs. In seeking to combine both, Mr. Gandhi fell between two stools.

The third great defect of Gandhism was the intrusion of metaphysics into the realm of politics; the confusing of spiritual with temporal aims; the obstruction of the dynamic play of mass-action by religious scruples and moral cowardice; the insistence upon soul purification as a means to win the political franchise. Revolution is not a religion, neither is Swaraj a "mental state". To undermine or overthrow British Imperialism is a material problem, and to build up a national state in which the condition of the people will be improved, is a question of economics, not metaphysics. The freedom of India depends upon the ability of her sons and daughters to face these problems squarely and to find their solution.

The fourth great defect of Gandhism is its reactionary economics. To run from the Machine-Age back to the Stone-Age may appeal to romantic poets and religious visionaries, but the mighty process of natural evolution cannot be checked by sentimental imagination. Mankind has progressed by painful stages from being the slave of Nature to the slave of the Machine, which his own intelligence has invented, to conquer natural forces. Let us go forward with this intelligence that has carried us so far to the day when Mankind will use the Machine and Nature for his own welfare and enjoyment, instead of, as now, for the selfish profit of the few and the enslavement of man by man. To go "back to the Vedas", back to the Charka, is to put away the progress of two thousand years and all the bright hopes of a future age when all men will be free to cultivate their spiritual side because they have conquered, not run away from, the tyranny of material laws. Mr. Gandhi and his disciples may set all India spinning, but they cannot prevent the industrialization of that country, which has already begun. "Not back, but forward", should be their cry.

The fifth grave error of Gandhism was its vacillations and inconsistencies, its lack of steady driving-power towards a given goal. To declare Non-cooperation with a satanic government, and then to seek compromise with its Viceroy; to pronounce modern civilization to be rotten to the core and "Parliaments are the emblems of Slavery", and at the same time to define Swaraj as "Home Rule within the Empire"; to promise Swaraj on a given date and then postpone it; to declare Mass Civil Disobedience and then renounce it,—these are a few of the innumerable and bewildering contradictions of Gandhism, which lost for it the confidence of the masses and respect of all thinking people. Not of such stuff are leaders made who can bring a people to victory; cool judgment and unflinching purpose must radiate confidence to the hundreds of thousands who follow. Gandhism is not revolutionism, but a weak and watery reformism, which shrinks at every turn from the realities of the struggle for freedom.

In criticizing thus frankly the political leadership of the Indian movement, its concrete achievements are not overlooked. Mr. Gandhi and the Non-cooperators performed gallant service in the last three years, by leading the Indian people out of hopelessness and confusion into the path of agitation and organization which embraced the entire nation. The contradictions and confusion of the leaders were but a reflection of the chaotic state of the movement itself, just emerging into consciousness. All honor to Mr. Gandhi that he found a way for his people out of the barbed-wire entanglements of governmental vigilance; that by slogans of Non-violent Non-cooperation, Boycott and Civil Disobedience, he was able to draw the wide masses into the folds of the Congress Party and to make the Indian movement for the first time truly nation- wide. But the movement had outgrown its leaders. The masses sought to forge ahead in the struggle, and their leaders vainly tried, to hold them back. The arrest of Mr. Gandhi means the disintegration of Gandhism, which is on its last legs, and the development of new ideas, new tendencies, new leaders. Mr. Gandhi and his metaphysical politics had become an unconscious agent of reaction; the Government could do the Indian Movement no greater service than by removing him from its active guidance and making of him a martyr, to spur the people on to greater activity.

Gandhi the Patriot

In closing what has been a dispassionate analysis of Mr. Gandhi's influence upon the Indian movement, heartfelt tribute must be paid to Gandhi the Patriot. We believe that Mr. Gandhi's political career is inspired by a deep love for his suffering countrymen, a love none the less noble for having made great tactical mistakes. His very utterance breathes a deep desire to free the motherland from thralldom, and to help her children find a happier life. Few scenes are destined to greater immortality in history than the court-room in which Mr. Gandhi read out his scathing indictment of British rule in India, and pleading guilty to the charge of promoting disaffection to the Government, asked the judge to give him the maximum sentence.

"From a staunch loyalist co-operator, I have become an uncompromising disaffectionist and Non-cooperator... To preach disaffection towards the existing system of government has become almost a passion with me... If I were set free, I would still do the same. I would be failing in my duty if I did not do so... I had either to submit to a system which has done irreparable harm to my country, or to incur the mad fury of my people, bursting forth when they heard the truth from my lips... I do not ask for mercy. I am here to invite and to submit to the highest penalty that can be inflicted upon me for what in law is a crime...Affection cannot be manufactured or regulated by law. I hold it to be a virtue to be disaffected to a Government which, in its totality, has done more harm to India than any previous system...It is the physical and brutal ill-treatment of humanity which has made many of my co-workers and myself impatient of life itself."

Mohandas Karamchand Gandhi will live in the annals of his country as one of its greatest saints and patriots, long after his political failures are forgotten. (June 15, 1922).

15

M.N. Roy and the Mahatma:
A Radical Critique and Assessment of Gandhi and Gandhism

Prof. Sibnarayan Ray

When Mohandas Karamchand Gandhi returned to India in January 1915 after nearly twenty-one years in South Africa he was a relatively obscure figure known to very few people in his own motherland. His acknowledged political mentor, Gokhale, advised him to devote a year to acquainting himself with the Indian reality.[1] Gandhi himself had remarked before leaving South Africa that India was a strange country to him. India was in the midst of war, and Gandhi pleaded for unconditional, and wholehearted support by Indians in the war effort.[2] In the New Year's Honours list of 1915 he was awarded a Kaiser-i-Hind gold medal for his proven loyalty to the British empire. He was then forty-six, and no-one could have foreseen that in a few years time he would establish himself as the most popular and powerful political leader of nationalist India.

But although his valiant efforts in South Africa had not achieved any just or enduring solution of the Indian problem in that country, his personal gain from that bitter experience was considerable. South Africa transformed him from a diffident and inconspicuous young man to a charismatic personality whose integrity and inner strength inspired not a few and commanded from them unquestioning devotion and discipline. After the cold and lonely night at Pietermaritzburg station which he later

* Reprinted by kind permission of Professor Sibnarayan Ray and the Indian Renaissance Institute from *The Radical Humanist*, 63:7 (October 1999), 4-14.

claimed to be the 'Most creative experience' of his life[3] it took him about ten years (1894-1904) to prepare himself for the leadership role which was to be his for the rest of his life. Not only did he re-mould himself, but he also got his self-image persuasively portrayed by his first biographer, Rev. Joseph J. Doke, who focused on the religious-ethical dimension of his politics and presented him as a patriot-saint. M.K. Gandhi: An Indian Patriot in South Africa was published in London in October 1909 with an introduction by Lord Ampthill. He had already discovered his very special method of organized nonviolent resistance to unjust laws and institutions - Satyagraha - and formed his welt-anschauung which he then boldly formulated as some kind of a manifesto, at first in Gujarati - *Hind Swaraj* - and subsequently in English. *Indian Home Rule* (March 1910). He sent copies of both his authorised biography and his manifesto to Tolstoy who gave his authoritative imprimatur by declaring Gandhi's experiments in South Africa to be of global significance. South Africa also made Gandhi an adept in both conducting a militant political movement involving many people and terms of imprisonment and in negotiating settlement with powers that be.[4]

With all these acquisitions Gandhi arrived in India, and although at that time his name was hardly known even to the politically minded public, within five years he was in overall command of the nationalist movement and Congress organisation. He had advanced step by step - establishing his ashram, making limited experiments in satyagraha, winning from the poet Rabindranath the epithet the Mahatma, assuming editorship of two weeklies Navajivan and Young India which enabled him regularly to propagate his views, getting published the first Indian editions of both Hind Swaraj and the Doke Biography, calling a nation-wide hartal which led to several outbreaks of mob violence, proposing non-cooperation at the All-India Khailafat Conference, then assuring the Khilafatists that the majority of the Hindus supported them, and finally by defeating his rivals and opponents at the Calcutta and the Nagpur sessions of the Congress and persuading that organization to commit itself to his programme of non-cooperation, boycott, charkha and swadeshi on the assurance that it would bring India swaraj within a year. He revised the Congress constitution and reorganized it in such a way that what until then was a political platform of mainly moderate-minded elite groups was transformed into a populist mass movement of which he was the supreme leader. To the masses he was not only the Mahatma but also an avtar or incarnation of God who would not only get rid of the British but also establish Ramarajya on earth. From this point onwards for nearly a quarter of a century Gandhi occupied the centre stage of Indian policy.

However, even during this period he was not without critics nor was his authority altogether unchallenged. I have elsewhere examined at some length the vital points of disagreement between Tagore and Gandhi, but although Tagore publicly differed from Gandhi on many major issues, their personal regard for each other did not suffer any decline.[5] On other hand, three of the most persistent critics of Gandhi, Jinnah, Ambedkar and Roy - not only rejected his method of satyagraha and the utopian vision of Hind Swaraj, but took a highly skeptical view of his widely publicized 'saintly' personality. Of the three, M. A. Jinnah, originally a liberal-secularist proponent of Hindu-Muslim unity, reacted so violently to Gandhi's mixture of religion and politics, that he eventually employed that explosive mixture himself to mobilize his own community, re-emerged from self-chosen exile to become the supreme leader of the Muslim community in the Indian sub-continent, and became the founder of Pakistan. Dr. B. R. Ambedkar fought Gandhi tooth and nail over the issue of caste and untouchability. In the end, shortly after Gandhi's death, he saw the legitimacy of his demands fully recognised in the Constitution of free India, which was drafted in the main, ironically enough, by Ambedkar himself. The most radical and thorough-going critic of both Gandhi and Gandhism was, however. M. N. Roy who had neither Jinnah's nor Ambedkar's political success, and it is to him and his critique that I intend to devote the rest of this paper.

II

Born eighteen years after Gandhi, Roy was the son of a Brahmin head teacher of Sanskrit at a school in the neighbourhood of Calcutta.[6] At birth he was named Narendra Nath Bhattacharya, but later he had to assume a string of aliases to escape detection and arrest by the police. M. N. Roy was the name he adopted at Stanford in 1916 and that is the one by which he is known. Between the two, Gandhi and Roy would seem to exemplify many of the contrasts which comprise India - the former a modh bania Vaishnava from the back waters of a princely state of Kathiawar Gujrat, married at the age of thirteen, sent to England to qualify at the bar after passing the matriculation examination; the latter, a brahmin Sakta exposed from his early boyhood to the strong intellectual-cultural cross-current and political turmoil in Bengal, especially in the metropolis of Calcutta, expelled from school at the age of eighteen for organising an anti-partition meeting, inducted shortly thereafter into a secret revolutionary nationalist organisation which had been formed in 1902 and of which the ideological leadership would be assumed by the Cambridge-educated Aurobindo Ghosh. Though Gandhi wrote and published a good deal in Gujarati, English and Hindi, he was not by temperament an intellectual, or a systematic thinker or a theorist. Roy, with the Brahmin tradition behind him and the rich inheritance of the Bengali cultural renaissance of the 19th century, developed into an outstanding intellectual and theorist and wrote and published his ideas in several modern European languages. (Spanish, German, French, Russian and of course, English, but not in Bengali or Hindi).[7]

Between 1908 and 1915 Roy was one of the principal organisers of the revolutionary nationalist movement in Bengal. With his associates he planned an armed insurrection in India during war.[8] To negotiate military assistance from Germany he went to Batavia in 1915, and from there to the Philippines, Japan, Korea, China and the United States till he finally landed in Mexico in 1917. The insurrectionary plan proved to be abortive, but Roy imbibed Marxism in Mexico, learnt Spanish, wrote and published four books in that language, became one of the leaders of the Socialist Party founded El Partid Communista de Mexico (1919), and was invited by Lenin to Moscow to take part in the Second Congress of the newly founded Communist International

(1920).[9] Although at the Second Congress Roy differed with Lenin on the National and Colonial Question (more about this later), he rose very rapidly in the International's hierarchy on account of his exceptional intellectual eminence and organisational ability. His work *India in Transition* (1920, translated in several European languages) came to be acknowledged as a Marxist classic and was followed by a succession of books, pamphlets, manifestoes. In 1920 he founded the emigre Communist Party of India at Tashkent, and from 1922 to 1928 edited a political Journal, published at first as *The Vanguard of Indian Independence*, then as *The Advance-Guard* and finally as *The Masses of India*. Although his books and journal were banned in India by the government, they reached clandestinely not a few people, and by 1922 he succeeded in forming five small communist groups in Bengal, Bombay, Madras, U.P. and Punjab. In December, 1925 the Communist Party of India was formally founded at a conference in Kanpur.[10]

By 1926 Roy had been elected as a full member of the Executive Committee and Presidium of the Comintern, its Secretariat and Orgbureau, Chairman of the Eastern Commission and member-secretary of the Chinese Commission, and he had offices and staff at Moscow, Berlin, Paris, Zurich and Amsterdam. At the end of the Seventh Plenum of ECCI, he was sent to China as head of the Comintern delegation there. Due to ambiguities in the Comintern's directives and confusions and conflicts within the Communist leadership in China, counter-revolutionary forces succeeded temporarily in crushing the communists.[11] Roy returned to Moscow after seven months in China to be caught in the midst of the deadly power struggle among Lenin's bolshevik successors in the Soviet Union, in 1928 when at its Sixth Congress the Comintern adopted an extreme left policy. Roy disagreed with it, and after the publication of his critical view of the official line in the Opposition press, the unavoidable break came in 1929.[12] Roy devoted the next year to completing his monumental work *Revolution and Konterrevolution in China* (Berlin 1930), returned to India clandestinely, and after seven months of incessant underground work for building a Revolutionary Party of the Indian Working Class, was caught and sentenced to twelve years' transportion which was reduced on appeal to six years rigorous imprisonment. He was released in 1936, joined the Congress, tried to build an alternative leadership to Gandhi, then broke with the Congress in 1940 over the issue of support to the 'anti-fascist war', formed the Radical Democratic Party which was eventually dissolved in December 1948 after much careful consideration. During the last eight years of his life Roy formulated and developed, in collaboration with several younger colleagues including the author of this paper, the philosophy of Radical or Scientific Humanism, the most detailed formulation of which may be found in his magnum opus, *Reason, Romanticism and Revolution* published in two volumes (Calcutta 1952, 1955). In June 1952 he met with a serious accident in Mussoorie, which resulted in cerebral thrombosis and partial paralysis. He recovered briefly, and his Memoirs began to be serialised in his weekly journal, but after a third and final attack of cerebral thrombosis, death came ten minutes before midnight on 25 January 1954.

From 1920 till the Mahatma's assassination at the hand of a Hindu fanatic Roy had been a consistent critic of Gandhi and Gandhism. Even after his break with the Comintern he continued to remain a Marxist till the end of the war, when, totally disillusioned with the Soviet Union, he had to re-examine his theoretical postulates. The philosophy of Radical Humanism which developed out of this re-examination is still basically very different from Gandhi's world-view, but with the advantage of hindsight it is possible to discern several pregnant features which Radical Humanism shares with Gandhism. I shall come to this in the last section of this paper, but at no stage do I find any evidence that Roy was remotely influenced by Gandhi or was even aware of any possibility of a confluence of ideas in future. However, Gandhi's martyrdom did make him reconsider his view of Gandhi's personality, ideas and method. He now recognized that Gandhi's was 'essentially a moral, humanist, cosmopolitan appeal', that 'the implication of the doctrine of non-violence is the moral dictum that the end does not justify the means', that Gandhi 'sincerely wanted politics to be guided by moral considerations' and his 'endeavour to introduce morality into political practice was the positive core of Gandhism'. He thought that the only way to immortalize Gandhi's memory would be for his followers to practice 'the precept of purifying politics with truth and non-violence'. Nevertheless, even when paying his homage, Roy did not forget to mention that the Mahatma himself allowed his humanist appeal 'to be heavily coloured by the narrow cult of nationalism', that he 'fell a victim to the very cult he preached', that he vaguely visualized a humanist idea, while still groping in the twilight of medievalism'.[13] Roy was no longer a Marxist, but to the end his humanism continued to be uncompromisingly materialist, rationalist, atheist and libertarian. Despite significant points of similarity towards the end, any scenario of reconciliation between the Mahatma and the heretic would be altogether far-fetched. Professor Dennis Dalton put much more meaning into Roy's homage to the martyred Mahatma than is warranted by available evidence.[14]

III

The year 1920 was a turning point in the life of both Gandhi and Roy. Gandhi formally launched non-cooperation on 1 August of that year. Roy reached Moscow in May having been invited personally by Lenin to take part in the Second Congress of the Communist International which opened on 19 July and continued till 7 August. In Mexico Roy had studied Marx and been initiated into the intricacies of dialectics by Michael Borodin, but his interpretation of Marxism was much more deeply influenced by the writings of Lenin's erstwhile mentor, George Plekhanov, than by Lenin. Moreover, during the months he spent in Berlin on his way from Mexico to Moscow he acquainted himself with the works of the recently assassinated great Marxist theorist Rosa Luxemberg, founder of the German Communist Party, and for many years a very severe and influential critic of Lenin,[15] and he developed strong ties of personal friendship with some of her prominent colleagues and followers.

On arrival at Moscow Roy was given a draft copy of Lenin's theses on the National and Colonial Question for his comments and observations. The theses were to be presented and adopted at the Second Congress. Roy, however, differed with the Lenin's fomulation on several major issues, and at Lenin's request, formulated his own Supplementary Theses. With some modifications both sets of theses were adopted by the Congress[16] but the differences were not really resolved and they would continue to haunt the communist movement long after the death of both Lenin and Roy. On a later occasion Stalin explained Lenin's acceptance of Roy's supplementary theses with modifications on the ground that when Lenin formulated his own draft, he was very inadequately acquainted with the Asian situation. Stalin subsequently supported Roy's position at the Fifth Congress of the Comintern (1924) against Roy's principal opponent at the Congress, D. Manuilski.[17]

It was during his discussions with Lenin before the Second Congress that Roy gave what was probably his earliest critical assessment of Gandhi. The Hartal of the previous year and subsequent developments had already brought Gandhi into prominence in Indian politics. Lenin saw in Gandhi a potential revolutionary who might lead the upsurge of post-war mass discontent in India against the British. Roy opposed this view by holding that while Gandhi might appear 'politically revolutionary' he was in fact a 'social reactionary whose popularity rested on his religious and cultural revivalist appeal. He drew upon the authority of Plekhanov who saw the Narodniks and the Social Revolutionaries in Russia in the same light as he saw Gandhi.[18]

Roy's assessment of Gandhi at this time and the following years has to be placed in the context of his Marxist interpretation of Indian history, and in particular, his analysis of contemporary politico-economic and socio-cultural developments in India. The bourgeoisie in Europe had at one time played a progressive role by overthrowing the ancient regime of feudalism and the Church and by bringing about a social revolution. In India the middle classes grew under the patronage of the foreign rulers. On the other hand, they were still very much rooted in a tradition-bound feudal society and, on the other, they were largely a creation of colonial rule. They were frightened of the prospect of a far-reaching social revolution, and despite their growing politico-economic aspirations, were prone to reaching a compromise with the British if the terms proved favourable to their interests and ambition. The exigencies of the war had forced the British to promote a measure of industrial development in India, but what they planned was some kind of a partnership with the rising Indian bourgeoisie in which control would remain essentially in British hand. Within India popular unrest against both foreign and native exploitation was growing fast since the end of the war, and the situation had become potentially revolutionary. Sections of the Indian bourgeoisie might cooperate in the movement for political independence, but faced with the threat of a social revolution they would prefer to come to terms with the British.

To Roy Gandhi, on the one hand, was the embodiment of the primitive, blind, spontaneous spirit of revolt of the masses', and on the other, he was a cunning bania-politician who, with his reactionary ideology and stress on non-violence, was bent on restraining the revolutionary forces and promoting a compromise between the indigenous vested interests and the British. Gandhi in his view 'endeavours to utilise mass energy for the perpetuation or revival of the heritage of national culture which has been made untenable by the awakening of mass energy'. It is the paradox of Gandhi that while he rejects western civilization, under his leadership the movement would at best succeed in establishing a capitalist society with a pre-capitalist culture.[19]

Gandhi, however, did not figure in the deliberations of the Second Comintern Congress. Roy's principal differences here with Lenin were on three points. According to him, (a) a revolution in Europe depended on the course of the revolution in Asia bringing about the break-up of the colonial empires, (b) in the colonies, especially India, there were two distinct movements, one bourgeois democratic limited to the middle classes, which sought compromise with the existing order and tried to bring under its control the second movement which was that of the exploited and ignorant masses for whom political independence to be achieved and made meaningful required at the same time a social and economic revolution, and (c) the Comintern should support revolutionary mass movements and not the colonial middle class movements. He pleaded for the Comintern's commitment to the principle of 'revolution from below'. Lenin rejected the first point, and after considerable discussion acknowledged in a qualified manner the validity of the second and third points, and as a concession to Roy substituted the term 'nationalist revolutionary' for the term 'bourgeois-democratic'. Roy on his part admitted that 'the cooperation of the bourgeois nationalist revolutionary elements is useful' in the early stage, but the emphasis should be on the organisation of peasants and workers and on a programme which would telescope political independence with a socio-economic revolution.

The position outlined by Roy at the Second Congress was elaborated and developed by him in his first major work as a Marxist theoretician, *India in Transition* (1922). This included a systematic critique of Gandhi and Gandhism. The work was followed by a succession of books written and published both while he occupied a peak position in the Comintern and after his break with it, - among them, *One Year of Non-cooperation* (1923), *Political Letters* (1924) *The Aftermath of Non-cooperation* (1926), *The Future of Indian Politics* (1926), *Our Task in India* (1932), *Whither Congress* (1934), *Manifesto of the Revolutionary Party of the Indian Working Class* (1935), *Fascism, its Philosophy, Professions and Practice* (1938), *Our Problems* (1938), *Letters to Mahatma* (1940), *Gandhism, Nationalism and Socialism* (1940), *Ideal of Indian Womanhood* (1941), *Freedom or Fascism* (1942), *Nationalism, An Antiquated Cult* (1943), *Nationalism, Democracy and Freedom* (1943), *Problems of Freedom* (1945), *India's Message* (1950) - in every one of which Gandhi is a major target of his attack. Instead of going through these writings individually, I shall, for the purpose of this paper, highlight some of the main points of his criticism which became sharper and went deeper with the passage of years.

IV

We have already mentioned that Roy underlined some of the glaring self-contradictions of Gandhi. Gandhi, in his view, was a product and historic expression of the seething discontent of the Indian masses at the end of the first world war, and total non-cooperation, if whole-heartedly pursued, could have been the prelude to the much-needed revolution in India. But by imposing on it his dogma of nonviolence Gandhi deliberately emasculated the revolutionary forces and reduced its leadership to impotence. All established orders, whether foreign or indigenous, rely on force and use it without hesitation when threatened with dislodgment. Whether violence is desirable or not, it is unavoidable in a revolutionary confrontation between the oppressor and the oppressed, Gandhi provided the aspiring masses with the potent weapon of all-out non-cooperation, and then called off the movement the moment it went out of the bounds set by him. He did this repeatedly, which to Roy could not but be interpreted, at the best, as Gandhi's self-deception, arising out of his self-contradiction, and at the worst, as cunning deception of the people who had accepted him as their messianic leader.

Again Gandhi professed to reject totally all elements of modern civilization - science and technology, factories and railways, medicines and hospitals, schools and colleges, parliaments and political parties - but at the some time he negotiated with the British imperialists to reach some compromise, and the net effect of his swadeshi movement was to strengthen the position of the Indian capitalists through boycott of foreign goods, and to prepare the Congress as a suitable instrument to which political power could be eventually transferred by negotiation. All this amounted to rejecting and accepting modern civilization at the same time. He preached the cult of poverty but relied heavily on his industrialist patrons to finance his various activities. He condemned untouchability but clung to Varna divisions or the caste system. A man of Bhakti, he proclaimed the agnostic Jawaharlal Nehru as his successor. In this Roy saw a certain deviousness on the part of Gandhi who thereby seriously reduced the chances of an alternative modern leadership emerging in Indian politics, and a lack of integrity and inner strength in Nehru's character, who with all his modernism, clung to the Little Father or Bapu. Gandhi proclaimed the ideal of sarvodaya of the people, but in concrete terms he relied on the so-called trusteeship of the elite (which would include benevolent landlords and millowners), and himself came to occupy for a quarter of a century the position virtually of the dictator of the Congress, who knew how effectively to suppress and eliminate any challenge to his absolute authority. It is not necessary to mention all the self-contradictions of Gandhi listed by Roy, but it should be clear that he gave little credence to the much publicized sainthood of the Father of the Nation.

Roy strongly objected to Gandhi's mixing of politics with religion. The secular political temper which the moderate leaders before Gandhi had tried with some measure of success to develop in the Congress and which extremist leaders like Tilak and Aurobindo had threatened to subvert, was virtually overthrown by Gandhi when first he championed Khilafat, and then introduced into the Congress his whole range of traditional Hindu religious beliefs, rituals and practices, including Ramdhun and Ramarajya, prayer-meetings and fastings, cow-protection, brahmacharya, Bhajans and recitals from the Gita. In Roy's view, Gandhi stimulated the growth of Hindu nationalism and, may be somewhat unwittingly, helped in the growth of Muslim revivalism by, on the other hand, alienating secularist Muslims like Jinnah and, on the other, encouraging Khilafatists and Muslim militants. By mixing religion and politics Gandhi became the Mahatma and avatar to the Hindu masses, steeped in ignorance and superstitions, and did incalculable harm to Indian polity.

While Roy saw in Gandhi's non-violent non-cooperation a strategy to immobilize revolutionary forces and help Indian vested interests in improving their position and bargaining power with the British, what he found most perverse in Gandhi was his persistent advocacy of a return to the past, his rejection of the achievements of modern civilization, his refusal to visualise a future where no one will be deprived of his or her right to the fullest enjoyment of the achievements of civilization. In his books and the critical essays published in his journal *Independent India* Roy exposed time and again the implications and practical consequences of Gandhi's rejection of science and technology, his distrust of reason, his asceticism and fear of sex and the senses, his cult of poverty, his panacea of the charkha, his refusal to see the basic conflict of interests between landlords and peasants, capitalists and workers, his total failure to grasp the far-reaching significance of the concept of fundamental human rights. During Roy's six years of rigorous imprisonment in jail in the thirties while he was writing his Prison Notebooks (about 3000 closely handwritten foolscap sheets of paper), it became increasingly clear to him that Gandhism was, paradoxically, very close in its ideology to Fascism which was threatening the very basis of modern civilization. In a segment from the Prison Notebooks published after his release under the title *Fascism : its Philosophy, Professions and Practice* (1938), he not only analysed the fearful phenomenon in Europe, but showed how many features of the Hindu tradition in general and of Gandhism in particular bore strong similarities with the ideas of Schopenhauer, Nietzsche and Giovanni Gentile, and the adoption of those ideas by their followers in contemporary Italy and Germany. The rejection of reason and reliance on 'inner voice', the glorification of the mysticism morality of suffering, the doctrine of superman or the avatar of the Gita, the merging of the individual in a deified collectivity called the Nation, the metaphysical justification of inequality and the systematic effort to make the workers accept their exploiters as benevolent trustees, -all these indicated an affinity which was skilfully covered by the advocacy of nonviolence which, in actual practice, was repeatedly shown to be ineffective. To Roy it came as no surprise that Gandhi would show almost total callousness to what happened to the Jews in Germany under Hitler. In 1938 while Hitler was planning total extermination of the Jewry in Germany Gandhi publicly advised the Jews to choose self-immolation as satyagrahis. 'The calculated violence of Hitler', he wrote in his organ 'may even result in a general massacre of the Jews. But if the Jewish mind could be prepared for voluntary suffering, even the massacre I have imaged could be turned into a day of thanks giving and joy that Jehovah had wrought deliverance of the race even at the hand of the tyrant'.[20] The same year Gandhi praised the Munich Pact as sound statesmanship, and advised the Czechs against an armed resistance to invasion by the Germans.[21] In 1940 he praised the

French surrender to the Nazi invaders as 'brave statesmanship'. French statesmen have shown rare courage in bowing to the inevitable and refusing to be party to senseless mutual slaughter.[22] A few days later, he appealed to the British (who were then fighting for survival) to :

> lay down the arms you have as being useless for saving you or humanity... Let them (Herr Hitler and Signor Mussolini) take possession of your beautiful island, with your many beautiful buildings ... If these gentlemen choose to occupy your homes, you will vacate them. If they do not give you free passage out, you will allow yourself man, woman and child, to be slaughtered, but you will refuse to owe allegiance to them.[23]

Roy who knew what had happened to Germany and Italy under Fascist and Nazi dictatorships and who had no doubt that a Fascist victory in the war would mean a terrible setback to human freedom and progress throughout the world including India publicly came out in support of Britain even though he had fought against the British for thirty-five years since 1905.

Roy traced the source of the affinity of Gandhism with Fascism to the fundamentally authoritarian nature of Gandhi's personality. In South Africa a different and inarticulate young barrister had transformed himself into a leader of people by developing an iron will which could not be deflected from its target. Like the yogis of India he had given away sex and the pleasure of the senses and material possession to achieve the kind of power which would risk death rather than acknowledge defeat and all is grist that comes to its mills. But the authoritarian personality is afraid of freedom and reason which it must avoid to maintain its self-image and hold over others. Even Nehru sensed this when in his Autobiography he spoke of a 'Kingliness' in Gandhi which compelled a willing obeisance from others. Consciously and deliberately meek and humble. Yet he was full of power and authority, and he knew it and at times he was imperious enough, issuing commands which had to be obeyed.[24] Following Erich Fromm's study of Luther and Cavin, Roy diagnosed that the fascist traits in Gandhi's personality and ideas were rooted in his 'fear of freedom'.[25]

Gandhi rarely engaged in public controversy with his critics (the only sustained debate over basic issues that he ever had was with Tagore). Once he had ensconed himself at the Mahatmic pinnacle of popular reverence and virtually absolute control of the Congress organisation, he presumably felt no need to refute criticism, although from time to time he would make strategic moves to outmanoeuvre potential political rivals. While Roy was his most persistent and radical critic for a quarter of a century, he was never a serious threat to Gandhi's political dominance like C.R. Das or B.R. Ambedkar or M.A. Jinnah or Subhash Chandra Bose. He could afford not to recognize the seriousness of his criticism. In 1924 Gandhi wrote in his organ *Young India* a brief article on "Bolshevism and Discipline", acknowledging that he "did not know the meaning of Bolshevism", and followed this in the same issue with another article defending charkha against Roy's attack on it in *Welfare* of May 1924. Subsequently he published in the same organ Roy's fairly long reply to Gandhi's piece on Bolshevism, along with a dismissive comment that Bolshevism, if correctly represented by Roy 'is a poor thing'.[26] At the Karachi Session of the Congress (March 1931), the draft of the Resolution on Fundamental Rights and Economic Programme which, according to Intelligence Reports, was prepared and given to Nehru by Roy (who attended the Congress session clandestinely under the assumed name Dr. Mahmood), was considerably modified and watered down at the instance of Gandhi and eventually adopted. The Congress also endorsed the Gandhi-Irwin Pact which Roy strongly opposed. After his release from jail Roy met Gandhi for the first time at Faizpur Congress (December 1936) where Roy's proposal for transforming the Congress into a fighting organisation against the British was unequivocally rejected by Gandhi. At that Congress Roy refused to join Gandhi's prayer meeting and was advised by him to eschew active politics. When Roy started his weekly *Independent India*, Gandhi replied to his request for a goodwill message with a postcard advising him "to render only mute service to the cause of freedom". Later in November 1939 there was an exchange of correspondence between Gandhi and Roy over their differences on various issues. Gandhi emphasized that the Congress had now become 'a non-violent army in war time ... Its will is expressed by its general whoever he may be. Every unit has to render him willing obedience in thought, word and deed.' Of course, Gandhi did not have to spell out that he was himself the general whose will would brook no questioning. And so here could be no compromise. The rupture became complete when, after a great deal of hesitancy and tight-rope walking, Gandhi eventually launched the Quit India movement in August 1942.

The war brought about drastic changes all around. Not only were the Axis Powers crushed, but the British Empire was left too exhausted to maintain itself. Roy had anticipated this quite early and prepared and published a Draft Constitution and People's Plan for independent India.[27] Meantime Jinnah had fully established himself as the Quaid-e-Azam of the Muslims of the subcontinent, and creation of Pakistan had been proclaimed as the goal of the Muslim League. The Congress leaders were in a hurry to reach a settlement with the British that will ensure peaceful transfer of power, even at the cost of partition of the subcontinent. And Gandhi, now in his late seventies, found himself bereft of his command over his long-time followers and the Congress organization, and left with his personal God and ethic of satyagraha. He told Louis Fischer that he was 'a spent bullet'.[28] He was opposed to Partition, he even proposed to the new viceroy Jinnah's name as the Prime Minister of an undivided India; he advised the Congress leaders to disband the organization, give up the struggle for power, and transform the Congress into an association of social servants. But neither Nehru, nor Patel, nor Rajendra Prasad, nor Kripalani found any of his proposals realistic or acceptable. The record of their conduct does not indicate that any of these trusted lieutenants of the Mahatma were ever really committed to the goal of Hind Swaraj or to the absolute principle of ahimsa. With Mountbatten as Governor-General they decided to be rulers of a truncated India. Gandhi's last years were his loneliest, but they were also his noblest. Alone he worked steadfastly for non-violence and truth in private life and public affairs, against powerful currents of aggressive chauvinism and cynical power-lust. He fasted and prayed and tried in vain to bring reconciliation between Hindus and Muslims, between the two newly formed rival states, India and Pakistan, to bring solace and courage and faith into the lives of the millions who had become victims of partition. And then he himself fell a victim to the fanaticism of a Hindu nationalist.

It was Gandhi's martyrdom and his moral praxis of the last lonely years, rescued from the ambiguities and manoeuvring of power-politics of the previous quarter century, which made Roy re-examine his long -held, poor estimate of Gandhi, and pay him public homage in unambiguous terms. But before that his own outlook (and to an extent, personality as well) had been changing under the impact of the war and his self-examination during the post-war years. I had the privilege to know and work with him closely during the last eight years of his life. Although there was a difference of thirty-three years between us, he accepted me not only as a colleague but also as a friend and had enough generosity and openness of spirit to welcome what contribution I was able to make to the development of the new philosophy of radical humanism.[28] During the early forties he had gradually become altogether disillusioned with the profession and practice of Bolshevism and the record of the party dictatorship in the Soviet Union. I do not think he ever totally rejected all the major premises of Marxism, but he increasingly emphasised the worth of many ideas and ideals which in no way could be reconciled with orthodox Marxism. He still recognized the importance of the economic foundations of social organisation, but culture, which included knowledge, art, morality and various finer and distinctive pursuits and achievements of homo sapiens, was seen as having its intrinsic and abiding value and creative significance, and he rejected its Marxist characterisation as superstructure. The worth of any institution or organisation was to be measured in terms of how it helped and advanced the free development of the creative potentialities of everyone of its members. Most significant, he now fully recognized the integral relation of ends to means, the urgent need for imbuing politics with morality, the utter unsuitability of political parties to the pursuit of human welfare and enlightenment, the pressing need for decentralization and devolution of power, the beauty and value and effectiveness of small units related to one another in voluntary cooperation.[29]

These realizations brought him closer to an appreciation of Gandhi, although I do not think he was ever really conscious of any kinship with the Mahatma.

During Roy's last years, on a number of major issues the differences between the two antagonists had significantly reduced. However, I do not think that between their total philosophical approaches there was any possibility of reconciliation. To the end Roy remained an unmitigated materialist (or physical realist, as he sometimes preferred to write), an uncompromising rationalist, a radical humanist who saw man not as a "sinful creature" who may through abstinence, devotion and prayer win his god's blessing, but as the peak of the evolutionary process, maker of history, rich in potentialities, gifted at birth with the urge for freedom and the spirit of inquiry which through proper development and application produce civilization and bring about material and cultural progress. He saw no virtue in privation, poverty, fasting or the fullest development of his or her personality. In a just and open society the basic physical and psychological requirements of every individual must be met, and at the same time people shall equip themselves to create evernew cultural resources which, unlike material resources, do not diminish by sharing. Roy thus belonged in spirit to the tradition of the humanism of the renaissance and saw in puritanism, devotionalism, distrust of reason and the senses, or obsession with moksha or the other world nothing but serious impediments to the proper development of the individual and society.

Nevertheless the issues on which they came closer to each other towards the last lonely years of their lives are not only significant for an understanding of the change in their respective situations, but are even more pointedly relevant to the national and global situation today. By obliterating almost totally from their consciousness and behaviour the integral relation of means and ends and the principle of basing politics on morality, our power-elites in India have enmeshed themselves and the country during the last few decades in all-pervasive corruption and cynicism. The terrible concentration of power in the hands of the multi-nationals and superstates, the systematic efforts to cretinise the common people through the mass media, the misuse of resources on rocketry, weaponry and big projects, on proliferation of bureaucracy and middlemen, on production and consumption of luxury goods, to the neglect of meeting the basic needs of the majority of mankind (food, shelter, education, medical service, clothing etc.) - can only lead to global disaster. The process which has brought mankind to the brink of a universal catastrophe requires urgently to be reversed. It strikes me that both in Gandhi and Roy there are insights and pointers which are likely to be helpful in confronting our fearful contemporary situation. Both Gandhi and Roy put their accent on a radical reconstruction of society in which some of the main guiding principles were decentralization and devolution of power, promotion of small and viable units and institutions of grassroots democracy, politics guided by morality, economy based on voluntary cooperation and directed to meeting the basic needs of the people, technology fully oriented to human welfare, and culture which would be creative, open and various while at the same time drawing upon the positive common past achievements and heritage of mankind.[30] Caught in the crisis of our age, we may yet find much succour and useful guidance from the voices of both who have currently been sidelined by our power-hungry politicians, unscrupulous finance-magnates and obtrusive mass-media.

References and Notes

1. Tendulkar. D.G., *Mahatma, Life of Mohandas Karamchand Gandhi* in 8 Vols, 1960-63; Delhi, Vol. 1, p. 109
2. Malhotra, S.R. *India and the Commonwealth* 1885-1929: 1965, London; p. 162.
3. *Harijan*, 10 December, 1938.
4. For details of the South African period, Gandhi, M.K., *Satyagraha in South Africa*, 1928, Madras; *Indian Opinion Golden Number; Souvenir of the Passive Resistance Movements in South Africa 1906-1914;* Phoenix; Natal; 1914; *The Collected Works of Mahatma Gandhi*, 1958, Delhi, esp., Vols. 9 and 10.

5. For a detailed examination of issues. Ray, Sibnarayan, 'Tagore-Gandhi Controversy' in *Gandhi, India and the World,* ed. Ray, Sibnarayan, 1970, Melbourne and Philadelphia; pp. 119-141.
6. For life of M. N. Roy, Karnik, V.B., *M. N. Roy : Political Biography*, 1978, Bombay. *M. N. Roy : Philosopher-revolutionary*, ed Ray, Sibnarayan, 1995, Delhi, pp. 264-295.
7. Several of these books have been translated from their original versions into English and edited and included in *Selected Works of M. N. Roy.* ed Ray, Sibnarayan, Vols I-IV. 1987-1997, Delhi.
8. Kerr, J. C., *Political Trouble in India 1907-1917*; pub. 1917, rept. 1973, Calcutta. Also *Sedition Committee Report*, omd. 9190, 1913 London.
9. Roy, M. N., *Memoirs,* 1964 Bombay; Adhikari, G., *Documents of the History of the Communist Party of India*, Vol. I, 1971, New Delhi; Degras, Jane, *The Communist International*, 1919-1943. Vol. I, 1956, London.
10. Kaye, Sir Ceul, *Communism in India*, pub. 1925. rept. 1971 Calcutta; Petne Sir David, *Communism in India 1924-27*; pub. 1927; rept. 1972. Calcutta. Adhikari, *Documents* Vol. 2, 1982. New Delhi.
11. North, R.C. and Budin. x J., *M. N. Roy's Mission to China*, 1963, Berkeley and L.A.
12. For details of the break and Roy's writings in the Communist Opposition press (Translated by me from the original German into English), Roy, M. N., *Selected Works* Vol. III, 1990, Delhi, pp. 229-448.
13. The quotations in this paragraph are from Roy's signed articles in his journal *Independent India* of 22 February and 18 April 1948, and 30 January 1949.
14. Dalton, Dennis, "Gandhi and Roy : the interaction of ideologies in India" in Ray. ed. *Gandhi, India and the World*, pp. 156-170.

15. Luxemburg, Rosa, "Organisations fragen der russischen Socialdemokratic", *Die Neue Zeit*, 1904. Stuthgart, pp. 484-492, 529-535; Luxemburg, *Rosa, Die Russische Revolution*, 1922 Berlin; Nettle, J. P., *Rosa Luxemburg*, 2 Vols, 1966, London.
16. For the texts of the theses and Lenin's and Roy's speeches on the Second Congress *Selected Works of M. N. Roy*, Vol. I, pp. 165-178; also Der Zweite Kongress der Kommunistischen Internationale; Protokol, 1921, Humburg.
17. For details, *Selected Works of M. N. Roy*, Vol. 2 pp. 279-308. Protokoll: Funtfer Kongress der Kommunistischen Internationale repr. 1973. Erlangen. Band 1 pp. 149-53. Band 11 pp. 638-651. Stalin, J. *On Chinese Revolution* 1975 Calcutta pp. 33-34; Ulyanovsky, R.A. ed. *The Comintern and the East* 1979. Moscow, pp. 169-70.
18. Roy. M. N . *Memoirs*, 1964. Bombay. pp. 375-382, for Plekhanov's view, Plekhanov, Georgi. *Selected Philosophical Works*, Vol. 1, *Our Differences*, 1977, Moscow.
19. Roy M. N. *Selected Works*, Vol. 1, *India in Transition* pp. 183-375.
20. *The Gandhi Reader*, ed. Jack, H. A .1956, Bloomington, pp. 319-20.
21. *Harijan*, 15 October 1938.
22. *Harijan*, 22 June 1940.
23. *Harijan*, 6 July 1940.
24. Nehru, Jawaharlal, *An Autobiography*, 1961, Bombay, p. 129.
25. Roy, M. N. *Gandhism, Nationalism and Socialism* 1940, Calcutta; M. N. Roy, *Problems of Freedom*, 1945. Calcutta Fromm Erich, *The Fear of Freedom*, 1952, London.
26. *Young India*, 21 August 1924, 1 January 1925.
27. Roy, M. N. *Constitution of India*. A Draft. 1944, Delhi. *Planning a New India*, 1944, Calcutta. *People's Plan* 1944. Calcutta.

28. See, Ray, Sibnarayan Ray *Radicalism*, 1946, Calcutta. *The World Her Village*, 1979. Calcutta, Roy, Ellen and Ray, S.N., In *Man's own Image, 1948*. Calcutta.
29. Roy, M.N. *New Humanism*. 1947, Calcutta; *Radical Humanism*,1952, New Delhi; *Reason, Romanticism and Revolution* 2 Vols. 1952-1955. Calcutta *Politics, Power and Parties*, 1960. Calcutta.
30. Ray, Sibnarayan, 'Tagore, Gandhi and Roy : three twentieth century utopians', in *Rabindranath Tagore, Three Essays*, 1987, Calcutta.

Index